A CODED CAKE?   WW2 REVEALED IN

PART 2b – HIS SECRET'S ACT WAR EFFORT(S)

PLUS AN APPARENT GOD FEARING DEVIL AND MORE SPIES

DR MYA XAVIER (SOUS CHEF EXTRAORDINAIRE!)

INTRO And here we are now in 2024, September 8th to be exact, and we celebrate the 2nd Anniversary of the end of her glorious *Régime...!* – As her eldest son undergoes his Cancer treatment!

BUT
*Today also came the **hopeful** Announcement of the end of her Daughter-in-Laws chemotherapy Régime...!*
*(This came 4 years after her husband's childhood female playmate's declaration that the Evil Big 'C' had also attacked her and a hopeful remission had put a **hopeful** end to it! (Later...*

And so this updated volume will start with both their 'Regal' ***Copyright*** photographs >>>

(Copyright Author's Personal Collection)

See Also Last Page of this Book...

AND SO NOW BACK TO BEFORE....

THE RELATIVELY SECRET GUINNESS LIVES WITHOUT A DROP OF STOUT IN SIGHT!

2026 AND HERE WE HAVE YET ANOTHER INTRO AND IT ONLY CAME ABOUT WITH THE AID OF OUR US DOJ AS A CERTAIN EPSTEIN'S HOUSE OF CARDS SLOWLY GET EXPOSED UNRAVELLING! (SEE PART 2 INSIDE LATER ON)

....

PLEASE NOTE: *Updated 2025/26 with the death of Tom Stoppard, Royal Scandals here and in related Norway, Epstein related scandal fall out + the connected historical Guinness WWII scandals, etc.*
SEE PART 16b: STOPPARD AND CRICKETTING PINTER
John thought old wicket-keeping hard stop would soon become a full stop! BUT he passed John's imaginary death by 80 goal post, which became a winning post until 29 November 2025, when at 88 not out, demon bowler death finally smashed his life wicket, bails, stumps and all!!! (So what now Dear 'Dorset' Again Single Sabrina???)
BUT THEN/NOW IN NOVEMBER 2024 WHAT DO THEY AND THEIR RICH SIMILARLY AFFECTED CONNECTIONS &/OR RELATIVES DO ABOUT THE NEW UK LABOUR GOVERNMENT SLAPPING A 20% INHERITANCE TAX ON FARMS LAND/BUILDINGS?
(Now only over £2 million!)(Small fry to our Book's principals!)
WILL THEIR TRUSTS * NEED URGENT UPDATING?
WE WAIT AND SEE IF THE NEW TAX PASSES!
<u>TRUSTS * ARE DEALT WITH AT LENGTH INSIDE... ></u>
BUT LATER WITHIN CAN YOUR USA &/OR USSR FRIENDS BE TRUSTED?
AND VICE VERSA!!!??

NB1:- I HAVE UPDATED THE ORIGINAL WITH ITEMS DISCOVERED FROM OLD ARCHIVED TEXTS.

I HAVE ALSO INTRODUCED MANY CHAPTERS AT THE BEGINNING SHOWING HOW HISTORY HAS ULTIMATELY LINKED ROYAL STORYLAND WITH GUINNESS PAST.

THE GUINNESS PAST WILL MAINLY FEATURE EVENTS IN THE SECOND WORLD WAR.

BUT THE EVOLVING REGAL STORYLINES WILL BE PRE & POST WORLD WAR ONE.

AND WE SHOULD EVENTUALLY ARRIVE AT QUEEN ELIZABETH'S CORONATION TIME.

SEPARATE ITEMS WILL ALSO SHOW THAT BEING RICH &/OR ROYAL DOES NOT EXEMPT YOU FROM PERSONAL PAIN &/OR DISEASE.

NB2:- MOST UPDATED MATERIAL WAS FINALLY ADDED DURING THE EARLY MONTHS OF 2026.

THE NAME DUPLCATIONS DROVE ME MAD!

I HOPE YOU WILL BE ASTOUNDED BY THE RECENTLY ADDED...

LIKE >>>>

>>>>>>>>>

Autumn 2022...

As **HER** death is everywhere you read/look/listen to the message(s) they are all complimentarily identical.

And so recalling her passing as my [H] Homage Introduction to this Book, but from a specific painful slanting point of view...

So as our *Regal Leader* has now left as and what one can imagine as her son's words as befitting, but not mentioned in any speeches made is a simple:

<u>*Did It Hurt, Mummy?*</u>

<u>*I Hope It Didn't!*</u>

<u>*Everyone is now in Bleak Black*</u>

<u>*But, and it is that Big Memorable But,*</u>

<u>*You Looked Real Great In White!*</u>

I make no apologies as her photo has also appeared in another of my Books, **It Hurts, Mummy! It Hurts Mummy!**

[H] *Here is a Story, amongst others, only a few (like John) know, where her funny side/giggle/smile radiated as her Corgi created Utility Havoc:-*

This is related by an ex Patient, John, who, when a wet around the ears 18 year old, a Cockney Raised North Londoner, whose vernacular would be far removed from those he was to work with!
But thankfully for all those around it was just a Temporary Government Secondment as his way of speaking was not a true fit for those who thought him below them, but perhaps not those High & Mighty Before Him Below?
.....

"It was my first posting helping one of the **#Cloth** there: Green yes, but definitively not of the baize variety, I had some success on that!"

He then showed me this **old** personal *'Cloth#'*, Regal Green Card from **Her**, as his grin broadened, whilst self-doubt eerily crept up upon me.
He continued as I gathered my thoughts...

The *Queen Bee Boss* has always had one special thing, even in her older state, which is the envy of all those US & Co plastic operated upon female faces, which is the state of her skin – immaculately smooth, if I say so myself.
And, as it also part of my following, funny story, that she had a wicked little innocent smile – if that combination is possible?
But, it was Christmases at Sandringham which might have elicited a special type of being wicked in her?

Ignoring the special entertaining guests like Cliff & Bruce, it was what went on before and after the Festivities where the, perhaps, little devil in her which came to the fore, or was it just her being concerned?

To check in her own particular way if the guests had enjoyed themselves *to the **full***, she had them weighed on their arrival, then on their departure – bit of a shock to those wobbling above average weight fillies I dare say?

But now back to the dogs...

It is likely you know about her first born's favourite dog, Tigger, and his encounter with one of the kitchen's warm ovens: Charlie remarked how warm he later felt, being unaware of where he had been thrown by an exasperated cook!

But, ^H here is one extra bit of frivolity I can relate between her & the gas man, where her Corgi took centre stage and I at the outer periphery, with them all giggling at the eventuality.

She hid a great little smile, behind her concealing hand.

If, like me, you'd have been/invited to those Garden Parties (!?), ^{BP} you'd've marvelled how each food serving counter could achieve such great results: hot food on tap, so to speak.

Well, each stand had its own supply of the essentials, gas, water & electricity...they, however, do break down and need special *Royal* attention.

One such time I was in the Garden overseeing **a British Gas Engineer struggling with a faulty mains-pipe.**

It needed replacing and he expected to only dig down a couple of feet.

He didn't expect the Electricity Board fellas to have wrapped their conduits around his large gas pipe.

It was too dangerous to fiddle with the obstruction, so he decided to dig much deeper and create a by-pass lower down.

He was about six feet down when it started to piss down, not cats & dogs, but a special Corgi type rain!

God, did he get a shock and thankfully not an electrical one at that.

The old girl was giggling unrestrainedly as she saw what had happened.

A so sorry came from her lips; he accepted it as he took off his shirt and continued his work in his string vest, unabashed!

••••••••••••••••••••••••••••••••

And why John's stay was a short one?

Well, his carefree cockney way his way of greeting **everyone** would be the same. And so his Gran would be his **Old Girl** of the family, but heads would turn when he was heard to refer to & even call the **Queen, Old Girl** too!

The Duke of Edinburgh would remark to him that *'You will incur the sign of her displeasure (?), her raised eyebrows!'*

Needless to say, he did, but as she slowly turned away he noticed the grin filling her smiling face – *'silly boy!'*

^{BP} And just to show she bore John no grudge...he did!

The Lord Chamberlain is
commanded by Her Majesty to invite

to a Garden Party
at Buckingham Palace
on Thursday, 19th July 2007 from 4 to 6 pm

AND A GOOD TIME WAS HAD BY ALL

AND NOT FOR THE FAMILY FIRST TIME!

ONE OF WHOM MAY HAVE EVEN WORKED FOR THE QUEEN!

Board of Green Cloth

Admit the Bearer to the forecourt of
BUCKINGHAM PALACE
from 10 a.m. on the occasion of
THE QUEEN'S BIRTHDAY
on Saturday 3rd June 1972

Maclean

Author Copy

INTRO...*followed by*...

PREQUEL (a) - WHERE THERE'S A WILL,
                                    THERE'S A WAY (*OUT*) –TRUST ME?
PREQUEL (b) - TRUSTING TO THE WILL OF OTHERS
                                                              PASSED AWAY
FOLLOWED BY AN INTRODUCTION TO HIS *BALLIOL ALMA MATER*
PART 1+ BANKING HENRY *SAM* GUINNESS+THE *EXTENDED* BREWING ARM
PART 1+1 AN ALEC GUINNESS TENUOUS 'LEGAL SANCTITY OF MARRIAGE LINK EXPLORED
PART 1+2: BANKING *TEMPORARILY* SUPPLANTED BY BONKING! – UNTIL?
PART 1a: BONKING *TEMPORARILY* SUPPLANTED BY MORE BONKING! – UNTIL?
PART 1ai: BONKING *TEMPORARILY* SUPPLANTED BY BANGING!
PART 1b - HIS *BALLIOL ALMA MATER* ROWING/FIGHTING CREW(S)
PART 1ci & 1cii: THE ONCE KING EDWARD VIII OF OLD!!!
      LIKE FATHER LIKE SON<>ONE NOT AFRAID TO PUT IT ABOUT!!!
PART 1d: THE 3Ws in WW2??? & 'ONE' NO LONGER KING!!!
PART 1e: THE 3Ws in WW2??? & 'ONE' NO LONGER KING <> SET STRAIGHT!!!
PART 2 - THE EPSTEIN INTERWOVEN FALLOUT HERE AND '<u>RELATIVELY</u>' ABROAD!
PART 2a – HIS/HIS GUEST'S POLICE FOREBODING!
PART 2b – HIS SECRET'S ACT WAR EFFORT(S)
                    PLUS AN APPARENT GOD FEARING DEVIL AND MORE SPIES
PART 2c: HIS *(FLUFF)* WIFE ALFHILD'S WAR EFFORT(S)
PART 3: SAM'S AUNT LUCY *LASZLO*
PART 4: THE GUN IS MIGHTIER THAN THE SWORD & THE WORD HAS NO CHANCE AGAINST THE BULLET!
PART 5: DAUGHTER MARIT EXCHANGING UNKNOWNS
PART 6: THE WOMEN ALSO SHOW THEIR YOUNGER METAL
PART 7: HELLO SABRINA – BUT SEE YOU LATER....
PART 8: HELLO MIRANDA – SEE YOU'RE JUST TRYING
                                                              TO BE ORDINARY
PART 9: HELLO JASMINE (+ HOLLY) – THE ORDINARY
PART 10: POOR MICHELLE BUT NOT THE PROPERTY
PART 11a: JULIA THE SAGE BEAUTY
PART 11b: ANITA THE BEAUTY THAT IS RICH
PART 12a: NATASHA THE SAGE FAILED NOT THE WORK
PART 12b: COMING & GOING WITH THE OTHER THREE SIBLINGS
PART 12c: THE SIBLING SPOTLIGHT NOW FOCUSES UPON
PART 13: ANNA TAKES OVER FROM DADDY FREUD
PART 14: MICHAEL ETHICAL COMPANY CHARITY MAN
PART 14a -NAT -URAL RICH PRE-THOUGHTS.
PART 14b -SAM'S HISTORICAL MUREX PAST
PART 14c -AND NOW FOR AN EXTENSIVE JOHN LED
                              TOUR OF THAT FAMOUS MELLS PARK PLACE.
PART 14d -AND NOW TO THE JOHN LED *RENEWABLES*
                                                  MONEY NITTY GRITTY >
PART 14e -TRUSTING TO TRUSTS BUT NOT THE SAM WAY
PART 14f -ANNA'S COMPLETE OVERHAUL COURTESY OF SOME VERY
                    SPECIAL FELLOW JEWISH (ETCETERI) PATRONAGES
PART 15: SABRINA – YOU CAN TRY VALIANTLY – BUT?
PART 16a+b: STOPPARD HUBBY AND CRICKETTING PINTER
PART 17: A POST SCRIPTED FANS-TASTICAL MALE FEMALE FINALE!
PART 18: JOHN's MEMORABLE (YCTV) REGARDS TO ALL - MYA

PREQUEL - WHERE THERE'S A WILL,
                                           THERE'S A WAY (*OUT*) –TRUST ME?

Like so many more out there – a veritable jargon hotchpotch; I kid you not!

- *Incidence of Tax on lifetime transfers,*
- *Personal Chattels Legacy,*
- *Agricultural Property legacy Fund,*
- *Life Interest Trust in Default,*
- *Discretionary Beneficiaries,*
- *Extended Power of maintenance…*

The Trustees, as usual, had all the powers of….

- *general management,*
- *investment,*
- *lending,*
- *borrowing,*
- *apportionment guaranteeing,*
- *insuring,*
- *trading,*
- *exclusion,*
- *appropriation,*
- *minor relationship,*
- *Charitable payments,*
- *agent, foreigner & nominee appointments,*
- *delegation,*
- *indemnification,*
- *charging,*
- *remuneration,*
- *variance of administrative provisions …*

(John paused, it wasn't worth any more effort, as there was still more **& more**, including several pages of *'interpretation!'*)

My God, Sam's was so much easier to *office* work with, there again the provisions were an education, which I needed to learn to pass my Probate *Taxing* Paper – admittedly, at the second time of trying."
Zzzzzzzzz

John made out he had fallen asleep with all the effort; he looked so innocently vulnerable to … lying there eyes closed, but the grin still apparent; *I could have* …but I couldn't, **or could I have?**

My thoughts were interrupted as the closed eye *sleeper* perked up,
"So, where's this frog's kiss then?"

*** *BUT needless to say the (Female) Psychiatrist said, "NO!"*

BUT
Here she says YES!

As we need his expert input ONCE...again:- So I needed search his old[old] Taxation Examination Study Notes. ([old] *apologies if they have changed much in the many years since my John qualified*!)
And so here come's an enlightenment to those who care to be *legally*
En-Lightened!

- The essence of a Trust is the imposition of an equitable[1] obligation on a person who is the legal owner of property (a trustee) which requires that person to act in good conscience when dealing with that property in favour of any person (the beneficiary) who has a beneficiary interest recognised by equity[11] in the property.
- The Trustee is said to 'hold the property on trust' for the beneficiary.
- There are four significant elements to the trust:-
- That it is equitable; [ET]
- That it provides the beneficiary with rights in property;
- That it also imposes obligations on the trustee;
- That those obligations are fiduciary[111] in nature!
- The trust comes into existence either by virtue of having been established expressly by a person (the settlor) who was the absolute[IV] owner of the property before the creation of the trust (an express trust);
- Or by virtue of some action of the settlor which the court interprets to have been sufficient to create a trust but which the settlor himself did not know was a trust (!)(?) (an implied [express] trust);
- Or by operation of law either to resolve some dispute as to ownership of property where the creation of an express trust has failed (an automatic resulting trust);
- Or to recognise the proprietary[VI] rights of one who has contributed to the purchase price of the property (a purchase price resulting trust);
- Or by operation of the law to prevent the legal owner from seeking unconsciously to deny the rights of those who have equitable interests in that property (a constructive trust).

I. *Equitable = means fair or impartial. In legal context it can relate to "equity" as opposed to "law". The distinction between equity and law originates from England where courts were divided into two kinds, courts of equity and courts of law.*

II. *Equity = is the particular body of law, developed in the English Court of Chancery, with the general purpose of providing legal remedies for cases wherein the common law is **inflexible** and cannot fairly resolve the disputed legal matter.*

III. *Fiduciary = is someone who 'by law' manages money or property for someone else for that person's benefit and not for their own!*

IV. *Absolute = NB The waters might get a bit muddied here later [V], but an absolute title confers upon the holder the right to use and dispose of the property as they wish, without any contestations that could hinder them. The owner can freely sell the property, giving the buyer the same title upon completion of the purchase, provided the seller had it in the first place. Additionally an absolute owner is/was known as the person holding the (mortgage) freehold title deeds!*

V. *Not always absolute however e.g. >Such that the property in question is best understood to be 'rights in property' & need not be absolute title in the property. Thus a lease over land may itself be the subject matter of* a trust even though it is not the largest property right in that land (Keech v Sandford 1726 – Yes they do go back that far – just as the Landed gentry Do?! – An equitable trust ^{ET} in trust may itself be the subject of a trust (Re Lashmar 1891).

VI. *Proprietary rights = are legal rights that an entity has to own property, whether tangible or intangible (like an easement). As with the absolute title above the owner has the right to accumulate, own, hold, delegate, rent, or sell their property.*

John's notes then said there were 4 main types of trust:- these being under the Law of Property Act 1925 s53(^{2})

1. *Implied trusts – rarely used.*
2. *Express trusts = declared intentionally by the 'settlor';*
3. *Resulting trusts = implied by the Court;*
4. *Constructive trusts = arising by operation of law*

John would much later also come across the Freud's 'Blind Trust!' (Below)
However, I shan't bore you much longer..
Although, wherever you look you will be flooded with the various types, although you might consider something different like > a Gifts out of Income declaration! So now starting with the Law Society....

➢ *Bare;*

➢ *Interest in Possession =* **Example** *You create a trust for all the shares you owned. The terms of the trust say that when you die, the income from those shares go to your wife for the rest of her life. When she dies, the shares will pass to your children. Your wife is the income beneficiary and has an 'interest in possession' in the trust. She does not have a right to the shares themselves.*

➢ *Discretionary;*

➢ *Mixed;*

➢ *A special one for a vulnerable person;*

➢ *Non-Resident;*

➢ *HMRC add a settlor-interested;*

➢ *Accumulation;*

➢ *Charitable/Non Charitable*

➢ *Then hunt around and you'll be inundated...*

➢ *But in the main they have no part in our story adventure.*

➢ *Although people with wealth and big business can thwart the taxman with Charitable contributions which are tax deductible and perhaps one of our principals later along the line has done that in one form or another?*

➢ *Then there are those non-scrupulous types who salt away their undisclosed income in foreign (fraud accepted) climes and with these their numbers dwarf the number of different Trusts you can find!*

➢ *BUT you'll find all them and the related Panama/pandora paper revelations expanded upon in my,* The Rich and Powerful don't give a shit *- (about us)? #*

On 30th July 2014 Judgment was handed down in the case of *Re The Estate of Lucian Michael Freud*, which followed a previous ruling in *Marley v Rawlings* (the scope of clerical error).

But here I might point out again a rich man who was quite dissolute # *(of a person or a way of life) overindulging in sensual pleasures!)* and so many about him were treated with disdain! So some elaboration... #
... Freud was infamous for fathering an enormous number of children while avoiding his responsibilities for

11

raising them - One daughter by one illicit affair was most scathing about the way he treated people/women in general! - *(There again the women took no precautions either? His fame and more importantly his wealth pull?).* The 14 of them, two from his first marriage and a dozen by various mistresses, might have expected a life of inherited clover on his death...

BUT...
The Will, which was drafted in 2006, apparently he left his entire residue estate jointly to his former Solicitor Diana Rawstron and one of his daughters Rose Pearce, also both appointed as sole executors...because they were bound by a secret promise that they would distribute certain amounts of it to a number of undisclosed recipients, who remained un-named!
I only added this for a bit of spice and that his other famous relatives might feature later on!

Many wiki 4.0 cc thanks to Simon Edwards Esq for his-Grave_of_Lucian_Freud_at_Highgate_Cemetery

(Clement Freud's Ashes are in the same Cemetery – See Later...Below)

Trusts raise selves again in PART 9: HELLO JASMINE (+ HOLLY) – THE ORDINARY#
RESTRICTION: No disposition by a sole proprietor of the land (not being a trust corporation) under which capital money arises is to be registered except under an order of the registrar or of the Court!?

So, what was that all about?

Old Sam's Trust Stuff rearing its head?

And who banked here?

Again to avoid the snoopy taxman?

Jersey/Guernsey Tax Havens, or perhaps even more Identity Protective?

<u>CONTINUING JOHN'S TRUST(ING) SAM'S EDUCATION...</u>
<u>PREQUEL (b) - TRUSTING TO THE WILL OF OTHERS</u>   **PASSED AWAY**

And here I will just give you snippet of a future Chapter relating to a certain 'Epstein' which he named after his birthday, the 1953 Trust, and so many are desperate to see within, and they had to wait until now – normally they would have no access!
Another intriguing Legal aspect which may have been at the centre of it all was the hiding of so many of his property dealings? BUT The use of a private trust means that the details of his beneficiaries are not normally released to the public. There again it may be pursued that the transfer of assets into the trust is a fraudulent transfer as Epstein was facing criminal charges at the time of his death.
BUT it all is slowly coming out in the DOJ revealed paperwork wash!
                                                                        ALL REVEALED IN PART 2 >>>>

Sam's story all began there...
                                                                                              *** Later

PLAIN JANE GUINNESS & I ONCE...CHAPTER Thirty Six:
Where There's a <u>Will</u>, There's a Way (*Out*) – <u>Trust</u> me? Part 1

Way back when... *wow how the other 1% live and possess: the only <u>lift</u> tour of the place (Sam, then nearing death, <u>could no longer cope with the stairs</u>) showed me to the rear, with that solitary upright sculpture, within the expansive greenery for which he was taxed! Then the upper floors, but the first, the most outstanding, to many displayed paintings and that, paintings surrounded, focal grand polished near thirty seater dining table, he smiled at me as he saw me take it all in.*

Then, Fluff, in her cultured soprano voice, called out to Sam, (she never called him his christened Henry) saying (red haired#) daughter, Marit had arrived... (#Contrary to Charlie Boy's Guinness Blonde ex, the dominant banking-arm hair gene was actually red/ginger!)... but back to that other day ... One afternoon, walking into their front living room for our standard tea & biscuit treat, <u>his</u> dearest sweet-petite Norwegian wife, Alfhild, (he called her, <u>Fluff</u>) warned him to be careful; <u>he</u>, still using his walking stick support, proffered the same advice about <u>her</u>, prompting the ever inquisitive me to ask as to <u>his</u> state of health. Like all people, at that age, becoming more frail, the truth is never on their lips, just a usual, OK, type response, hiding reality from the listener, but, her expression said there was something more serious than <u>he</u> would let on – <u>then he only had but 2 more years## to live!</u> (Alfhild survived him by 8 years) Pity, he missed another (minor) milestone, if he had lived 3 more years he could have celebrated 50 years in his Cheyne pad!

Subconsciously drawn by death, I raised the subject of Wills!?

Well, being one of the local tax officials for old Sam's area...Perhaps, old Sam may have been worse## than he let on! He was to die shortly primarily of Prostate Cancer, although, the Cancer had spread to many parts of his body by then, *poor* man! His daughter, Marit, like me, saw her/my father die in pain : it is not something a loving someone should suffer!

See, *rich* and having had it all, disease is not selective about the dying prisoners it takes! Nor, the pain it inflicts: there is only so much morphine the doctors could medically/legally allow injected into him!

<u>**GONE, BUT NOT FORGOTTEN!**</u>

Sam Guinness [signature]

Sam, the ever charming and open minded host asked if I wanted to view his!? (I had previously broached the subject of his wealth, or apparent lack of it, relatively, at his late stage of life, living on a seemingly strict allowance* and was interested what happens next, sort of thing)!?

"It's about the same length as my Dad's!" I said incredulously.

"So, that's the critical aspect!" Sam nodded, with cheeky grin.

"My mates at the Tax/Probate Office are gonna be disappointed!"

And so they were, Sam left this earth less than a couple of years after, as the Estate grossed short of *£2k, netted just over the £1k mark! Yet, the premises he and I shared tit-bits in, his, was valued (then) well in excess of the million mark; so what happened there?

The fascination stayed with me, not that I would ever be in that envious position, *albeit my place is valued also in excess of a million, though this is over 30 years on*, but my office position gave me access to so many more and so convoluted, as to be mazes within mazes! Trusts can be such virtually, unravellable puzzles: Let confusion reign!" … And so I allowed free spirited John, free reign over all he surveyed! >>>

"Strange, Dad had his old war buddy as Executor; others use Solicitors, but **his** was apparently a *River* based Limited Trust Company; the Will a few pages long started highlighting new methods & legal terms I needed to acquaint myself and be truly versed in – my future exams depended on it.

All his property, unlike Dad, he didn't leave it simply all to his wife, but to her via that Trust, then to the daughters via that Trust again, or to their/any children offspring *per stirpes*. (That was one thing had me stumped at the time!) (It would have been quite different if his beloved Georgeson hadn't *mishandled* a loaded gun at 15 years, 3 months, 3 days, old/young! And still his Landed descended/related Gentry play at killing, whether, across the water, or here down South, or north of my Pitlochry Castle roots?!"

John paused and returned to the lesson at heart.

"Amazing the power that some Trustees have, if they see fit:

- *sell any, or all of the assets;*
- *provide funds for security/property;*
- *manage property whether freehold, or leasehold;*
- *determine buying/selling share business, with this sole exception where investment in* certain *alcoholic shares was still to be maintained.*

This ex Irish-Eire ** resident declared that all within was free of all duties – How clever he was, as the whole thing would be in other's hands; there again the will was made in the spring of 69, (not the Summer, as with Bryan Adams') – sorry couldn't resist that one – just one month short of six years off his death, so little legislatively changed within the intervening period. ** And no mention of Non Dom Status!

> *(** This, perhaps, exclaims why he apparently wasn't called up for WWI*
> *- like his since very long departed slaughtered Oxford colleagues?)*

The will though seemed quite simplistic as it was all down to Trustees to carry on doing what they did best, but it still took over 3 years to settle!

His relative's, ** a Non Dom, three times as long, made just seven years & a few days before his own demise, took less than a year?! Oddly enough, from his choice of Executors, you could see who were the business brains in the extended family and passed them on to … a her!

Couldn't believe my ears/eyes when told by a colleague of the money in our tax coffers – apparently she said, '£4 million plus gross and all we got was £20!'

I had a laugh to myself – *It's all those infernal trusts, again!* I just wondered how the place, a few miles from St. Tropez, was designated; also the long lease on the swimming pool/tennis court equipped elite, overlooking Holland Park, London pad leased-long in his name; then there was that hilly farm, including trout stream and its neighbouring sporting rights of 2000 acres – he, like so many of his kind, liked his outdoors > hunting/fishing/shooting.

The pecuniary (if you don't know Latin, you're no lawyer) legacies were interesting, having met one of the beneficiaries outside his home when I visited that time; contrary to Police reporting (later), she *wasn't there at the time*...but we'd already met a few times by then.

The other (Trust Fund) beneficiaries, apart from his wife, who were not the millionaire marrying types and worked to pay the bills?!

Seems all had to? Funds out of their control, perhaps not totally?

Maybe, the Trust stated that money only when married?
Or, until demise of his still existante wife?
Or, whatever some distant Great Grand-daddy deceased sorted and put in motion, still a nuisance, those Trust conditions!
Again the old *per stirpes* language surfaced. But, then something new to me, something called a *Nil Rate Band Legacy Fund?*

And, by *Carlo Collodi* Jiminy Cricket, there was more!

"That will was so short and undetailed, but the Trust was the significant aspect; his nephew's was longer, yet took less to finalise! Trusts reminded me of the tax avoidance schemes which were later to become the vogue, particularly the loan terms which could be anything the parties wanted to be. But, I might bore you with that sometime later, but not now."

That statement actually takes place in a *later* session in this tale, but, in view of what he discusses next, your introduction will begin here, much sooner than *later*...
Just as later, after John had retired, did a certain Secret Trust raise its Legal Wrangling > Rawstron v (That Illustrious Family) Freud!

(Later)

But, not too late for John's personal involvement – now qualified – was there a certain House of Lords Case (Sam related, but he, now sadly deceased) > Guinness Mahon v Kensington < where John learned that 'subrogation was a restitutionary device, not just an equitable one!'
'Yes, I too have no idea what that all meant – but, John then did!

(Oh, John, that Rich Language you had to learn to use!)
....

AND THERE'S SO MUCH MORE!

> **1906-7**   BALLIOL COLLEGE REGISTER
>
> **GUINNESS, Henry Samuel Howard.**—b. June 22, 1888; e.s. of Howard Rundell Guinness, of Co. Dublin. *Educ.* Winchester; Balliol 1906-9 (H.B.H., G.W.S.); 3rd Nat. Sci. (Zool.) 1909; B.A. 1910. Torpid (head of river 1907), Eight (Henley). Hon. Finl. Adviser, Foreign Office, 1919; Senior partner in Guinness, Mahon & Co., Bankers, London and Dublin; Dir. of Nat. Discount Co. Ltd. and of Provincial Bank of Ireland; London Chm. Commercial Banking Co. of Sydney; Viking Investment Trust Ltd.; Chev. Order of St. Olav, Norway. m. 1913. Alfhild Holter of Oslo, Chev. of St. Olav.; one son (d. 1930), three daughters. Benefactor of the College. Founded a Scholarship from Shrewsbury in memory of his son, George Guinness.

AN INTRODUCTION TO HIS *BALLIOL ALMA MATER* FAMILY

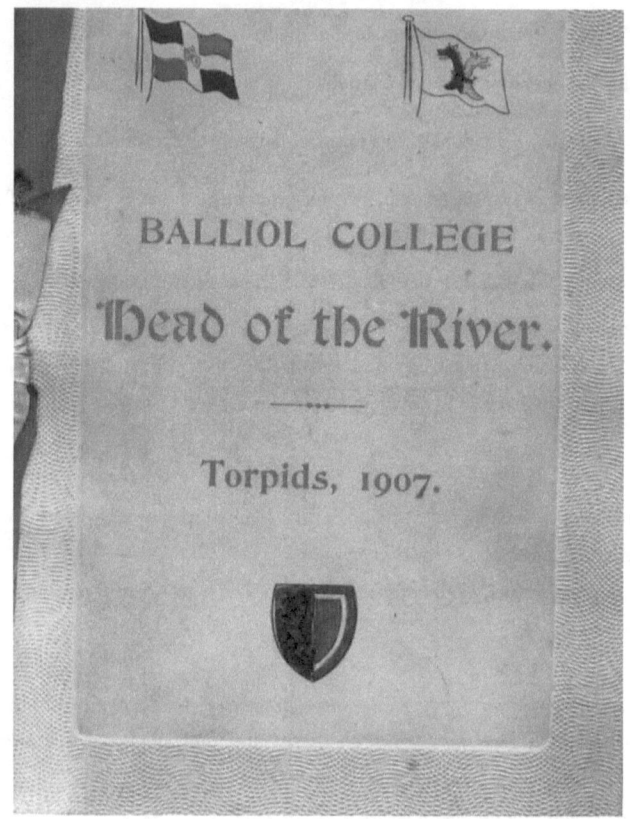

THIS BOOK IS *PLAINLY* SOME SORT OF BIOGRAPHY...

BUT GOING BACK GENERATIONS

INSIGHTFUL? PERHAPS?

WITH AN UNKNOWN SNIPPET HERE

– ANOTHER THERE...

AND PERHAPS SO MUCH MORE TO FOLLOW...

Something unknown to so many *(Like those Royal Story before?)*, but a certain Guinness Brewery Man was a renown Blue @ Rowing for Balliol, long before any of you readers were born!

Who?

Keep turning over...for an insight written by a University Fellow/Friend...

PART 1+:BANKING HENRY *SAM* GUINNESS+THE *EXTENDED* BREWING ARM

I used the word **'extended'** as I will now take you all on a rather convoluted Rich/Royal 20th Century linked tour starting and ending with a certain Lord Moyne (A Guinness), *who was born 29 March 1880 – died 6 Nov1944), who will be one of the focal 'W' points in the –* **'There are 3Ws in WW2!?'**

The first Guinness my John met was Henry Samuel Howard (k/a Sam to his family and friends) down at his No 6 Cheyne Walk 'tall extended' house premises and his story will unfold later:
Introductory Historical Note:- Henry Samuel Howard Guinness was born on 22 June 1888 in Dublin, his father, Howard, was 20 and his mother, Mary, was 25.
He married Norwegian Alfhild Holter on 8 October 1913.
They had four children during their marriage.
He died on 10 April 1975 in Cheyne Walk, Chelsea, London, at the age of 86.
His neighbours about him were the Rolling Stones and their manager, plus Channon + another Guinness staying in further down the road...

He should not be confused *with another* >>>>

And so this part of the Book will start *with another* 'Henry' Guinness....

Henry Eustace Guinness (22 Sept. 1897 – 19 Feb. 1972) an Irish banker and politician.

His place of education was at Winchester College, in Hampshire, England.

He fought in World War I and gained the rank of Lieutenant in the service of the Royal Artillery.

In addition, he was a partner and later of managing director of Guinness & Mahon bank.

He was an Independent member of Seanad Éireann from 1954 to 1957.

Henry Eustace Guinness was nominated by the Taoiseach, John A. Costello in 1954 to the 8th Seanad.

But there is so much more that my patient John discovered!

>>>

If you venture down Norfolk/Suffolk UK way you'll come across a place called 'Elveden' which many will associate with the 'Centre Parcs' resort location.

But in reality the resort is small financial fry compared with the largest landowner in that vicinity: The Iveagh Family ^{IF} *which is part of the Guinness Dynasty – BUT the Brewery Arm - and it is from there they also sell their locally produced foodstuffs etc.*

^{IF} *See Part 2 for more scandalous behaviour!!!*

But there is another place nearby called 'Lakenheath' which many inside the USA will not be aware is where part of their Air Force is located!

And the link here is that the Guinness owners leased this Air Force Occupied area for something like £60 million annually – that was the figure John ascertained many years ago! Now it is?

And we miniscule fry complain of the amount we pay for our Housing!

But there is so much more that my patient John discovered!

His Guinness family homes were at <u>Farmleigh</u> near Dublin, and at <u>Elveden Hall</u> in Suffolk.

>>>

Elveden and its surroundings have been used for filming on a number of occasions. These films include:

- <u>Agatha Christie's Poirot</u>: <u>Cat Among the Pigeons</u> (2008)[5]
- <u>All the Money in the World</u> (2017)
- <u>Dean Spanley</u> (2008)
- <u>Eyes Wide Shut</u> (1999)
- <u>Gulliver's Travels</u> (1996) TV / DVD
- <u>Heart of Stone</u> (2023)
- <u>Lara Croft: Tomb Raider</u> (2001)
- <u>Stardust</u> (2007)
- <u>The Living Daylights</u> (1987)
- <u>The Moonstone</u> (1997)

Such an impressive list is reminiscent of those I enumerated upon in my Scotland travels, contained in part within my,

Legal Sanctity of Marriage – Part 10 <
*> **Where green with envy***
Is a colour match made for more than two!

Whose Back Book Cover resonated with the following, below, which just reflects the goings on with the following selection of Rich Pampered yet still Unhappy Individuals!

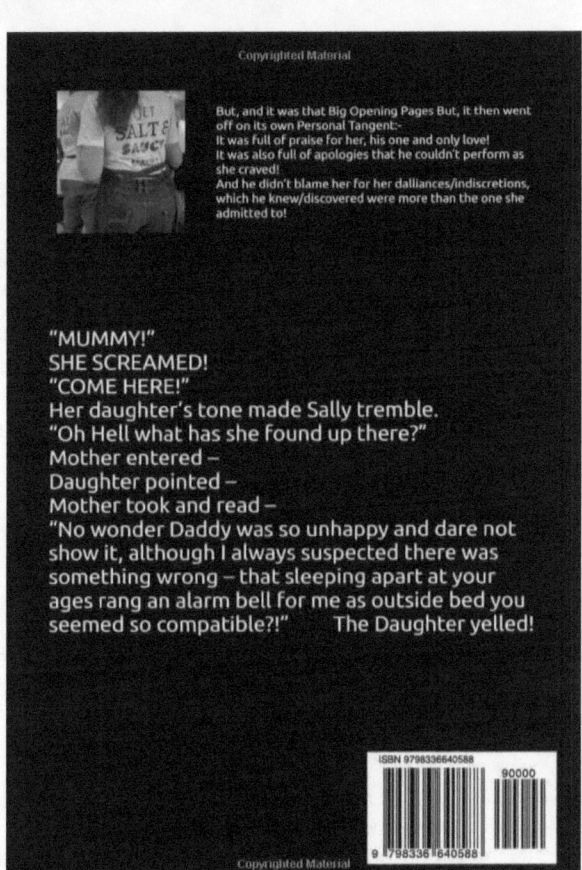

BUT *the Brewing Arm is not on my Chart below?!*

Of which Henry formed part of the second level down...

WHY?

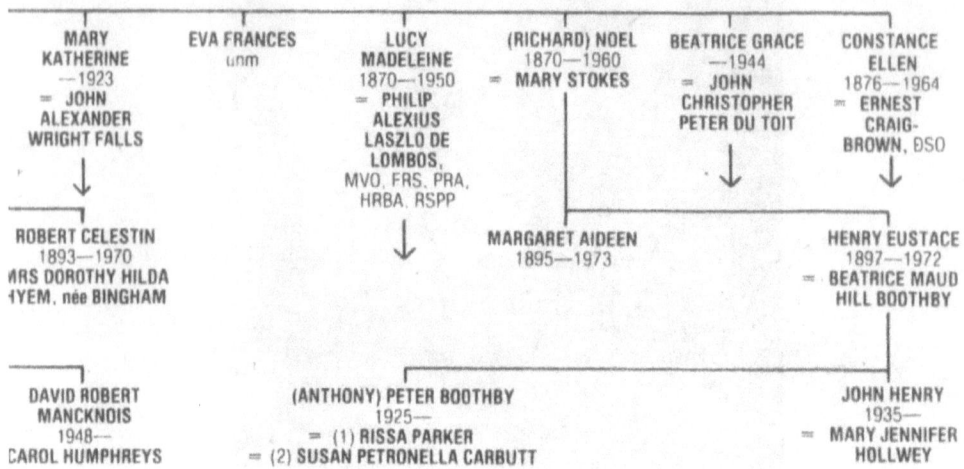

It was the **Boothby link** here that was sought.

Who you can see also married a Guinness!

BUT
Later in the Book it would be the Mitfords...and below...
And what bound them was another Guinness...with that Elveden Iveagh connectivity:-

Walter Edward Guinness, 1st Baron Moyne, DSO & Bar, TD, PC was a British Conservative politician, soldier and businessman.
He was a British Minister of State in the Middle East until November 1944, when he was assassinated in Cairo by the Jewish terrorist group named Lehi.
The assassination reverberated through Palestine and the rest of the world. And the effect on the 1948 # Agreements one can only surmise!?
     (See my ...# **The Legal Sanctity To A Peaceful Life: But Tell That To The Takers/Breakers/Killers!** *(Also in Italian).*

And the resurrected fighting now?

He [H] was the third and youngest son of Edward Guinness, 1st Earl of Iveagh;<> At a certain point in time, Edward was one of the richest men in Ireland. Edward married his third cousin Adelaide Maria Guinness in 1873; this helped concentrate family wealth and maintain tight control of the brewery before it became a public company. They went on to have three children together. He died 1927.

[H] His brothers were Rupert Guinness, 2nd Earl of Iveagh and Hon. Ernest Guinness. His family homes were at Farmleigh near Dublin, and at Elveden Hall in Suffolk. (SEE ALSO PART 2 SCANDALS)

BUT even though a male he did not inherit that special interest in Elveden as according to the Rich (unwritten ?) Rule?/?Law, the first born male always seems to inherit!

And never the female even if first born – a perfect example The Spencer Estate and what the Royal & Guinness Families strive(d?) for also!

At Eton, Guinness was appointed as Captain of Boats. *(And here our link with that other Guinness of particular interest – a Fellow Oxford Student, but a Rowing Blue, Sam - Later)*

Walter was married with 3 three children <> His story will follow below after these snippets...

BUT it was who his son (d.1992) Bryan married, which will be of much later interest – a certain Hon. Diana # Mitford, one of the Mitford sisters – See Part 9 of this Book...(The other # Dianas will get a mention later.)

The point to be made here is how personal opinions/connections can split family ties/bonds!

On the one hand we had amongst others in a certain Private Members' Club >our Walter Guinness, Lloyd George, Bob Boothby and notably Winston Churchill who apparently went bananas when he heard the news of a policy so **'sordid, squalid, sub-human and suicidal'**! *

*Many Munich Treaty thanks to the German Federal Archive for this file is licensed under the CC-BY-SA 3.0 Germany license. Attribution: Bundesarchiv, Bild 183-R69173

- The Munich Agreement * was an agreement reached in Munich 30 September 1938, by Nazi Germany, the UK, France & Italy, who were fascist led!.
- The agreement provided for the German annexation of part of Czechoslovakia called the Sudetenland, where more than three million people, mainly ethnic Germans, lived.
- The pact is also known in some areas as **the Munich Betrayal** because of a previous 1924 alliance agreement and a 1925 military pact between France and the Czech Republic.

And my picture below echoes the local sentiment when Germany later rolled over that Country...

Author Copyright <> WW2 Prague homage to those who died assassinating the Butcher Heydrich – the many bullet holes showed they were showed no mercy!
As were the villagers chosen to join them in their graves!
*(This Book's Czech link will follow later...**Part 16b**)*

What was of particular interest to me was that in Parliament the majority agreed with Moyne's cousin-in-law, except such as Chips * Channon MP, (d.1958), who apparently rejoiced – BUT he would, wouldn't he: he was a supporter of and belonged to Chamberlain's administration plus he loathed America, despite that's where his family wealth came from!

But American wealth came back to seduce him later as he became friendly with that (in)famous Mrs Simpson & her partner, King Edward V111. *(He died in 1972 of throat cancer).*

And another perhaps sordid link with Boothroyd above was they were both openly bi-sexual – perhaps that's why Channon's brewing heiress spouse, Lady Honor Guinness, (d.1976), eldest daughter of Rupert, the 2nd Earl of Iveagh, took up with so many (? Local) lovers ending up with a local farmer close to her new home, Kelvedon Hall * - meantime old Channon was buggering the local landscape gardener Peter Coats (d.1990)!

The irony of it all * Kelvedon Hall was his recent country purchase to get away from **it (?)** all at London's Belgravia!

BUT **it** _never left him_ as a certain Terence Rattigan *took his amorous rear entry attention!*

NB * One of the Channon residences happened to be in the 90s the other end from Sam's who was in 6, with the so many of the Rolling Stones + their manager with various Houses within!

EXPANDED FROM MY, LEGAL SANCTITY OF MARRIAGE – PART 8 'SOLE OR SOUL?':-

....CHAPTER 3 LOVE AT FIRST SIGHT Part 1

LOVE AT FIRST SIGHT:- *'No Matter What You Read/Hear There is Nothing k/a Love at First Sight, because Without Subsequent Conversation the Love Base Cannot be Established!'*

I think that notion is best exemplified in the Peter O'Toole/Petula Clark version of 'Goodbye Mr Chips', where the soubrette, Miss Bridges, doesn't initially pay Chippings any mind.

But on the second occasion at Naples and Pompey when spending time alone talking, she recognised his, now, 'first love felt attraction' which was confirmed in a later scene at her home when his true character persona blossomed before her!

Although, our book hero Michael's second occasion venture, he thought disastrous!

There again one thing mentioned is that much sung about, *'Power of Love'*, by so many!

But, not the Power of Lust, which brought us our famous (Sir) Alec Guinness, who was conceived when his mother prostituted herself on/in a boat at one Cowes Regatta with one, or all three of a male only Guinness Party plus a certain Scottish Mr Geddes!

And possibly the crew members, according to Alec's memoirs!

Agnes Cuff, most times drunk[ML] *and short of cash, according to Alec's memoirs, was either turning up at his stage doorstep cadging cash off him, or had to do other 'illegitimate' things to supplement her meagre legitimate income, had worked at Cowes on the Isle of Wight as a barmaid at the Royal Yacht Squadron clubhouse at the time of the Cowes Regatta in 1913, which was attended by several members of the Guinness family including Edward Guinness, 1st Earl of Iveagh, and his sons Ernest and Walter.*

Members of the Guinness family claimed a "distinct resemblance" between Alec and one or other of the Guinnesses at Cowes that year; Honor Guinness, who made Alec's acquaintance in 1950 and invited him to tea with "his cousin", later visiting Alec's family with photo albums and diaries to point out the similarities she perceived, believed either her uncle Ernest or his brother Walter ("a celebrated seducer") was Alec's father, while her cousin Lindy considered Alec closely resembled her father, Loel >> This Guinness had tragedy follow him as so many others:- first marriage had a son, Patrick Benjamin Guinness, who was killed in an automobile accident in Switzerland! One of many tragic episodes:- Lady Henrietta Guinness – Her husband was the younger brother of Lord Ardilaun, Lady Plunket, and The Earl of Iveagh - she once famously said 'If I had been poor, I would have been happy' – fell from a bridge in Italy in 1978. That same year, her relative Peter Guinness, aged just 4, was killed in a car crash in Norfolk. What gives this story poignancy is that the car was driven by his father, Sir John Ralph Sidney Guinness CB (1935 – 2020).

And so, Alec Guinnes himself had son tragedy, as his only son contracted polio and to add another to his metaphorically 'unfinished' Agatha Christie novel, Alec thought his father was a Scottish banker named Andrew Geddes (1861–1928):- Geddes, a friend or business acquaintance of the brewing family, it was he who paid for Guinness's education at boarding schools in Southbourne and Eastbourne.

NB Geddes was a guest on that infamous sexually current swaying 1913 Cowes boat!

Alec himself caught that (? Drink/Excess) ^{ML = Mother Lush} disease killing duo combo prostate + liver cancer!

For the conception event, about his mother, Alec uses the word *'whore'* in one of his Biographies!

Hence a one 'IN' four chance one of the celebrated Guinness 'elite' was the father – So that's where that nickname, 'Chips' ^{CH} makes its connected entrance as one related to the above famous family was one known as Chips * Channon MP, (d.1958)

Chips Channon 1930

Public Domain HMSO has declared that the expiry of Crown Copyrights applies worldwide -

Channon's brewing heiress spouse was Lady Honor Guinness, (d.1976), (NB She was never Lady Channon. Her first husband was knighted several years after their divorce, so when she was married to him she was known only by her courtesy title as the daughter of an Earl, i.e. Lady Honour Channon, not by the style of a woman married to a knight, i.e. Lady Channon.)

However, as wives go, because 'Chips' was gay this _naturally_ (?) followed? >> Peter Coates, the upper-class rent boy, who he took up with & who was known by those in the know as 'Petticoats', but by the more venomous/nasty amongst them as 'Mrs Chips'.

More to the sexual point Alec Guinness himself liked the male connection, yet called himself a Bi-Sexual, yet there is no mention of any extra marital curricula female activity, which one might find strange in the acting profession circles where inter-connectivity was acceptably rife!

Public Domain Edward Cecil Guinness, 1st Earl of Iveagh (1847–1927)

Lady Honor Guinness was the eldest daughter of Rupert, the 2nd Earl of Iveagh, ↓↓↓

At 11 May 1937 (Public Domain) https://www.npg.org.uk/collections/search/portrait/mw137418/Rupert-Edward-Cecil-Lee-Guinness-2nd-Earl-of-Iveagh?LinkID=mp55972&role=sit&rNo=5

One of those on the Cowes Boat! Another = His brother Walter…

Walter Edward Guinness, 1st Baron Moyne, DSO & Bar, TD, PC (29 March 1880 – 6 November 1944)
Public Domain Author Unknown

PART 1+1 AN ALEC GUINNESS TENUOUS 'LEGAL SANCTITY OF MARRIAGE LINK EXPLORED

EXPANDED FROM MY, LEGAL SANCTITY OF MARRIAGE – PART 8 'SOLE OR SOUL?':-

....CHAPTER 3 LOVE AT FIRST SIGHT Part 1

LOVE AT FIRST SIGHT:- *'No Matter What You Read/Hear There is Nothing k/a Love at First Sight, because Without Subsequent Conversation the Love Base Cannot be Established!*

I think that notion is best exemplified in the Peter O'Toole/Petula Clark version of 'Goodbye Mr Chips', where the soubrette, Miss Bridges, doesn't initially pay Chippings any mind. (Chips has another user [CH]

But on the second occasion at Naples and Pompey when spending time alone talking, she recognised his, now, 'first love felt attraction' which was confirmed in a later scene at her home when his true character persona blossomed before her!

Although, our book hero Michael's second occasion venture, he thought disastrous!

There again one thing mentioned is that much sung about, *'Power of Love'*, by so many!

But, not the Power of Lust, which brought us our famous (Sir) Alec Guinness, who was conceived when his mother prostituted herself on/in a boat at one Cowes Regatta with one, or all three of a male only Guinness Party plus a certain Scottish Mr Geddes!

And possibly the crew members, according to Alec's memoirs!

Agnes Cuff, most times drunk [ML] and short of cash, according to Alec's memoirs, was either turning up at his stage doorstep cadging cash off him, or had to do other 'illegitimate' things to supplement her meagre legitimate income, had worked at Cowes on the Isle of Wight as a barmaid at the Royal Yacht Squadron clubhouse at the time of the Cowes Regatta in 1913, which was attended by several members of the Guinness family including Edward Guinness, 1st Earl of Iveagh, and his sons Ernest and Walter.

Members of the Guinness family claimed a "distinct resemblance" between Alec and one or other of the Guinnesses at Cowes that year; Honor Guinness, who made Alec's acquaintance in 1950 and invited him to tea with "his cousin", later visiting Alec's family with photo albums and diaries to point out the similarities she perceived, believed either her uncle Ernest or his brother Walter ("a celebrated seducer") was Alec's father, while her cousin Lindy considered Alec closely resembled her father, Loel >>

This Guinness had tragedy follow him as so many others:- first marriage had a son, Patrick Benjamin Guinness, who was killed in an automobile accident in Switzerland!

One of many tragic episodes:- Lady Henrietta Guinness – Her husband was the younger brother of Lord Ardilaun, Lady Plunket, and The Earl of Iveagh - she once famously said 'If I had been poor, I would have been happy' – fell from a bridge in Italy in 1978.

That same year, her relative Peter Guinness, aged just 4, was killed in a car crash in Norfolk.

What gives this story poignancy is that the car was driven by his father, Sir John Ralph Sidney Guinness CB (1935 – 2020).

And so, Alec Guinnes himself had son tragedy, as his only son contracted polio and to add another to his metaphorically 'unfinished' Agatha Christie novel, Alec thought his father was a Scottish banker named

Andrew Geddes (1861–1928):- Geddes, a friend or business acquaintance of the brewing family, it was he who paid for Guinness's education at boarding schools in Southbourne and Eastbourne.

NB Geddes was a guest on that infamous sexually current swaying 1913 Cowes boat!

Alec himself caught that (? Drink/Excess) ^{ML = Mother Lush} disease killing duo combo prostate + liver cancer!

For the conception event, about his mother, Alec uses the word *'whore'* in one of his Biographies!

Hence a one 'IN' four chance one of the celebrated Guinness 'elite' was the father – So that's where that ^{CH} nickname, 'Chips' ^{CH} makes its connected entrance as one related to the above famous family was one known as Chips * Channon MP, (d.1958)

Chips Channon 1930
Public Domain HMSO has declared that the expiry of Crown Copyrights applies worldwide -

'Chips' Death Example =
His friend Princess Marthe Bibesco sent him a telegram, using "Goodbye Mr. Chips" (referencing the 1934 novella of that name by James Hilton). Channon, who smoked and drank heavily, died from a stroke at a hospital in London on 7 October 1958, at the age of 61.
BUT before the end, he was the toast of celebrities, where his party attendance became a must-do!

Well when you attract such as these, what else would you expect? >> *a guest list headed by King Edward VIII and Mrs Simpson, of whom Channon was a friend and admirer, Prince Paul of Yugoslavia, then Regent and his wife Princess Olga of Greece and Denmark, the Duke of Kent and his wife Princess Marina of Greece and Denmark . (So many of these are covered within…later)*

Such an elite' richesse' attendance was matched by his wedding present list!

Channon's brewing heiress spouse was Lady Honor Guinness, (d.1976), (NB She was never Lady Channon. Her first husband was knighted several years after their divorce, so when she was married to him she was known only by her courtesy title as the daughter of an Earl, i.e. Lady Honour Channon, not by the style of a woman married to a knight, i.e. Lady Channon.)

The marriage was doomed since…see later…but his acidic barbed comments displeased so many, examples being, January 21, 1941, following a conversation with Philip's aunt, Princess Nicholas of Greece, Channon noted in his diary regarding Philip, "He is to be our Prince Consort, and that is why he is serving in our navy... but I deplore such a marriage. He and Princess Elizabeth are too inter-related".

The Familial Context: Channon's concern, which was shared by some others at the time, stemmed from the fact that both Elizabeth and Philip were great-great-grandchildren of Queen Victoria (third cousins) and were also related through the Danish Royal line. (this is also covered in this book).

However, as wives go, because 'Chips' was gay this *naturally* (?) followed? >> Peter Coates, the upper-class rent boy, who he took up with & who was known by those in the know as 'Petticoats', but by the more venomous/nasty amongst them as 'Mrs Chips'.

More to the sexual point Alec Guinness himself liked the male connection, yet called himself a Bi-Sexual, yet there is no mention of any extra marital curricula female activity, which one might find strange in the acting profession circles where inter-connectivity was acceptably rife!

Public Domain – Author Unknown
Sir Alec Guinness – London, Old Vic, 1938.

We all are aware of his auto/biographies, but one departure from such was his mish-mash collection under the title banner – A Commonplace Book.

My only 'personal' reason for mentioning is that on page 104 Alec made an error when copying my current club tennis doubles partner's Chekhov leaflet comment on a then forthcoming production of The Cherry Orchard.

So with Nick's permission I'd like to put the record straight:- Nick's surname has two 'l's! = Worrall
— not Worral!

From *LAMDA* leaflet on forthcoming production of The Cherry Orchard:

'The dying Chekhov appears to contemplate a world in which humanity is exhausted, reduced to a futile pattern of physical gestures, squeaky boots, pratfalls, conversations with bookcases or with the setting sun. Here the absence of humanity can seem a consummation devoutly to be wished.'

Nick Worral

Now back to those (apparent) naughty Cowes Yacht occupants…

Public Domain Edward Cecil Guinness, 1st Earl of Iveagh (1847–1927)

Lady Honor Guinness was the eldest daughter of Rupert, the 2nd Earl of Iveagh, ↓↓↓

At 11 May 1937 (Public Domain) https://www.npg.org.uk/collections/search/portrait/mw137418/Rupert-Edward-Cecil-Lee-Guinness-2nd-Earl-of-Iveagh?LinkID=mp55972&role=sit&rNo=5

One of those on the Cowes Boat!

Another = His brother Walter…

Walter Edward Guinness, 1st Baron Moyne, DSO & Bar, TD, PC (29 March 1880 – 6 November 1944)
Public Domain Author Unknown

PART 1+2: BANKING *TEMPORARILY* SUPPLANTED BY BONKING! – UNTIL?

<u>Conversely</u>, sexually speaking, his father was Frank Rattigan CMG, a diplomat whose exploits apparently included an affair with Princess Elisabeth (not Eliz...) of Romania *(below)* (future consort of King George II of Greece) which resulted in her having an abortion. *(Although it was officially covered up/explained as a miscarriage by other reports!)*

And a certain Elisabeth would not object as her husband had!?

Public Domain Author unknown Crown Prince George and Crown Princess Elisabeth of Greece 1921

....

BUT IT IS HERE WE TAKE A BREATHER TO REVIEW THE HEREDITARY LINE CHART

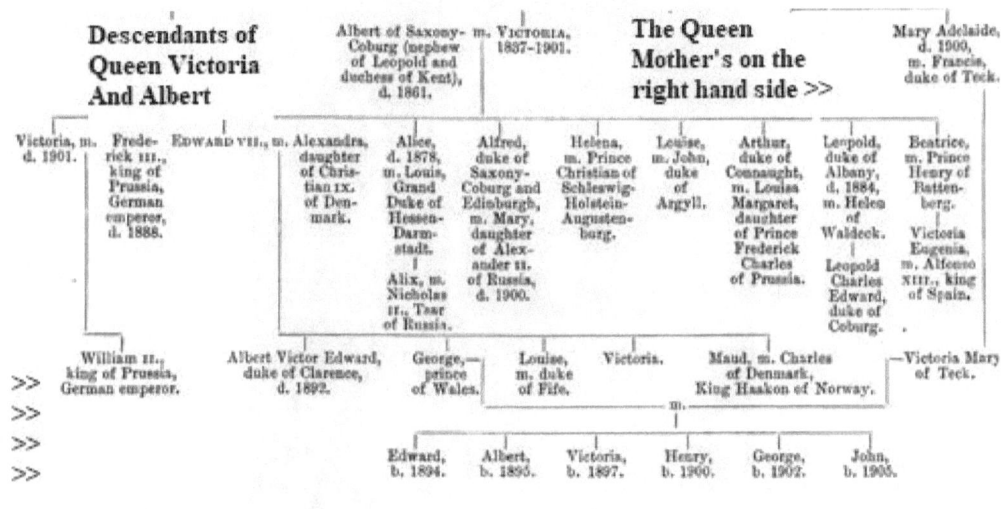

So starting with the bottom line:- Edward was to become Edward VIII and ended up childless, despite being married to Wallis! Additionally he abdicated, as I have written about here and there, so his brother George took over and had his two girls by his Queen Mary – the one who became Queen, we all know to be Elizabeth II:- again I have written about her, here and there.

And what stares you in the face in the names of the 6 children, 4 of their Christian names were straight from their recent relatives – so confusing people when they speak OR WRITE of an Edward, Albert, Victoria or George! E.G. There are 4 Victorias above!!!

Princess Victoria of Hesse and by Rhine, then **Princess Louis of Battenberg**, later **Victoria Mountbatten, Marchioness of Milford Haven** (5 April 1863 – 24 September 1950), was the eldest daughter of Louis IV, Grand Duke of Hesse and by Rhine, and Princess Alice of the United Kingdom, daughter of Queen Victoria and Prince Albert of Saxe-Coburg and Gotha. – mother of >>>>

Public Domain painter de Lazlo-Prinzessin d.1937 Victoria Alice Elisabeth Julie Mari-von-Battenberg, 1907
*This work is in the public domain in its country of origin and other countries and areas where the copyright term is the author's **life plus 70 years or fewer**.*

Coincidental linked past/future name use > Victoria <> Elizabeth?

NB The 'Battenburg' cake was purportedly named in honour of the marriage of Princess Victoria, granddaughter of Queen Victoria, to Prince Louis of Battenburgh, (1884).
The name refers to the German town of Battenberg, Hesses: Countess Julia Hauke became the 1st Countess of Battenberg on her marriage to Prince Alexander of Hesse – k/a Mountbatten in the UK since the 1st World War.

The same war which took so many of Sam Guinness' & others' friends and relatives...

(See Later Chapters...)
For John, he and Terence shared a sporty link – cricket: John, once against Pinter & his fellow writers who played alongside Harold plus Stoppard when he could (later) and Terence also a fellow writer & cricketer, played against Uncle Sam's (and the Guinness') old school # = Rattigan represented the Harrow First XI and scored 29 in the # Eton v Harrow match 1929. Naturally Terence then went on to Oxford Uni! # (The Guinness' University of choice!)

*Terence was also part of a group of writers k/a **the angry men**, to which 'angries' belonged Harold Pinter above!*

For John, his own other Channon/Guinness Cheyne Walk link:- amongst other things down Chelsea way, my John was, at Election time, the Chief Presiding Officer and had access to all the electoral voting records, in addition to his full-time job, all the tax records.
And on his many inspection visits noticed Sam's Cheyne Walk place the other end of another Channon's, who happened to be allowing another young Guinness girl to stay at his/this place!

(No (John) names mentioned here though!)
Coincidental Links <> Everywhere! Or just such select rich/royal bands keeping themselves to themselves?
Coincidentally more:- Cheyne Walk - where a majority of the Rolling Stones and their Manager had homes!

BUT
Now we go elsewhere where sexual predator (?) Frank **_Rat_** (above) had trodden, where only another had ventured **_upon & into!_**

And a certain _Elisabeth_ would not object as her husband had!?

Public Domain 1906 -Crown_Princess_Marie_of_Romania_with_her_daughter_Elisabeth

....

It all starts here:-

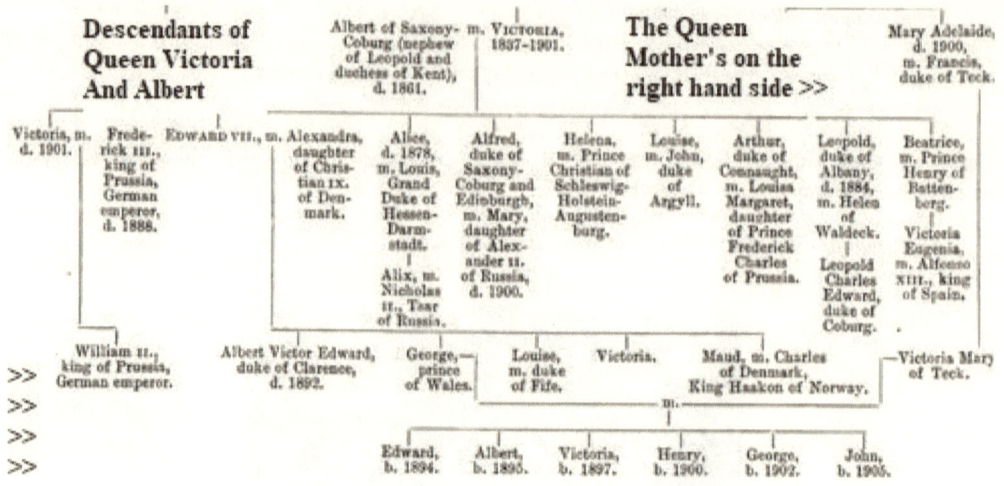

For those not in the know the chart does not show that Queen Elizabeth's Mother and her Husband's Mother were related via Queen Victoria:- The Queen via Mary Adelaide * on the top right, across from Victoria's Parents > *Her mother was Princess Mary Adelaide, a daughter of Prince Adolphus, Duke of Cambridge, and a granddaughter of King George III and first cousin of Queen Victoria of the United Kingdom. Her father was Francis, Duke of Teck*; **Philip's via the line descending from Victoria's Alice, but elaborated thereafter below.**

Victoria married Albert (d,1861) and their children were:-
1. Victoria (d.1901) * (photo below)
2. Edward VII (d. 1910) ↓
3. Alice (d.1878) (photo below)
4. Alfred (d.1906)
5. Helena
6. Louise
7. Arthur
8. Leopold
9. Beatrice

Public Domain 1856 Photo of Victoria, the Princess Royal, later Empress of Germany (1840-1901), and Princess Alice, later Grand Duchess of Hesse and by Rhine (1843-78)

Victoria * was (Queen) Victoria's first child and her life had its downs:- Her husband, Frederick III died in 1888 – 99 days after his accession – from laryngeal cancer; she died of breast cancer in August 1901, less than 7 months after the death of her mother, January 1901!

*(NB The Grand Mother, Princess Victoria * of Saxe-Coburg-Saalfeld <> 17 August 1786 – 16 March 1861 <> Christened as Marie Louise Victoire; later Princess of Leiningen & then Duchess of Kent & Strathearn was a German Princess & the mother of UK Queen Victoria *. Her 2nd husband, Prince Edward *, Duke of Kent died suddenly of pneumonia in January 1820, six days before his father, King George III.)*

And it continued as follows:-
a) *Edward VII (m. Alexandra of Denmark 1863)* **was the father of:-**
  i. George V (d.1936) #
  ii. Princess Victoria of the UK (d.1935)
  iii. Maud of Wales (d.1938)
  iv. Prince Albert Victor (d.1892)
  v. Louise Princess Royal & Duchess of Fife (d.1931)
  vi. John Alexander (d. 1871 at birth)
b) *George V # (m. Mary of Teck 1893) was father of:-*
  i. Edward VIII (Abdicated 1937 - m. Wallis Simpson 1937)
  ii. George VI (d.1952) (m. 1923 Elizabeth Bowes-Lyon)

c) George VI was father of:-
i. Princes Margaret (d. 2002)
ii. Queen Elizabeth II (d. 2022)
d) Princess Victoria Alexandra Olga Maria - unmarried although had suitors
i. one cousin, the future Christian X)
ii. another cousin (first - which was not then unusual) (her mother's sister's son) = Nicholas II of Russia, who apparently sad something unusual – 'He like her <u>unfeminine mind!</u> Which links us back to Marie Bonaparte's thought of herself – being more male than female! So it might not come as a shock that she though Mary of Teck (above) (another connection to our late Queen Mother) as 'terribly boring'!?

Princess Victoria late 1900s (public domain photo)

e) Maud of Wales – (k/a Harry) future Queen of Norway (Guinness linked *)

By Alice Hughes - Royal Collection RCIN 2807432, Public Domain, https://commons.wikimedia.org/w/index.php?curid=80028018
i. m. 1896 Haakon VII of Norway
ii. Their son became Olav V *

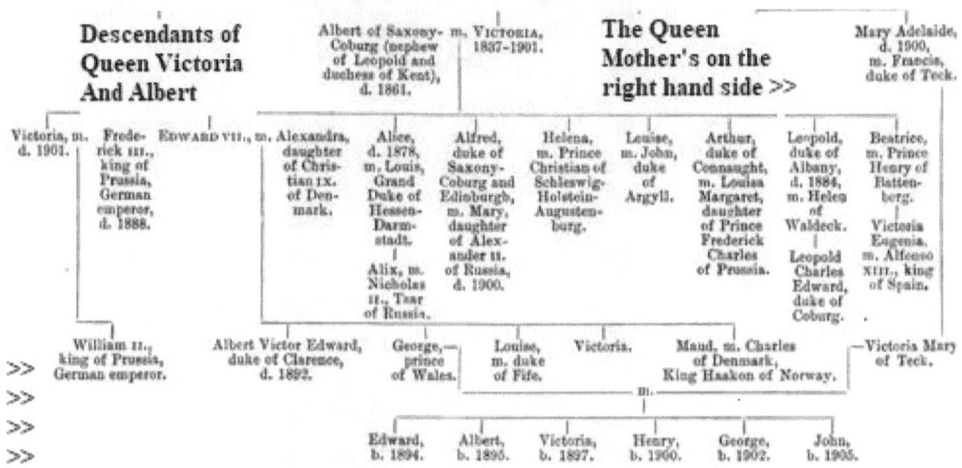

From before...
Victoria married Albert (d,1861) and their children were:-
1. *Victoria (d.1901)*
2. *Edward VII (d. 1910)* ↓
3. *Alice (d.1878)*
4. *Alfred (d.1906)*
5. *Helena*
6. *Louise*
7. *Arthur*
8. *Leopold*
9. *Beatrice*

And so now you'll be introduced the Greek element – let's see how it ultimately fitted in with now, with just so much/many foreign blood lines included!?
But with blood already out in the open:- be warned being Royal guaranteed you neither happiness, good health nor a painless death – sometimes at another's hands!
First we need venture back 2 centuries or so...

<u>then end up with another Regal Guinness Link!</u>

But here we must Royally commence with our first Right Regal Couple:-
View the chart again and you will see Edward VII to whom we have already been introduced – BUT – it is a Very Big But that we must be introduced to his younger sister:- **ALICE,** *who is shown, but only one of her 7 children: Alix who married Nicholas, Tsar of Russia* <> .

Princess Alice below and her bearded beau Louis IV further below!

39

Public Domain -Alice,_Princess_Louis_of_Hesse in 1871 (d.1878)
By Franz Backofen - Royal Collection RCIN 2902405, Public Domain,

From before above...that bearded spouse...
Public Domain Photo by unknown of Grand Duke Ludwig IV of Hesse and by Rhine. Hesse, Darmstadt, German Empire, 1878 (from Mrlopez2681's connection)

In German he was known as, *Ludwig IV. Großherzog von Hessen und bei Rhein.*

Born 12 September 1837- deceased, unlucky for some/him the 13th March 1892!

His other title was the Grand Duke of Hesse and by the Rhine from again that unlucky (?) 13th June 1877, until his death.

He married Alice in 1862 and created a British linkage:- she was Queen Victoria's 2nd daughter, although two of his daughters ended up marrying into the House of Romanov, BUT with tragic consequences!!!

Unfortunately, dear Alice, born 25 April 1843 as Alice Maud Mary, known now as Princess Alice of the United Kingdom, although being Queen Victoria's 3rd child, was the first to die 14 December 1878 – even before her older sister *(below)* & her celebrated ageless mother!

So, from the above, she was married for only 16 years but bore 7 children, and their names and future spouses had similar names to their so many related others * (? Confusingly) down the ages:-

1. *Princess Victoria of Hesse and by Rhine, then Princess Louis of Battenberg, later Victoria * Mountbatten, (5 April 1863 – 24 September 1950) Marchioness of Milford Haven...*
   More will follow after the siblings' brief histories...

2. *Grand Duchess Elizabeth * Feodorovna of Russia = born Princess Elisabeth of Hesse and by Rhine; (1 November 1864 – 18 July 1918); an older sister of Alexandra, below, the last Russian Empress. Sadly, after the Socialist Revolutionary Party's Combat Organisation assassinated her husband with a bomb in 1905; Elisabeth in 1918, was arrested and ultimately murdered by Bolsheviks!*

3. *Irene *, Princess Henry of Prussia = (Irène Luise Marie Anne; 11th July 1866 – 11th November 1953), previously k/a Princess Irene of Hesse – She married her first cousin, Prince Henry of Prussia. Sadly she was a carrier of the haemophilia *** gene as did her sister, Alexandra (below)! Irene's first son, was the haemophiliac Prince Waldemar, born in 1889; her 2nd son Prince William did not; BUT little 4 year old Henry Victor Louis Frederick did and a fall from a table head first did for him:- the haemorrhage would not have been fatal if not from his inherited disease!*
   Irene not considered the beauty of the girls – see below for your own decision making:- She's on the left....

Public Domain 1885 daughters of Louis IV, Grand Duke of Hesse and Princess Alice of the UK Princesses Irene, Victoria, Elizabeth and Alix of Hesse and by Rhine
And here another photo of the same year, but here including 3 cousins. What is striking is the similarity between them:- they could have been mistaken for sisters! BUT was it as a result of intermarrying too close cousins etc down the ages? U Judge

Left to right (back row): Princess Alix of Hesse; Princess Irene of Hesse. (front row): Cousins Princess Marie Louise of Schleswig-Holstein; Charlotte, Princess Bernhard of Saxe-Meiningen; Princess Helena Victoria of Schleswig-Holstein.

4. Ernest Louis *, Grand Duke of Hesse and by Rhine = Ernst Ludwig Karl Albrecht Wilhelm; 25 November 1868 – 9 October 1937 was the last Grand Duke of Hesse and by Rhine, reigning from 1892 until 1918. On 19 April 1894, at Schloss Ehrenburg, Ernest Louis married his maternal **first cousin**, Princess Victoria Melita of Edinburgh nicknamed "Ducky", the daughter of his mother's brother, Prince Alfred!

(As has befallen so many of the associated family members, like his two young siblings, Ernest also lost children young:- a daughter, (? Another?) Elisabeth in 1903, at the age 8 of typhoid fever; preceded by a stillborn son on 25 May 1900. But more woe in adult life followed him: The couple were divorced 21 December 1901 on grounds of **'invincible mutual antipathy'** by a special verdict of the Supreme Court of Hesse. After the divorce had come through, Victoria apparently told some close relatives that Ernest was a ** homosexual. Supposedly, she had caught her husband in bed with a male servant when, in 1897, she returned home from a visit to her sister Queen Marie of Romania. Victoria later chose from the opposite side and married another first cousin, BUT this time on her mother's side!

I make this homosexual ** reference here, as it is to be replicated by others over the centuries, there, hence! And the accusation seemed true as during Ernest's 2nd marriage he maintained a close friendship with the bisexual Karl August Lingner, the inventor of Odol, one of the first liquid mouthwashes. When Lingner died of tongue cancer of all things, he bequeathed Tarasp castle in Switzerland to Ernest Louis. However, the Hesse family never lived in it, and it was sold in 2016.

5. Prince Friedrich = b.1870 - his premature death as the younger of their two sons, Frittie, who was afflicted with haemophilia *** + suffered a fatal fall from a palace window before his third birthday in 1873!

6. Alexandra Feodorovna *, Empress of Russia = Unfortunately, Alexandra was one of the most famous royal carriers of haemophilia *** and passed the condition to her son, Alexei! <u>She was born Princess Alix of Hesse and by Rhine, 6 June 1872 – d. 17 July 1918)</u>, was the last Empress of Russia as the consort of Tsar Nicholas II, until his forced abdication in March 1917. Following her husband's abdication, the royal family were placed under house arrest by the Bolsheviks during the Russian Revolution. On 17 July 1918, they were executed!

(Some suggest the Romanov demise was accelerated by their association with an Evil Rasputin!? Either way late December, 1916, Rasputin was assassinated by a group of conservative Russian noblemen who opposed his influence over the imperial family. The rest is Russian Revolutionary History!)

7. *Princess Marie* * = *(1874-1878) as just a 4 year old, (below) contracted and died from diphtheria along with her mother, Alice – the father survived. From then on, he reigned and raised his five surviving children alone.*

Public domain author unknown Princess Marie of Hesse and by Rhine – just before her death in 1878

....

And so back to *Princess Victoria of Hesse and by Rhine, then Princess Louis of Battenberg, later Victoria* * *Mountbatten, (5 April 1863 – 24 September 1950) Marchioness of Milford Haven, would be the mother of Queen Louise of Sweden, Louis Mountbatten and Princess Alice of Battenburg, who was the mother of Prince Philip, Duke of Edinburgh.*

Victoria (back row, second from right) at the marriage 1894, of her brother Ernest Louis (back row, right) to Princess Victoria Melita of Saxe-Coburg and Gotha (seated, second from right),. Nicholas II of Russia and his fiancé Alix are on the back row left,
Irene and Elisabeth are seated front row left,
and Grand Duke Sergei Alexandrovich of Russia (Elisabeth's husband) is seated right.
AND SO NOW ONTO TWO SPECIFIC DAUGHTERS- STARTING WITH A VICTORIA:-

Alice's first daughter was named * after the grand mother:- Princess Victoria * Alberta Elisabeth * Mathilde Marie * (née Princess of Hesse), Marchioness of Milford-Haven

(5 April 1863 – 24 September 1950)
↑ *c1878 Princess Victoria Alberta Elisabeth Mathilde Marie
(née Princess of Hesse), Marchioness of Milford-Haven by Alex Bassano d.1913*

Her godparents were Queen Victoria, Princess Mary Adelaide of Cambridge, Louis III, Grand Duke of Hesse & by Rhine, the Prince of Wales and Prince Heinrich of Hesse & by Rhine.

Over her father's disapproval, 1884, she married his morganatic first cousin Prince Louis of Battenberg, (24 May 1854 – 11 September 1921), an officer in the British Royal Navy. Who later became Louis Alexander Mountbatten, 1st Marquess of Milford Haven and thus a German Prince related by marriage to the British Royal Family.

> (<u>Morganatic marriage</u>, sometimes called a left-handed marriage is between people of unequal social rank, which in the context of royalty or other inherited title prevents the principal's position or privileges being passed to the spouse, or any children born of the marriage.) (Mainly Germanically linked!)
> (There will be more of this/these)

Louis & Victoria had four children: (# Again name duplications with past relatives!)

- Louise Alexandra Marie Irene Mountbatten (13 July 1889 <> 7th March 1965), (born **Princess Louise of Battenberg**: was closely related to the ruling families of Britain as a great-granddaughter of Queen Victoria and of Russia as a niece of Empress Alexandra Feodorovna of Russia, wife of Tsar Nicholas II of Russia. She was also an older sister to Lord Louis Mountbatten (below). As the assumed Queen of Sweden she was noted for her eccentricity and progressive views! (Something her nephew, Philip, may have inherited and continued?)

- George # (6th November 1892 <> 8th April 1938); born Prince George of Battenberg & like his brother linked to the Royal navy: he was a Captain. But, significantly an accomplished mathematician, especially handy in solving complicated gunnery problems in his head! And to cap it all casually studied his calculus books on train journeys to pass the time amusing himself thus! And significantly our Dear Elizabeth II, his niece-in-law, spoke of him as "one of the most intelligent and brilliant of people". (Well apparently according to > Richard Hough (1984) in his 'Louis and Victoria: The Family History of the Mountbattens' <> So perhaps we now know where the brainy side of the Royals emanated from? As we might do within the Guinness & their related... (see later inside)>

- Louis (25 June 1900 <> 27th August 1979); NOW WE COME TO THE RECENT BIG HITTER:- **Louis Francis Albert Victor Nicholas Mountbatten, 1st Earl Mountbatten of Burma** (born **Prince Louis of Battenberg**; known to all as **Lord Mountbatten**, was a British statesman, also like his brother, a naval officer, colonial administrator and 'in' close with the UK British Royal family, well he was a maternal uncle of our Prince Philip + a second cousin of King George VI! But unlike the loosely related George II and his Homosexual Naval Uncle Lover Valdemar – that's where Louis' Naval Experiences end – so none of the 'Royal Yacht Brittanica' Gay Party ** Scene' and so no such influence over Male Royal family Members!

NB 'Royal Yacht Brittanica' Gay Party ** Scene' = The homosexual orgy, which supposedly included several (5 or so) members of the navy who were later dismissed, reportedly took place in 1981, when homosexuality was still illegal in the British military! But that hid a few more cracks **1968** - The 'Bermuda case': The owner of a gay brothel on Bermuda had made a record of the names and ships of more than 400 Royal Navy sailors who had visited the brothel, potentially making them the targets for blackmail. (Expanded upon later..)

And so we come to Philip's mother, who adds her own 'Psychological History into the Hereditary Line!

- Alice # (25 February 1885<> 5th December 1969); (Prince Philip's Mother)...

*Public Domain 1920 author unknown Princess Alice of Battenberg,
Princess of Greece and Denmark
Pity she was so deaf! Which may have contributed to her Psychosis?
Although she learned to sign language in 4 languages!*

Like so many Royals the parents were often stand-offish and farmed off their offspring to nurses/tutors etc rather than fully engage. Then when older the poor saps were farmed off to Private Schools etc! But Philip lost his mother early and not to death!

Prince Philip was born in Corfu in 1921 eight years after the assassination of his grandfather, King George I of Greece – calamity 1....

He was the youngest child and only son of Prince Andrew of Greece (another name coincidence with ours – but disgraced prince Andrew) and Denmark and Princess Alice of Battenberg. He was little more than a year old when his father was sent into exile by an army court martial following Greece's calamitous defeat in a war with Turkey – calamity 2....

Philip attended a small day school nearby, but in 1930 his world was again thrown apart when his mother, whom he had always adored, suffered a severe mental breakdown # – calamity 3....Gordonstoun then welcomed!

Calamities did not end there:- later years there were overshadowed by the death of his sister Cecilie, and her family, in a plane crash on their way to London for a family wedding in 1937. – calamity 4......

Six months later, Philip suffered yet more sorrow when his guardian Georgie Milford Haven died from cancer at the age of 45. – calamity 5!!!!

There were hints # that part of his mother's problems were due to Post Natal Depression which if real actually happened well before she was finally diagnosed 'schizophrenic' by Psychoanalysts including additionally by the most celebrated, Sigmund Freud, who featured greatly with another distant royal relative, Marie Bonaparte – expanded upon below & another later Chapter....
Eventually, Alice's mother (Philip's grandmother) bowed to the advice of psychiatrists, and agreed that her daughter should be committed to a secure sanatorium.
And she then began her time in the company of Nuns!
But fame found her in he end:- during the war-time Nazi German occupation of Greece, she hid Jews in her house in Athens, earning, like Oskar Schindler, Israel's award of Righteous Among the Nations.
Not bad a conniver for such a declared 'nutter'!

>>

And so with Philip being mentioned above another under a man's wing and a naval one at that but not of the George II ilk! (later below)...

Mention the Guinness Sabrina link and you'll find her Philip's favoured of all the earlier Son's lady friends and always welcome at the Palace but perhaps not as a future Bride material and so many grateful for that as then there would be no YCTV (later) – although there again any person would scupper their chance seen as one who palled around with such as the Bi-Sexual ** Steve Strange (see also George II & Uncle ** again)... although not she was not Steve's heart's desire as this belonged to his forbidden fruit, *** a certain **von Thyssen-Bornemisza,** *but the names who played/attended his club(s), so many though being Homosexuals, but others who weren't, were perhaps those females may have wanted to latch onto!? Or simply the place to go & be seen @?*

NB To connect the points of the triangle:- Steve and Sabrina palled around; Steve was on David Bowie's Video, 'Ashes to Ashes'; (Drug addiction killed Steve off in his 50s!) David would later do a guest stint for Sabrina's YCTV! They met up at one of Steve's Clubs.

Bisexual Steve, he was then in a relationship with Francesca *** 'Chessie' Thyssen (daughter of the German steel tycoon Baron Heini Thyssen) with whom he skied in Gstaad and 'played elephant polo in India with Ringo Starr and Barbara Bach' – well he was certainly adaptable!? Prince Andrew and his then girlfriend, Koo Stark, were frequent visitors to Strange's flat in Chelsea.

But any chances of marriage were scuppered by the older relative generation, who had more high & mighty goals?! ***

So once again it's who you know which determines who you really can be pally with!? (Perhaps another 'Rich' entrant to the Samuel Dynasty discovered see much later..)

Baroness Francesca Anna Dolores von Thyssen-Bornemisza de Kászon et Impérfalva *(born 7 June 1958), formerly* **Francesca von Habsburg-Lothringen**.
By birth, she is a member of the House of Thyssen_Bornemisza.

She is also the former wife of *** Karl von Habsburg, who became head of the House of Habsburg-Lorraine
.
AND YES, the Habsburgs are related to Queen Elizabeth II through various connections in European royal lineage.

The Habsburgs were a prominent royal family in Europe, especially known for their rule over the Austro-Hungarian Empire, and they intermarried with many other royal families.
Queen Elizabeth II is a descendant of Queen Victoria, and the Habsburgs also have connections to Queen Victoria's descendants. For example, through her daughter Princess Alice, Queen Victoria is related to various European royals.

The Habsburgs, like many European royal families, often intermarried to solidify political alliances, creating a complex web of relationships among royal families across Europe.

Thus, while there may not be a direct line of descent, the connections among various royal families, including the Habsburgs and the British royal family, create a familial link.
....

And since I have mentioned him more than once, Greek George needs a full-on introduction who took on the might of the Bonaparte female line and stayed the full course, until natural death defeated him!

>>>>>>>>>>>>

<u>Olga, Princess Paul of Yugoslavia</u> Olga was just 16 years old when she married his father, also called George, in St Petersburg on 27 October 1867. After a honeymoon the couple left Russia for Greece Over the next twenty years, they had eight children:

- <u>Constantine</u> (1868–1923), who married <u>Princess Sophia of Prussia</u> and had six children, including three subsequent kings of Greece: <u>George II</u>, <u>Alexander</u>, and <u>Paul</u>;

- <u>George</u> (1869–1957), who **'*managed*'** to have two children via his marriage with Princess Marie Bonaparte! (Later)

- The word **'*managed*'** is in bold italics for a specific sexual oriented reason – read on...

   <u>(More below)</u> about his wife, future author & psychoanalyst ...~~~.
   (Source: Flickr Commons project, 2012)

- https://www.loc.gov/pictures/item/2014698927/, Public Domain,
  https://commons.wikimedia.org/w/index.php?curid=90916496

George I of Greece (ante ↑) and Olga Konstantinovna of Russia

And the enviable marriage name dropping continues apace:-

- Alexandra (1870–1891), who married Grand Duke Paul Alexandrovich and had two children;
- Nicholas (1872–1938), who married Grand Duchess Elena Vladimirovna of Russia and had three children;
- Maria (1876–1940), who married firstly Grand Duke George (another George!) Mikhailovich, with whom she had two children, and secondly Admiral Perikles Ionnadis;
- Olga # named after her mother,(1880), BUT who died aged seven months;
- Andrew (1882–1944), who married Princess Alice of Battenberg (remember her from above?) and had five children, including **Prince Philip, Duke of Edinburgh!**
- Christopher (1888–1940), who married firstly American widow Nancy (Nonnie) Stewart Worthington Leeds (a wealthy American heiress having married into 2 wealth off families) and secondly Princess François of Orléans, with whom he had one child.
- But, just to show how brittle a rich person's life was then:- this was Nonnie's final (3rd) marriage –another like Edward & Wallis = a morganatic union + Nonnie was 10 years older and a cancerous death took her 3 years later – then she was k/a Princess Anastasia of Greece and Denmark.
- But her husband seemed to attract death's attentions as he was to die one year after the birth of his son!

....

And now for more of that Rich Involved/entwined notoriety!

THE SON:-   Prince George

Prince George of Greece and Denmark (24 June 1869 – 25 November 1957) was the second son and child of George I of Greece (ante ↑) and Olga Konstantinovna of Russia, From 1883, George lived at Bernstorff Palace (Copenhagen) with his uncle, Prince Valdemar of Denmark.

The Queen, who had a number of European Royals living in her palaces, had taken the boy there to enlist him in the Danish royal navy and consigned him to the care of Uncle Valdemar, who was an admiral in the Danish fleet.

*(And we all know what went on on/in the UK modern day Royal Yacht Britannia!) > From Before:- The homosexual orgy, which supposedly included several (5 or so) members of the navy who were later dismissed, reportedly took place in 1981, when homosexuality was still illegal in the British military! But that hid a few more cracks **1968** - The 'Bermuda case': The owner of a gay brothel on Bermuda had made a record of the names and ships of more than 400 Royal Navy sailors who had visited the brothel, potentially making them the targets for blackmail.*
The case led to three sailors and two Bermudians being jailed for indecency and to at least 40 sailors being discharged. The incident was discussed in Parliament. The Navy Department Homosexual Discharge Advisory Panel was temporarily set up to advise on the discharge of those involved in the 'Bermuda case'. Personnel were dismissed from aircraft carrier HMS Eagle for homosexuality.
AND
(Britannia was decommissioned in 1997)!
....

And *it was raised here because of that aforementioned 'Guardian', Valdemar:-*

MORE HOMOSEXUAL DEPRAVITY IN A BISEXUAL PRODUCING FORM!

Feeling abandoned by his father, (like so many other Royal Sons/daughters) George would later describe to his fiancée the profound attachment he developed for **his uncle** from that day forward.

And that Modern Mentor Mountbatten's history showed himself also to be the fly in the Royal Palace's Ointment – affairs et al! (later)

Shock-Horror Gorge was *'Primarily'* a homosexual, who lived most of the year with his uncle, Prince Valdemar of Denmark with whom he had a life-long relationship!

Hence my '<u>managed</u>' conception comment above!

BUT, Regal Duty Obligations Called and so he *'Secondly'* did the minimum month's courting, then *proposing/being accepted – then getting hitched.*

Then like Diana and such, the truth came out – I suppose with Diana one could say it was discovering she'd always be 2nd fiddle:- perhaps so glad to have her best friend in the psychology business! And at least she kept all her wealth to herself...

With Marie it was not that they went from going at it like rabbits then a steady decline to zero, it was that the one 'thumping' her was of the opposite persuasion, then not, as the number of children she + him sired proved!

Diana found out over time; Marie on her visit to Valdemar's Bernstorff Palace, where his wife, Marie d'Orléans set her straight.

BUT there was enough manhood, some satisfying !? to go around at the relevant times – thank God the two Guys were Bis!

BUT here we now go into such realms as in my, *'The legal sanctity of marriage (part 7) the cuckold? The cuckoo in the matrimonial nest!'* ###

This file is licensed under the Creative Commons Attribution 2.0 Generic license:-
(Marie Bonaparte Princess Giorgios of Greece:- Author The Lost Gallery...)

(1982) Marie Bonaparte: A Life by Célia Bertin, *who seems to have access to Marie's innermost and secretive diary thoughts on paper. Whether fantasy or not, what the 'False Happiness' Chapter sets out is possibly too depraved to be credible – fantasy time?*
Well to be engaging in her/their own form of a 'Ménage-à-Trois, where George just watches as his Uncle and his wife 'enjoy' each other in front of him?! = **'The legal sanctity of marriage (part 7) the cuckold? The cuckoo in the matrimonial nest!'** ### Although in walks together as a 'threesome' she treats them both as her 2 husbands! Though from what was 'diary' implied there was no sexual intercourse paraded, nor indulged! And whatever the Uncle's wife thought about this was not mentioned – nor that she was made aware! Why not? (Revisited later!)

BUT
It didn't end there..
Well not seemingly with an orgasm for her as this was her 'own sexual problem to overcome!'
And try as she might with so many lovers thereafter she didn't seem to master the task!
Hence her assailing dear old Sigmund! ~~ **Frigidity Expert Anyone?**

I WILL HOWEVER COVER SIGMUND AND DAUGHTER SOME CHAPTERS LATER AND THE GUINNESS LINK!

PART 1a: BONKING *TEMPORARILY* SUPPLANTED BY MORE BONKING! – UNTIL?

A Diana Deja Vu Life/Love Affair
(With similar tragic consequences, introduced here as Di was friends with certain of the Guinnesses & Samuels, as her son & daughter in law continued to be!)
NB The principal's name being **ELISABETH** AND NOT to be confused with our late QUEEN – who only formed the introduction of this Book to you!

*According to historian Marlene Eilers Koenig, George was in love with his cousin Anastasia de Torby, (not aware if first or second?), however their relationship was opposed by George's mother, Sophia, as Anastasia was the result of **a morganatic marriage!***

*(**Morganatic marriage**, sometimes called a left-handed marriage is between people of unequal social rank, which in the context of royalty or other inherited title prevents the principal's position or privileges being passed to the spouse, or any children born of the marriage.) (Mainly Germanically linked!)*
(There will be more of this/these)

(See next page for an example....)

Public Domain Charles Ferdinand, Prince of Capoua, with his <u>morganatic</u> wife, Anglo-Irish commoner Penelope Smyth (left), and their daughter, Vittoria (right).

....

And here we yet again get confused by the name/title duplication - Here another poor in the sack George II.

Meantime, Elisabeth of Romania (Lizzy) above caught his 'appropriate status' eye... Prince George (a Diadochos^{D↓} *and heir of the throne) became engaged in October 1920 to be married in 1921 - They first met in 1911. George had previously asked Elisabeth to marry in 1914, he was refused that first time!*

And what might have swayed it was his expected route to the throne (?) plus that her options might have shrunk considerably:- (?) Now considered fat by her mother, and apparently of very limited intelligence, Elisabeth decided to accept the marriage. *(Like Diana's apparent 13 date courtship, perhaps the (blinded/blinkered) marriage consequences were not totally thought through!?)*

The wedding took place in great style in Bucharest on 27 February 1921, *although perhaps not on such a grand sale as Diana's (?).*

*And like Diana's it all ulti-**mate**-ly went pear shaped, but so swiftly after her great pregnancy day – the consequential shock was to resonate thereafter...*

And in 1921 it was back to Warring for the Spouse...

Public Domain author unknown 1921 Arrival of Crown Prince George
(later George II of Greece) plus troops in Smyrna (Izmir),

In Greece, Elisabeth had great difficulty integrating into the royal family, *(Like Diana?)* and her relationship with Queen Sophia was particularly awkward:- perhaps reflected in her inability to mingle (shy ? [see hubby below]) (withdrawn ?) (stubborn (? ◇ *see her face when young above...)* character.

Elisabeth felt out of place amongst her in-laws, who regularly conversed in Greek in her presence, to show her up because she had not yet mastered the language - *(As perhaps Diana was, say regarding her one GCSE pass intellect dwarfed by say her hubby and sister-in-law? – amongst others!*
Perhaps even/especially when playing competitive games:- I mean both Charles & Anne were winners in their own selected sporting arena!)

BUT
She had *not too much time* to suffer this discomfort....

In a complete upside turn, Elisabeth was upstaged by Crown Prince Carol of Romania, her elder brother, who married George's younger sister, Princess Helen of Greece! *(That's what I call keeping it in the nearly sanguineous family way!)*

Crown Prince and Princess of Greece and family. Clockwise from far left:
Paul, Alexander, George, Helen, Irene, Constantine and Sophia.
(John thought her quite a pretty Rich/Royal as opposed to ..Much later)
This work is from the George Grantham Bain collection at the US Library of Congress. According to the library, there are no known copyright restrictions on the use of this work.

BUT
Lizzy had the *initial* last laugh as her brother's marriage only lasted 7 years!
I mean to say everyone, even Helen knew of his bad reputation!
With her regular, ever extending visits to her parents abroad, she let her husband get on with **it**!
And expectedly his multiple affairs led to his one true love, Magda Lupescu and he abandoned his wife **and did a King Edward 8th & renounced the throne in order to live openly with his mistress.**
Distraught, Helen tried to persuade her husband to return to her but eventually she accepted the divorce in 1928.

And then hammered by a right regal kidney punch:- her hubby, k/a *Diadochos ^{D},* was shunted off the future throne by his Dad, and adding insult to injury, he was replaced by his younger brother, the future King Alexander 1..., *(The irony here being that ^{D} in old Greek meant successor (which he wouldn't be now) but also meant substitute, which he was until his younger brother was back to take over the role, or subsequently relinquish it!?!)*

The usurping executioner's cut was deep and nearly life ending financially speaking:- George was exiled, penniless apart from a small annual legacy, but with no future prospects!

And money would be tight for one who expected it to be free flowing for her own self- extravagance! Although a future financial hole get out clause would subsequently materialise in the form of... her brother, Carol 11, of Romania, as, the former queen *'quietly'* amassed an important fortune, partly due to financial advice given by her lover, the banker Alexandru Scanavi.

But her physical hammer blow manifested it below her belt, as her apparently shy in this department ^{hubby} *Diadochos* was disappointing wife, Elisabeth, who wanted him to sexually continually spice up her now dullard life relationship. *(Future Déjà Diana Marriage Doom Vu after initially behaving like rabbits?)*

And as it happened after the first Frank *Rat* *'miscarriage'* there was no further issue and the marriage disintegrated as each went his/her separate European adulterous ways!

On 6 July 1935, George learned through the newspaper that Elisabeth had filed for divorce after she accused him of '*desertion from the family home*'.
A court in Bucharest processed the divorce without inviting George to attend.

NB Strangely enough George II wasn't able to satisfy his Elisabeth, YET went on to have many affairs!
England was to be his scene(s) of triumph(s)!
Obviously his subsequent female lovers didn't have Elisabeth's demanding sexual scope?! Although that had diminished somewhat after her post miscarriage illnesses =

Public Domain 1931 German Archives Bundesarchiv_Bild_102-12092,_England,_London,_Georg_von_Griechenland_im_Exil
This file licensed under the creative commons attribution share alike 3.0 Germany license.
Attribution: Bundesarchiv, Bild 102-12092 / CC-BY-SA 3.0

::

AND JUST TO GILD THE GEORGE LILY!

More George(s) II !? + In Ernst!? And yet another Victoria!
Just another way of showing just the title doesn't give you the answer you search >>>

Public Domain Portrait 1855

Princess Feodora Victoria Adelheid of Hohenlohe-Langenburg *(7 July 1839 – 10 February 1872) was the daughter of ERNST I, Prince of Hohenlohe-Langeburg and Princess Feodora of Leiningen. She married GEORG II, of Saxe-Meiningen, and was the Duchess of Saxe-Meinigen from his accession as Duke Georg II on 20 September 1866 until her death in 1872.*

Family >>> *Feodora was the youngest of six children. Her mother was the older half-sister to QUEEN VICTORIA, thus making the younger Feodora the niece of the Queen. Her siblings included Prince Victor of Hohenlohe-Langenburg and Adelheid, Duchess of Schleswig-Holstein.   (Time for a Holstein Pilsner anyone?).*

....

....

PART 1ai: BONKING *TEMPORARILY* SUPPLANTED BY BANGING!

The Germans having made their entrance in the previous Chapter – it was now the Guinness' turn to introduce their 'special' War Efforts!

A few Chapter parts later on Sam Guinness will show how both World Wars affected him and how he and his 'Fluff' wife affected the 2nd one – both here in England AND certain Foreign Involvement(s) abroad!

BUT
First some John type secret documentation revelations about Sam's distant relative, a certain special person mentioned a while back = Walter Edward Guinness, Moyne, (detail above) who - mainly by reason of his travelling, coupled with certain travails in the West Indies, Lord Moyne was appointed Secretary of State for the Colonies by Walter Churchill, serving from 8 February 1941 to 22 February 1942. (detail above)

And it is this stint which John will update us all on the goings on behind the political scenes during those times of War Strife!

I have already made reference to internal family feuding and here with his former daughter-in-law it went so much further!
There will be more in Part 9, but for now her introduction and how a family can be split by Political leanings – hers + her Unity's were towards Hitler And Co!
So much so that it was considered a form of Treason.
And father-in-law Walter sought her incarceration: she had left his son and re-married a certain Fascist Leader here in England, k/a a certain Sir Oswald Mosley!
What rubbed salt into her English patriots' war blooded wounds was that both Goebbels AND Hitler were the Wedding Witnesses!
Originally the then Home Secretary decided not to imprison...

BUT
Lord Moyne's letter seems to have swayed him back to the prison term conclusion!

Coincidentally like Sam & Fluff Guinness he supported those Europeans fighting on our behalf – he the Polish, (he was Chair of the Polish Relief Fund <> Sam/Fluff the Norwegians – giving over of their London premises when required.

              Sadly Lord Moyne had only a few more years to live....
BUT
  I'll soon introduce you to some Ex-Regal 1940s News... .....with a welcome back to our *Secretary of State for the Colonies*
BUT
First an introduction to someone who needed no introduction to our Dear departed Queen Elizabeth...

Sir Walter Monckton & Admiral Sir Andrew Cunningham, CinC Mediterranean, on the quarterdeck of the flagship. January.1942 IWM_A_6697
Public Domain author unknown- HSMO State Crown Copyright Expired

He chose to enter Balliol College, Oxford, as a commoner, despite in 1910 having won an 'Exhibition' to Hetford College, Oxford.

Whilst at Oxford, he represented the combined Oxbridge Universities cricket team in 1911.

And, as perennial coincidences go he like Tom Stoppard played in that specialist fielding role = Wicketkeeper!

In 1912 he obtained a third class in Classical Moderations *(Honour Moderations in Classics has been called one of the hardest examinations in the world. However, in recent years, the subject matter has been changed so that proficiency in both Latin (John's forté) and Greek languages is no longer required and the number of papers in the exam has been reduced, along with an extension in the time allowed to finish)*

And in 1914 he got a second in modern history.

In 1913 he was elected president of the Oxford Union.

Although, he would not have been known to Sam Guinness and/or *his Crew* as their stays at Balliol did not cross.

BUT

As likely Sam would have got to know of him via The Times – the newspaper of all the well-off choosing – when they wrote of **Fowler's Match** a historical two-day Eton v Harow cricket match held at Lords on 8-9 July 1910. The match is named after the captain of Eton College, Robert St Leger Fowler, whose outstanding batting & bowling stints allowed Eton to win that match by 9 runs!

And another famous cricketing episode to add to our other 'Rattigan' mentioned before!

BUT

The sad 'Eton/Oxford' note to end with, also ended Sam's (later) as 1914-1918, WW1 cannon ended so many friendly faced lives:-

1. *Of the Harrow Team the following were taken from us by the trench warfare across the Channel!* <> **TB Wilson**, *2nd Lieutenant, Irish Guards;* **GWV Hopley**, *2nd Lieutenant, Irish Guards;* **TLG Turnball**, *Private, 1st, Artillery Company; And sadly, if the first one doesn't get you, then...War death waited patiently for* **CHB Blount**, *Air Vice Marshall, RAF, killed later in an aircraft crash (WWII - 1940)!*

2. *Of the Eton Team the following were taken from us by the trench warfare across the Channel!* <> **CW Tufnell**, *2nd Lieutenant, Irish Guards;* **AI Steel**, *Lieutenant, Coldstream Guards;* **AR Stock**, *Lieutenant, Ayrshire Yeomanry;* **JN Manners**, ** Lieutenant, Irish Guards;* **WGK Boswell**, *Captain, Rifle Brigade!*

3. *Subject * of a poem in The Muse in Arms = Poem* **LIV**: *To John by William Grenfell (d.1915) – a tribute to Lieutenant the hon.* **John Neville Manners** ** Regiment & Unit/Ship, Grenadier Guards, 2nd Bn. Died 01 September 1914, Age 22 years old, Buried or commemorated at La Ferte-Sous Jouarre Memorial, France*

LIV

To John[1]

O HEART-AND-SOUL and careless played
   Our little band of brothers,
And never recked the time would come
   To change our games for others.
It's joy for those who played with you
   To picture now what grace
Was in your mind and single heart
   And in your radiant face.
Your light-foot strength by flood and field
   For England keener glowed;
To whatsoever things are fair
   We know, through you, the road;
Nor is our grief the less thereby;
   O swift and strong and dear, good-bye.

                WILLIAM GRENFELL.

[1] The Hon. John Manners.

BUT DEAR OLD SAM
WAS NO STRANGER
TO THE ROWING
AND
WWI FIGHTING
AND
DYING
FRATERNITY
!!!

↓

PART 1b - HIS *BALLIOL ALMA MATER* ROWING/FIGHTING CREW(S)

QUADRANGLE BALLIOL COLLEGE

OXFORD UNIVERSITY

ITS FOUNDER

JOHN de BALLIOL 1263

ITS OUTER GARDEN AREA

↑ **ITS CHAPEL & ALTAR** ↓

But we must temporarily leave Central Oxford and return to Central London to a Psychologist's couch where our Story Tour Guide, John, is opening his memoried heart to his female Doctor *looker*, revealing all before her of all that he had experienced within that Famous Family 's Conclaves, interwoven with his own life's eventful occurrences.

But there is an apparent *spark* there!

What transpires is obviously a different story!

Here just a glimpse.... *"I notice that you ask for very little personal detail, even omitting names, just allowing people to create their own pseudonym?"*

"So to you I can be just Baker John, that Harrods Cake man?"

And so he too will be just plain John to us and we follow him...

....

I took the Herts job.

Unfortunately, it meant leaving *Uncle* Sam, a really nice, kind & gentle man, to await the outcome of his/our (*jointly prepared*) Tax Appeal, a copy of which I retained...

_P

Gone, but never forgotten – death has an unnatural hold on the future of people's life:- Sam only became head of the banking arm due to the death of his father, who left half of the business to him!?

I found out later the successful appeal went without a hitch, but I had lost contact and regretted the move, if only for the fact he died the year later...*(But, many years prior, here is one 'man' who made his own splashing entry & 'rowlockingly' definitely succeeded!)*

If you were ever fortunate to receive a letter from him: he loved his fountain pen ^P *and would boldly sign* >>>

#Sincerely Sam – definitely!

John, at those times of visiting, would have been at University age, which you'll have been told, he never did make.

So, it would be interesting to see a certain Balliol Oarsman, of the same age, but at his athletic prime – recognisable to him and a certain few, but deserving of so much credit and praise for a job well done! Hello, the Young Handsome Henry **Samuel** Howard Guinness....et al! #

*1907/1909 Sam: That 3 Year Dark Blue ↓
* Head of the River Team Winner in 1907↓
Congrats Great Uncle Sam & Co!

Take it from me > A tall strapping lad, but, as you will observe, already wearing Specs... As did the Cox, who had to, so he could see the 'winning' way' he was taking them!

'THE HEAD OF THE RIVER' 1907' *** GUINNESS (No 7) + **Fellow Rowers: Messrs Bell (Bow) (Nicknamed Keech), Barrington-Kennet (No 4)** * *(Who was one of 4 sons to die in the Great War. Although, ironically not in any dreaded trench, but in the air! Regrettably, the Germans had the superior planes, then!) (They could shoot through twirling propellers! We couldn't!)* *_____**Macdonnell (No 5), Orr (No 6), Stapledon (no 2) **, Grenfell (No 3), Higgins (Stroke) & Plimsoll (Cox).**

First Torpid.
Head of the River – 3 Bumps.

		st. lbs.
Bow.	K. N. Bell	10 12
2.	W. O. Stapledon	9 9
3.	Hon. J. Grenfell	11 6½
4.	V. A. Barrington-Kennett	12 12
5.	J. M. Macdonnell	12 8
6.	J. Orr	13 6
7.	H. S. H. Guinness	11 5
Str.	M. B. Higgins	11 2
Cox.	S. R. Plimsoll	9 13

Second Torpid.
3 Bumps.

		st. lbs.
Bow.	M. L. MacCallum	9 9
2.	R. G. Barnes	13 4
3.	Hon. J. N. Ridley	11 10
4.	V. L. Armitage	12 1½
5.	K. J. Backhouse	13 13
6.	W. R. Reynell	13 13
7.	P. L. Mitchell	12 7
Str.	K. V. Myers	12 1½
Cox.	E. W. Clifton	9 3½

NB Winning 'Bumps' are scored by catching the Boat in front of you and nudging its Rear.
Catching up '3' was an achievement in itself!
Thus a winning one!

**OTHERS WHO ROWED WITH HIM DURING HIS 1907/09
↑THE LIGHT + TORPID DAYS ↓
WERE MESSRS FLETCHER ↑ (No 4), HEARD ↑ (No 7),**
TREVOR ↓ (Bow), HORNER ↓ (No 4), MORRISON ↓ (No 2),
SHAW ↓ (No 7), FINDLAY ↓ (Nos 4 & 6), MACLEHOSE ↓ (No 2), HEINEMANN ↓ (No 5),
McCALLUM ↓ (No 7), POOLE ↓ (Stroke), FRASER ↓ (Bow) & PLOWDEN ↓ (Cox) ◇ ** *STAPLEDON
was also* ↓*1908 Stroke * BARRINGTON-KENNET was also* ↓ *1909 No 6.*
*** Henry S GUINNESS was thereafter (No 3)↓ in both the Light & Torpid Boats!

LIST * OF THOSE WHO DIED:-

Barrington-Kennett, Victor Annesley
Primary Service (as stated on memorial)
- Service: Air Force (RFC/RAF)
Rank: Major
Unit: Royal Flying Corps
Primary Service (IWM reference)
- Service: Air Force (RFC/RAF)
Rank: Major
Death and burial details
Date: 1916-03-13
Country of death: France
....

Findlay, Robert Scott
Primary Service (as stated on memorial)
- Service: Army (British)
  Rank: Captain
  Unit: Argyll and Sutherland Highlanders
  Primary Service (IWM reference)
- Service: Army (British)
  Rank: Captain
  Death and burial details
- Date: 1915-05-22
  Country of death: Scotland
  Town of death: Gretna

....

Grenfell, The Honourable Gerald William
Primary Service (as stated on memorial)
- Service: Army (British)
  Rank: Second Lieutenant
  Unit: Rifle Brigade
  Primary Service (IWM reference)
- Service: Army (British)
  Rank: Second Lieutenant
  Death and burial details
- Date: 1915-07-30
  Town of death: Flanders

....

Heinemann, John Walter
Primary Service (as stated on memorial)
- Service: Army (British)
  Rank: Captain
  Unit: Royal Fusiliers (City of London Regiment)
  Primary Service (IWM reference)
- Service: Army (British)
  Rank: Captain
  Death and burial details
- Date: 1916-03-06
  Country of death: France

....

Higgins, Mervyn Bournes
Primary Service (as stated on memorial)
- Service: Commonwealth
  Rank: Captain
  Unit: Australian Light Horse
  Primary Service (IWM reference)
- Service: Commonwealth
  Rank: Captain
  Unit: Australian Light Horse
  Death and burial details
- Date: 1916-12-23
  Country of death: Sinai

....

Horner, Edward William
Primary Service (as stated on memorial)
- Service: Army (British)
Rank: Lieutenant
Unit: 18th (Queen Mary's Own) Hussars
Primary Service (IWM reference)
- Service: Army (British)
Rank: Lieutenant
Death and burial details
- Date: 1917-11-21
Country of death: France

....

Macdonell, Alasdair Somerled
Primary Service (as stated on memorial)
- Service: Army (British)
Rank: Second Lieutenant
Unit: Queen's Own Cameron Highlanders
Primary Service (IWM reference)
- Service: Army (British)
Rank: Second Lieutenant
Death and burial details
- Date: 1915-10-13
Country of death: France

....

71

From above > **'THE HEAD OF THE RIVER' 1907'**

Yet none of the above could have then forecast a hundred years on it would be the Female Rowers who would then equal...

Oxford's Women's Top Women Rowers 2007

...*then eclipse Sam & his fellow male rowers!*

Women's Headship of the River Retained 2011

....

Keeping it in the family, in the early sixties, his grand-son, David also became another Balliol Oarsman!

Sam was so proud!

Similarly, his grand-daughter, Juliet, around the same time, using her expertise, the College used her to clean-up several of their important pictures. Handy, eh? And to have another grand-son, a supplier of literary work via his firm – Graham Greene owned, (Handy, eh?) who just happens to be another ex-Balliol! So, still keeping it in the family, so to speak! (ALL ABOVE INCLUDED IN THE LETTERS BELOW! ↓

Kindness In Memoria Personified

Mansion House 6141.

HSH Guinness

3, GRACECHURCH STREET,
LONDON, E.C.3.
30th October 1967

Dear Master,

PERHAPS KNOW HIM AS SOME SORT OF SECRET SANTA BUT FOR ALL THOSE PREVIOUS NORWEGIAN ROWERS AT OXFORD IT WAS SAM WHO BOUGHT THEM, THE STUDENTES ROKLUB, THEIR FIRST 8 OARED BOAT!

THAT THE PAINTINGS HIS GRAND-DAUGHTER CLEANED UP WERE HOLDING UP WELL!

HIS GRAND-SON'S GRAHAM GREENE LITERARY HELP

BUT THE HEART TOUCHING TALK ABOUT ROWERS WHO HAD SINCE LEFT THE WORLD BUT WOULD ALWAYS BE REMEMBERED SUCH AS, CLOSE FRIEND KENNETH-BELL, WHO TOGETHER FORMED PART OF THE 'BEST TOGGER'! THE BEST 'FIXED EIGHT - EVER!'

Yours sincerely,
H. S. H. Guinness

The Master,
    Balliol College,
        Oxford.

6 Cheyne Walk,
London, S.W.3.

TELEPHONE
FLAXMAN 4774

30th October 1961

Dear Master,

RE KING OLAV VISITING YOUNG HARALD AT HIS ALMA MATER ...

AND HOW HAPPY HE WAS TO SEE HIS GRAND-- SON DAVID NOW HIS OLD COLLEGE MAINTAINING THE FAMILY TRADITION.

Yours sincerely,
Iam Guinness

Sir Lindsay Keir,
    Master's Lodge,
        Balliol College,
            Oxford.

Above highlights one of the Guinness Family Royal Ties! There are more!

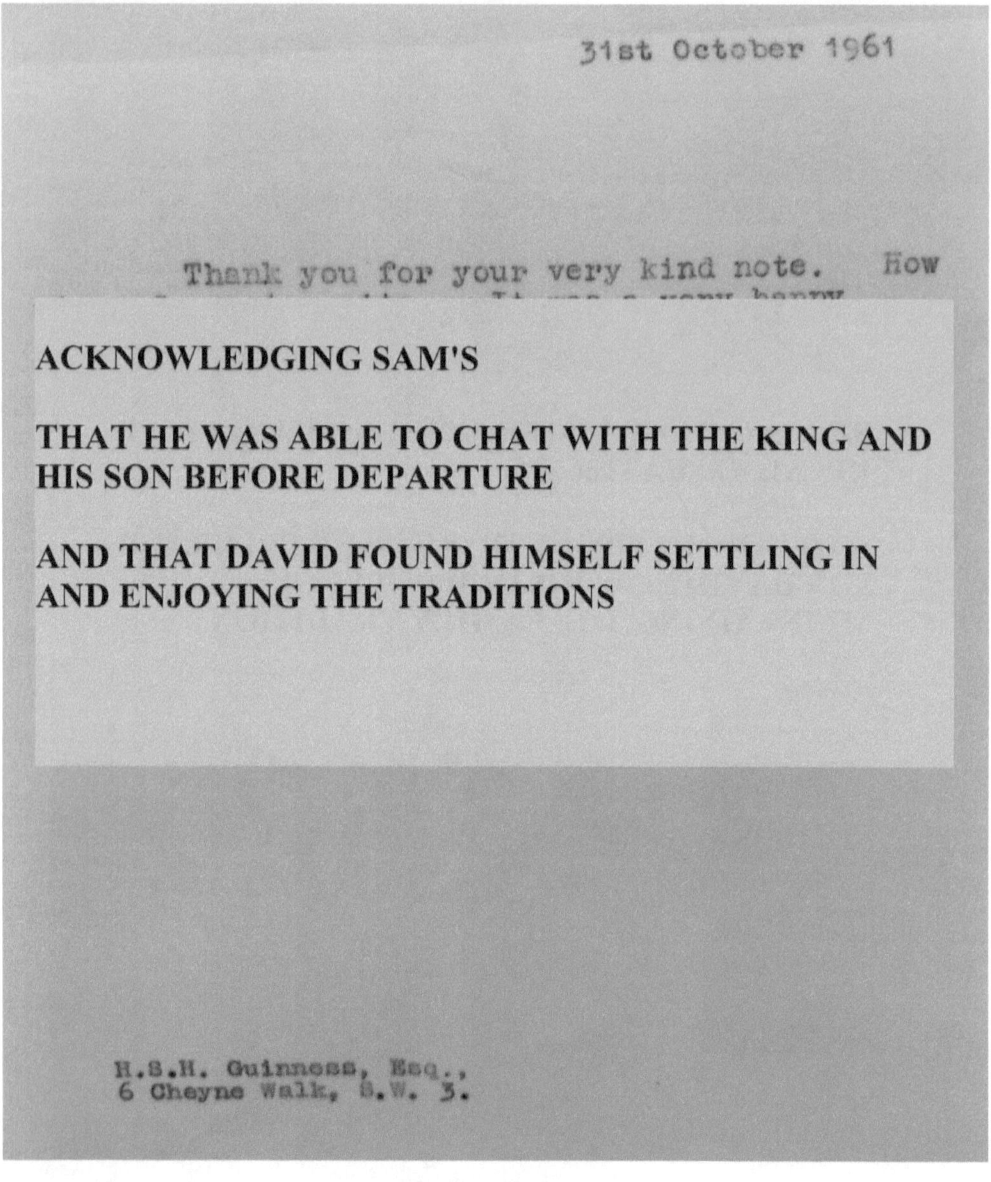

31st October 1961

Thank you for your very kind note. How

ACKNOWLEDGING SAM'S

THAT HE WAS ABLE TO CHAT WITH THE KING AND HIS SON BEFORE DEPARTURE

AND THAT DAVID FOUND HIMSELF SETTLING IN AND ENJOYING THE TRADITIONS

H.S.H. Guinness, Esq.,
6 Cheyne Walk, S.W. 3.

Their friendship expanded – see ...

PART 1cii: THE ONCE KING EDWARD VIII OF OLD!!!
LIKE FATHER LIKE SON◇ONE NOT AFRAID TO PUT IT ABOUT!!!

13th November 1961

Dear Mr. Guinness,

SAM
AGAIN
THE EVER
PHILANTHROPIC
BENEFACTOR
THIS TIME DEAR TO HIS HEART
THE DAVID KEIR TUTORIAL FELLOWSHIP
QUEEN'S UNIVERSITY BELFAST
WAS TO BENEFIT

Yours sincerely,

H.S.H. Guinness, Esq.,
17 College Green,
Dublin.

Interestingly enough and just another Regally Connected coincidence, down the Guinness married Hungarian Laszlo line I met at Sam's Cheyne Walk Place, another with the same skills who could have done Juliet's work was namely Sandra de Laszlo, who married Damon de Laszlo, one of the Great Artist's 7 Grandsons: the Royal Connection being she went to School with Princess Anne!

Small World Annie related to me, meeting for the second time, as so many times she would give out gongs to those she had, unknowingly, met before on her many down the years previous official outings.

See the deserving ultimately get their just rewards, but I didn't, sadly, only the Queen's Garden Tea Party Invitation/Attendances – he said ironically!

But underneath it all he really enjoyed that Family Day!

And with the mention of Royalty – the Queen herself – it is with her husband linked memory that we delve back in History which will take us back to WWII and the Guinness War Efforts!

Where...

**LIKE A CERTAIN OTHER GUINNESS MEMBER
DEAR OLD
SAM & FLUFF
WERE NO STRANGERS
TO THE WWII
EFFORT/SUPPORT
FRATERNITY
AND
SORORITY
!!!**

↓

**BUT FIRST A STOP
AT THE QUEEN'S
LINKED REGAL ANCESTRY**

Public domain c. 1908 - one current + three future UK Kings:-
Edward VII (far right) his son George, Prince of Wales, later George V (far left) and grandsons Edward, later Edward VIII (rear; and Albert, later George VI (foreground),

(WITH LATER A GUINNESS THROWN IN HERE/THERE FOR GOOD MEASURE!)

PART 1ci: THE ONCE KING EDWARD VIII OF OLD!!!
LIKE FATHER LIKE SON◇ONE NOT AFRAID TO PUT IT ABOUT!!!

And yet whilst all were defending & dying about them in those muddy coffins...somebody special (?) was on the prowl to overpower another type of defensive resistance!
Here an example of what he wanted to conquer!

Courtesan of Prince Edward = Marguerite Alibert c.1920

And here below her lay the answer...

Public Domain Portrait c. 1920 by Reginald Eves, (D. 1941)

OUR FUTURE TEMPORARY RULER – AN OFFICER LEADING BY EXAMPLE!!!

1917 was a significant year in this young man's gallivanting years:- On leave from the western front, this regular Paris party animal was introduced to a courtesan named Marguerite Alibert, *(above)* with whom he had a relationship until the following year.

Here the significance was his initial infatuation which was reflected in personal letter exchanges:- his were sought after by the British MI5 agency to avoid a scandal – **as it always seems to be**!

The talk is that their significant handing over was of paramount importance to so many in high places!

And the apparent opportunity arose in 1923 where Alibert was on trial at the Old Bailey accused of shooting her then husband.

Contrary to public expectations she was acquitted; Edward's name was not mentioned; the letters ended up in the UK Secret Service hands!

While he was all over Alibert, he found time in the same 1917 year to court a certain Rosemary Leveson-Gower, youngest daughter of the 4th Duke of Sutherland, whose family had their own relative notoriety claim to fame, which scuppered the apparent marriage proposal from Eddie!

The namely culprits being maternal auntie Daisy Greville, Countess of Warwick and maternal uncle James St Clair-Erskine 5th Earl of Rosslyn, but let us focus on 'Daisy'.

It seems that this and before chapters show how promiscuous and possessing little respect for marriage vows the males showed, but Daisy perhaps had so many beat – perhaps because the '60's pill was not about, although the 'rubbers' were:- *Daisy's first child, and probably the only one fathered by her husband, was Leopold Guy, who later became the sixth Earl of Warwick; Daisy's second child Marjorie Blanche was fathered by Lord Charles Beresford as was possibly her third, Charles Algernon who died aged 16 months?!*

Daisy's fourth child was Maynard and the fifth, Mercy were fathered by Joseph Frederick Laycock <u>a millionaire naturally</u>, but he too was an unfaithful, to her & his future wife! = Mercy was fathered by Laycock after he had married Katherine Mary (Kitty), after she had been divorced by Arthur Hill, Marquess of Downshire, citing adultery with Laycock.

Coincidentally like her niece a possible future spouse for Edward VIII, talk was that Aunty Daisy had also been put forward before as a possible spouse for 'Eddie's dad Edward VII: added to this she may have also been another of his concubines/mistresses?

Following the Edward VII's death, facing increasingly large debts, she attempted a private sale of the late King's letters to her, to the new king George V. This was thwarted as it was adjudged that the letters were Edward VII's copyright!

A second attempt in 1928, to avoid imprisonment in the women's prison in Holloway, North London, succeeded, but with certain conditions:- The subsequent memoirs were heavily censored as far as any correspondence was concerned, although became a glorified success: 'Life's Ebb & Flow!'
And ultimately copies of the love letters were later released to the public by Daisy's daughter; rather than being the passionate love letters claimed by Daisy, they were found to be <u>a mix of gossip and affectionate banter.</u>
*So actually on reflection had posed <u>no revealing **threat**</u>!*

Public Domain 1897 Daisy Greville, Countess of Warwick, by James Lafayette (1853–1923)

Public Domain 1906 Lafayette Portrait of Frances Evelyn Daisy Greville, Countess of Warwick, her son Maynard Greville (1898-1960) fathered by Joseph Laycock

So with M/s Leveson-Gower out of the running, during the subsequent decades, Edward started running after all and sundry, but in particular, with married women.

Here the question to be posed were the husbands then purely cuckolds *(see my 'Legal Sanctity of Marriage Part 7)?*

And perhaps the succession seed was sowed, if circumstances ever merited it, which we all now know, they did!

Another Brother was truly in the frame:- George V actually favoured his second son Albert ("Bertie") and Albert's daughter Elizabeth ("Lilibet"), later King George VI & Queen Elizabeth II – to confuse historian writers, Elizabeth's mother was also named/called Elizabeth, but ultimately she would be known by all as Queen Mary!

However, the succession end was in sight as Edward, in his new private abode, k/a Fort Belvedere in Windsor Great Park, first went with Freda Dudley Ward, then the married wife of an English Peer, Lady Furness, below...who initiated the Edward/Wallis meeting.

The rest is succession history as George V had wished for!

With Thelma Furness 1932 (Public Domain – Author Unknown) –
(HMSO has declared that the expiry of Crown Copyrights applies worldwide-)

NB Prior to this... *A little known fact ? about Wallis and her former spouses:- Did you know she met, in April 1916 and married soon after November 1916, Earl Spencer!?*

So we can then have a contrived link to our future Diana via a related marriage!?
Well I'll take the wool from your eyes – just a bit of title/name as he was actually, Earl Winfield Spencer Jr. a drunken American pilot, but of significance as airplane crashes about him, in Wallis created her future fear/aversion to flying anywhere!

BUT..

PART 1cii: THE ONCE KING EDWARD VIII OF OLD!!!
LIKE FATHER LIKE SON◇ONE NOT AFRAID TO PUT IT ABOUT!!!

It doesn't end there as with previous and future randy male Royals whose dilly dalliances were in their main hidden from the Public's (Eye) Sight, as they have now until some young woman cries Rape!
Then all the revealing flood gates are sprung open for all to savour!

So Eddie boy VII, like son Eddie boy VIII was not satisfied with just rich & regals, he had to have his way with another type, a famous prostitute (His son would later make it 2 in a row)!

Agustina del Carmen Otero Iglesias *(4 November 1868 – 10 April 1965), better known as* **Carolina Otero** *or* **La Belle Otero***, was a Spanish actress, dancer and courtesan.*
She had a reputation for great beauty and was famous for her numerous lovers.
Within a short number of years, Otero was said to be the most sought-after woman in Europe. She was serving, by this time, as a courtesan to wealthy and powerful men of the day, and she chose her lovers carefully.
***(How** didn't STD's have a Royal Field Day – I cannot fathom!?) >*

Public Domain 1890 photo of La Belle Otero by Leopold Reutlinger (d.1937)
(She accumulated an enormous fortune, but stupidly gambled it all away)!

She associated herself with Kaiser Wilhelm II, Prince Albert 1 of Monaco, Prince Nicholas 1 of Montenegro, & from above, our King Edward VII, <> The second child and eldest son of Queen Victoria & Prince Albert:- Edward, nicknamed "Bertie", was related to royalty throughout Europe.
He, like our Charles, was an heir apparent for an apparent eternity (he 60 years) and being excluded form any real Political dealings, he came to personify the 'dissolute', leisured elite. And fitting time amongst his various professional prostitute connectivities, he still managed time and his sexual attention to sire 6 kids by his 1863 marriage to Princess Alexandra of Denmark!

One of those children was Maud Charlotte Mary Victoria **(B. 1869 – d. 1938)** *k/a* **Maud of Wales** *as her father was the infamous Prince of Wales at the time, she became Queen of Norway as the wife of King Haakon VII –*

And it is this Norwegian Guinness link which will be expanded upon later when we discover Dear (Henry) Sam's and Fluff's WW11 secret activities!!!

But until that time some more Norwegian inter-connected history...her ONLY son OLAV...

We begin with Maud's picture.....

Public Domain Queen Maud of Norway (nee Princess of Wales) 1910 Author unknown

And here Annie+kids & Charlie eat your hearts out as Olav's sporting accomplishments were legendary as they were varied:- He was an accomplished ski jumper and regatta sailor, culminating in his winning 'gold' in the 1928 Olympics!
And with sailing being his passion it was no coincidence that he and Sam would share fond memories and Harald's introduction to that specialist sport! **(To follow)**...
Olav V was the first heir to the Norwegian throne to be brought up in Norway since 14th Century, Olav IV:- he attended both civilian and military schools. In 1929, he (?consanguineously?) married his first cousin, Princess Martha of Sweden (d. 1954).

He became king in 1957.
But before then, it is during the second world war that his involvement (mirroring Sam + Fluff) was particularly significant where he was appointed Norwegian Chief of Staff in 1944. And like Edward and Mrs Wallace sheltered in the USA whilst the war raged in Europe!
(As did Harry & Megan as the tabloid war here waged against them!)
There Olav & Maud rubbed shoulders with President Roosevelt, whilst Edward and Wallace moved in lower fashionable circles – (to be expanded upon later...) Olav (d.1991) (16 years after (Uncle) (Henry) Samuel Guinness – part of this Book) –

Olav & Maud had 2 daughters and one son Harald (born 1937) succeeded to the throne 1991, who will be another Sam Guinness Family post war link.

And maintaining the rich/regal connectivity one of Harald's god-parents was none other than our, King George VI.
His marriage to Sonja Haraldsen was considered in Germanic circles as being Morganic (see definition above):- marrying a commoner was not the regally accepted liaison/union way, but it was allowed to pass and made acceptable by his father, who relented seeing the love in their eyes, mirroring Sam's & Fluff's – she was also a Norwegian!! (Link already explained).
Interesting for me is that the boy's name, Harald, is fully contained in his mother's surname!?

*Public Domain 1943._Prins_Harald_-_no-nb_digifoto_20160108_00334_bldsa_pk_kgl0090 **National Library of Norway***

Like Henry Samuel Guinness (friend of family see letters..) In 1960, Harald entered our famous Balliol College, Oxford, where his free time was enjoyed in his handed down watery choices - rowing! (Which Sam encouraged also (see later..) coupled with sailing where, like father, like son, he represented Norway in 3 Olympics, 1964, 1968, 1972 and carried the Norwegian Flag in 1964!
And last but not least of his accomplishments, he came second in the 2016 sailing world championships!

BUT
Serious Disease/Illness/Sickness knows no Regal Boundaries <> As our own Princess Kate & King Charles know only too well fighting off their own cancerous infection!

At the start of the twenty-first century, this prolific sporting type has been unable to perform his duties as sovereign due to ill health on certain occasions as the doctors operated on his urinary bladder cancer, aortic stenosis (picture below) and covid time, in 2020 due to cardiac surgery (replacement of a heart valve).

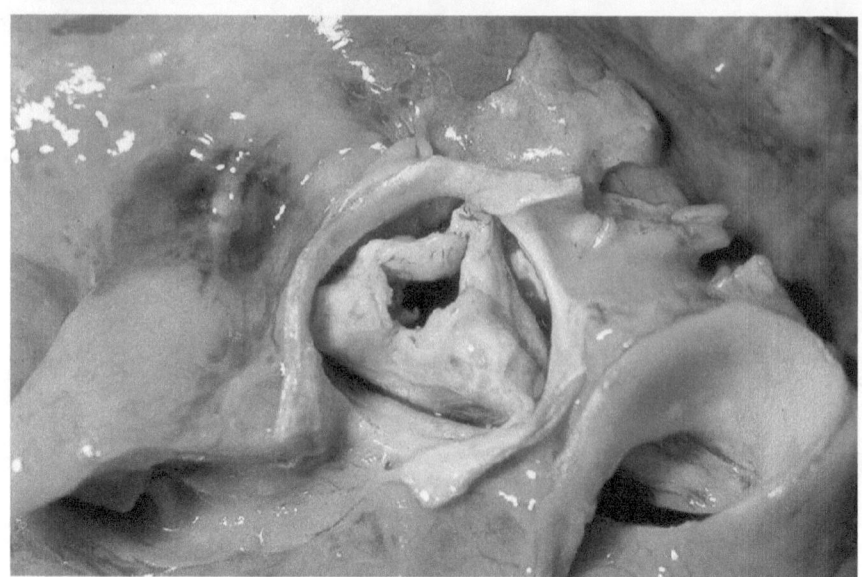

Public Domain thanks to US CDCDr. Edwin P. Ewing Jr.Aortic_stenosis_rheumatic,_gross_pathology_20G0014_lores

And back full circle to Sam who also had disease to have its final say...he died in 1975.

PLUS
Our Sam's Balliol and WW2 Histrionics will follow sooner rather than later!?

PART 1d: THE 3Ws in WW2??? & 'ONE' NO LONGER KING!!!

The Truth is/will Out!?

Whatever was written or said before those papers (below **) were published could have been classed as hearsay, or just fabricated as there were no definitive personally noted writings on the subject: a case of believe none of what is said, or half of what has been read, as Sabrina once told my John, the first time they met in her YCTV office!
There again if someone close, yes, but if a friend quoted by the media, then, no!
As manufactured friends by the press are ten a penny and not worth that penny, as she pointed out when denying the article he laid before 'by a friend'!?

So we are now at an arena where Mr. M. was up close and personal with Edward and Wallis: so his quotes carried great weight and merit – here are some pertinent ones I had come across...

"To him she was the perfect woman. It is a great mistake to assume that he was merely in love with her in an ordinary physical sense of the term. There was an *intellectual companionship* and there is no doubt that his lonely nature found in her a spiritual comradeship."

For me the phrase '*intellectual companionship*' had a special significance AND resonance when we compare and contrast Charles & Diana's relationship – this phrase mentioned aspect was to me sorely missing and finally contributed to the split!
M. further wrote, reinforcing his belief in his ex sovereign's, "For myself I am free to confess that I always underestimated the depth and strength of the king's devotion and of their united will." This reinforcing that this was not a passing phase as were his previous historical dalliances!

   And here we need back track many years to the apparent 'W' triumvirate men of old!?

Here a certain Wx2 Intro!?

Grania Maeve Rosaura, Dowager Marchioness of Normanby died peacefully at home on 15th January, aged 97 years.
She was the daughter of Lord Moyne, who as Minister in the Middle East had been murdered by the paramilitary Stern Gang in Cairo in 1944 #.
A descendant of the Guinness brewing family – her grandfather was Lord Iveagh –
but the war took her father # and before the loss of her mother to cancer, left indelibly painful memories plus...
Like other privileged Guinness in this book, she did her WW2 bit, joining the Women's Auxiliary Air Force, she was put to work <u>analysing photographs from reconnaissance planes of German military installations</u>.
At home in Grosvenor Place, close to Buckingham Palace, a bomb blew her bedroom shutters across the room. (Like another future diplomat's wife, the future Mrs Pinter was to experience!)
Fearing more for her life, her father gave over the house for the use of Polish officers and she found herself on the family estate on the Sussex coast, taking pistol-shooting lessons from him – until he was sent to the Middle East # by his friend and ally, Winston Churchill.

Monckton papers lists 2000
The couple subsequently moved to Portugal where the Duke ignored Churchill's instructions to return to Britain. He was finally persuaded to take up a governorship of the Bahamas in 1940.
German 1950s published old, biased documents suggesting the Ex King had sympathies with the old Nazi Regime created UK W. Churchill extreme resent ensuring a UK intro rebuttal:-: "The duke was subjected to heavy pressure from many quarters to stay in Europe, where the Germans hoped that he would exert his influence against the policy of his majesty's government.

BUT

His royal highness never wavered in his loyalty to the British cause or in his determination to take up his official post as governor of the Bahamas on the date agreed – as far as I have 'Monckton & Co' read!?

And so onto the man himself....

Public Domain (Guinness) Lord Moyne Secretary of State for the Colonies (February 1941/42) entertaining recruits from Jamaica on arrival in London for RAF training. CH4432

Monckton served as advisor to King Edward VIII during the abdication crisis, having been Attorney General to the Duchy of Cornwall since 1932.

So it is no surprise to find Lord Moyne later in letters correspondence with him subsequently re King Edward, which were retained by Monckton..

And here one of Walter's Colonial personal responses in 1941...re the Ex King!

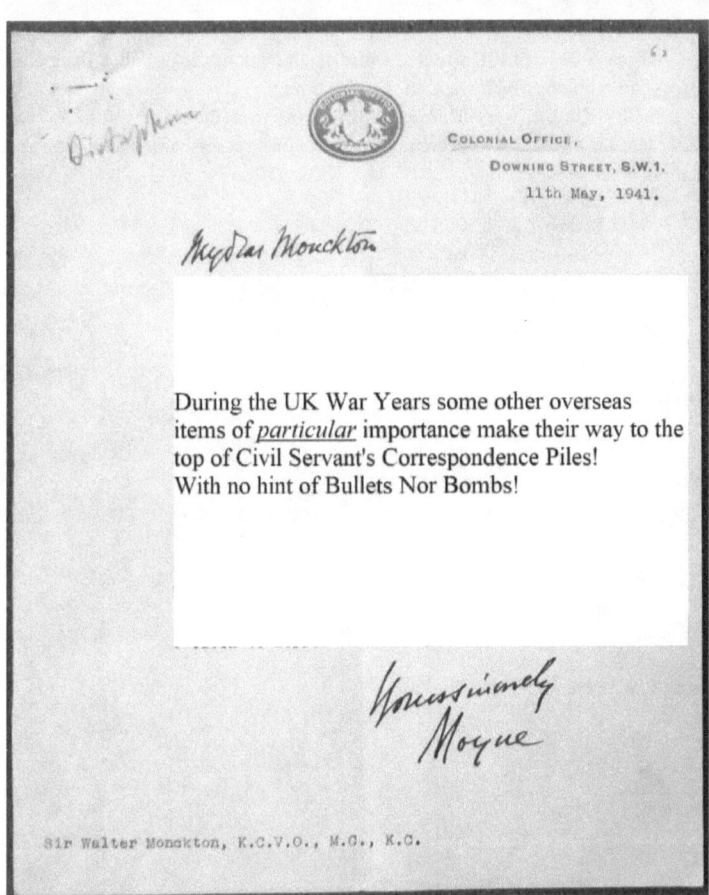

In view of all the attention and possibly flak that Wallis & Eddy, as he was known amongst the family, were receiving, the Ex King had suggested he might be given a Press Secretary.
Strangely enough the Davidson gentleman suggested was not found as the most suitable for the role and ended up a Commander of an Anti-Tank Regiment!
But, a candidate had to be found as the US Mis-Representing Press were having a Field Day and what was needed was someone at the Front to Re-But such scandalous nonsense!

Later below I will highlight one such print scandal monger!

But first an internal travel update plus ???

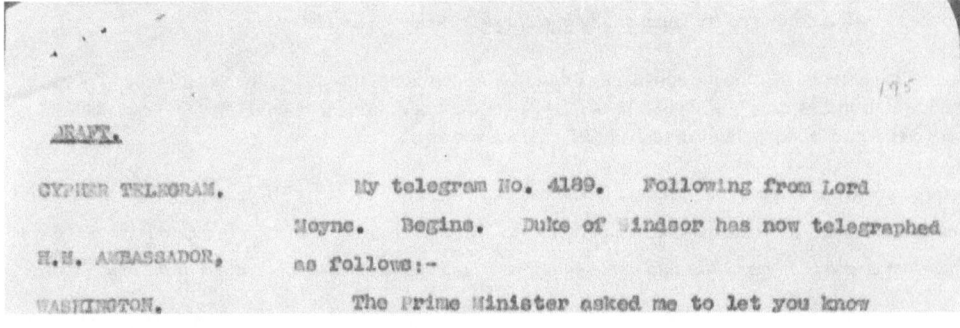

But
Whilst all in Europe/Africa/Asia were struggling to avoid death by bomb &/or bullet, there came another Edward+Wallis **Press**-ing problem which was 'title' orchestrated!
First may I point out the Ex-King +1 were *'Bahamas'* well away from the Bombs/Bullets:-
Although there was a fear they might have become the subject of an assassination attempt, hence the British Cruiser escort mentioned below...

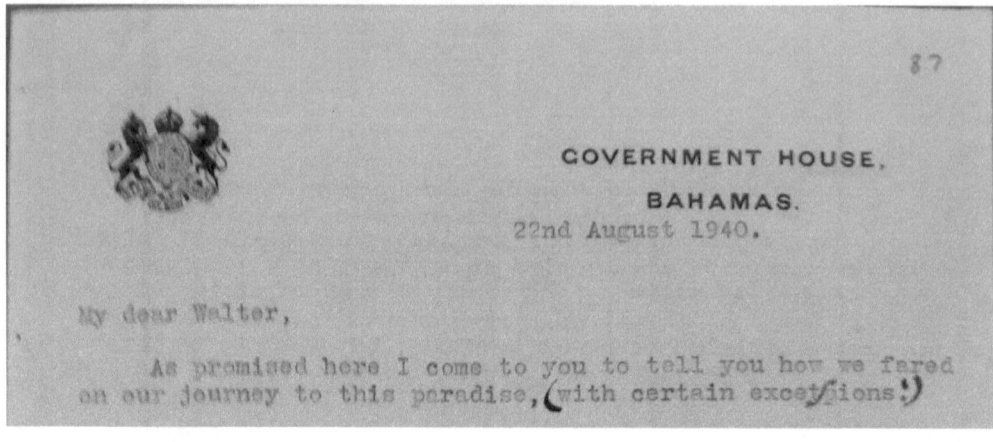

Lord Moyne +1 were also about then (Later Below).

And here I gained some insight which I shall share with you.

The aspect of Edward + Wallis support of the Nazi Régime has been, well, albeit not always ***accurately***, depicted – well according to the Duke totally ***inaccurately***!(below)+(And later↓)

And as one example of/from the above may I first may I introduce you to something called 'Liberty' a weekly periodical, launched exactly 100 years back in 1924 and continued off and on until some 50 years ago!
It covered stories about politicians, celebrities, authors, and artists.

Before I get to the article(s) in question I would just copyright point out that, 50+ years ago, they *'innovately'* went about proprietary rights in a very thorough way:- *In 1968, Dr Seuss sued Liberty over a copyright dispute regarding cartoons an artist had sold to the magazine in 1932. Unlike most publications at the time, Liberty* typically bought not only first serial rights, but all publishing and distribution rights to the work of their contributors. Liberty won the case, and their copyrights were apparently solidly established by a landmark ruling in copyright law!?

English: Liberty Magazine Cover (10 May 1924) –
The author died in 1949, so this work is in the public domain in its country of origin and other countries and areas where the copyright term is the author's life plus 70 years or fewer. This work is in the public domain in the U.S. because it was published (or registered with the U.S. Copyright Office) before Jan 1, 1929.
A possibly contentious celebrity tabloid and it still existed in full flow when the cypher telegram above was sent. (It ceased publication many years since.)

Its reporting veracity was questioned by the Ex King himself as his fears were just as they are for so many, false reporting, or without substantiating facts first creating a monster out of someone who claims they are not.
Here that apparently totally inaccurate article in the Liberty edition dated 22 March 1941, ↑↑ which was copied by the Germans and published over there in occupied France, purporting to be the truth!?
This followed on another false German report of Edward's being arrested in July 1940!
Edward went to great lengths to explain it was all an 'Aryan' propaganda plot to cause rifts here and gossip amongst those not in the know: He wrote:- "...*that it was taken for granted that the Royal Family AND the British Government attitude towards him and his wife had embittered him against his Country!*

    ....It was up to the PM to issue a denial if he so wished..."

BUT
Moreover Edward thought was that it might be easier/better if he & spouse were issued a Press Officer to accompany them in America.
Hence the discussion in the Moyne Colonial Office (letter above).

And for those not in the know, the Americas were where our couple were 'touring', where they felt welcomed, albeit under protective custody:- so currently topical/controversial in view of the pro & con argument for the UK to maintain payment for our Royal Protection Squad looking after, originally Prince Harry, post Meghan US move, but now apparently, Prince Andrew, post Jeffrey Epstein trial!
....

BUT
There was more Moyne had wished to impart...(From Above)

NB Originally Monckton Trustees available to view/comment upon correspondence sifting between the two caused a problem:- I mean they were both **Walters**!

The 22nd August 1940 letter was written by Moyne, who only had a couple of more years to live, before an assassin's bullets ended it!

And here I would add Monckton served as advisor to King Edward VIII during the 1936 abdication crisis, and although there was much about his involvement re that situation, the holders (? In Trust?) <> "Oxford's Bodleian Library released 10 boxes of the Monckton papers in 2000, but held back material in a file labelled "Box 24" and some like Historian Mr Roberts *claimed one of missing letters from the then Queen to Sir Walter in August 1940 may have been related to the arrival of Edward and Mrs Simpson in the Bahamas, where the former King was to become governor.*

It was sent just days after Queen Elizabeth had written to the Colonial Secretary Lord Lloyd expressing unhappiness that the Duke of Windsor was being made Governor of the Bahamas.
<u>*It won't apparently be released until 2037!*</u>
John's obtained August 1940 correspondence above ↑↑ does mention '<u>Queen Mary</u>'!

<u>BUT</u> *I shan't elaborate upon it here – just keep it to myself!*

Although (re the above) I can confess on Walter's behalf that the Canadian Boat Bahama bound trip suffered from a surfeit of Mosquitos, Sandflies, Cockroaches & <u>other annoying little blighters</u>! Not to mention the oppressive heat!

Everything went according to convivial plan: Edward and Wallis were hits with the locals!

<u>BUT</u> *keeping low under the Radar they also suffered not from enemy attack!*
Although I assume the Cruiser Sea Escort had a significant part to play in that aspect!

<u>And here I must add that 'Regal Title' fly in the Political Ointment:-</u> Wallis was called 'Duchess' by Edward as he detested the official submitted – Her Grace!!!
('Her Excellency' was also off the table! And his brother seemingly wouldn't relent:- he was the only one with the Power to sanction a change to the preferred <> Her Royal Highness!
Ah well perhaps it was just a case of sibling 'revenge' (?) rivalry at its worst?

Walter's sign off now merits a minor discussion...

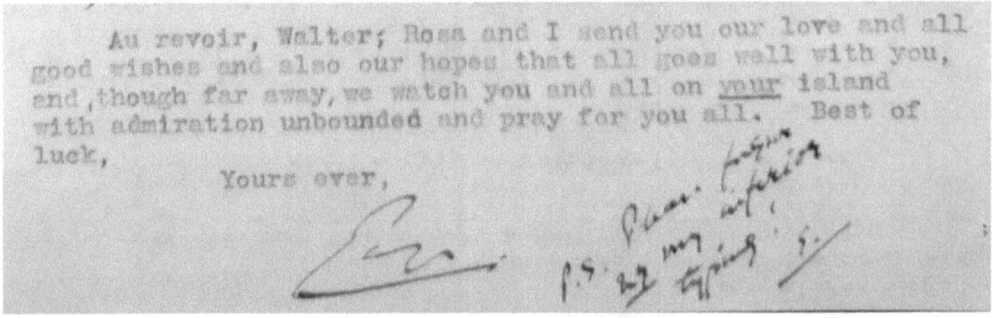

Lord Walter Moyne died a few years later!
↓
WHICH ROSA?

The Honourable **_Rosa-mund_** Monckton, born 1953, has an aristocratic background and influential connections of her own. As an adviser to Edward VIII, her grandfather, **_Walter_** Monckton had drafted the 1936 abdication speech.

Many years later, another link on high, Princess Diana agreed to be Godmother to Rosa's daughter Domenica, who was born with Down's syndrome – *and John recalls meeting another Down's syndrome sufferer who made John envious as she retold the story how Diana gave her a long hug! (She did away with a supposed getting too close taboo!?)* <> John gave her a hug too and they each got the reciprocating smiles they deserved!

NB **_Walter_** Moyne also had a daughter called Grania Maeve **_Rosa-ura_** Guinness, born1920!

And significantly, not the only time with Edward AND Co:- *According to Wallis, it was during a cruise on Lord Moyne's private yacht, which features later in WWII, named Rosaura, in August 1934 that she fell in love with Edward.* <> *So wrote Greg King 1999 in his book, 'The Duchess of Windsor'. New York: Citadel Press.......*

And so like their grandfather/father who shared the name Walter, these ladies shared the name Rosa, which was confusing as I wrote – Added to all the other duplications which initially threw me:-

King George I AND II of Greece (Father <> Son); on top of our King George V AND King George VI (Father <> Son)!

Not forgetting, King Edward VII AND King Edward VIII (Grandfather <> Grandson)!

And the Elisabeth v Elizabeth above also!

And a couple of Marys along the way! (Later)

....

And so now you have seen the Royal Links, some rather tawdry, others (im)purely promiscuous, we can now come upon the significantly more upstanding and scandal free Phillip & Elizabeth, whose descendants (children/grandchildren) still maintain a Guinness Link – to follow that of Lord Moyne (a Guinness) and his well to do family...which contrasted with so many other Royals, highlighting that a Title does not guarantee wealth and the hope is that it will attract the benevolence of the Current Monarch who can decide the other's financial fate.

Similarly, criminality & sickness ignores social boundaries...

Here below a few examples of each >>>

Poor Rich/Royal Types Prior Examples	Early Rich/Royal Deaths Prior Examples	Sick Rich/Royal Types Prior Examples
Daisy Greville, Countess of Warwick Holloway Prison beckoned her for unpaid Debts!	*Edward VII at 77 years of age died of (laryngeal) throat cancer*	*Princess Alice of Battenberg, Princess of Greece and Denmark Born severely deaf*
Agustina del Carmen Otero Iglesias lover of many Royals incl Edward VII, but penniless at death	*Olav V - urinary bladder cancer, aortic stenosis, heart attacks*	*Elisabeth of Romania (Lizzy) Fat and dim!*
Diana Mitford (Mosley) was imprisoned during WWII as a suspected Nazi sympathiser.	*Grania M. Rosaura lost her parents too young: mother to cancer; Father Lord W. Moyne to a terrorist attack.*	*Prince Wilhelm of Prussia (1882-1951) first daughter. Alexandrina was born 1915 with Down's syndrome.*
Sister of the above called Unity Mitford chose to put a bullet in her brain, rather than face imprisonment!	*Charles Bedaux (Below), who had hosted Edward's wedding, with charges of treason in 1943 committed suicide in jail in Miami*	*Princess Alice of Battenburgh mother of Prince Phillip was seen by many Inc. Sigmund Freud, but finally diagnosed with paranoid schizophrenia, & committed to a Sanatorium.*
Th Queen Mother Princess Mary below – was not a wealthy Royal:- when 16, her the family were heavily in debt, and in the 1880s stayed abroad with relatives to make pennies meet!	*Edward's youngest brother, Prince John, died at the age of 13 on 18 January 1919 after a severe epileptic seizure.*	*Philip suffered yet more sorrow when his guardian Georgie Milford Haven died from cancer at the age of 45. Then Mountbatten was assassinated.*
George II he was replaced by his younger brother, the future King Alexander 1 was exiled, penniless apart from a small annual legacy!	*In 1937, Phillip, 16, lost his sister Cecilie; her husband, Georg Donatus, Hereditary Grand Duke of Hesse; their two sons; and Georg Donatus's mother who were killed in an air crash.*	*George VI had a long lasting stutter; beaten as so many because he initially wrote left handed; suffered chronic stomach problems as well as knock knees, for which he was forced to wear painful corrective splints.*
Opposite NB The Queen Mother died 6 weeks after her daughter, Margaret's death in 2002! >>>	*Queen Elizabeth, the Queen Mother lost her husband early: He had died in the night from a coronary thrombosis at the age of 56.* <<< >>>	*Princess Margaret's heavy smoking and linked lung operation + pneumonia + strokes for most of her adult life, resulted in death at 71 in 2002 on her fourth stroke. Her mother lived until 101!*
Not to be confused with ↑↑ Queen Mother Princess Mary: she lost >>> Plus she died weeks before her Grand Daughter ascended the throne But she survived her sons >>>	*Her 13-year-old son, Prince John, in 1919, suffered a fatal seizure; Another son, in 1942, Prince George, Duke of Kent was killed in an air accident at the age of 39. Plus - In 1952, a third son, George VI also pre-died her!*	*Her betrothed, Prince Albert died a few weeks before their wedding–the influenza pandemic of 1891-92.*

BUT NOW BACK TO OUR 3Ws in WW2 or Thereabouts >>>>>>>..

PART 1e: THE 3Ws in WW2??? & 'ONE' NO LONGER KING <> SET STRAIGHT!!!

Yet as there are &/or were those 'Monckton Papers ** in &/or out of Public Circulation, there is another corroboratory source which John delved through and perhaps the definitive as having been publicly revealed:- let's start back with that 'Abdication' matter...and opinions...

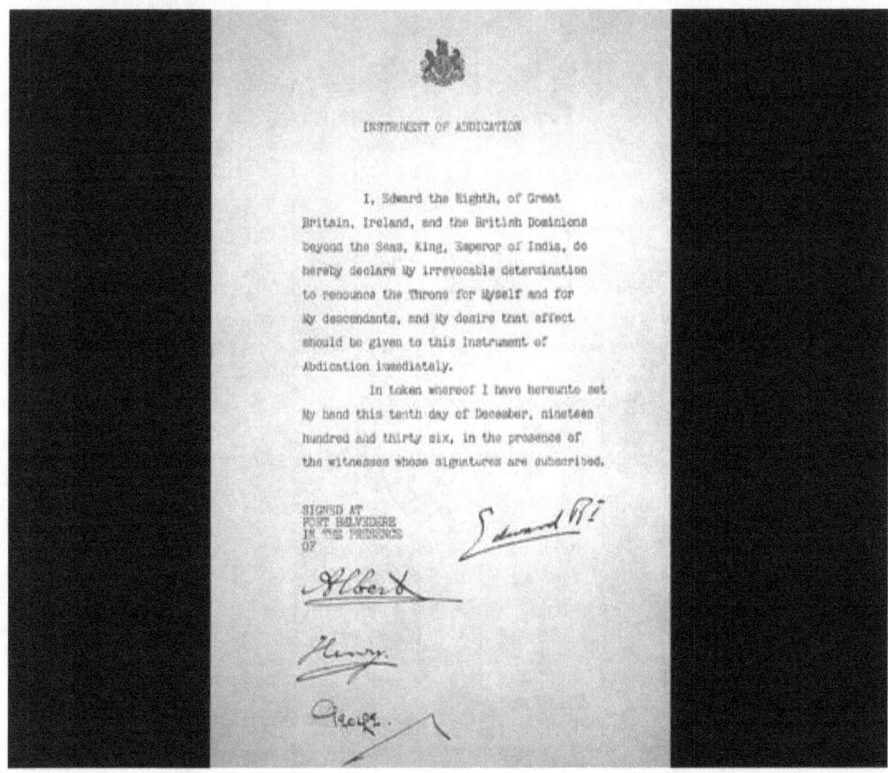

Instrument of Abdication signed by King Edward VIII and his three brothers, Albert (later George VI), Henry and George, 10 December 1936
public domain crown copyright only 50 years-Edward abdication 1936

Edward VIII became king following the death of his father, George V. He abdicated the throne in order to marry divorcee Wallis Simpson and became known as the Duke of Windsor. Fort Belvedere is a house situated in Windsor Great Park in Surrey where Edward lived as Prince of Wales. The Instrument of Abdication was witnessed and signed by his younger brothers: Prince Albert, Duke of York; Prince Henry, Duke of Gloucester; and Prince George, Duke of Kent.

HRH Prince Edward created Duke of Windsor

AND IN A BLAZE OF GLORY ANNOUNCEMENT THE ARCHIVES HAVE IT!
AND THEY LET THEIR SECRET CATS OUT OF THEIR BAGS FOR US ALL TO SEE:

By Dr Susan Williams (Research Fellow in History at the Institute of Education, University of London), historical adviser to The National Archives does the Intro:-

"This is the largest, richest and most comprehensive set of papers on the subject of the Abdication. It contains a wealth of detail that will fill many gaps in knowledge, as well as shedding new light on material available elsewhere.
The files provide essential source material for the understanding of relationships between the Crown and Government during the interwar period, in relation to constitutional and political issues.
Although some of the material appears in Ziegler's life of King Edward VIII, the fact that he was writing a biography, rather than a study of the Abdication, limited his scope.
The minutes and verbatim reports of Cabinet meetings ... flesh out the background to the Abdication and reveal the Government's determination not to let the King marry Mrs Simpson, **morganatically** # ↓ *or otherwise.*
They confirm that although Cabinet trusted the King to behave with propriety, they feared that Winston Churchill would exploit Edward's popular support to form a King's Party that would challenge the government (Prem1/457) (CAB 23/86 Vol LIII) >

the word has been fully explained and exampled elsewhere in this Book. ↑.

These files are of value not only to constitutional and political historians, but also to social historians. The transcripts of interviews with servants contain information about domestic service and social attitudes, and a set of letters to the King's Proctor from members of the public reveal opinions on the laws relating to divorce.

These records are also significant in terms of what they do not say.

They do not provide any evidence to substantiate allegations that the Duke and Duchess of Windsor were at any time Nazi traitors.

Nor do they link the Duchess of York (later Queen Elizabeth, the Queen Mother) to the events that led to the abdication, although they do show that some members of the Royal Household, cooperating with Ministers, high ranking civil servants, and some members of the press, had an influence on the course of these events.

Abdication Papers
Document reference: PREM 1/461
A minute to the Prime Minister from Sir John Simon, the Home Secretary, 28 April 1937.
It refers to the Letters Patent which deprived Mrs Simpson of the title 'Her Royal Highness', and comments, 'You are aware how strongly The King [George VI] and Queen [Elizabeth, later the Queen Mother] desire this situation to be established; I believe Queen Mary also has strong views that it should, if possible, be done.'

It also explains that,
'She would acquire it [that is, the title HRH] unless something is done about it.'

At this meeting the Prime Minister began by pointing out the impossibility of the marriage so long as His Majesty remained King. Public opinion, neither in the United Kingdom nor in the Dominions, would stand for such a marriage, if only for the reason that the wife of a King automatically becomes Queen.

After considerable discussion of the matter, the King made it clear to the Prime Minister that his mind was made up; he was determined to marry Mrs. Simpson; he recognised that the Prime Minister was right in his description of opinion in the country; the King therefore would be prepared to abdicate.

In the course of the discussion the Prime Minister drew attention to the state of feeling throughout the Empire, on which he had received some very direct and significant information from the Australian High Commissioner, as well as a good deal of indirect information through the Secretary of State for the Dominions and through others.

The Prime Minister pointed out that if events should, in the end, result in such a conclusion it was important that it should be arrived at in a manner that would avoid any constitutional struggle, so as to make matters easy for the King's successor.

The Prime Minister told the King that there was an uneasy feeling about the circumstances of the divorce, more especially as the King was not justiciable in his own courts. Finally the Prime Minister told the King that he did not then wish for any decision; on the contrary he would like the King again to think the matter over.

ANON....

PART 1f – SUBSEQUENTLY THE OTHER (DEVIL(s)?)
A ONCE KING AND DIVORCEE TOLERATED!:-

Edward was no stranger to (cultural?) visits to the good ole US of A.... *
American General, Oscar Solbert had suggested that the Duke take a tour of Germany, which was soon intended to be the first of several planned international tours. Solbert had been with Edward on his 1924 * tour of the US and had been impressed by his gravitas and professional demeanour.
The latter had also been remarked on in Official Correspondence above...SO in effect he was not really a Nazi sympathiser as some mooted that his visit might future cement a liaison between the UK & Germany with Edward as our connecting Monarch!
AND – the timing was off:- if it were when he was King and had the necessary Political Clout, then some quarters suggest relations between the UK and Germany may have not gone to future War,
BUT as likely that political **chicanery** would have fallen flat on its proposed Regal Engineered Use face!
French-American Millionaire Charles Bedaux offered to organise the Duke's side of the arrangements.
(Unfortunately their acquaintance, Charles Bedaux (above), who also had hosted their wedding, was arrested on charges of treason in 1943 but committed suicide in jail in Miami before the case was brought to trial.)

German Archives - Duke of Windsor inspecting SS troops at Ordensburg Krossinsee 1937
(Leys on the left)

Coincidentally on their visit <u>the Windsors may have suffered a same fate as Diana</u>: On one journey, their liaison, Dr Robert Leys ↑, head of the German Labour Front - Bedaux and he worked together earlier in the 1930s – dear Robert was drunk at the wheel of the Windsors' Mercedes while he was driving at speed <u>and crashed them into the gates of the Munich factory</u> that they were visiting.

But two further points that the views of the visit could be differently recalled and that would be down to the possible (purposeful) mistranslations by Hitler's translator who was more than once criticised by the Duke's own!

"Finally all this talk of being Nazi sympathisers??? **I THINK NOT!!!**"

How could either/both be accused as such when their opinion of the leader was as such:- the Duchess wrote how she was both 'fascinated and repelled' by Hitler; Edward later said that he had thought Hitler was 'a somewhat ridiculous figure, with his theatrical posturings and his bombastic pretensions!'

The couple returned to France and retirement after the defeat of Nazi Germany....

NB:- After all the Hoo-Ha died down and there was no more WWII dying, Edward & Wallis moved to Paris and remained there whilst eventual death took them one by one...
BUT
Lo & behold who should buy their Mansion?
Well none other than that female molester, Al-Fayed!
Perhaps part of his plan to infiltrate the inner circle of our Queen & Co, or perhaps rather use it to Inveigle himself into the 'Royal Enclosure(s)?
It worked as the Royals were welcome within his Famous Harrods Store's inners, just as he expected the Royals to welcome him into theirs!
And when Diana was friendless and alone with no man in her life to lean on... this is where wealth again played its part for his son, Dodi, to make his move.
And here that newly purchased Paris mansion had its small part to play: it had already played host to the Rich/Elite/Famous such as Liz Taylor and Dietrich AND the Rothschilds #, who get mentioned more than once in this Book:-
Here is one # of theirs >>>

AND THEN ANOTHER >>>>

Author Copyright

They were also Commercial rivals of sorts to Marie Bonaparte's illustrious, Monaco casino owning Grandfather, François Blance. (Her father was >
Roland Napoléon Bonaparte, 6th Prince of Canino and Musignano (19 May 1858 – 14 April 1924)

BUT
Apparently, when introduced to this future, perhaps permanent bolt hole, Diana only gave it a cursory, disinterested glance!
BUT
If only she stayed over then perhaps the car death which awaited her might not have happened!?
 now no longer had his 'Insidious' means of Royal Connectivity and auctioned off its contents for a mere >> $20 million plus!
BUT
As luck would then have it, he returned the place to the Paris French!
Expect it to open up in 2025 as a 'glorified' Museum!

Historical Note: *Commentators did not reckon her a 'beauty' BUT as a young girl she looked OK to me?!*

Public Domain photo of her @ 10 years of age.

<u>TO REITERATE</u>

<u>These (ARCHIVED) records are also significant in terms of what they do not say.</u>

<u>They do not provide any evidence to substantiate allegations that the Duke and Duchess of Windsor were at any time Nazi traitors.</u>

<u>Nor do they link the Duchess of York (later Queen Elizabeth, the Queen Mother) to the events that led to the abdication, although they do show that some members of the Royal Household, cooperating with Ministers, high ranking civil servants, and some members of the press, had an influence on the course of these events.</u>

>>>>>>>>>>>>

And since I mentioned her, perhaps she needs a few history lines of her own!?
Our **LATE QUEEN MOTHER**:-

Elizabeth Angela Marguerite Bowes-Lyon was the youngest daughter and the ninth of ten children of Claude Bowes-Lyon & Cecilia Cavendish-Bentinck.

Elizabeth Bowes Lyon (4 August 1900 – 30 March 2002) –
Public Domain Photograph Lafayette portrait of then Lady Elizabeth Bowes Lyon.

*Public Domain portrait by **Philip** de László d. 1937 of the future Queen in 1925*

*(This dear ole (yet another) **Philip** has and will himself feature in this Book)*

Public Domain 1931 Portrait by Philip de Laszlo d.1937 of Claude George Bowes Lyon, 14th Earl of Strathmore and Kinghorne

Her father was Claude Bowes Lyon, 14th & 1st Earl of Strathmore & Kinghorne14th –
He was well decorated:- *possessing, a KG = The Most Noble Order Of The Garter, KT = (the Scottish) Most Ancient And Most Noble Order Of The Thistle, GCVO = (For services to Queen Victoria) The Royal Victorian Order – where the seeds for his daughter's future betrothal were sown? The Grand Master of the Order is currently Princess Anne; + TD = the Territorial Decoration – currently known as the Territorial Army.*

(NB Like some other Royals one of his family siblings had a sporting interest/ambition which came to fruition when the brother won Wimbledon Men's Doubles 1887).

Upon succeeding his father to the Earldom on 16 February 1904, Claude inherited **large** estates in Scotland & England – *as they all seem to have down the centuries*!?

After her husband died, she was officially known as Queen Elizabeth the Queen Mother, with her daughter, the now also departed, Queen Elizabeth II.

And all I need now is look at her hubby's lineage where names are too shared!
....

So here I bid you welcome to the **TECKS!?**
....

AND HERE WE GO BACK THREE CENTURIES!

Princess MARY Adelaide of Cambridge,
(Mary Adelaide Wilhelmina Elizabeth) 27 November 1833 – 27 October 1897) -
Later known as the Duchess of TECK

She was one of the first royals to patronise a wide range of charities and was a first cousin of Queen Victoria.

The young Princess was baptised on 9 January 1834 at Cambridge House, by Revd John Ryle Wood, Chaplain to the Duke of Cambridge.

(TECK (German Heritage) = In 1863, the title "Prince of Teck" was conferred as a courtesy title by King William I of Wurttemberg upon the children of his cousin Duke Alexander (1804–85) by his morganatic marriage (Definition provided before) with Countess Claudine Rhedley von Kis-Rhede (1812–41), ennobled as countess of Hohenstein.)

> *Her mother had a suitable candidate found for herself by her parents, the Prince of Wales & his wife Princess Alexandra on a visit to the Austrian court at Vienna in 1865.*

> *During the visit, they met and took a liking to a young officer in the Austrian Army, Prince Francis of Teck, a minor member of the royal family of Wurttemberg.*

> *Francis was of lower rank than Mary Adelaide, was the product of a morganatic # marriage (Already elaborated upon earlier above # Prince William & Kate?) and had no succession rights to the throne of Württemberg, **but was at least of princely title and of royal blood**. Perhaps here chosen on principles similar to Diana a century later?*

> *He was also considered to be "the most handsome man at the Austrian court", where he was known as Der schöne Uhlan, "the handsome cavalry officer". Again a similar 'handsome' compliment had been paid our late Prince Phillip?*

> *6 March 1866 arranged for him to meet Mary Adelaide. "The wooing was but a short affair" - Again a future Diana similarity - according to Mary Adelaide: the pair were introduced on 7 March 1866.*

> *A month later were engaged, - Again a future Diana similarity? much to the satisfaction of Mary Adelaide's family. "Everyone seemed to think it would do", Mary Adelaide's daughter Mary, but called May, would later say:- The couple were married on 12 June 1866 in Kew, Surrey.*

And once again that filthy lucre (money) decided the future: The family resided here rather than abroad, mainly because Mary Adelaide received £5,000 per annum as a parliamentary annuity and carried out royal duties + extra cash from her mother + Granny Victoria allowed them housing at BOTH White Lodge in Richmond Park & Kensington Palace, London - Again a future Prince Philip similarity - Her mother, the Duchess of Cambridge, also provided her with supplementary income.

*The Tecks had one daughter and three sons: the daughter was **Princess Victoria MARY** of Teck, who married the future George V in 1893: their sons Edward + George would also attain the throne.*

Mary of Teck (Victoria Mary (May) Augusta Louise Olga Pauline Claudine Agnes; 26 May 1867 – 24 March 1953) was until 20 January 1936 Queen/the wife of King George V. Her godmother and paternal aunt was another Liz, Princess Elizabeth, landgravine of hesse-Homburg – from all this you can see the German UK linkage!

Mary, as queen consort (wife) from 1910, was at George V's side through WWI, but what of note is that he suffered consistent ill health!
He was to die a quarter of a century later and she became queen mother in 1936 when her eldest son, Edward VIII, ascended the throne.
He soon abdicated and so she was then duty bound to support her second son, George VI, until he died in 1952. Sadly, she passed in 1953 - ten weeks before her granddaughter was crowned, Elizabeth II.

Edward VII, their other son's wife, the future Queen Mother-Princess Mary was born at Kensington Palace in London on 26 May 1867- Her mother was Princess Mary Adelaide, above.

BUT

And here back to our Guinness Stars:- You'd think with their Regal/Political Links, the Heads of Breweries/Banks carried some clout with the Authorities during War Time?

I'll here show you not!

↓↓↓

Be careful Sam what you say & do at Airports during War Time!

Similarly so many up there in the Rich/Famous/Powerful Strata have found to their Epstein Cost that loose lips, talk &/or emails, costs lives AND reputations AND hitting hard in so many's pockets too!

>>>>>>>>>>>

PART 2 ◇ THE EPSTEIN INTERWOVEN FALLOUT HERE AND 'RELATIVELY' ABROAD!
(Here the 'relatively' will refer to Norway, whose Guinness connection has been established – But so many others get drawn into a symbolic Stoppard's Squared Circle!
- Here the impossible where the Elite thought themselves untouchables! – As the dispelling Truth materialises!)

RECOLLECTING >>> The Early Unabating 2026 Spring Scandal Fall Out!   BUT
PLEASE NOTE: We start here with an updated 29 Nov 2025 with the death of Tom Stoppard.......

From PART 16b: STOPPARD AND CRICKETTING PINTER >>>>
John thought old wicket-keeping hard stop would soon become a full stop! BUT he passed John's imaginary death by 80 goal post, which became a winning post until 29 November 2025, when at 88 not out, demon bowler death finally smashed his life wicket, bails, stumps and all!!! (So what now Dear 'Dorset' Again Single Sabrina???) (See also *'You can try valiantly'* **Chapters)**

Although his departure news was well and truly hit out his metaphorical cricket ground as another, now most infamous person of that certain ever recurring male species ^{S}, took all the centre stages and mock applause!
(^{S} a group subordinate to a genus and containing individuals agreeing in some common attributes and called by a common name = ***SCUM****!)*
AND so 2026 news welcomes us with something truly sinister as a certain Epstein's Web stretches further and further afield, snaring so many who thought they were free as a bird only to find their wings trimmed and brought 'unceremoniously down to earth to be set upon all at the base level they once were well and truly way above!

……………………..

We will begin this insightful Chapter as we will finish it at BLEAK BLENHEIM PALACE -
As the news is NOT GOOD!...

Author Copyright

Within the lower floors there is a memoria/historical museum setting where Winston Churchill's historic moments are on display: (SEE ALSO **PART 1+**)

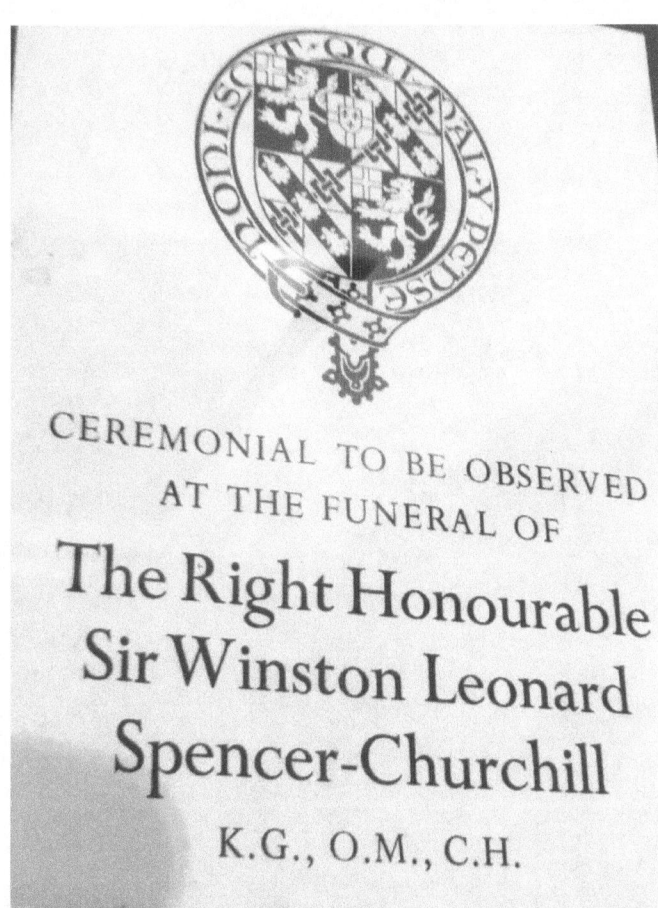

AND now the main part of their then (? Unworked for?) Wealth Source >>>

Author Copyright

AND the lady on site who transformed the whole Blenheim Palace Stage >>

Anne Countess of Sunderland v Northumberland Estates

Author Copyright

AND The Man himself from on old:-

Author Copyright
John Churchill, 1st Duke of Marlborough, painting attributed to Michael Dahl 1702
Winston's father was the British Lord Randolph Churchill.
The youngest son of John, the 7th Duke of Marlborough.

Anymore? Yes, the Duke of Marlborough is a distant relative of Princess Diana through the prominent Spencer family, (SEE ALSO PART 4) as both descend from common ancestors within the extended Spencer-Churchill lineage that holds the dukedom and the Earldom of Spencer. They are related through the Spencer line, with the current Duke, Charles Spencer-Churchill, being a member of the same aristocratic family that produced Diana, Princess of Wales, and Winston Churchill.

Marlborough House – St James Park - In 1817, it became Crown property.
This view of the entrance front published in the 1850s before Pennethorne's additions shows an additional storey on the wings. The wings later gained a fourth main storey, and the central section gained a third.

The current holder of the title, Duke of Marlborough, is Charles James Spencer-Churchill (born 1955), who is the 12th Duke of Marlborough. (See end of Chapter)
He inherited the title and the family seat of Blenheim Palace in 2014. (SEE ALSO NB ENDING)

(NB info –behind here is St James Palace ◇ that is where all her letters were delivered and pre-selected for her personal attention!)
Here is St James should you wish to visit….

Many Wikipedia thanks to https://commons.wikimedia.org/wiki/User:Ricardalovesmonuments

Following on from the photos, the 2 most blue blooded English families have been linked historically through marriage, Sunderland ◇ Northumberland (estates):- Yes, the 9th Earl of Northumberland (Henry Percy, 1564–1632) and the Dukes of Sutherland were related through the long-standing, interconnected lineage of British aristocracy – lately most specifically, Diana Evelyn Percy, sister of the 9th Duke of Northumberland, married John Sutherland Egerton, 6th Duke of Sutherland, in 1939 – related as fourth cousins.

BUT back to Winston and John's perennial lamenting: yes and you have never been able to contract such a disease, you good boy, but Winston's dad reputedly died of that naughty boy disease, syphilis. **(Explanation >)**

Alright he may have put it about into women of ill repute BUT I have it on good authority at least this fellow born with a speech impediment and a hearing problem was taken from us via another 'sick' route:-
"While syphilis may have been a reasonable diagnosis in the absence of modern techniques, the patient's temperament, combined with his speech and articulation problems and absence of dementia, is more consistent with a tumour deep in the left side of his brain." (Per The International Churchill Society) BUT they added…
"It is not possible to be certain; but this is far more likely to be the proper diagnosis."

Following on from the photos, the 2 most blue blooded English families have been linked historically through marriage in reality the linkage c/b expanded to 4 – we need add the Spencers as well as the Churchills! *(Or Even More - See later Part 11b)*

…. So now back to insignificant John!

A 'late' utterly disillusioned patient of mine once questioned the whole life thing and left a pause for thoughts:-
"What's the point of it all?
Why has a combination of loneliness and desperation made me grab at the first sexual partner straw, only to find it would quickly sink taking the future satisfaction with it?
Why have I never experienced this thing people call a friend?
Why have I never found my 'belonging' peer group?
Why does my 'questioning all' individuality create antagonism from those I wish to get to know better?
And why was I put on this earth as a 'true intrusive loner'?
Why does one feel that after every first encounter opportunity, that would be the last?
It seems being brainy with it makes one question whether relationship success was always a no-no?
And so would I continually feel as the irritating stone inside the sock which needs immediate ejection?"
So John some pain caused? BUT you died painlessly in the sleep disease free at 93!
And the reason for including his depressing comments on life?
Well so many might actually be reflected in the life experiences of those on high he desired to cultivate!

And cultivation (expense) does not always mean you end up with the best crop – metaphorically speaking! So John boy, those on high can also hit rock bottom, given the appropriate <u>inappropriate</u> circumstances! NB John died peaceably in his sleep, unlike so many of those 'well above him' who experienced slow painful deaths, some well before their envisaged time! Proving yet again those with the wealth could not buy themselves out of an early &/or painful life departure! Their control ended there, at that juncture!

One final statement before we go full blooded/bodied into total dysfunction, another patient mentioned that whilst on security secondment at the newly built Home Office Building (2MS) the Security Officers were located on floor 2, whilst the big-wig Ministers on floor 3 above, where those above thought them better at the job of vetting their 'personal home' 'foreign' cleaning staff, only to discover they were here in the UK illegally!

BUT those who really knew better could not prevent that faux pas and the subsequent episode where the contracted out company providing their own vetting of their Home Office Building Cleaner Staffing, ended up another batch of employed illegal immigrants!

Both instances proving you should leave the experts to deal with such issues, to avoid personal embarrassment!

Such episodes will be replicated by those again who thought themselves above the lowly security staff detail who would have highlighted whose *'friendship'* they should cultivate – BUT would the stubborn, vain ones on high take the advice?

……….

Important FUTURE READING Context

No Direct Evidence of Crimes: The appearance of a name in the Epstein files, including the "black book," does not necessarily mean that the individual engaged in any wrongdoing or was complicit in trafficking.

From before this Introductory Historical Note:- (SEE ALSO PART 1+) Henry Samuel Howard Guinness was born on 22 June 1888 in Dublin, his father, Howard, was 20 and his mother, Mary, was 25.
He married Norwegian Alfhild Holter on 8 October 1913.
They had four children during their marriage.
He died on 10 April 1975 in Cheyne Walk, Chelsea, London, at the age of 86.
John's last visit was in late 1974, where Fluff made it clear he, cane et al, was not a well man anymore!
His neighbours about him were the Rolling Stones and their manager, plus Channon + another Guinness staying in further down the road...

The Channon Pad

Author Copyright

....

During one therapy session, John once lamented, "How come I can initially inveigle myself into the upper-class echelons, only to be un-majestically booted out as an unwanted intrusive intruder? And yet the female gets a free pass as her moronic bouncing bosom come-on continually/historically provenly trumps my pursuing, enquiring insatiable intellect?"

NB 1 - He is obviously wrong since as far as the Elitist Families within are concerned, the Goldsmith Patriarch managed to court/wed a South American Millionaire's daughter/heiress AND they wouldn't be in the positions they occupy in the hierarchy if it were not for those perennial French Strikers:- this time it was the Postal Workers which gave him grace-time to rectify his precarious position and stave off Bankruptcy!!!

NB 2 As many 'unscrupulous' males have managed what he found impossible, yet their trail of 'insinuation' could have/had a more significant bitter after taste, than John's enquiring trail of 'personal' questioning!

That life comment has significance in his personal eyes, BUT also in so many scandal ridden episodes affecting those very apparently well up the prestigious privileged life ladder.

As his past encounters with Cheyne Walk-Welcoming ole Uncle (Henry) 'Sam' (Samuel) Guinness and in the main here in this book his relayed WWII History and connectivity with the Norwegian Royal Family, as shown briefly with his correspondence exchanges etc. with the King Olav, regarding his son, Harald, whose rattled regal life is exposed later, and his Balliol College Oxford experiences. (Balliol was Sam's Alma Mater!)

And on the subject of interconnectivity, the book shows over the past/future how the inter-marrying between cousins, especially 1st cousins, is something which could lead to medical 'critical' speculation as to the future gene crop, Sam then might have welcomed his Balliol protégé, Harald, marrying a commoner?***

AND it was no shock in this Liberal Monarchy, ours rather stuffy in comparison, that son should follow father..

Picture is from the Norwegian National Library's picture collection. Remarks on the picture were: Prince Harald posed as a mascot for the Norwegian Air Force in Canada during the war. According to Ivar Ulvestad: Norwegian postcards. Cultural history and collectibles, 2005, p. 89, the photo was taken in the training camp Little Norway in 1943 and probably published by Mittet til julen 1945. (SEE ALSO **PART 1cii)**

THEN AND NOW >>>

Born 21 February 1937   **Photo on 10 December 2025**
Author   Presidencia de la República del Ecuador
https://commons.wikimedia.org/wiki/File:REUNI%C3%93N_CON_EL_REY_DE_NORUEGA_HARALD_V_Y_HAAKON_MAGNUS,_PR%C3%8DNCIPE_HEREDERO_DE_NORUEGA._OSLO,_10_DE_DICIEMBRE_DE_2025._(54975098432).jpg

This work AND the next two have been released into the public domain by the author on Flickr, where the author has declared it as a "Public Domain Work" and tagged it with the Creative Commons Public Domain Mark
The reign of King Harald has been marked by modernization and reform for the Norwegian Royal family. The King has cooperated closely with Queen Sonja and the Crown Prince in making the royal household more open to the Norwegian public and the Norwegian media, the latter may have proven costly!? – read on …
King Harald's decision to accept two more commoners into the royal family, Crown Princess Mette-Marit and Ari Behn, has been interpreted as a sign of modernization and adjustment. (But that would change…)
Under King Harald and Queen Sonja's leadership, comprehensive renovation projects on the Bygdøy Royal Estate, the Royal Palace, the royal stables and Oscarshall have also taken place.
The latter three have also been opened to the public and tourists. ^{Below #} *Together with Queen Sonja, the king has also for decades attempted to establish a palace museum in Oslo.*

Born 21 February 1937   **Photo on 10 December 2025**
Sonja (nee Haraldsen) is Queen of Norway as the wife of King Harald V >>

** Born 20 July 1973 **Photo on 10 December 2025**

(** John was already visiting old Sam, and his health was somewhat poor, although at death's door if you knew which diseases he was afflicted with/attacking his inners! So he would never have been able to attend, the Christening, if invited?!)

At this christening, 20th September 1973, were various Euro Royals, but one much closer to home, further connecting within this Book, **a certain young, Princess Anne**, now The Princess Royal (his paternal cousin, highlighting the Euro Royal previous historical marrying partners, expanded within).

(ANTE…*** *Sam then might have welcomed his Balliol protégé, Harald, marrying a commoner?*

AND it was no shock in this Liberal Monarchy, ours rather stuffy in comparison, that son should follow father..

BUT it was a shock to all & sundry at his choice of future 'Princess t/b Queen' Spouse!

AND the scandals thereafter began to mount up and up and up >>>

So in view of John's self-plea, how did such a low ranking female get to socialize with a Prince?

AND where they first & subsequently met and paired up was at no Royal Garden Party, where John was once invited and brushed shoulders, albeit at arm's length, mingled within touching reach of the Regal hierarchy – the Matriarch whom he already had previous contact with, plus daughter Annie, whom he had met twice up close and personal, plus son Charles, both the latter in their splendid eye catching, specially chosen for this day, attire!

BUT imagine a muddy Glastonbury and imagine our Regal Hierarchy there mingling with all the scruffy pop fans?

BUT here in a VIP area such as this? I doubt it! > ….at_Quart_Festival_2009….AND there is more >>>

Many thanks to Rockman at 'wiki loves folklore' for the photo memory

NB For those not in the know the/our Royals, plus the/their selected elite personnel, congregate on an Island within the Palace garden grounds, with just one *'guarded'* path in/out!

BUT how come a prince was allowed at such a notorious festival? (See before ↑ *Below #)*

Examples of its notoriety > <u>There have been some scandals during the years</u>.
- A local band Flying Crap fired a shotgun from the stage in 1995.
- <u>Marilyn Manson</u> ripped a bible on stage in 1999.
- <u>The Kovenant</u> burned a bible on stage in 2000.
- <u>Mayhem</u> threw pigs' heads at the audience in 2001.
- Eight musicians from hiphop group Equicez were arrested for drug offences in 2003.
- Kristopher Schau attached an engine to a dead pig and used it as a boat in 2003.
- Two persons from rainforest charity group <u>Fuck For Forest</u> **had live sex on stage** during a concert with <u>The Cumshots</u> in 2004.

<u>Would our Charles attend such a venue?</u>
<u>If yes, then certainly the press would have made him out to be a Proper Charlie!</u>

Ah well back to the Royal Couple's Historic beginnings:-

Mette-Marit Tjessem Høiby first met Crown Prince Haakon of Norway in 1999 at a garden party during the Quart Festival, a music festival in her hometown of Kristiansand.
While they formally met and began their relationship in 1999, reports suggest they may have briefly crossed paths earlier in the mid-1990s at the same festival.
(So John, unlike you it was a case of the mountain venturing to its female admirer!?)

<> *This expression has been traced back to Francis Bacon's Essays (1625): "Mahomet made the people believe that he would call a hill to him, and from the top of it offer up his prayers for the observers of his law. The people assembled: Mahomet called the hill to come to him again and again: and when the hill stood still, he was never a whit abashed, but said, "If the hill will not come to Mahomet, Mahomet will go to the hill." - Francis Bacon.*

This tale would seem to be apocryphal as there is no source for it in the Quran or any other Islamic teachings.

NB From John's personal involvement with the Royals (before) e.g. at his Garden Party Invite experience, only but a few got the nod to say high within handshaking distance to the Queen!

BUT the Liberal Royal Norway modus operandi meant as likely the Prince would have freely mingled amongst his subjects until she caught his eye!

Years later, after becoming a mother, she met the prince again at another party related to the festival – so a case for him of being twice smitten!

Mette-Marit Tjessem Høiby and Prince Haakon announced their engagement in December 2000. The crown prince thus became the third step-father of Høiby *# – (See later *# this/her son's chequered past/present!) ....

The fact that Mette-Marit was a single mother and the fact that Høiby's father was a convicted felon created controversy. TV 2 later wrote that "...merely by existing, Marius Borg Høiby was seen by many as a scandal for the royal family." The couple married on 25 August 2001. Høiby was four years of age.

BUT some might say in response that might well have become the beginning of the end of the Norwegian Monarchy as the Norwegians knew it?

-
- *Sam's friend, Harald's future daughter-in-law, Mette-Marit Tjessem Høiby, a one-time waitress* *** Expanded later below*, raised speculative eyebrows in view of her drug associated past with Morten Borg, who was one of the first convicted cocaine dealers in Norway and incarcerated several times.*
- *He was the father of her child, Marius Borg Høiby (born 13 January 1997), although they did not stay together as she had other subsequent relationships.*
- *Her relationships were unspectacular to say the least:- from the fiancé she had before she went with Borg, a certain John Ognby, a man convicted of violence and drug-related offences; to a relationship with a disc jockey/self-described "life artist" from Oslo; then when back in Kristiansand, with her new partner, another disc jockey, until the couple separated apparently in early 1999, just before Harald got hooked!.*
- *I suppose with all such drug related & violent criminality about him as he grew up it would come as no surprise that her son, Høiby, was charged in August 2025 with 32 criminal counts, including rape and domestic violence.*
- *It is no surprise then that he admitted during the trial to his alcohol AND drug abuse!*
- *Perhaps, nor that Høiby was detained for a fourth time for violating a restraining order and new allegations of assault and threatening someone with a knife.*
- *His trial is scheduled to take place from 3 February to 13 March 2026. Høiby was arrested the day before his trial on new, separate charges and was held as a remand prisoner.*
- *He faces an array of 38 charges!*

>>>>>>>>>>>>>>>>>>>>>>>>>>>>>>>

(ANTE) …BUT it was a shock to all & sundry at his choice of future 'Princess t/b Queen' Spouse!

BUT not her beauteous attraction for him >>> although she like our own Princess was not without her health demons – BUT here many more:-

- *So in many ways resembling the Kate/Wills meeting/parting/re-meeting AND regrettably for the females disease mirrored itself in their life:*
- *Kate with her publicised cancer.*
- *BUT worse still for her opposite number, in October 2018, Mette-Marit was diagnosed with* **pulmonary fibrosis** *– much younger than the usual sufferer! She indicated that she would undergo treatment at Oslo University Hospital.*
- *This poor, now rich privileged lass has dealt with many ever increasing health problems:- including*
- *pneumonia,*
- *several instances of norovirus,*
- *low blood pressure, falls,*
- *concussions,*
- *a neck injury*
- *AND a herniated disc.*
- *In December 2025, the palace revealed that Mette-Marit's pulmonary fibrosis was approaching a point where she would require a lung transplant – interestingly her future brother-in-law (Later in this Chapter) also had a transplant, of a different sort!*
- *Although nothing apparently could point at her earlier lifestyle having contributed to any of the above.*

Many thanks for photo goes to...
httpscommons.wikimedia.orgwikiCategoryPhotographs_by_Frankie_Fouganthin –

Mette-Marit of Norway on the way to the castle church at the Royal Palace in Stockholm before the wedding between Princess Madeleine and Christopher O'Neill June 8, 2013.
(Interestingly enough, Sam & Fluff, much before her time, also named their first born daughter, Marit – she is also featured much later in the Book)

>>>>>>>>>>>>>>>>>>>>>>>>>>>>>>

(ANTE) …BUT it was a shock to all & sundry at his choice of future 'Princess t/b Queen' Spouse!

BUT – putting the sickness aside as this was not the real concern of those below her and especially any who respected the Monarchy as was (is?) it was her 'self' outside activities and their promotion which were an additional cause of shock/scandal mongering:- ?????? Did some of our Royals replicate this? (Later to follow)

BUT back to what one might now call the **'black sheep'** stepson of the family!? And his charges and trial >>>

Høiby who is also referenced several times in the Epstein files in conversations between his mother and Epstein. When he was 15, his mother and Epstein discussed pictures of naked women she wanted to give him. *faux pas ↓*

His array of charges:
- *rape with sexual intercourse while a woman was unconscious in October 2023*
- *three counts of rape by sexual assault on incapacitated women - considered rape in Norway - in December 2018, March 2024 and November 2024*
- *six counts of sexually offensive conduct without consent - including filming of victims*
- *causing bodily harm*
- *repeatedly abusing a current or ex-partner through threats, coercion or violence*
- *violating a restraining order against him*
- *transporting 3.5kg of marijuana*
- *speeding*

Some of the charges involving abuse and threats in August 2024 relate to the so-called "Frogner woman", and it is understood that his latest arrest is linked to her too.
He is expected to give evidence for the first time sometime in February 2026. The case will be decided by three judges - if they find him guilty he could go to jail for at least 10 years. BUT betting man John thinks different!

So we can leave that major scandal in Limbo as it evolves before the World Press!

Haakon's first official girlfriend was cosmetics heiress Celina Midelfart, with whom he was in a relationship from 1994 to 1996. Midelfart later dated Donald Trump.

>>>>

Midelfart was a friend, according to some sources a one-time girlfriend, of Jeffrey Epstein, who claimed that he had "given" her to Trump as his girlfriend.

(This is one of 2 references to such incidents which I found and all it seems to tell me is that perhaps the women, like those below them in such pecking order, were perhaps willing to go be exchanged as chattels to where the money was i.e. metaphorically speaking one multi-millionaire must be just as good as the next? Otherwise they would have refused?
Unlike those below where the money was just a means to a (living) end? And more importantly they were insignificant cast off chattels for many, not just a select one!)

>>>>

Haakon met Epstein once in St. Barts, but his wife Mette-Marit was a close friend of Epstein over several years, meeting him many times after his release from prison, apparently just like our UK Fergie!?

Both as likely deeply regret, as so many more found/find out, terming him as a 'friend' = a ginormous faux pax!

BUT her faux $^{see\ also\ faux\ pas}$ $^\uparrow$ *pas was not as great as our Duchess, who as a parent must have her lack of responsible care questioned, who also the convicted paedophile just 5 days after his release…(Email 27 July 2009) all flights paid + free stay! The Royal Protection tagged along in his own car. The venue was 358 El Brillo.* ^{BRILLO}

BUT she brought her now (? Impressionable?) daughters along with her! Why?

BUT seemingly Epstein had helped pay bills etc for some time:- examples possibly when she needed £20k to pay her rent arrears (2009) and another time to keep her Charity, Mothers Army, going (2011) – it is unknown how much he paid both Fergie ^{X} AND Andrew ^{X} over the years, but alleged suggestions are so much more!?

AND Fergie, Andrew AND Mette-Marit are mentioned several hundred times in released Epstein files!!!

Seemingly this is one of several 'Groundhog Parallel Universe examples where the same type of elitist replicates the same acts of a neighbour across EU way! Or relative past v present! (Later)

^{BRILLO} AND not considering any long term consequences? AND now poor Beatrice's husband, has apparently claimed to have lost a number of previously expected work contracts! AND so will Eugenie's husband's Wine Merchants suffer similar ('financial') losses?

^{X} From those interminable DOJ trickled files we see a linkage between the two and a certain bank – J P Morgan…and those evil Epstein goings on…

When the name JP Morgan cropped up in the DOJ files then my mind went back to my book, 'The Rich and Powerful don't give a shit!" and within there the series of fines that bank incurred over the recent years:-

2018 Citigroup Inc and **JPMorgan** Chase & Co would pay $182.5 million to settle U.S. investor litigation claiming they violated antitrust laws.

....

FOREX FINES TO THE SAME OLD SAME OLD?

(NB Michael knew the Bank's Payment Master and she was always telling him on such occasions: *"I've just drawn another 7 figure fines payment cheque!"* Obviously they had millions to burn!?

1. Commodity Futures Trading Commission hit Barclays for $400 m; Citibank for $310 m; HSBC for $275 m; **JP Morgan** for $310 m; RBS for $290 m; UBS for $290 m!
2. New York State Department of Financial Services hit Barclays for $635 m.
3. US Department of Justice hit Barclays for $650 m; Citibank for $925 m; **JP Morgan for $550**; RBS for $395.
4. UK Financial Conduct Authority hit Barclays for $441 m; Citibank for $358 m; HSBC for $343; **JP Morgan for $352 m**; RBS for $344; UBS for $371!
5. The Federal Reserve hit Bank of America for $205 m; hit Barclays for $3421 m; Citibank for $342 m; **JP Morgan for $342 m**; RBS for $274; UBS for $342!
6. Swiss Financial Market Supervisory Authority hit UBS for $145!
7. Office of the Comptroller of Currency hit Bank of America for $250 m; Citibank for $350; **JP Morgan for $350**!
8. A Grand Total of $10,181 Million!

Fines above by UK USA & Swiss Authorities in US Dollars (Millions)

AND Yes,

JPMorgan Chase agreed to pay $290 million in June 2023 to settle a class-action lawsuit brought by victims of Jeffrey Epstein. The lawsuit accused the bank of knowingly facilitating and benefiting from Epstein's sex trafficking, with the victims alleging the bank ignored warnings about his abuse while keeping him as a client.

Key details regarding the settlement:

Re Settlement Amount: $290 million.
Liability: **JPMorgan** did not admit to wrongdoing in the settlement, which is par for all such settlement courses, though they expressed regret for their association with Epstein.
Approval: The settlement was approved by a U.S. judge, with funds overseen by a court-appointed administrator to determine payouts for the survivors.
The class-action lawsuit covered a period from 1998 to 2013, during which Epstein held accounts at **JPMorgan**, even after being convicted of soliciting a minor for prostitution in 2008.
AND Yes, there's still more…
Additional Payments: In September 2023, **JPMorgan** agreed to a separate $75 million settlement with the U.S. Virgin Islands to resolve claims that the bank enabled Epstein's sex trafficking operations.

JPMorgan Connections e.g. Epstein connected Prince Andrew to Jes Staley, a senior **JPMorgan** executive, and arranged for them to meet on several occasions, including at the World Economic Forum in Davos in 2011- to do what?   And what more behind the scenes? Before/After?

BUT IT ALL GOT WORSE NORWAY WAY!

Down the daughter's/sister-in-law's way!

Like Harry & Megan they got paid blame pointing airing via Netflix –

Here it was Harald/Sonja's daughter Martha & son-in-law Durek Verrett slagging them off in their documentary called Rebel Royals!

Poor Sam Guinness would turn in his grave…

"We have to connect with Mother Earth"
https://commons.wikimedia.org/wiki/File:Princess_Martha_Louise_of_Norway_in_2019_(cropped).jpg
Public Domain Author Richter Frank-Jurgen
https://en.wikipedia.org/wiki/Frank-J%C3%BCrgen_Richter
Frank-Jürgen Richter (born 1967) is a German entrepreneur, economic advisor, and commentator. He is best known as the chairman of Horasis and founder of the Horasis Global Meeting, as well as a former director of the World Economic Forum.
This file is licensed under the Creative Commons Attribution-Share Alike 2.0 Generic license.

Märtha Louise is a certified physiotherapist, but never practised that profession, but established her own commercial entertainment business giving public and televised performances reciting folk tales and singing with well-known Norwegian choirs.

In December 2003, she took part in Oslo Gospel Choir's Christmas concert with a solo performance.

All commendable so far?!

BUT

And it seemed to have begun here:- On 1 January 2002, Märtha Louise started her own business, *(Later)* in order to work with more freedom from her constitutional role as a princess.

(Like Prince Harry/Megan?) She began paying income tax, and the King, after consulting her, issued a royal edict that removed Märtha Louise's title of Royal Highness (she is conventionally accorded the lesser title Highness abroad, although this title has no legal standing in Norway). Märtha Louise retains her place in the line of succession.

After several postponements due to family births and her father's illness, during which the princess took on some representation duties, Princess Märtha Louise and her husband moved to New York City in October 2004. In 2004, her first book, a children's story about the first royal family of Norway was released – *Why Kings and Queens Don't Wear Crowns* - Book signing October 2005

(How come she like Fergie found writing children's books so easy? Outside help? Well I mean so many famous people's autobiographies were Ghost Written?) (AND mine personally scribed made nil child impact!?)

BUT

Another certain Harald related book - **The Escape** *is a thrilling love story where we follow Princess Märtha of Sweden and Norway and see the important part she played in Norway's liberation, and her unwavering diplomacy during the war to ensure constant support for Norway across the world. Martha was Harald's mother and not Martha Louise above/below:- another example of confusing research people with mother & granddaughter having identical Christian names!* **Further expanded upon here in Part 1cii: The once king Edward viii of old!!! <> like father like son<>one not afraid to put it about!!!** Martha like so many in this Book, either attacked, or was taken, here at that young 54 by that ever alive, life taker = The Big 'C' (Cancer)

AND so down a strange path:-

Märtha Louise trained as a Rosen therapist*, and studied at an academy for holistic medicine. She claims she can communicate with animals and angels and started her own alternative therapy center named* Astarte Education*, after one of the oldest goddesses in the Middle East. Astarte Education offered a three-year course on healing, readings, and angels!??*

NB Critics of Rosen Method:- Bodywork (RMB) primarily argue that it lacks robust scientific evidence, relies on potentially flawed exploratory research, and carries risks of emotional re-traumatization. Quackwatch, a group that investigates questionable health claims, has categorized the Rosen Method as an "unnaturalistic method".

Key criticisms and concerns regarding Rosen Therapy include
- *Lack of Rigorous Evidence: Studies on the effectiveness of the Rosen Method have been described as exploratory or based on weak experimental designs (e.g., small, non-blinded samples). Critics argue these studies often rely on self-reported improvements rather than objective measures, making them prone to bias.*
- *Questionable Scientific Basis: Critics argue the theoretical framework—that emotional trauma is physically stored in muscle tension and released through specific touch—lacks empirical validation.*
- *Rebecca Rosen, a mother of two, who lists her profession as "psychic medium," and her specialty is communing with the dead, acting as "the bridge between the spiritual and the physical world."*
- *Others might say phooey!? Hokum pokum? And for those interested I would point you to* tessajean84 https://www.reddit.com/r/Mediums/comments/166z8y2/maybe_im_overthinking_or_looking_at_it_wrong/ *– for her own personal opinion <>*
- *"I'm not a fortune teller," she said. "I don't work with ghosts either, spirits who are trapped in limbo between here and the other world.* **I work with those who are happily crossed over** *and want to ease the anxieties of the living."*
- *And her clientelle is as likely mainly the rich who want to contact their loves now dead!*
- *Well Group sessions would include 12 clients and cost $500 per person for two hours, garnering Rosen $6,000 a session. I rest my spiritual case.(There is a Rosen/Samuel Wycombe property link later in the Book)*
- *Such a pricing system is endemic in so many rich elite circles where the ordinary souls are priced out of that market! But hey if it eases the wealthy troubled mind which is willing to pay, then who am I to criticize – clientelle such as celebrities Jennifer Aniston, Courteney Cox Arquette and Vanna White.*

…………

Martha's claim to be able to communicate with say angels, similar to so many US/UK practitioners listed under the Rosen certified banner, was relayed in a September, 2023, BBC interview,
https://www.bbc.co.uk/news/world-europe-66804252
And her connection with British clairvoyant Lisa Williams *raised concerned Norwegian eyebrows!*
For me for all this spiritual healing talk I thought her facial skin looked very markedly spotty as if she had a skin infection, or something?(Heal that lady!) (Her mother has had a history of medical problems - Ante). There again I could be wrong? I usually am about such things!
Needless to say, the princess drew criticism in Norway after the announcement that she would begin Astarte Education. Astarte Education was an alternative therapy school founded in 2007 by Princess Märtha Louise

and Elisabeth Samnøy, focusing on healing, readings, and connecting with angels. Located near Oslo, it offered a popular three-year "angel school" program designed to teach spiritual skills, although it faced significant criticism.

- Controversy: The institution was dubbed an "angel school" by the Norwegian press and drew scrutiny regarding the Princess's involvement in alternative, non-scientific treatments.
- Closure: Needless to say, despite early success, the school faced declining revenue and ultimately closed in 2018 after its founder, Princess Märtha Louise, shifted focus to other projects, notes Norway's News in English.
- It was named after Astarte, one of the oldest goddesses in the Middle East. In 2015, Swedish author Jan Guillou questioned her mental health.

On 11 August 2007, Märtha Louise defended the school on NRK, the Norwegian public service television network. In the interview, she regarded her relationship with angels as "creatures of light, which gave her a feeling of a strong presence and a strong and loving support." She responded to criticism that she should leave the Church of Norway by stating she still considered herself a Christian that was thankful the Church still had room for her.

On 2 October 2007, Princess Märtha Louise became the first member of the Norwegian royal family to ever appear in a court of law, as she wanted to halt sales of a book entitled Martha's Angels, which used her photo on its cover without permission. She stated that she felt "commercially exploited" by the book's use of her photo, which she regarded as misuse of her name and picture. Film critic Pål Bang-Hansen stated that Märtha Louise was a *"thief and hypocrite"*, claiming that she had stolen translated texts from his father's books.
        BUT The princess succeeded in her legal proceedings, stopping the sales of the book in Norway.

AND so what type of man did she attract as husband material?

First marriage – perhaps here the 'awkward' questions began? ## Like his wife there was his/an unstable family life # +## so perhaps divorce was not unexpected?

On 24 May 2002, Princess Märtha Louise married author Ari Behn (1972–2019) in Trondheim. The couple had three daughters: Maud Angelica, Leah Isadora, and Emma Tallulah, none of whom have royal titles. The family lived in Islington, London, (not far from John's Hornsey home) and Lommedalen, Bærum.

(Like our dear old Anne + daughter = showjumping experts) Emma Tallulah Behn, a junior member of the national equestrian team and won a bronze medal during the Norwegian National Horse Jumping Championships in 2021.

The couple divorced in 2017. In 2016, the Royal Court had announced that Märtha Louise and Behn would have joint custody of their three daughters.

Behn was born as Ari Mikael Bjørshol in 1972 in Aarhus, Denmark, to Olav Bjørshol (b. 1952) and Marianne Rafaela Solberg (b. 1953), Bjørshol was baptized and confirmed in The Christian Community and attended the Waldorf School # in Moss from 1979.

Waldorf education, also known as Steiner education, is based on the educational philosophy of Rudolf Steiner, the founder of anthroposophy. Its educational style is holistic ###, intended to develop pupils' intellectual, artistic, and practical skills, with a focus on imagination and creativity. Individual teachers have a great deal of autonomy in curriculum content, teaching methods, and governance. Qualitative assessments of student work are integrated into the daily life of the classroom, with standardized testing limited to what is required to enter post-secondary education.

Many Waldorf schools have faced controversy due to Steiner's connections to racist ideology and possible magical thinking, apparently]

Others have faced regulatory audits and closure due to concerns over substandard treatment of children with special educational needs.

Critics of Waldorf education point out the mystical nature of anthroposophy and the incorporation of Steiner's esoteric ideas into the curriculum. Waldorf schools have also been linked to the outbreak of infectious diseases due to the vaccine hesitancy of many Waldorf parents.

In 1983, his parents divorced and married a couple who had been among their friends, Jan Pahle and Tone Bjerke, who had previously been married to each other.

Crazily surprisingly, in the 2000s his parents divorced Pahle and Bjerke, and they married each other for the second time in 2007.

In the 1990s, he studied history and religion at the University of Oslo, from which he received a bachelor's degree.

Behn's original surname was Bjørshol and he was known by family and during his childhood and youth under the given name Mikael.

In 1996, he seemingly changed his name to Ari Behn when he took his maternal grandmother's maiden name.

Crazily surprisingly, in 2009, it was made public that Behn's de jure paternal grandfather, the Tromsø lawyer Bjarne Nikolai Bjørshol, was not his biological grandfather!!!???. Behn's father met his biological father, Terje Erling Ingebrigtsen (1933–2009), a retired car mechanic from Tromsø, for the first time, but Ingebrigtsen died before Behn had a chance to meet him.

(Waldorf ## A parallel to the Gunness education within <u>Montessori schooling method</u> which is also a comprehensive, holistic approach to education designed to develop the "whole child". It nurtures a child's physical, social, emotional, and cognitive growth by fostering independence, self-directed learning, and hands-on exploration, rather than focusing solely on academic achievement.)(SEE ALSO PART 11A)

Behn died at his home in <u>Lommedalen</u> on 25 December 2019. A statement from his family said Behn had died by suicide. He had struggled with alcoholism and mental health problems. Not surprising in view of his later 2009 interview, he said he was chronically depressed and lonely:- the surprising fact was that it took 10 years!.

<u>He was yet another who was able to write children's books</u>! **(Here I should point out my only entrance into the child book arena is on Amazon, originally entitled, 'The Legal Sanctity of Present Giving – Part 13A Unlucky for One or More Som? As Santa Claims His Sleigh was Robbed on his way to WHO? YOU!**

    BUT this was superseded/replaced by >>   **'WHO STOLE OUR CHRISTMAS PRESENTS?**
                                          SCREAMED SETH & JUDE!: V3 = THE THREE DAY HEISTS!'
>>>>>>>>

Controversy

Märtha Louise + future 2nd husband, Durek Verrett - The political editor of Nettavisen, Erik Stephansen, criticized Märtha Louise's complaints about the coverage of her and Verrett, and wrote that she has "actively sought the spotlight with her entire family, exploited the princess title in every conceivable way – including commercially – and is now fully engaged in milking her own glamorous celebrity wedding in Geiranger for all it's worth." **And here in the UK were any of the related Royals' weddings, male &/or females low key?**

The way Märtha Louise + new hubby acted has raised similarity aspects of how Megan + new husband acted.

BUT without the Royal Coffers financing you, what would you expect? I mean they have to live up to the previous Regal Status?! So financial gathering means MUST!

>>>>>>>>>>>>>>

So onto this, her Second marriage choice:-

Awkwardly, Verrett is often characterised by Norwegian media as a "conman" and "conspiracy theorist" and has also been accused of being a cult leader and selling bogus cancer cures.

Public records confirm that Verrett was convicted of felony arson and trespassing and sentenced to five years imprisonment in 1991 in his native California.

Verrett, who previously identified as gay but now identifies as bisexual, served prison time again in 2015 after a domestic incident with his former male partner Hank Greenberg.

It was in the year 2019 (7 months prior to her first husband's death) that she announced that she was in a relationship with an American citizen, apparently a conspiracy theorist and self-styled shaman named Durek Verrett (born 17 November 1974 as Derek Verrett).

Again as her first choice before > His parents divorced when he was three, and he lived with his father, David Benjamin Verrett (1929–2017), and his stepmother.

"The Princess and the Shaman[1]," ([1] See later) for which they also received widespread criticism. Specifically, Verrett has suggested that cancer is a matter of choice and has sold medallions, said to ward off Covid-19 online and without any scientific evidence to support such claims.[64] This reference '64' is what specifically drew my eye:-

"A Generous Heart, Repaid". *SooperArticles. February 17, 2012. AND it is here that it gets really intriguing!?*

Like others mentioned in this Chapter this self-proclaimed healer, he has not lived sickness free and nearly died at 30, due to kidney failure!

So after it was a case of regular dialysis sessions!

His previous contracted HIV-positive status further complicated matters, although his 'Angel' by name sister, Angelina donated her kidney to him and here he is now surviving!

The operation was apparently afforded by a fundraiser k/a *'The carnival of magic medicine'?!* (So not a rich man as has been claimed?!)

I am not aware if his previous 5 year male partner, Hank Greenberg, also contracted the disease, from him, or from another, or not at all? Although some time thereafter things did not go well = Derek served prison time again in 2015 after a domestic incident with this former male partner!!!

So interestingly, originally a gay man and then how long post-operative did he self-categorize bi-sexual so to attract the ladies, too?

Criticisms of shamanic practices cover a wide spectrum, ranging from ethical concerns regarding cultural appropriation to safety, efficacy plus ideological disagreements. While traditional [1] shamanism is deeply embedded in indigenous cultures, modern "neo-shamanism" is frequently scrutinized for lack of training, commercialization, and the potential for psychological harm.

[1 (From before] *What is a shaman?*
a person regarded as having access to, and influence in, the world of good and evil spirits, especially among some peoples of northern Asia and North America. Typically such people enter a trance state during a ritual, and practise divination and healing. e.g. like an African [2] type witch doctor, or medicine man!
Note here Verrett has at times claimed a different descent = Verrett has claimed that his mother, Sheilah G. Farmer (1943-2026), who goes by the alias Veruschka Urquhart, is of Norwegian-West Indian descent, although he has alternately described her as being of Native American heritage, and he has also claimed "she was white." He has sometimes claimed that his father was of African [2] and Haitian origin, while at other times stating his father was "Native American Blackfoot Indian." You pays his money and takes your choice!

Here are the primary criticisms of shamanic practices:
1. Cultural Appropriation and "Plastic Shamans"
Misappropriation of Heritage: A major criticism, particularly from Indigenous communities, is the adoption of shamanic rituals,, and titles by Westerners who have no, or shallow, connection to the indigenous culture from which they originate.
 "Plastic Shamans": This term refers to self-proclaimed shamans who sell, often for significant profit, ceremonies (like sweat lodges or ayahuasca rituals) that are inauthentic or misrepresented.
Decontextualization: Critics argue that removing shamanic practices from their original cultural, social, and spiritual contexts—which often involve lifelong apprenticeship and community validation—strips them of their meaning and safety.

2. Safety and Psychological Risks
 Inadequate Training: Many modern practitioners lack the rigorous training, mentorship, and initiation required by traditional practitioners to handle intense spiritual, energetic, or psychological states.

Psychological Damage: Improperly guided, intense experiences—especially those involving psychoactive substances like Ayahuasca or Bufo—can trigger psychosis, severe anxiety, depression, or PTSD in participants.
Dangerous Rituals: In rare, extreme cases, poorly managed, unregulated ceremonies have resulted in the death or physical harm of participants.

3. Ethical and Financial Misconduct
Commercialization: Shamanism is increasingly commodified, turning spiritual healing into a high-cost luxury service (e.g., in "Ayahuasca tourism" in South America).
Power Imbalances: Some shamans may use their position of authority to manipulate or exploit vulnerable, traumatized, or dependent clients, including for sexual or financial gain.

4. Lack of Scientific Evidence
Denial of Physical Reality: Critics from a scientific or medical perspective argue that relying solely on shamanic healing can cause people to ignore, delay, or reject necessary modern medical treatment.
Faith Healing Mechanism: Many, including sceptics, argue that any perceived benefits of shamanism are solely due to the placebo effect or psychological suggestion, rather than the manipulation of spirits or energy.

5. Theological and Religious Rejection
Occult/Demonic Association: Major religions, such as Christianity, Islam, and Judaism, frequently condemn shamanism as paganism, sorcery, or the worship of evil spirits, viewing the practices as dangerous to spiritual well-being.
Idolatry Concerns: Critics may view the reliance on a human "shaman" for spiritual healing as elevating a human above God.

6. "Core Shamanism" Criticisms
Superficiality: "Core Shamanism," popularised by Michael Harner and designed to be a universal, de-cultured method, is criticized for being shallow or a "watered-down" version of complex, diverse, and deep-rooted traditions.
Homogenization: Critics contend that Core Shamanism falsely lumps together diverse indigenous practices into one generic, "cookie-cutter" approach!

So following on from those claims it is no great leap of (disbelief?) faith (if there is such a phrase?) which can lead you to such as claimed by his new female partner:-
Märtha Louise has claimed she can communicate with angels. Verrett also claims to have been initiated spiritually by an American woman who calls herself "Princess Susana von Radić of Croatia", whom the fact-checking site Vantrú describes as "a fraud who claims to be a princess."

Headlines like ' The royal family cannot be for sale' seems somewhat silly/hypocritical as here, perhaps just like there, there have been many biographical exposes. Although the use of Netflix is most modern! [3]

Märtha Louise's marriage to Verett, who is a Black American, [3] has generated controversy. Märtha Louise has accused former friends of racism for their criticism of Verrett.(See a few lines later here...) [3]

BUT most disturbing for any righteous person would be the following:- In November 2024, Norwegian media published recordings of three voice messages of Verrett amongst other incidents, where during sessions he admitted he performed oral sex on one of his male clients after their session and helped a woman 'clean' her vagina after she had 'violent' sex with her partner to sexual assault during shamanistic sessions, and apparently claimed that his wife knew about his actions.(See audio recordings obtained by Norwegian paper Se og Hør)

Märtha Louise and Verrett were featured in the Netflix [3] documentary Rebel Royals, in which Verrett accused the Norwegian royal family of not being aware of racism. The royal family said the documentary violated an agreement not to use the couple's connection to the royal family.

A similar relationship controversy was Guinness/Rothschild related where daughter..
Based on reports from 2012,
[3] **Kate Rothschild** [4], a British heiress and member of the Rothschild banking family, was involved with an African-American musician. (SEE ALSO PART 11b)
The Individual: Kate Rothschild was reported to be in a relationship with rapper **Jay Electronica** (Timothy Elpadaro Thedford) around 2012.
Context: At the time, this was reported alongside the breakdown of her marriage to Ben Goldsmith, son of tycoon Sir James Goldsmith.

Historical Parallel: The 2012 reports noted a parallel to her great-aunt, Kathleen Annie Pannonica Rothschild (the "Jazz Baroness"), who famously left her husband for jazz musician Thelonious Monk in the 1950s.
THE parallels between Kate and Nica are uncanny. Both married in their early twenties to rich, handsome, ambitious, young men with whom they seemed to be much in love. They became enraptured with unconventional musicians who turned their lives upside down. Most tragically, as young girls, each lost their father to suicide.

[4] *Kate Emma Rothschild is the daughter of the late British financier <u>Amschel Rothschild</u> (1955–1996) and <u>Anita Patience Guinness</u>. She is a member of the prominent Rothschild banking family and was previously married to Ben Goldsmith. Her sister is Sabrina Guinness, a one-time girlfriend of Prince Charles and as likely a possible regular Palace visitor with her late departed husband, Tom Stoppard – Their Linking later in the book. Charles and Camilla on hearing of his death expressed that they were "deeply saddened" to learn of the death of playwright Sir Tom Stoppard, calling him "one of our greatest writers" **and a "dear friend"***
Seems Sabrina opened one door for him, that he couldn't without her 'personal 'privileged contact!?
(SEE PART 13 + others)

…………………………..

BUT NOW BACK TO A CERTAIN REGALLY CONNECTED TRIAL:-

Høiby affairs

Harald has refused to answer questions about the <u>relationship of Mette-Marit and Jeffrey Epstein</u> and the criminal trial of <u>Marius Borg Høiby</u> for rape.

- A year and a half after Marius Borg Høiby was arrested by police over a violent episode at a woman's flat's in Oslo, the son of Norway's crown princess has gone on trial, in the biggest case to come to court here for years.
- Høiby pleaded not guilty to four charges of rape, as the public prosecutor read out the 38 charges against him.
- The seven-week trial opened at Oslo district court against a backdrop of almost daily revelations surrounding him and his mother, Crown Princess Mette-Marit.
- The crown princess is facing increasing criticism after it emerged that she was cited in hundreds of emails showing extensive contacts with the late US sex offender Jeffrey Epstein.
- She has admitted showing "poor judgement", but the fallout has already begun, with one organisation dropping her as patron for its annual prize.
- On the eve of the trial it emerged her 29-year-old son had been detained again, in circumstances not unlike his initial arrest, on suspicion of assault, making threats with a knife and violating a restraining order.
- As police have placed him on remand for four weeks, he began the trial in custody.
- His defence team intends to appeal against the decision.
- Marius Borg Høiby appeared in court wearing a brown sweater and white T-shirt, green trousers and glasses, his blond hair cut short. Heavy court restrictions have been imposed on the trial, with a ban on any pictures of the defendant inside or outside court. The judge broke into English at one point to emphasise the rules to international media.
- As the charges against him were read out, he pleaded not guilty to the four accusations of rape, speaking very quietly.
- He partially admitted charges relating to a woman in Frogner in western Oslo in August 2024, admitting bodily harm but denying abuse, He admitted several other charges, including violating a restraining order, transporting marijuana and speeding.
- BUT AND IT IS MY USUAL BIG BUTS:- What may do for him is the following >>> Damning Evidence!?
- <u>The prosecution has presented videos and images from Høiby's phone, which they say show sexual acts performed on an incapacitated victim. Høiby has claimed he does not remember filming the videos and did not intend to commit assault.</u>
- <u>The eldest son of Norway's crown princess has denied that videos on his phone showed acts of rape as he broke down during his first day of testimony in his trial for rape and domestic violence.</u>

>>

Epstein Link: The trial has coincided with scrutiny over Crown Princess Mette-Marit's past contact with Jeffrey Epstein, for which she expressed regret. (Don't they all when found out!?) As also in the UK/USA!

Mette-Marit had a long-standing association *with the American convicted sex offender* Jeffrey Epstein

In 2026, the Epstein files *showed that she had far more extensive contact with Epstein and over a longer period than she had previously admitted. (As others equally implicated!?)*

Her father was also a felon who had twice been convicted of violence.

Her parents divorced, and her father later married professional stripper *Renate Barsgård.*

She has a sister and two older brothers, including Per Høiby. Trond Berntsen, her step-brother by her mother's 1994 marriage to Rolf Berntsen, died in the 2011 Norway attacks.

And yet, most of her ancestors were cotters *and small farmers.*

As a part-time student, Mette-Marit took six years--longer than usual--to complete her high school education. She went on to take preparatory college courses at Agder College *and *** worked on and off as a waitress at the restaurant* Café Engebret *in Oslo.*

Mette-Marit Tjessem Høiby had little higher education when she met and later married Norway's Crown Prince Haakon. The former waitress and single mother from Kristiansand has been catching up ever since and now, as Crown Princess, *but it is not clear if in resulted in any degree, if one then the exact subject matter not clearly disclosed, although she wasn't a University drop out like her son in the US.*

………

Like others she had stayed at Epstein's infamous beach home, but apparently not when he was there!

BUT not being there does not mean he didn't see what was going on whilst away – motion sensor cameras!

Epstein killed himself in 2019 while awaiting trial on charges that he sexually abused underage girls at his homes in the U.S.
In a 2010 deposition, Palm Beach Detective Jo Recarey described covert material from a hidden camera which was found on Epstein's computer: "It was basically motion-activated *(Evidence suggests one clock may have been the hiding place for a spy camera in his office area. One of 2 that we are told about!).* **When there was motion, it would start to record. So, there was, there were images of Epstein at his desk. BUT none in any bedrooms! (Yet?) (My Legal Sanctity of Marriage Part 7 – The Cuckold? Interestingly enough no wife performing on camera for her partner has ever made its way onto any Epstein files, but as likely there were videos which certain select male members may have viewed together/individually?!)**

>>>>>>>>>>>>

Her quite lacking in common sense and care in such a privileged official position meant she would be both an embarrassment to others and those she holds dear! Examples below…
Although some might claim you can take the person out of ???? yet not the ???? out of the person!
Her upbringing being spectacularly family chequered and associated with various low lifes/criminals!

In addition to the smutty naked women picture for her son comment mentioned before, in a separate email, Epstein told Mette-Marit he was in Paris "on my wife hunt" but that "i prefer Scandinavians."

In response, Mette-Marit said Paris was "good for adultery" but that "Scandis" were "better wife material".

In a statement following the documents' release, the crown princess said she felt "deep sympathy and solidarity" with the girls abused by Epstein.
Such smutty talk not really becoming of a future Queen some might say?!
Hundreds of emails from 2011-14 involving Epstein and the crown princess came to light in the cache of files published by the US justice department Jan 2026. Although few published so far (Feb 2026)

Norwegian newspaper Dagens Næringsliv's December 2019 previously also reported/revealed that Crown Princess Mette-Marit had ties to Epstein, >> "I never would have associated with Mr. Epstein if I had been aware of the seriousness of the crimes he committed," Mette-Marit said. "I should have investigated his past more thoroughly, and I am sorry that I didn't." *Which unsurprisingly was the same old, same old, all those incriminated stated prior & subsequently!* <> *Even Prime Ministers in 2 European Countries when the associated Mandelson/Epstein scandal re – re – re – surfaced!!!*

DN reports that the Crown Princess met "several times" with Epstein between 2011 and 2013—years after his 2008 conviction and subsequent registration as a sex offender.

BUT I cannot end without our current UK competing for press room scandal in high political places!

…………..

DEAR OLE MANDY…*(SEE ALSO YCTV Hunky Dory)*

October 2023 - Lord Mandelson has married his long-term partner at a wedding attended by guests including Kate Garraway, her husband Derek Draper ##↓ nearer to death than anticipated, in his wheelchair, and former prime minister Tony Blair # – so the latter was still close then and made no issue of it e.g. boycott the wedding? As likely Mandy made no issue reference to that Epstein individual as he hadn't been publicly tainted just yet!

Although other Blair & Co boycotting came concerning another very rich party when the US CAATSA (Countering America's Adversaries Through Sanctions Act) lists were published (SEE MUCH LATER PART e – TRUSTING TO TRUSTS)

So it seems # he thought nothing of any Mandelson/Epstein links? (See his wife's times v Mandelson below) or like all others was unaware? Though the cynics might say how is it possible that they never spoke of the man since that 2002 meeting! I mean he was again in prison in 2019 on sex-trafficking charges!?)
I leave you all to make up your own minds on the millions of released ?damning? /incriminating evidence! Epstein died in prison suicide infamy according to Official Records = 10 August 2019 with a timestamp of 06:49 local time, around 16 minutes after he was found unresponsive in his cell.
(NB (suspiciously) the prison guards failed to carry out routine 03:00 + 05:00 checks, prison documents show, and the camera system in the unit was also down!) (Although the next morning check did take place!)

Suicide has been/will be mentioned about this book, but the interesting 'sexual services connectivity' is that another depraved male took his own life IN Prison, again when find out and tables turned upon him, was a certain, perhaps not well known to you, but he was to all the models he manhandled and entered IN, Jean-Luc Brunel was his name and his MC2 modelling agency:- let me inside You, or You will get No work! And NO was not a word so many dared not use!

And one who worked on similar lines:- In December 2022, Harvey Weinstein was convicted in Los Angeles, California, of three counts of sexual assault: forcible rape, forcible oral copulation, and sexual penetration by foreign object!
He was sentenced to 16 years in prison for these crimes, which involved a Russian-born model in a 2013 Beverly Hills hotel incident.(With his deteriorating health he faces a retrial in New York!!!
Another powerful male individual of repute, Sean "Diddy" Combs, he is currently serving a 50-month (4 years, 2 months) federal prison sentence, handed down on October 3, 2025, for transporting individuals for prostitution which is something Epstein could have been accused of!
Oddly Epstein was not the wham bang IN YOU man as say Brunel, as he had other sexual means of being satisfied which did not necessitate the use of insertion, although the use of all those recruited were made to perform for him in one way and another – in front of the camerawoman or the hidden ones! (Later/Ante)

Oh it's not a nice world for any up and coming female who wants to get on – seemingly in so many instances ONLY by getting it on with the male-InComing who bars her progress!?

…..

##↑ *Derek Draper <> Michael/he met at a labour party seminar post 1997 successful election of which Michael was one of the local team supporter workers – he thought him a cocky bastard who bragged a lot as to what/who he knew to do what/whatever he was asked, so much on the QT:- his comeuppance happened shortly afterwards where he was embroiled in the 1998 "Lobbygate" scandal, where he was caught boasting about his*

access to government ministers and lost his job! (Apparently another around at the same time, whilst lecturing them claimed a similar ability, yet apparently (? Behind the scenes!?) got off with a slap on the wrist?!) *Derek's hedonistic drug style/preying on younger female staff whether in HQ or at Clubs then precluded his nervous breakdown! AND perhaps his excess lifestyle may have made him one of the many with underlying problems which might have contributed to his ultimate, but drawn out, Covid related death!*
NB Tony only had good words to say about him when asked.

It was about the same type Michael was in Government/Civil Service Circles then and he first came across 'Peti' (Epstein's nickname for him noted in correspondence with JP Morgan -multi-fined bankers) outside his Department's Office complex, when (Secretary/Officer) Michael had UN business across the way at the UK National HQ at, 3 Whitehall Court: he didn't like how he looked and doubted he could trust him!? Although what Michael heard about Mandy's involvement in how his boyfriend was able to get across to the UK and stay extendedly may have pre-influenced his opinion?

Tony Blair and Peter Mandelson have maintained a long-term political alliance and personal friendship, spanning from the creation of New Labour in the 1990s through to the present day, despite Mandelson being forced to resign from the cabinet twice during Blair's premiership, although it might be that Tony had Starmer's ear re Mandelson and his 'Political' abilities!

Though press reports say it was in the main Starmer's Chief Adviser, who was later sacked! Hey, whatever, apparently it did not prevent more of Bair's cohorts entering Starmer's inner sancta?!)

Cherie Blair has also historically been close to Mandelson, relying on him for advice, although they had a notable disagreement in 2010 regarding his inclusion of her private letter, which criticized Gordon Brown, was included in his memoir, The Third Man.

*Copyright would have been the issue here and perhaps Mandy relied on a defence such as **in** some cases, if the letter is used for criticism, review, or quotation, it might fall under fair dealing (*Section 30 of the CDPA*).*

BUT whatever, the case seemed to have died a death and no Court outcome.

A year prior to that November 2009: Cherie Blair spent a shooting weekend with the Rothschild family, an event that also reportedly included Peter Mandelson. Although her lawyers confirmed she had been with the Rothschilds, but clarified she was not present at the same time as certain other guests reported in the media. ˣˣ ↓

Quirkily enough, the next month, December 1, 2009, Tony Blair visited Azerbaijan during which he met with President Ilham Aliyev in Baku. During this visit, he discussed energy cooperation and praised the country's economic growth, a visit that was noted for taking place despite some international controversy, the last aspect doesn't interest me, but the next year's Mandelson connection does.

AND here, jokingly put, was the singular outcome of Tony's visit:- Carpets!?

Lord Peter Mandelson, Evgeny Lebedev and many connected others attend the reception for the opening of an exhibition on Azerbaijani Carpets at One Marylebone on November 15, 2010 in London, England. (Ha Ha Ha - Like I said in jest BUT >)

And if we coincidentally stay with that year (2009) and visit the Raisa Gorbachev Foundation Annual Fundraising Gala Dinner on 6ᵗʰ June at Hampton Court Palace Gardens (just a stone's throw over the river from one of Michael's family homes) we can see that aspect of sharing the same event attendances, as Evgeny was there again with Boris – the PM who gave this (Russian) Lebedev his Lordship Title!

A certain lady, an ex-employee of his was also in attendance, but Sabrina's more significant storyline is for much later!

(Below is the Hampton Court Garden Location for the Event <> Evgeny owns the adjacent neighbouring property and at one time passed his property & the palace had an adjoining large Wooden Door for access).

The other controversy amongst friends = Media Context: In 2009, when Evgeny Lebedev and his father were looking to acquire the Evening Standard, it was noted that then Business Secretary Peter Mandelson would not be holding an inquiry into the sale (? To Russians?), as he had "no plans" for such an inquiry!?
Presume he had good reason not to!

While they were both key figures in Tony Blair's circle, their relationship was often described as strained, XX ↓ *particularly when Mandelson was at odds with other allies or when Cherie felt his actions caused public humiliation for the Blairs.*

But whatever, neither Blair has been shown to keeping up the friendship perhaps they don't want to be asked the same awkward questions about what did you know/when did you know etc!

Especially in as late as 2023 # Tony was still palling about with him?! (Ante)

There again like so many before/after Epstein seems to have pulled the 'sexual scandal' wool over so many eyes?

So no wonder they could not relay such to all those the palled about with!?

There again with his Business Acumen it is no wonder he still attracted individuals for the best business way to proceed!?

Note:- Michael, a one-time avid Labour supporter and Secretary of one of its principal National Peace Organisations, admired Tony and especially when the Irish Peace Accord was signed – Michael was privileged to be part of a select group to dine after with one of the signatories > John Hume, subsequently Nobel Peace Prize winner 1998!

Author Copyright

Although after he read the small print something bugged him and it would come back to haunt many UK soldiers many years hence.

And on a minor irk point Michael and his peace campaigning cohorts were very unhappy when their oldest member and long life Labour Supporter was ceremoniously turfed out of a Labour Party meeting hall <>

The Incident: In September 2005, 82-year-old Walter Wolfgang, a veteran Labour Party member and anti-war activist, shouted "nonsense" and "That's a lie and you know it" during Foreign Secretary Jack Straw's speech on Iraq at the Labour Party conference in Brighton.

Michael had a soft spot for Cherie and they exchanged favours – nothing untoward I assure you, just that his experience in UN Uk in Westminster could make him a mentor for those females on her Charity Foundation books.

The first National (Government) Congress together, although she got railroaded into being dragged about on some sort of public relations viewing stands etc!

Author Copyright <> Conference Bored lass!

SPEAKING FOR MYSELF

The Autobiography

MICHAEL

NOT THE STANDARD DAILY MAIL REPORTER I'M USED TO

CHERIE BLAIR

Michael, Not the standard Daily Mail Reporter I'm used to! Best wishes Cherie Blair

Little, Brown

BUT THE ABOVE IS ANOTHER STORY

Author Copyright

The first meeting was on her birthday where he found himself the only one giving her a bunch of flowers!

But subsequently, more importantly was ECHR:- The rights were incorporated into domestic law through the Human Rights Act 1998, which took effect in October 2000 AND significantly Cherie Booth (Cherie Blair) co-founded Matrix Chambers in 2000 which seemingly were the premier to hold Seminars/Tutorials on the subject.

Michael was there through his UN work and had lunch with her and all her Junior proteges, one female preparing for her stint researching for a Senior EU Judge! Plus so many now Seniors on the subject, although she later left that behind (?for greener/richer pastures?) as 2014 she formed Omnia Strategy.

Great George Street which facilitates such meetings/seminars can be reached via the back door or side doors through Downing Street +another, and so just a hop and skip to take the meeting(s).

>>>>>>>>>> Property Concerns >>>

Whilst researching this Book, I came across foreign ownership of one of the premises in Phillimore Gardens – Title Number NGL353202, whose lease was apparently shared by a Rundell Guinness & a Mosley. BUT what interested me more was the ownership = a company called, Almetingo, seemingly abroad, as not on the UK Company register!

Michael was visiting her chambers on a personal matter, but said he would drop off an enquiry letter to them to see if they could shed light upon the 'personal' ownership of the company: I mean he told me that they proudly displayed the plaque in the reception area, that they were the winners of the award as they had been the most successful UK legal company at recovering 'proceeds of crime!'

Well he was sorely disappointed at the helpless answer – they had no idea! "Well they're not what I thought them cracked up to be!" was Michael's response, although the Offshore Companies are cesspool minefields where the big buck in say USA Delaware can get your company registered showing Mickey & Minnie Mouse as Directors! (Greatly expanded upon in my, 'The Rich and Powerful don't give a Shit!')

The dodge in the UK as Michael had experienced in his field of work was that these type of companies having interest would always show their registered office as via their solicitors who would divulge nothing to investigators!

Though, thank goodness we now have that oft touted 'Register of Foreign Companies with property interest in the UK!?' to look through where all is revealed!? Well no, as Michael found another not on the list!

Cherie moved on from there and formed another Chamber Set Up:- through her legal reputation, even being a Beak at some times, arbitration was her next legal port of call, seemingly a lucrative one perhaps matching her hubby who was/had been on the lucrative' speeching' circuit, then more via his own organisation, onto such that he could give advice to Country Leaders here in the UK and abroad! It is no wonder their property portfolio it is what has amassed to now.

AND if you are aware of such, their (publicized) Marble Arch Town Houses, back to back *?* properties, are not that far from Marylebone Registry Office, where the wedding ceremony took place.

? Originally the Blairs bought one in Connaught Square *!!*, overlooking the private communal gardens at the front, but their official positions made them fearful of prying eyes from the property at their back – so they bought that too!

Author Copyright

<u>(My Autumn central private garden overlooked by residents picture does not do it Summer *?* justice!)</u>

Author Copyright

[11]*Nearby neighbours, who moved on to Mells Park, their Country seat neighbouring Lord/Lady Asquith [G1], were the Samuels, the wife of whom, Sabrina Guinness sister [G2], and their middle sister [G2] who married into the Goldsmiths - her daughter into the Rothschilds! (Then divorced -Ante)*

[G1] *(See also **And now for an extensive John Led Tour**)*
[G2] ***(See also Chapters Part 11a Julia & Part 11b Anita)***

AND so the obvious link here is property wealth and wealth of its own:- Cherie and mingling with the Rothschilds (Ante/Later) she and Tone's portfolio runs to many millions, although their Wotton House cannot match one of Rothchild's French Riviera pads >

Author Copy - A TRULY MAGNIFICENT SPECTACLE

UNLIKE THE US DOJ OF MANDELSON IN BRIEFS >>>

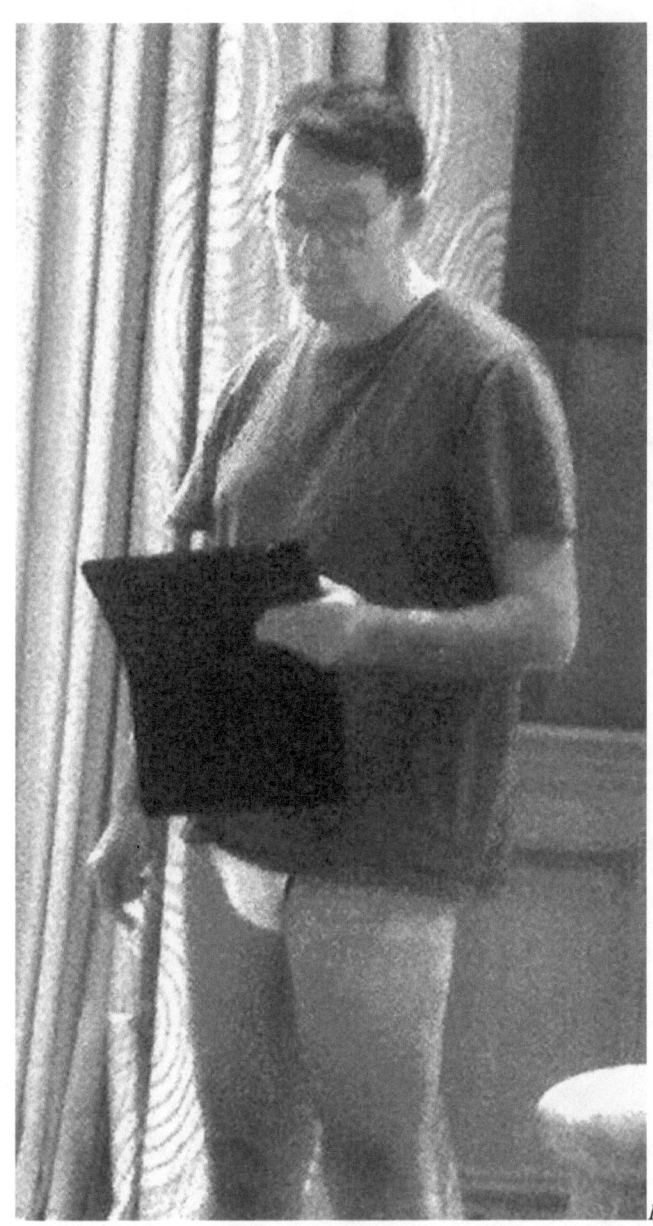
DOJ Public Domain

For all those in or linked to the 1997 steamroller Labour party election winning/winners The Blairs and Mandelson were the blissful friendship.

How long it continued I have no idea nor did a certain Michael, one of her ex Charity mentors, at **Dentons** one evening, who on their last meeting was more concerned as to her mother's health amongst other personal matters. (**Dentons**, their advertised claim is, "How can the world's largest global law firm help you today?" They are based on upper floors at, 1 Fleet Place, London)

....

BACK to the Intermingling rich & famous **From Rothschild Above...**

Cherie Blair has had multiple social and professional interactions with members of the Rothschild family over the years, most notably in 2002, 2005–2008, and 2009.
- **September 2002:** *Cherie Blair was photographed with Lord Jacob Rothschild at the opening of "Masterpieces From the Walpole Collection" at the Hermitage Rooms in Somerset House.*
- **2005–2008:** *Cherie Blair was known to attend the annual Christmas sing-along hosted by Lynn Forester de Rothschild* (**wife of Sir Evelyn de Rothschild**)(**see later Epstein/Rothschild linkages**) *at their Ascott estate in Buckinghamshire.*
- **March 2010:** *Cherie Blair attended the "Women In The World" summit in New York, an event associated with Lynn Forester de Rothschild.* (**SEE ALSO PART 11b**)
- See also ˣˣ ↑

 *Author Copyright*

Regrettably her special 'wealthy' colleague, Lynn, has had husbands who were not 'exemplary' pillars of society as would be expected of such?! And it all stars with a Epstein connected German...

....

German financier David Stern has resigned from the Cambridge Judge Business School (JBS) advisory board over his links to Jeffrey Epstein.
JBS was established in 1990. The school delivers programmes including the Cambridge Management Studies Tripos, Master of Business Administration degrees, and 8 PhD pathways.
It ranked second in the world in the Financial Times' ranking of post-experience Master of Finance programmes in 2024.
Stern was just another who shared explicit sexual pictures with Epstein, as also a go-between such as Andrew and Epstein.
Stern was so trusted that he was placed next to the late Queen Elizabeth at an event at St James's Palace in 2016.
Sir Evelyn de Rothschild flanked her on the opposite side.

BUT more to the point, he too was accused of sexual abuse of his position!
"This case was investigated immediately, dealt with appropriately, with full support for the colleague concerned, and led to Sir Evelyn de Rothschild leaving the group in March 2004." A spokesman said!
Mr. De Rothschild, died aged 91.
BUT multiple sources claimed that this kind of misconduct by De Rothschild went unchecked for decades.

Ex Wife whose (2 of 3) Ex husbands enjoyed their own form of scandal notoriety - Lynn Forester, Lady de Rothschild is an American-British businesswoman who is the chair of E.L. Rothschild, a holding company she owns.
Born: 2 July 1954 (age 71 years), Oradell, New Jersey, United States
Children: Benjamin Forester Stein, John Forester Stein
Education: Columbia Law School (1979), Columbia University, Pomona College, The Graduate Institute, Geneva
Spouse: Evelyn de Rothschild (m. 2000-2022), **Andrew STEIN** *(m 1983-1993 – New York Inhabitee also) (Prior to that to Alexander Hartley Platt)*

*It is claimed, although disputed, via the Epstein files etc Rothschild was friends with disgraced financier and later convicted sex offender Jeffrey Epstein. He said he had given her financial help in the 1990s during her divorce from **Andrew Stein**, although a spokesperson for Rothschild said this was "one hundred percent false." According to Epstein's lawyer, Alan Dershowitz, he was introduced to Epstein by Rothschild, who referred to him as an "interesting autodidact" who he would enjoy getting to know.*
According to Ghislaine Maxwell, it was Rothschild who introduced Prince Andrew to Epstein.
Mandelson was introduced to Epstein around 2001 at a summer house in Martha's Vineyard owned by Lynn Forester de Rothschild and her husband, Evelyn.

AND then > On May 27, 2010, STEIN was indicted and arrested for lying about his involvement during the investigation of the multimillion-dollar Ponzi scheme involving Ken Starr, a financial advisor to various Hollywood celebrities. He pleaded guilty to a misdemeanour tax evasion charge and was sentenced to 500 hours of community service.

In 2010, former New York City Council President Andrew Stein and financial adviser Kenneth Starr (not the independent counsel who investigated Bill Clinton) were prosecuted in federal court for their roles in a $50 million-plus Ponzi scheme and related tax crimes.

    Kenneth Starr's Conviction: Starr, who managed money for celebrities like Uma Thurman, Martin Scorsese, and Wesley Snipes, was accused of swindling clients to support a lavish lifestyle. He pleaded guilty in September 2010 to wire fraud, money laundering, and investment adviser fraud. He was sentenced to over 7 years in prison.
    Andrew Stein's Plea: Stein was arrested for lying to the IRS and federal agents regarding a shell company, "Wind River, LLC," which he set up for Starr to hide money. He pleaded guilty to a lesser misdemeanour tax charge, admitting to failing to pay taxes on more than $1 million in income.
    Outcome for Stein: Stein avoided prison time, instead being sentenced in March 2011 to 500 hours of community service and probation.

Starr was arrested in May 2010 after being found hiding in a closet in his Manhattan apartment. Prosecutors noted that while Stein was involved in hiding assets, he was not directly charged with participating in the underlying Ponzi fraud scheme, but rather with lying about it.

BUT I presume nobody really cares about the above?

\>>>>>>>>>>>>> **Rothschild + another female** \>>>

...

Emails from Ghislaine Maxwell in August 2010 warned Epstein to "be careful" of Neilson. In one email, Epstein asked "Any thing cute for after", Neilson replies "Cute as in cuddle toy? or cute as in badly behaved English girls." She added "There is a little thing for my very young friend who is lunching? launching her bikini range at Morton's but that might just drive you made!!! I have a friend I might call."

(former model) Annabelle Neilson (formerly Rothschild) was identified as having emailed Epstein numerous times between 2010 and 2012, after his 2008 conviction for soliciting prostitution from a minor.
In the emails, Neilson agreed to 'put together a group of girls' for Epstein and noted that some were 'unfortunately past their sell-by date'. Another email from a redacted sender to an account named Annabelle Neilson on 26 January 2011 reads "Hey Annabelle, let's you and I try and find something cute for JE tonight.

Iona Annabelle Neilson (formerly Rothschild; 31 March 1969 – 12 July 2018) was a British socialite, fashion model, author and television personality.

Editor's Note:- *NB Sorry Mya, but yet another who managed to write children's books: Neilson was the author of the 3 part Me Me Me children's and teenage, picture book series: Angry Me, especially poignant as it dealt with problems (her) growing up!*
But take heart Mya they were only a couple of dozen pages long, nowhere near your, 'Who Stole our Christmas Presents! Screamed Seth & Jude!'

Neilson and financier Nathaniel Rothschild, from 2024 the 5th Baron Rothschild, from the Rothschild banking family of England, eloped to Las Vegas, US, on 13 November 1995, following a four-year relationship. They separated in 1997. Their divorce was finalised in 1998.
NB1 More addiction/painful family deaths linked:- Nat's cousin Raphael de Rothschild, who died of a heroin overdose on a New York pavement at 23, and his uncle Amschel, who hanged himself in a Paris hotel room in 1996.
NB2 <> A former heroin addict, she remained sober from 1999 after attending Narcotics Anonymous meetings, perhaps as a result of an attack & beating by a man during her gap year in Perth, Western Australia, at the age of sixteen which lasted two hours before she broke free. She received facial reconstructive surgery in the aftermath, having been left disfigured:- She fell into a deep depression and thus became a heroin addict; she was sober by the end of her twenties.
NB3 She had been travelling in Australia with her paternal cousin, Guy Greville, 9th Earl of Warwick <> the 9th Earl Brooke who in 1978 sold Warwick Castle to the Tussauds Group. His mother another (fashion) model (seems the profession to snare male nobility!?)
His maternal great-grandfather was the American mining magnate Alfred Chester Beatty (the "King of Copper").
His paternal grandfather was Charles Greville, 7th Earl of Warwick. So all taken into account money literally pours through his family pores!
BUT so did the blood as his brother-in-law was killed in Tanzania by a charging buffalo and similarly with so many others in this book, he needed two wives i.e. his first he divorced.
His father, a some much more than old Sam Guinness exploits, WWII hero had a worse death(s) experience = Lord Lovat experienced a great deal of sadness in his final years; two of his sons predeceased him in accidents within days of each other (Sam's died barely 12 years old by a self-inflicted playing with guns bullet!).
In 1994, a year before his death and seemingly not covered by a protective Trust # the family's traditional residence, Beaufort Castle, had to be sold by his eldest son, Simon Fraser, to pay inheritance taxes # (Trusts well covered earlier in this Book...)

Neilson was found dead at her home in Chelsea, London, on the evening of 12 July 2018. She was 49. The Coroner's Court stated that her cause of death was a "cerebrovascular accident" (stroke)

PS The 15th-century "Kingmaker" Earl of Warwick (Richard Neville) was not directly related to the Spencer family, but he was married to Anne de Beauchamp, daughter of Isabel le Despenser. Anne Beauchamp, 16th Countess of Warwick (1426–1492), was a key late-medieval English noblewoman and wealthy heiress, born to Richard de Beauchamp and Isabel le Despenser.
Married to Richard Neville ("The Kingmaker"), she was the mother of Anne Neville (Queen to Richard III) and Isabel Neville (Duchess of Clarence), navigating extreme conflict during the Wars of the Roses.
The modern Earls of Warwick (Greville family) and the Spencer family are now separate aristocratic lines.
...

**Epstein advised Ariane Rothschild during Luxembourg money laundering probe (Luxembourg times) <>
Regulatory Fine: The Edmond de Rothschild Group's Luxembourg entity was fined nearly €9 million by Luxembourg regulators for money laundering failures in relation to the 1MDB scandal.**

Extensive Contact: The documents show years of correspondence and multiple arranged meetings between Epstein and de Rothschild from 2013 until shortly before his arrest in 2019 - with serious implications ↓

Bank's Statement: A bank spokesperson stated that Epstein was a business acquaintance and de Rothschild was unaware of his personal conduct, unequivocally condemning his crimes and regretting not learning of the full scope of the allegations earlier. <u>Although he had well publicised already been in prison before this!</u>

Ariane de Rothschild is related to the late Sir Evelyn de Rothschild by marriage, not by blood.
As the wife of the late Benjamin de Rothschild (who passed away in 2021), Ariane joined the Edmond de Rothschild branch of the family, while Evelyn belonged to the London-based banking branch.

STOP PRESS:- Swiss bank Edmond de Rothschild said, on Wednesday, February 25, 2026, that it had ↑ taken "measures" to protect its clients and staff after its chief executive, Ariane de Rothschild, was revealed to have links with convicted American sex offender Jeffrey Epstein.

De Rothschild established a professional relationship with Epstein from 2013, some five years after the deceased tycoon first pleaded guilty to soliciting a minor for prostitution, according to documents released by the United States justice department on January 30.

But and so IT GOES *'Rothschildsingly' on & on & on:-*
……………………..

Seems Epstein was a special friend to so many willing to enjoy his lifestyle and mode of playtime!

The Blairs seemed to steer clear when his name came into the conversation or into the vicinity.

BUT

Still his spectre shadow seems to cover so many, so many unsuspectingly – simply by crossing paths.

There again his apparent close friends continued the tainting of others, simply by association, whether vile or not.

One wonders how Cherie takes hubby's apparent innocent long term friendship with Mandy?

Will that title, special friend, lose its **glitter** *as Mandelson's own 'Gary* **Glitter** **' type, innocent friend to so many until criminally exposed, has already, but not without taking so many down with him? (* Gary Glitter, here in the UK, was also convicted of sexual abuse against minors!)*

There again as our UK Legal System states, innocent until proven guilty, so will anything stick and Mandelson will become our own ** Teflon Jamie? We can only wait and watch with wonderment!? Just as we do with baited breath regarding our disgraced Royal Male!

** Jamie Dimon, the Chairman and CEO of JPMorgan Chase, has been referred to as the "Teflon" CEO, particularly around 2012–2013.
Why the nickname? The nickname was coined by media and analysts because, despite facing major crises, significant trading losses (such as the $6.2 billion "London Whale" debacle), and intense regulatory scrutiny, Dimon often avoided personal blame and maintained his reputation, allowing the bad news to "bounce off" him.

 *Author Copyright*

Mandelson - His Confidante Relationship with Tony Blair
- **Key Ally:** Mandelson was crucial in getting Tony Blair elected as Labour leader in 1994, backing him over Gordon Brown, and was a key architect of the New Labour project.
- **Close Contact:** Despite resigning in 1998 and 2001, Mandelson remained a close ally whom Blair relied on for political and personal advice.
- **Was Cherie less receptive?** >> XX ↑
- **Support:** Mandelson has continued to support Blair's political legacy. As of late 2024 and 2025, Mandelson remained a key figure in the Labour establishment, close to the *(APPARENT UNSUSPECTING)* leadership.

Recent Context
As of early 2026, Peter Mandelson is in the news due to revelations regarding his friendship with convicted sex offender Jeffrey Epstein, which led to his resignation from the House of Lords and from the Labour Party, while Mandelson has been a long-term ally of Blair,

Based on documents released by the National Archives and reports confirmed by the BBC in October 2025, yes, Tony Blair (Prime Minister) met with Jeffrey Epstein at 10 Downing Street in 2002 at [BB (below)] Mandelson's instigation:- interestingly though, Epstein's illegal sexual activities were not known publicly then and strangely how Mandelson still had contact power from/to high & mighty even though he had resigned as Northern Ireland secretary resignation the preceding year!?

A spokesperson for Tony Blair stated that he "never met or engaged with him subsequently".

But the interesting statement being, in view that an ex-President & his wife were compelled/asked(?) to testify [&], Clinton is claimed by Mandelson to have previously told Blair he wished to present his 'travelling friend' Epstein to him!?
AND what must be really irksome for Tony is that apparently (? Unbeknown to him?) later investigations in 2026 revealed that Epstein continued to boast of his close relationship with Blair years after the 2002 meeting!?

AND in the same year Mandelson's scandalous Epstein past caused a third UK Prime Minister even more grief than they, the 2 previous Labour incumbents, had experienced:- the revelations nearly caused the overthrow of our dear old Sir Keith Starmer!

& Bill and Hillary Clinton have agreed to testify before the House Oversight Committee regarding the Jeffrey Epstein investigation, scheduled for videotaped depositions on Feb. 26 and Feb. 27, 2026 – BUT they were actively pushing for all hearings to be held in public to avoid what they term a "kangaroo court"

However nothing untoward seems to have ended up pointing their way!

………………………

[BB] With this big blot on his 'escutcheon' Mandelson has become 'persona non grata' AND under investigation, especially for what he supplied Epstein whilst in his position of UK Ministerial trust.

BUT it is always the same old, same old, as something, perhaps one might class as more serious is the War x Ukraine and Western world sanctions against Russia and its characters of dubiously acquired extreme wealth.

AND this is where under the Radar those who do not want to be tainted by association, having received funds from such sources, slowly begin to divest themselves of any linked association to such -

CAATSA Section 24 l(a)(2)-(5) requires a report on Russian parastatal entities, including an assessment of their role in the economy of the Russian Federation; an overview of key U.S. economic sectors' exposure to Russian persons and entities; an analysis of the potential effects of imposing additional debt and equity restrictions on parastatal entities; and the possible impact of
additional sanctions against oligarchs, senior political figures, and parastatals on the U. S. and Russian economies.
Russian parastatals have origins in the Soviet Union's command economy. After the dissolution of the Soviet Union, the Russian government conducted large-scale privatization of these entities; in the early 2000s, it began to renationalize large companies.
The Russian government has responded to economic shocks, including the financial crisis in 2008 and the imposition of sanctions in 2014, by increasing its role in the economy and ownership of parastatals.

As of 2016, Russian parastatals accounted for one-third of all jobs in Russia and 70 percent of Russia's GDP . For purposes of this requirement, Russian parastatals [X] are defined as companies in which state ownership is at least 25 percent and that had 2016 revenues of approximately $2 billion or more.
A list of such parastatals and the required analysis specified in Section 24 1(a)(2)-(5) are included in the classified annex of this report.

And here *Embarrassingly (?) for so many* - **situated in Appendix B, Oligarchs @ No 35 is > Vyacheslav Kantor…Who?   Read on and Discover (Later) > here of prime importance…**

BUT **October 2022** <> *His Tony Blair Institute, that not-for-profit organisation, has announced its severing of links/funding relationship with Billionaire, Moshe Kantor! (SEE ALSO PART f - Anna's Complete Overhaul)*

Michael Samuel (above ante) who got so much via that source to build the new Anna Freud related Mental Health Institute near Kings X London, achieved the same, noticeably with a change of Building name etc! (Later)

So with Kantor & Epstein in a different sphere:- CAN YOUR USA &/OR USSR FRIENDS BE TRUSTED?
                                                                                                                            AND VICE VERSA!
Although perhaps unbeknown to the public, Michael is godfather to Prince William, and his Freud Mental Health Charity is supported/sponsored by Wills & Kate! (Michael was at its (1st) opening – (see much later).

So it is not unexpected that the Royal Couple, despite doing all they can to put 'related' Epstein History behind them, they are continually feeling dismayed, as whilst they, our Wills Kate combo are up to all types of ASSOCIATED GOOD whilst Uncle/Aunt Andrew/Fergie combo apparently have been up to all types of ASSOCIATED BAD!?

(Above subject to Author Copyright)

....

AND so now here, what is the significance of the number 66?

<u>*Angel Number 66*</u>*: Focuses on relationships, home, and family, encouraging the expression of love and nurturing. It suggests finding balance in thoughts and reducing worries about material aspects.*

<u>*Symbolism*</u>*: Often linked to Venus (relationships, wealth) and Jupiter (power)*

Biblical Significance: Some interpretations connect it to the 66 books of the Bible or the idea of "upright" in certain contexts. It is sometimes associated with the concept of man's imperfection or, alternatively, the reign of Christ.

BUT the significant significance is that (1 February 2026) the now ex-Prince Andrew has been arrested on his 66th Birthday, of all days! (AND shortly afterwards Mandelson's arrest happened? A flight risk so someone claimed!)

AND if you study the 3 interpretations above, each has its part to play in this Stacked Royal Pack of cards about to be toppled!?

As this Royal family follows its Norwegian relative counterpart into the scandal laden mire!

....

AND in all those many individual/personal 'Epstein' dealings before; and all those recriminations AND denials, Shakespeare springs to mind >>>

"The lady doth protest too much, methinks" is a famous line from
William Shakespeare's play Hamlet (Act 3, Scene 2), spoken by Queen Gertrude.
She says it while watching a play-within-a-play, commenting on a character's insincere, exaggerated vows of love.
It implies someone is hiding the truth by protesting too much.

- Context: Gertrude is commenting on the Player Queen's over-the-top promises in The Murder of Gonzago, a play Hamlet stages to test his uncle's guilt.
- Meaning: The phrase is used to indicate that someone's excessive denials or affirmations suggest they are actually lying or insincere. **Although any lies above can be hard to prove with so much USA DOJ redacted!**#
- Common Misquote: It is frequently misquoted as "Methinks the lady doth protest too much".
- Significance: In the play, it highlights the irony of Gertrude's own hasty remarriage to her husband's murderer

Misinterpretations of the most innocent of actions seem rife if you take them completely out of context, or you are willing to twist them to taint/condemn:-

Example one > a picture of a man in a hot tub with a bikini clad younger woman just means they happened to have shared it at the same time, which is quite common at many Spa resorts; or the following >>>

Example two > French Composer, Frédéric Chaslin stated "With regard to the reference in a 2013 email to a 'young woman,' I wish to be absolutely clear, that Jeffrey Epstein asked me to put him in contact with an American translator who could assist him during visits to major Parisian museums: she needed to speak perfect English to visit the Louvre and other museums in Paris. I did nothing more than connect two email addresses — this was the one and only favour I ever did for him in this context.. Later, the translator called me to tell me that she wasn't happy with the telephone conversation with Epstein and wrote to him to reject the assignment offered to her (which, I repeat, was an interpreting assignment). The emails in the Epstein files appear to confirm the student's versions of events, in which she never Skyped with Epstein but emailed briefly with his assistant. The content of these exchanges (2013-2019) was neutral, social, or professional in nature and took place in a context in which he was, at the time, widely perceived in international cultural and artistic circles as a potential arts patron."

So the latter too, all quite innocent!?

However, following these revelations, the Metropolitan Opera reportedly withdrew Chaslin's contract.

You wonder why?

Continuing with the last aspect > ...*he was, at the time, widely perceived in international cultural and artistic circles as a potential arts patron..*

However, perhaps Chaslin, if he only knew now what he didn't apparently know then, was that Epstein was a sexual predatory shark and sought new waters to supply/enhance his young girls for all stock!

From revealed history young models were the main source, but here young UP and INspiring, or should that be aspiringly-appealing and seeking a perhaps swifter way Up the musicians ladder might be willing to be participants IN his personal invitational musical AND otherwise soirees!?

Or alternatively classed as a tete-a-tete = face-to-face, or in Epstein's parlance, a one-on-one for whomsoever he selects for the young female musician to entertain privately AND intimately, for a price?

Well according to such as he, **"Every girl has her price!"**

....

BUT here on a cheerful note:- More Lebedev friends – here Sir Ian McKellen:- they went into joint pub ownership when they purchased The Grapes Pub in Limehouse.

Author Copyright

However, like so many men, he was diagnosed with <u>prostate cancer</u> *in 2006, but thankfully over it now. The other dear old Boris, who ended up his UK Premiership giving Evgeny a Peerage – Well he had become a UK Citizen already!*

Author Copyright
AND here poor Boris looked stressed!? BUT not as much as the following, another Ex UK PM!!!

Author Copyright <> *Seems Gordon is not impressed by the latest DOJ redacted official file revelations as to what official sensitive document his past appointed official might have revealed to Epstein!?*

<u>**Time will out**</u>....

BUT perhaps more importantly Epstein's Russian Links?

So many of his girls came, financed by him, from Moscow to Paris; plus those from Moscow to New York, plus via UK Stansted, which also acted as a cheaper interchange/girl transporting (private charter?) airport!

Do you suppose Putin and his cronies knew?

Then what was their part in all this?

Some suggest a big Russian Honey Trap waiting to explode into a massive perhaps no holds barred exposition!

Well first we need look into his specific needs Russian connection i.e. a certain young Russian woman it was who supplied his whore harem; then there is another certain female individual named Maria Drokove aka Masha Bucher who became extremely wealthy c/o Epstein.

BUT there is another who became extremely wealthy also and contrary to common belief this woman was his true girlfriend (apparently?) well she is to inherit approx. $100 million from his estate :- let me introduce you to a certain Belarusian, Karyna Shuliak, whom he apparently seduced in his own inimitable style.

AND if totally the truth, a right kick in the teeth for loyal Ghislaine!?

Especially as she ended up inside with him for her part in all his sexual machinations!

There again some might say like father like daughter:- he, Maxwell, literally was not a nice man! <> His death exposed huge debts and missing pension fund money (around £450 million)! AND the Court Case involved more of his Family:-

Epstein and Robert Maxwell had been business acquaintances Pt1: *EACH AS INIQUITOUS AS THE OTHER!*
>>>

DTI inspectors 1991 report in the Maxwell probe.
Robert Maxwell was found floating in the sea near the Canary Islands in proximity to his yacht Lady Ghislaine in November 1991.

British courts determined that Coopers & Lybrand made gross errors during their 1990s audit of the Maxwell group of companies and fined the company a record 3.3 million pounds.

Kevin Maxwell and his brother Ian Maxwell, both Oxford Graduates(!), sons of the late media tycoon Robert Maxwell, were accused and arrested for helping to embezzle hundreds of millions of pounds from the Mirror Group pension funds. Both got Legal Aid! In the end totaling millions of pounds! See also [B!]

Here are the key details of the case based on reports from the 1990s:

The Accusations: Following Robert Maxwell's death in 1991, it was discovered that over £450 million (roughly $700-$800 million at the time) was missing from the pension funds of his companies, including Mirror Group Newspapers.

Role of the Sons: Kevin and Ian Maxwell, who were directors in their father's companies, were accused of conspiring with their father to use pension fund assets as collateral for loans to prop up their failing private businesses. Their American Financial Adviser, **Larry Tractenberg**, also accused (see next 2025 update where he again apparently is involved with Authorities regarding Pension Funds!) [PFP↓]

Arrest and Trial: In June 1992, Kevin and Ian Maxwell were arrested and charged with fraud and theft. After a long and complex investigation, they stood trial in 1995.

And incredibly legal aid was granted!

Outcome: In January 1996, all 3 were unanimously acquitted of all charges of conspiring to defraud the pension funds.

Aftermath: Although cleared of criminal charges, a 2001 Department of Trade and Industry (DTI) report heavily criticized Kevin Maxwell, describing his conduct as "inexcusable" and noting he provided "substantial assistance" to his father. Kevin Maxwell was declared bankrupt in 1992 with debts of £400 million. [B!]

While they were not convicted of criminal fraud, the investigation found they were deeply involved in the management of the companies that raided the pension funds.

BUT AND A VERY BIG FINE(D) BUT:- Goldman Sachs

The US investment bank that acted as Maxwell's broker on a number of transactions and its partner Eric Sheinberg were singled out by the inspectors in their conclusions. He made a total of £23m from Maxwell-related trades for Goldmans.

Goldman Sachs was among the financial institutions investigated and penalized following the collapse of Robert Maxwell's publishing empire. In 1993, Goldman Sachs ^{GS} (Jewish Company operating in New York) & Lehman Brothers (Collapsed 2008)(Jewish Company operating in New York) were fined for violations of British securities laws related to their dealings in shares of Maxwell-owned companies, which involved, in part, failing to disclose stakes held as collateral

BUT such acts don't stop there as Morgan Stanley although not apparently fined were heavily criticized – (See Euan placements etc.) However this banking leopard like so many others never seemed to change its spots:-
Further search results show Morgan Stanley has faced numerous fines for other issues, including:
  £1.4 million in 2009 for failing to supervise a rogue trader (mismarking).
  $150 million in 2019 to settle charges they misled public pension funds.
  $249 million in 2024 to settle a criminal investigation into block trading.
  £5.4 million in 2023 for WhatsApp messaging failures.

BUT they pale into comparison with the fines relating to the 2008 subprime market collapse:- $3.2 Billion Settlement (2016): Morgan Stanley agreed to a $3.2 billion settlement with federal and state authorities (including the US Department of Justice and New York Attorney General) to resolve claims related to the packaging and sale of toxic mortgage-backed securities.

NB Goldman Sachs ^{GS} says it has reached a deal with US authorities over charges that it used fraudulent marketing material to sell mortgage bonds before the financial crisis. The bank agreed to pay $5.1bn (£3.5bn) in civil penalties and consumer relief.

All the above just form a small sample of banking institutions being cavalier(And perhaps ?un-trustworthy/underhand?) in their way of working – See my, The Rich & powerful don't give a Shit! – there the extent of fines is mind boggling with all institutions blameworthy at one time or another <> even Auditors who failed in maintaining their independence where the almighty dollar was involved!

Trachtenberg ^{TR} was a £200,000-a-year executive of Bishopsgate, the fund manager that looked after some of the pension funds from which Robert Maxwell stole hundreds of millions of pounds.

The report showed he also netted a bonus of £250,000 in 1990, then worked for Kevin Maxwell at Telemonde. [X]

Kevin's bankruptcy was lifted three years later, and he co-founded media company Telemonde, [X] which later failed.
        He entered into a further arrangement over debts he accrued subsequently.
After his discharge from bankruptcy in 2005, Maxwell went into the property industry where he has been involved in establishing large property deals, including the sale of Earls Court Exhibition Centre and Olympia, and the purchase of Stables Market in Camden Town.
On 8 July 2011, as a result of an Insolvency Service investigation into the collapse of Syncro, a Manchester-based construction company, Maxwell was disqualified from being a company director for eight years!

………………

NOW NEARER NOW >>> ^{TR}
        TRACHTENBERG DID NOT COME UP TRUMPS!

PFP ↑ >>> NOW NEARER NOW >>>

Neutral Citation: [2025] UKUT 00206 (TCC)
Case Number: UT/2024/000093
UPPER TRIBUNAL
(TAX AND CHANCERY CHAMBER)
The Royal Courts of Justice,
Rolls Building, London

INCOME TAX – Unauthorised payments from pension scheme – whether HMRC have power under section 29 Taxes Management Act 1970 to assess amounts chargeable to income tax under sections 208 and 209 Finance Act 1994 – yes – appeal dismissed

Heard on: 2 April 2025
Judgment date: 26 June 2025

Before
JUDGE THOMAS SCOTT
JUDGE ASHLEY GREENBANK

Between
LARRY TRACHTENBERG
Appellant
and
THE COMMISSIONERS FOR HIS MAJESTY'S REVENUE AND CUSTOMS
Respondents

Representation:
For the Appellant: Keith Gordon, instructed by Simmons Gainsford LLP
For the Respondents: Rebecca Murray, instructed by the General Counsel and Solicitor to His Majesty's Revenue and Customs

……………

In the case of Trachtenberg v HMRC [2025] UKUT 206 (TCC), the UT has dismissed an appeal against the FTT's earlier decision that Mr Trachtenberg was liable to income tax in respect of unauthorised payments made to him by his pension scheme

Upper Tribunal confirms HMRC's power to issue assessments under TMA 1970 regarding Pension Scheme Unauthorised Payments (Trachtenberg v Revenue and Customs Commissioners)
>>>>>>>>>>>>>>>

Another from New York!?

Not in the greatest of health 2026 — doctors say he will likely need an aortic valve replacement in the next few years — Trachtenberg, 67, passing the winning line in 2025 said he might not yet be finished running New York marathons: he was the first to compete, since its inauguration, 50+ years apart!

He has always been an exceptional athlete!

A PERENNIAL WINNER

And a Princeton Brainbox!

Unlikely this time v our UK Tax men!

A ONE TIME LOSER

>>>>>>>>>

AND so back from her kick in the teeth above....

Ghislaine Mugshot

February 2026 she is trying to wriggle out of prison:- Ms. Maxwell is prepared to speak fully and honestly if granted clemency by President Trump," her attorney, David Oskar Marcus, said.

Again what about the innocent girls & others get out of this?

Well the estate paid out $121 million in victims' compensation to over 135 women from 2019 to 2021. So all s/b paid out by now?

Epstein's assets will not pass into his specifically created 1953 Trust until all of the victims' claims are resolved. NB The estate could face tax claims if authorities such as the Internal Revenue Service challenge his domicile.

Well Late Epstein's Estate Will named his lawyer, Darren Indyke, and his accountant, Richard Kahn, as joint executors of his estate, which is organized under a trust called the 1953 Trust. Epstein's estate was worth over $577 million at the time of his death, but it has since decreased in value to around $120 million. The estate has been the subject of numerous lawsuits and legal inquiries, including two Congressional subpoenas by the House Oversight Committee <>

The executors of Jeffrey Epstein's estate, lawyer Darren Indyke and accountant Richard Kahn, were subpoenaed to testify before the U.S. House Oversight Committee in early 2026, with scheduled appearances on February 25, 2026 (Kahn), and March 5, 2026 (Indyke).

NB Karyna Shuliak - In early 2013, Jeffrey Epstein's apparent new ex-girlfriend, Karyna Shuliak, was stressed about her US visa status. later that year she married a woman named Jennifer, who had been in a relationship with Kimbal Musk after Jeffrey Epstein connected them. Now her worries were gone. A Green Card followed, and, in 2018, citizenship.

Then Shuliak divorced her spouse: a woman named Jennifer who had been in a relationship with Kimbal Musk after Epstein connected them!!!??? >>> Although subsequent emails seem to contradict his version especially:- "Kimbal — just fyi — you better be nice to [the woman] ;)" Nikolic responded to Musk. "Jeffrey goes crazy when someone mistreats his girls/friends."

AND incredibly for all the charges he faced, he seemingly cared for his 'charges'!? Or did he, really?

DOJ revelations:- if you read here how 2 certain women (who ended up truly wealthy, were signaled out to have all their fees, Unit/Lodging + Whatever paid by Epstein 'cos he favoured them in some way, this was just the tip of the iceberg:-

Other Findings on Foreign Women:
Student Visas: The files indicate that Epstein often used enrollment in English-language courses, such as at the Spanish American Institute in Manhattan, to help other women in his orbit obtain I-20 forms for student visas.
Work Visas: Epstein's team pursued work visas (O-1 visas for "extraordinary ability") for other associates, often citing modeling or, in some cases, work for his foundation.
Funding: A former bookkeeper for MC2 Model Management stated in a deposition that Epstein was "paying for the visas" through the agency.

With all those young, give me easy money girls, he used the tried and tested grooming gang methods, which have been well documented, but with all this illicit (And unprotected?) sex it is strange that the DOJ papers only refer to one instance of somebody contracting an STD! The now ex-wife is saying zilch as she wants that abhorrent married time well behind her!

BUT if you are really interested what went on amongst such/any grooming girl gang party time and what was expected:-Read the end of my, <u>SO WHAT IS ABNORMAL? Subtitled - WOULD FEMALE NORMALITY SUPREMELY REIGN IF THERE WERE NO PENIS ABNORMALITY KINGPIN PAIN?</u>

However, Karyna's seduction mirrors a certain Guinness who was not part of the Epstein limelight.

The late Countess of Iveagh died apparently before her time at the youngish age of 51 aka The late Clare Hazell

Similarly to how Fergie's Epstein scenario panned out and that of Matte-Marit, it appears he seduced such with monetary opportunities and/or connections!

Unlike those like the Clintons, Mr. never attended that infamous Isle; Mrs. never flew the Lolita Express, however this Guinness certainly did on many occasions, and Epstein's home were no strangers to her!

(But is there a US DOJ cover up – 'Where are all the 'Lolita fly me' Republican supporters in the files?

And like Karyna, our Clare Hazell had more than her tuition fees paid for, as the travel was extensive as were the Elite doors open to her.

And all 3 when the shit hit their respective family fans, the Charities disassociated themselves from them – Fergie's Companies then seemed to disappear from Companies House!

Matte- Marit is still about, but sick Claire disappeared from this earth (Dec 2025) just a few years after the scandal broke, dying four years after her divorce was finalized

And as her house of cards tumbled about her, John would again ask how a model made it through elite doors to this multi-millionaire type? Perhaps Epstein had more to do with it than we imagine – money opens so many doors! > She the now Countess filed for divorce in 2021

Clare Hazell, also known as the Countess of Iveagh, was a British interior designer/model and socialite who was identified in 2020 as having a significant, direct, and close association with convicted sex offender Jeffrey Epstein

She divorced her millionaire Guinness landowner the year later, 2021,or was it initiated by hubby when her Epstein shit hit his fan!?

NB You can buy his farm produce down Elveden way, whilst taking a neighbouring Centre Parcs break!

Here are the key details regarding her connection to Epstein:

   Romantic Relationship and Social Orbit: Hazell dated Epstein in the 1990s. She was deeply embedded in his inner social circle during the period when he was actively cultivating powerful, high-profile connections.

   Flight Logs and Travel: Flight logs revealed that Hazell travelled on32 occasions on Epstein's private plane, often referred to as the "Lolita Express," between 1998 and 2000.

   Association with Ghislaine Maxwell: She was known as a close friend of Ghislaine Maxwell, who was Epstein's longtime accomplice.

   Allegations: Reports indicate she was sometimes at the "beck and call" of Epstein and Maxwell. Epstein allegedly bankrolled her tuition at Ohio State University in the 1990s. Further, it has been alleged that she helped introduce Epstein to women.

   Post-Epstein Life: She later apparently came across at some hoity toity bash, then shortly after married Edward Guinness, the 4th Earl of Iveagh in 2001, and became a prominent figure in UK society.

Response to Allegations: While she has been the subject of intense scrutiny regarding her role in his circle, she had not been charged with any crimes and had denied wrongdoing, as they all do/did – she died of brain cancer in 2026.

Another who piggy backed Epstein's millions and got off with her own rich guy!

………………....   *Conclusions suggested >> ???*

Feb. 2026 Andrew interviewed conclusion: 'Look at the money trail' - <> Epstein links possible next stages for ex-duke and Sarah Ferguson over Epstein links

Poor guy suffered a mini-stroke (transient ischemic attack)= (a brief episode of neurological dysfunction resulting from an interruption in the blood supply to the brain or the eye, sometimes as a precursor of a stroke) in May 2018 while giving a speech in London, added to another prior near death experience, in November 2012, he and his wife were involved in a serious head-on collision on their honeymoon in South Africa, whilst being driven to the Airport.

"He certainly aged a lot in the last few years since our meeting, before his collapse," Michael added + photo

. *Author Copyright*

Author Copyright

And now we end, where we started, Bleak Blenheim Castle >>

Author Copyright

**The dark clouds still now linger over Regal Sites such as this Blenheim!
WHY?**

Just that another scandal breaks…linking our Royals and late Diana's Family, as Blenheim is the accused Ancestral Home > And he is 70-year-old Charles James Spencer-Churchill, the 12th Duke of Marlborough, who is accused of striking/strangling his 'estranged' wife!

Ah well, just like the Norwegian trial mentioned before, we can only sit and wait, even forget, especially as this is not due in Court until 10 Jan 2028!!!!!!!! If it even makes it there?

>>>>>>>>>>>>>

Epstein's Web Expansion World-Wide is covered in my, 'The Rich and Powerful don't give a Shit!'

>>>>>>>>>>>>>

Now back to Guinness through and through Chapter 2a…

PART 2a – HIS/HIS GUEST'S POLICE FOREBODING!

Today was different for, not yet known, notable reasons.

"You're quiet this afternoon?"

"What!?!…" I seemed to have startled him.

"Got a couple of strange e-mails to my personal account and non-personal Facebook pages. My computer went bananas, with red flags all over the place!"

"From anybody you know?"

"The surname yes, but not the Christian name. I was being asked about my involvement with *the family:* the family and a select few of mine are only privy to both my e-mail addresses."

"From her, toying with you?"

"Hardly, everything her *Charitable* end came in the third person – via an underling, she says etc. **except one**."

"Perhaps, it's a sign you should …?"

He interrupted me,

"There's something not quite right about this all!?"

A future early morning Police telephone **call** would enlighten him!

As it did Old Sam during the Second World War!

....

A couple of generations later he was successfully introducing his & his wife's Royal Family Friend, the King Olav of Norway's future Crown Prince Harald, to the University's Rowing Fraternity Watery Arena!

But, before all this there comes their Joint WWII Allied Efforts, in this next story session.

....

PART 2b – HIS SECRET'S ACT WAR EFFORT(S)
PLUS AN APPARENT GOD FEARING DEVIL AND MORE SPIES

And hereonin be agasp at John's Open Government Licence & other REDACTED Discoveries!

Or that John knew the places to look for the real meaty stuff? *(From my, Plain Jane Guinness & I Once...##)*

Then, afterwards came the interminable waiting...
Unlike in Sam's War Experience, where Justice Was Extremely Swift!!!

> **1941**
> Josef Jakobs captured parachuting into England and tried as a spy. Committed to Tower overnight in east turret room on top floor of Waterloo Block before his execution the following day

But, and it is a Big Uncle Sam But:
Henry Samuel's Own **Secret** Run-In with
The Police
AND
The **Secret** Service!
But, he told John!
AND
He too got a **call**! (Although many years later).

From above... *(Plain Jane Guinness & I Once...##)*

– where we join John and Sam Guinness at his Cheyne Walk home:-

"There's something not quite right about this all!?"

Today, we had heard nothing more on the/his/our Appeal, *so the conversation got rerouted via my family War Escapades/Escapes, to his own War Escapes/Escapades*!

Like John he had put his oar where it was not welcome and so was ignored!

Interested?

Read on...

I don't suppose the name, Mozzoni, means very much to you, but it did to Sam, and others of more import!

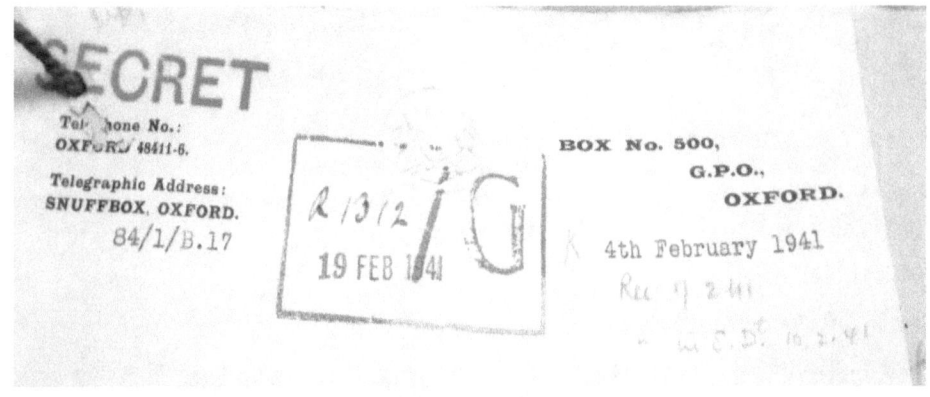

So, rather than a tale of 3 little Piggies, here, before you, are three Mozzonis.

1. Imagine the scene in War Torn 1940 England and a bunch of certain privileged, who wanted to board a plane at Heston Airport, Sam's foreign friend, being one, who had been staying with him: Cesare Cigogna-MOZZONI, whom we shall call the one made of straw. Needless to say, he was blown away, by an Official Wolf, k/a, an Immigration Officer, who denied him leave to access the plane. Sam offered to vouch for his colleague's character, but his word was ignored! (Later #)

2. But, for some, flying here and there was unhindered by Officialdom, especially if you were linked to the Vatican, as was Monsignor MOZZONI, whom we shall call the one made of wood, who openly proclaimed it was the easiest thing in the world for him to communicate from Britain with Italy, via the Vatican Pouch! And, so it was with all the posters, which proclaimed, *'Loose Lips etc.'* someone overheard his boast and reported him to MI5: his UK World crumbled under the Diplomatic Pressure, as their request to have him removed from here was accepted as his next, immediate posting was to the Nunciature in Lisbon!

3. Then, we come to the UK Brick Stalwart, Guglielmo MOZZONI, who had many aliases*: suspicious and so you might enquire?

159

NAME   MOZZONI, Guglielmo.   23.11.45
Alias GUGLIELMO MINOll; MASSIMO;COSTA;GUGLIELMO;AMBROGIO;GUGLIA;GUGLI
       MORONI;GUGLIELMO; M.232
Nationality Italian   Date & Place of Birth   28 Mar 1915 - MILAN
Description
Address   PIAZZA MOZZONI 1, VARESE
Means of Contacting   Via MARTELLI 10, ROME
Occupation   Architect - Doctor, Own practice.
Political Leanings
Estimate of Potential Value
History Commenced Service as below. Crossed into SWITZERLAND 12.9.43.
         Returned to Italy 31.12.43 and contacted CLNAI in MILAN. Acted
         as courier for the CLNAI up to MARCH 44 and made repeated
         journeys across the Italian-Swiss frontier. Continued work
         with PARTISANS and as courier, PIEDMONT, LOMBARDY, SWITZERLAND.
         Captured 20 Jan 45 by Republican Guards near MOLTRASIO.
         Interned in SWITZERLAND. Returned to Italy 25.1.45. MARCH 45
         went to S.Italy via SWITZERLAND. Engaged by No.1 Special Force
         w.e.f. 20/3/45 and trained. Infiltrated to MILAN at the end of
         April 45 with OP ORGAN 11. Always considered himself to have
         the status of a "MILAN CLN Officer". Was discharged on
         7.9.45 with a Letter of Commendation.

So, the code number M.232 might give you a clue as to why the Officials were jumpy at the Airport.

Unbeknown to innocent Sam, who, like John, was always for the seemingly hard-done-by, his friend's name had been found in the possession of another Italian suspect!

Hence, he was stopped. # But, and here is the Big But, it was essential MI5's real life spy of the same surname was not brought into this and there should be no further references to any Mozzonis.

And so * alias Guglierlmo Minoli, Massimo, Costa, Ambrogio, Guglia, or, Gugli, our solid, dependable, reliable information rock would not be discovered acting on our behalf: -

He was *liquidated* 7/4/45 ** –

** No, not *killed* off = just discharged from further duties!!

His Letter of Commendation was Issued 16/8/45!

> MI/P/27/257
>
> PART 11   FILE
>
> TO: ~~[redacted]~~
>
> Name... MOZZONI GUGLIELMO ... Alias... MINO II: MORONI
>
> Action in accordance with the Liquidation Committee's CL/.J/.290 ...has be[en]
> fully implemented. The Agent was discharged on ...7. Sept. 45...
>
> Date... 7. Sept. 45...   H Boutigu[?]

4. And so to that extra British one, made of sterner, stiff upper lip stuff, he got his own call 2 years later on, Flaxman 4774, to say he was now officially part of the War Effort!
5. And so codename 6995 & his Cheyne Walk Home were to act as Host to the Norwegian Forces ***, even though MI5 knew all about the *'Heston Affair!'*.

From above... *(Plain Jane Guinness & I Once...##)*

John being John and so conversant with those Secret HO Files popped up the following week, paper in hand, as in the past and 'Hello Sam!'

Date 9.11.1942.

22806/A C.R.

S.O.2.

SURNAME. GUINNESS
(State name at birth if different or if known by any other names.)

FULL CHRISTIAN NAMES. H.S.H.

DATE & PLACE OF BIRTH.

NATIONALITY. British

NATIONALITY AT BIRTH. (If different from above.)

PRIVATE ADDRESS. 6 Cheyne Walk, Chelsea S.W.3.
Tel. Flaxman 4774
PERMANENT ADDRESS.

NATIONAL REGISTRATION NUMBER.

BRIEF PARTICULARS OF PREVIOUS EMPLOYMENT. [Present] Director Of Guinness

FULL NAME, NATIONALITY AT BIRTH AND PLACE OF BIRTH OF FATHER, MOTHER, HUSBAND/WIFE.
NOTE—If applicant or parents naturalised, state Number, Date and Name In which Certificate was granted.)

PARTICULARS OF RELATIVES NOW IN ENEMY OR ENEMY-OCCUPIED OR CONTROLLED COUNTRIES. (Husband, wife, father, mother, brothers, sisters, sons or daughters only.)

NAME	RELATIONSHIP	PRESENT ADDRESS

APPLICANT FOR EMPLOYMENT AS— Host to the Norwegian Forces.

....
(With his Wife's Regal Connections there) Host to the Norwegian Forces – then did not come immediately:-

FULL CHRISTIAN NAMES.	H.S.H.
DATE & PLACE OF BIRTH.	
NATIONALITY.	British

S. GUINNESS — Henry, Samuel, Howard. 6994

P.T.C.	11.11.42
Traces	See below
Nationality	British
Born	
Occupation	Co. Director.

11.11.42	P.T.C. as he has offered to act as host to the Norwegian Forces.
17.11.42	Special Branch advised: On the 20.4.40 an Italian, Cesare CICOGNA-MOZZONI was refused permission by the Immigration Officer at Heston Airport to embark for Paris. (Apparently this man's name had been found, amongst others, in the possession of another Italian suspect and the instruction to refuse these persons leave to embark was issued by Home Office). Whilst the above mentioned suspect was waiting at the Passport Control a man of the same name and initials as 6994, born Dublin 1888, described as a Banker (and of the same address as 6994) approached the Immigration Officer and offered to vouch for the respectability of CICOGNA-MOZZONI. No attention was paid to him.
1.11.42	M.I.5 advised: There is no objection.
3.11.42	SN advised: 6995 is to act as Host to Norwegian Forces.

....

THE OTHER (DEVIL?)

MONSIGNOR MOZZONI INTRIGUE EXPOSED:-

one day last week when I mentioned the Mozzoni case and in this letter he is trying to be helpful. His point is that if we are not careful Mozzoni will be recalled to the Vatican where he will be appointed as a British expert and then, out of revenge, take the opportunity accorded to him, of damaging our interests to the best of his ability. This, as British expert, he might well be in a position to achieve. Clearly we should prefer that he was appointed to another post abroad rather than that he should return to the Vatican; but the first thing to do is to get rid of him from London.

AND CONFIRMED (?) ANONYMOUSLY

I have been tipped off privately that Mozzoni, the Vatican assistant of Monsignor Godfrey, is not by any means sticking to his ecclesiastical duties but engaged in Italian & [...] activities

THE DESIRED (?) VATICAN ORCHESTRATED RESULT!

Many thanks indeed for your letter of 18th April telling me that you have learned from the Vatican that Monsignor Mozzoni is being transferred to the Nunciature at Lisbon. We shall certainly see to it that all the necessary formalities are accomplished in good time. Perhaps you will kindly let me know the approximate date of departure you have in mind for Monsignor Mozzoni. It will of course be realized that the congestion of passenger traffic by aeroplane is enormous at the present time, and that it may well be some weeks before there is a vacancy.

AND STILL MORE SPIES NOW REVEALED BY DEAR JOHN:-

Now the War is over we can start rebuilding – eh Winston?

Post World War 2 - Winston laying foundation stone for House of Commons rebuilding

And reveal our WW2 undercover activities:-

DOUBLE CROSS AGENTS
Background to the Double Cross System

The Double Cross System was one of the greatest intelligence coups of the Second World War. J C Masterman, Chairman of the Double Cross Committee, concluded that 'we [MI5] actively ran and controlled the German espionage system in this country [Britain]'. Because a double cross, read as Roman numerals, is twenty, the Double Cross Committee was known as the Twenty Committee. In the Near and Middle East, Double cross was run by the Special Section of SIME (and its sub-section CICI in Persia and Iraq).

Due to a combination of counter-espionage work prior to the war and signals intelligence during it, MI5 were in a position to monitor and pick up German agents as they were 'dropped' into Britain. These agents were then 'turned' and began working for the British authorities. The preferred communication was via wireless telegraphy (W/T), although secret ink, microphotography and, in some cases, direct contact with the agent were also employed.

Initially the Double Cross System was used for counter-espionage purposes, but its comprehensive success provided an excellent conduit for strategic deception, culminating in the D-Day deception operation, known as FORTITUDE. This plan misled the Germans into believing that the Pas de Calais was the real landing area of the Allied invasion, rather than Normandy. Further successes were achieved in U-boat and V-weapon deception, and during operations HUSKY and TORCH.

A good summary of the most significant Double Cross cases may be found in JC Masterman's book, The Double Cross System.

GELATINE
(Archive Reference KV 2/1275-1280))

The female double agent GELATINE was born in Raithern, Austria in January 1911. Married to a Jew, she left Austria for Palestine in 1934. Arriving in the UK in 1938, she began informing on the activities of German organisations in Britain to the authorities. She was introduced to the German secret service by TRICYCLE in 1941 and for the rest of the war sent messages written in secret ink to her contact in Portugal. Initially these were political in content, but from 1942 her handlers began to introduce military misinformation into GELATINE's letters.

KISS
(Archive Reference KV 2/1281-1285)

KISS was a Persian national who went to Germany in 1936 to study electrical engineering. Recruited by the Abwehr in 1941, he was sent to Turkey, where he made contact with the British agent BLACKGUARD and revealed he had no intention of carrying out the Abwehr mission to report on Allied activity in Persia. BLACKGUARD persuaded him to continue his journey but allow his codes and transmitter to be passed to the allies. KISS complied, eventually arriving in the Soviet-controlled part of Persia where he worked in an armaments factory. Meanwhile, unknown to him, the British played back his transmitter to the Germans, initially with low-grade material. As the Germans asked specific questions about the situation in Persia and, particularly, the Tehran conference, KISS was required to provide more and more detail, which lead the British to reveal his existence (but not BLACKGUARD's) to the Soviets. The deception of the Germans was continued to the end of the war and beyond, as the link was watched for any signs of post-war Germany attempting to re-establish contact with its supposed agent in Persia.

KV 2/1281 is the main file on the KISS case, covering 1942-1945.
It contains the initial reports on KISS from BLACKGUARD, SIME reports on the KISS case, and full details of the decision to reveal KISS's existence to the Russians.
The Soviets were initially obstructive, but suddenly changed their attitude (in December 1944) and moved to open collaboration.
The file contains full reports on meetings between British and Russian agents and includes the text of some of the messages sent to the Germans using KISS's transmitter.

Double Agent policy files
(KV 4/210-215)

This release also sees the opening of a number of files on the policy behind the operation of the Double Cross system, including the following highlights.
The system depended for its effectiveness on the quality and quantity of information passed back to the Germans through the agents. Files KV 4/213-214 set out the policy on this, recording many of the messages sent and detailing who authorised the sending of certain messages.

A further file KV 4/211 sets out arrangements for securing the Double Agents in the event of a German invasion.

The plans, known as "Mr Mills' Circus", included the arrest of some agents, with others being escorted to out-of-the way locations in Wales (hotels in Llandudno, Llanwrst and Betws-y-Coed are mentioned).

The file covers the period 1941 to 1944, and ends with a receipt for the return to New Scotland Yard in May 1944 of seven pairs of handcuffs required for the plans.

The security of the agents in TRICYCLE's organisation in Yugoslavia after the defeat of the German occupying forces is the concern of file KV 4/210.

The file details the Security Service's efforts to safeguard the agents by liaison with various anti-German Yugoslav agencies, and includes a hand-written memo by the Director General Sir David Petrie.

....

AND TO ALL THOSE WHO THOUGHT THE HIT UK SERIES 'ALLO, ALLO' WAS A FIGMENT OF ITS AUTHORS' IMAGINATION?

THERE WERE SUCH CAFÉ/SHOPS WHICH HELPED/SUPPORTED THEIR LOCAL RESISTANCE WAR EFFORTS:-

AND HERE OUR CAKE FROM PAGE 2 IS *'MISTILY'* RESURRECTED...

My John's mother's best friend had a Cake Shop and did requests for all and even such ordered by the German Occupying Forces and advertised them in her shop window.

BUT

Little did anyone know, other than those <u>in the know</u>, that in the specially adapted cake inscriptions in the shop window were actually in a special code to pass on messages to/from the Resistance and the British Secret Service.

She regrettably only got her Medal Posthumously, as a sniper bullet took her life as the US forces charged into Paris!

PART 2c: HIS *(FLUFF)* WIFE ALFHILD'S WAR EFFORT(S)

*** Sam's wife, Alfhild, was Norwegian and ran the Norwegian Red Cross; their daughter, Marit, married Carl Nils Gunnar William Aschan, Swedish born; once a British Intelligence Officer & Spy: recruited by MI5 – he was fluent in Scandinavian languages & German.

Alfhild was also used for her multi-lingual capabilities.

<u>Including being there for interrogations</u>!!

Sam (And his wife too!) was awarded the Chevalier, Order of Olav of Norway in 1947.

Both Sam & his wife, pet named Fluff, were unbeknown to so many [F] that they were also local Air Raid Wardens – Wow!

All that was needed then was that they helped direct the Arc Lights and man the guns, which shot down the German Enemy Planes!

NB [F] Sam's wife, Fluff, also kept it Local and under the radar, as she spent so much of her earlier years' time in the poorer areas of West/Central London giving away food to local impoverished sleeping it rough residents.

Later, in another session, John recalled another Guinness introduction:
But, <u>in part</u>, <u>it wasn't</u>!?

Funny, one day, I was introduced to this 'foreign' woman and bearing in mind her parentage # (below ↓) I cried out, 'So, I've also met a Hungarian Guinness!'

'Yes, we're everywhere!' Alfhild said.

Oddly, that's what Pauline G. said to him, down at their farm, about Guinness properties many years later!

....

PART 3: SAM'S AUNT LUCY *LASZLO*

There was no internet then, nor those Ancestral Tree sites...
So it was a few years later I discovered that that Hungarian link was none other than Philip Alexius Laszlo do Lombos #, a renown Regal/Celebrity Portrait painter!

Sam's Aunt Lucy was his Guinness wife. What was coincidental about him & Sam was the War/MI5 link, which was publicly well documented: **Philip ended up in prison** *for trying to smuggle money to his Hungarian colleagues via the Diplomatic Pouch!*
It was also covered by Alfred William Brian Simpson in his book, 'In the Highest Degree Odious: Detention Without Trial in Wartime Britain'.

But, ultimately, with friends in high places, including his brother-in-law, Howard and his connections, after his release he was granted British Citizenship.
A full account is found in The de Lazlo Archives.

➢ *Delving more, much later, not publicly well documented, I discovered what Pope Leo X111 said to Philip about his Portrait likeness,* **perhaps he wasn't totally enamoured of it – to put it lightly;**
➢ *the so Droit de Seigneur, Hungarian Snobbish Upper-Class attitude to infidelity, that Lucy ascertained from a certain Diplomat;*
➢ *Alfhild, with her daughter & grand-daughter created a unique 3 generational Parisian artistic landmark.*
➢ *And, lastly, but not leastly, be especially careful post wartime whom you invite to dinner, unbeknown to you he might be an Englishman Wolf, dressed up in a Russian Foreign Spy's Sheep's clothing!*

See Revelations Below REV
....

Funny, you know how I like my coincidences and it was so with old Laszlo: his prison incarceration ᴶ site was in Cornwallis Road, not far from my place. ᴶ *His would be the second if you recall Mitford's*?

Its situation made it the apex in a triangle of 3 prisons: the other two, to the right, Holloway prison, to the left, Pentonville Prison. So many in such a small Islington location: seemed needed to accommodate all those, too many, crooked elements! Me? Perhaps? But?

He, then, paused for a self-chuckle.

Suppose it's not too much of a stretch of the imagination-link to jump from crooked to warped.

He, then, paused for a self-recognition.

None came.

So, then, we crossed verbal swords.

Me, warped?

You, lovely... Well, I have been called a *looker*... Not in the conventional way... I think convention went out the window some time ago... It must be hard for you to... I'd've thought the hard would be on you...Well, yes, your *enclosed* proximity has a big say in the matter... Yes, you do, do a lot of talking... So, you're sort of goading me into some sort of physical **action/reaction**... But, you won't, will you?

I was surely tempting fate, as the next time we would be alone in this empty building behind closed doors, with no avenue of escape should the opportunity manifest & present itself and he consider it time for the he/me physical **action/reaction**!

His past recollections had a lot to answer for...

....

\# But, now back to the present....And, off to the Races!
ALONE with HIM!!!
But, and it was my Big But, I had a countering-assault plan!!!
But, and it was his Big But re-**but**-all: **it failed**!!!

....

Countering-assault plan!!!
\# Oh, God! That Promised Kiss: I forgot all about *that* Bet way **in**!!!
\# (From Plain Jane Guinness & I Once... <> Chapter Thirty Seven: Rich Chapters Past – 30th

....

PART 4: THE GUN IS MIGHTIER THAN THE SWORD & THE WORD HAS NO CHANCE AGAINST THE BULLET!

Historical Note:
Hello 'Carolus Magnus' the 2nd

> *FREE John's history also had him being a Freemason
> and he had also came across Earl Spencer
> at this Royal One's select 3rd Floor Lodge, Room 14,
> situated within the Freemason's Central London HQ!*
>
> ....

"Sorry, do you mind a history *FREE* lecture today?"
"Do I have a choice?"

"When I first heard the young him speak I had my back to him and thought he was gay! Furthest from the truth and his latest wife certainly is a looker!"

"Like me?"
"Yes, but more so!"
(Oddly that comment hurt – again I couldn't explain it at the time)
He went on …

"Now, chubby (reddening) cheeks, like his Dad, (who would supplement his Income by having paid outsider guests at his Dinner table @ £80 a head!) and just like his father before him, the Estate's Caretaker, which would be passed down to his only male progeny, by his previous wife.
It might so easily not have been so, just as Washington would not have defeated the British in the American War of Independence?!
Fate and Money stepped in as it always seems to do with people like themselves.

The knack seemed to have been in that bygone era to marry a rich widow and take control of the purse strings, as was the husband's right – one wonders why rich widows ever bothered to re-marry?

One great, great, great, etc. grandfather was a past master at this, marrying a rich widow, then on her demise, 6 months later marrying a twice rich widowed woman, to save and then foster the estate.

So why would any self-respecting female do this?

Simply that many marriages were entered into because they were either politically, financially, or otherwise correct; arranged to unite two warring factions; generally to produce male heirs; to obtain titles; to move further up the royal pecking order; this **elitist** chess-gaming **list** is endless and the women just the pawns – impregnation usually <u>quickly</u> followed!

So it will come as no surprise that love does not factor into these Unions and if it were so then it would be one sided as, perhaps, people might say in <u>his</u> sister's own *'heady'* betrothal and subsequent unhappy marriage.
But, if all else failed the wealth of a rich related benefactress would do nicely.
So it would come to pass with Duchess Sarah, another Countess de Burgh of Pride and Prejudice infamy, but far better connected and far more opinionated – <u>do as she says or there will be consequences</u>!

She, it was, those centuries back, who first tried to get her grand-daughter, Lady # Diana to marry the Prince of Wales, coupled with a dowry of then (a fortune) £100,000, but it was vetoed by the, then, Prime Minister – no mention of love here like I said above.

She failed there, but without her, George Washington would have undoubtedly failed too: her daughter, Anne Churchill, married Charles Spencer # and after she died Sarah saved the family with her wealth and the sole grand-child benefactor was lazy young John Spencer, and it was the Spencer's inherited wealth which ended up saving the Washingtons from bankruptcy and if they didn't there would have been no George!

<u>So the Churchill's' money saved the Spencers, whose wealth saved the Washingtons.</u>
However, the Guinness brewery trade was saved by a brick wall preventing my Ancestral Co-Workers, the HM Revenues Men, checking up on their water usage; but, so many of the family later weren't so able:

- Sarah couldn't save her son, John, Marquess of Blandford, from smallpox!
- Nor, Sam Guinness, hundreds of years later save his son from the bullet!
- Nor, Anita, her 1st from the noose! + Another family Child tragedy!

- And there were so many more tragedies ...

Interestingly enough the Spencer family were connected to the Washington family in England and in Virginia: those tea? tobacco? slave? plantation days of *'yore'* making a vast future fortune!
If you manage to check the Northamptonshire Historical records you can find a complex interrelationship between the two families going back centuries!
(The links had been made and never severed thereafter.)

Strange, how, centuries apart, there was *another* Diana & Charles alive at the same time!? Even stranger, that Diana tried for her Prince so long ago <u>and failed</u>: one wonders if the modern day one <u>had</u> wished she had failed too?
History tells us that her rival (*in love?*) had her own established ancestor at turning the Royal eye her way!
Cynfillaness comes in many guises!
And there were so many more tragedies ...but not to be related here.

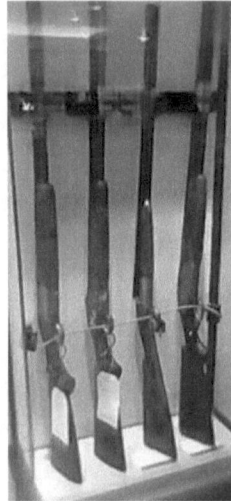

GUN

Here the Gentry's Favourite Past-Time Sport, but no fun if their kid handles any loaded with the safety off: then Death calls time on the kid's life here on earth! The pain of pains is that Sam & Fluff only had daughters thereafter.
<u>So, no male Heir which all those types crave</u>!

·····································

··

PART 5: DAUGHTER MARIT EXCHANGING UNKNOWNS

I dropped Marit a line, oddly like her father, frail & only a few years to go, seeing how I had the idea to write up her *celebratory* (once, or twice removed?) niece's Charity Work/Story, having met her a few times in her office.

Marit a horn of plenty of historical snippets came out with a handful which I thought you'd be amazed at:

1. Pope Leo X111 was indignant that (Marit's famous Great Uncle) Philip's Portrait likeness was more akin to Voltaire (A person the Pope detested!), than his own!
2. Lucy (Marit's Great Aunt) could not have been more embarrassed, if John had intimated this, when a certain Hungarian Ambassador enquired of her the identity of her husband's Mistress, as if that was the 'de rigueur' way of life for all in their privileged position!
3. With her daughter, Marit, like her mother Alfhild, all had showed in the Paris Salon: Where they had 3 generations of one family, a unique female first!
4. At one Wedding Party, Marit's invitee came and left suddenly? A strange way of doing things until it was discovered it was a certain **Blunt (Russian)** a **(future)** spy, on the run!
5. And, additionally, lastly, but not leastly, there was another **Diana** in the family history, who like her successor, died in a car crash. But, the least said the better.
6. And, pertinent to John himself, Marit had a Damien in her family life – a brilliant Chemist! Which coincidentally, "Just like me," John's second wife would say!
7. **But Marit's real sob story comes at the end of this Book!**

NB From all I have revealed before, **you can also see why her parents were War Heroes and recognised as such!**

....

PART 6: THE WOMEN ALSO SHOW THEIR YOUNGER METAL

One of my other Amazon publications is entitled, **The Rich Don't Give A Shit!**
But from all the aforementioned, you can <u>*see not all are hewn from the same cloth*</u> and so, so many of the Brewery Linked female line have temporarily gone out of their way for the good of lesser lights >>>
Starting with Sam's Grand Niece, who with her Twin Sister never did experience those particular female labour pains, (By choice or otherwise, I'll let your minds do the imagining?) but both ended up in ready-made families and historically had done their bit for the disadvantaged kid: I always admired King Charles 3rd ex - arm candy? Or a future Princess/Queen in the making? involving the YCTV kids & staff inviting them to that/those Estate(s), or her place - so many Patrons ignore those who keep the Charity afloat.

Her involvement, all hands to the pump so to speak, although, as Charitable acts go, her twin, Miranda, another Montessori *graduate,* felt she too could make a difference for disadvantaged kids # when, still in her teens, getting involved in a child rehabilitation scheme in the Gorbals Slums of Glasgow. <u>*John elaborates....*</u>

#*A sort of ballsy thing to take on, although, as putting yourself in the deep end goes, their mother beat them hands down, adventurously hitch-hiking thousands of miles from South Africa to Egypt – <u>sort of thing we all do when we have some spare time on our hands</u> – though must've been harsh on those model knees ^{T} who must have discovered perhaps painfully that the catwalk had nothing on those stony, undulating roads travelled!*

^{T} *In later life they were replaced by Titanium ones.*
She died at 90, (likely as not hopefully after having enjoyed her favourite pastime, another knitting session in the back drawing room) and the irony of it was that one of daughter's love rivals (?) for Charlie's attention, and others later (?) a certain Tara died in the same year but at 45 was half her age: the older died naturally, the younger, not drug filled according to what the Media had us believe, but **,** *having in 2016 been diagnosed with a pituitary tumour and an autoimmune condition, it would perhaps be no surprise she died 8th Feb, 2017, the following year, but oddly enough from a perforated ulcer!?*
Coincidentally another of Charles' Rich Set, Eva, also seems to have suffered the same fate!
Perhaps showing that we all share 2 simple facts of life: good/bad relationships and good/bad health – if the last named, then that arbitrary scythe carrier death takes them away – rich or poor, it doesn't really matter to ***it!***

#seems a consistent complimentary family thread/trait with the companies/organisations her youngest sister, ## Julia, and her family get involved in, their niece, Natasha, straight out of University even went to teach in an apparently rough around the edges school in Barnet, during which stint she was even promoted!. (It's in the middle of all the Council Estates...not dissimilar with the Islington Council Estate but with the advantage, perhaps just down the road from her then (?) £1 million + home). (See Much Later)

#but, Great Grand Uncle Sam's wife, Fluff, also kept it Local and under the radar, as she spent so much of her earlier years' time in the poorer areas of West/Central London giving away food to local impoverished sleeping it rough residents.

#but, Fluff's **Great** Grand Niece continues expansively as she seems to beat them all: the Morpurgo Farms for City Children; her helm ?inherited clothing Company regularly dropped off coat seconds for UK refugee children in the UK and Calais via her local Charity drop-in Charity work, albeit just seconds!

but poor Nat (Julia's Daughter) has one problem in that the Big C has visited her body and left its mark and she not yet 40!?

But in 2022 still in remission: let's hope the Big C doesn't return with a vengeance & call upon his mate Death to end it all for her!?

##But perhaps Daddy Michael outperforms them all?

Their Charitable Stories will come around, later.

....

PART 7: HELLO SABRINA – BUT SEE YOU LATER....(At the end?)

#And so here seems the appropriate time to introduce you to her _ballsy_ Charitable Adventure...(The YCTV Intro)
Her Own Youth Community TV STORY Insight
BASICALLY PUT
BUT FIRST A PICTORAL HISTORICALLY LINKED SCENE SETTER >>>
The Paparazzi's ideal of Her Own One True Blue Royal Beau Choice!?

Author Copyright

But HE HAD TO favour another True Bluer to the fore!?

Author Copyright

John Adds – June 1997 - *Strange all that hassle she was supposed to have encountered she was in great chirpy mood as she left with the other (male) guest speaker to parade before the baying media types who preferred to get the extremely scandalous photos, but today it would be just another meet & greet day! The scandalous would come in a couple of months' time!*

But he had already had a sampling taste of his True Brew in the Wings!?

Author Copyright

....

And so for <u>Her</u> <u>Own</u> <u>Guinness</u> choice way forward

it was a case of going down that Charity Avenue

like that of <u>Her</u> <u>Own</u> youngest sister:

Author Copyright

Whose husband favoured support was, Annie, Sigmund's daughter?!

Their Charitable Stories will come around, later.

Author Copyright

Such that the offices became ginormous!?

Author Copyright

With a little financial clout from him!?

Author Copyright

Such that it would attract his God-Son's Regal Parents!?

Author Copyright

Author Copyright

Who unknowingly to so many was once playmates with (Guinness Related) Nat, the God-Father's Muddy Puddled Daughter!?

Author Copyright

Whose auntie just so happens to be a certain

the Twin Sister of the Youth Community TV Founder >>>

Sabrina Guinness

Who once wrote...

Re: ex yctv students comments about you and YCTV

x

AND SO FULL CIRCLE

WE COME TO THE BEGINNING OF IT ALL!

With a Special Introduction to a Specific Page in Her Life

↓

(Again from, Plain JANE Guinness & I Once...) On the Psychiatrist's Couch!

"So, that old lady said life & relationships; you've said health & relationships. I have another for you – dreaming!"

He looked up at me in his *familiar* way, with his *familiar* grin, with his *familiar* eyes, in that *familiar* cognizant way.

"I shouldn't be letting you know what I might talk about in future sessions, as there won't be any surprise."

"Well, don't you concur?"

"And with a bit of that high-brow lingo!"

I could have taken over then, but, here, it wasn't my time to say: here, it was his time to say, when.

He recognised this, although no word was spoken, he knew where he had to go and when was now!

"Yes, it is not only those who are without who **dream** of getting it. Just cos you're either rich &/or famous, or, from this, well-connected, **you can dream** of achievements, which apparently are out of your compass, even out of your comfort zone, but you can still give it a try!

She did.

But new technology **within her dream bubble** eventually caught up & burst it!

Or, was it just those *beneath her*, who just didn't cut the mustard for those *above her*, either rich &/or famous, or, from this, well-connected, whom she wanted to *financially* attract?

Or had the edge just gone from her resolve?"

I'LL LEAVE YOU TO DECIDE WHEN WE EVOLVE HER PERSONAL JOURNEY STORY – LATER –
BUT FIRST

HER EIRE ISOLATED/INSULATED TWIN SISTER....

....

PART 8: HELLO MIRANDA – SEE YOU'RE JUST TRYING TO BE ORDINARY

And like her twin or the ordinary user, the Computer might not be an Asset if one doesn't know what it conceals from you? [x]

For the Charlie-Boy Ex. It was potentially her Password failings?
I'll enlighten you all when her Chapter turn arrives...

Here if you press the wrong button each and everyone you had contact with, will be included in this all-encompassing request...

<><>

On behalf of Miranda Payne via [x] LinkedIn member@linkedin.com
Tue 06/09/2011 14:28

LinkedIn

Miranda Payne requested to add you as a connection on LinkedIn:

I'd like to add you to my professional network on LinkedIn.

- Miranda

| **Accept** | View invitation from Miranda Payne |

<><>

[x] **A cautionary note from our IT AL(EX)pert:** https://haveibeenpwned.com/

[x] LinkedIn: In May 2016, LinkedIn had 164 million email addresses and passwords exposed. Originally hacked in 2012, the data remained out of sight until being offered for sale on a dark market site 4 years later. The passwords in the breach were stored as SHA1 hashes without salt, the vast majority of which were quickly cracked in the days following the release of the data.

Compromised data: Email addresses, Passwords – Visit the Web page above ASAP for advice!

Then, perhaps this/their niece is
a different **solecistic** *puddy muddle?*
Which I might reveal later?!
....

So, as *settlements* go, the UK is not one fit for all: unlike a distant relative, her overindulgent boozer/drug taker brother, as his female twin reported, could not, rather, did not want to get on the banking ladder, so escaped to the Manhattan Climes, where his (originally kitchen table stuff...) *elite purchasing* doodling paid off, handsomely? And later *'Budapest'* Film Work!

His elder sister sibling too went abroad to a humbler sunny part of French climes and didn't follow the elitist path, as there, she was just another *Plain Jane* and simply more at home on her *Rural French* **Lot** of crop producing land – no designer ball gowns for her here, as there, pinafores were the order of the day – home grown vegetables for dinner, anyone?

This Guinness Lady is more of a gentle Irish Country Lass, where husbandry would have been her chosen subject, not the limelight, although she has made the occasional appearances like at her Twin's YCV Fund raisers calling out the bids etc.

But, generally more the sat at home type.
BUT - She is the *(delicate (?)* one who you should treat with kid gloves unless you want her hubby to *Shillelagh* knock your block off!

She married her Cork Keith in 1990 and settled on Ireland's its West Coast just over from The Renown Burren.
Ret (South of the Galway Coast above, where John Houston had his getaway pad - Later)

But some years later they upped roots and went over to France.
They settled in a small village called Baladou, where not much happens.
And so if you wanted to do the Touristy thing and travel towards the Dordogne Valley, via Sarlat, you had only one public transport option: the school run bus 8am & return 3pm, otherwise you're on your own!

Dordogne is a department in southwest France, set between the Loire Valley and Pyrenees mountains.

It's known for prehistoric cave paintings in the Vézère Valley, like those in Lascaux Cave, and it is this type of subject Keith, in his sort of Jurassic mood, was after.

The town of Périgueux is home to the Cathedrale St-Front, with its 5 domes, and the Vesunna Museum, built around Roman ruins.

The medieval town Sarlat-la-Canéda centres on the Rue de la Republique and the Cathédrale St-Sacerdos.

The handy thing for him was that his wife had been brought up to learn French and it was she who did all the verbal interaction between them and the locals – Hubby not having bothered to really adapt learning their tongue. *(See the benefit of learning a second language!)*

But his *Gallerie Pomié* Exhibitions were not thwarted because of this.

Miranda hit it off with the locals and often there would be home grown produce exchanged, for which she was adept.

She was just the type you could have a good natter over a garden fence with.

Despite its out of the main highway location, she let part of their 2-building cottage/farmhouse set up.

The one-bedroom annex plus pool could be had springtime, for a mere £125 p/wk.

Regards Miranda

Coincidentally, when I visited her mother's farmhouse down Hants way: the cobbled drive passed by the other Cottages to the left.

You always knew somebody (? Sabrina?) was in/about in the chillier times because the billowing log fired smoke would be seen rising above the chimney pots.

where I was greeted by the manager and his daughter exercising the horses...

The sheep rearing upon their hilly slopes; Pauline's expanded upon chicken battery barn to the left of the house; the trout fishery was some way behind; the Sporting Rights further down the road.

Thanks to vectorolie at FreeDigitalPhotos-100269198

For those who throw all these vast estimations as to each member's relative worth, the inside was quite basic, with none of the grandeur associated with her daughter's place at Mells Park, where the right-angled staircase is a true feature.

Here, because of the Grand-Mother's walking problems, you would be greeted by a bending staircase stairlift, thankfully a downstairs loo! Although, as mentioned before, she spent more time knitting in the ground floor lounge at the rear of the premises.

And if lucky you might find an assortment of Son-in-law's paintings strewn about in the hallway!

But the Irish in him dictated his/their next move: nostalgic own family linked Cork called out his name in a language he fully understood and so return to off the Atlantic coast they did.

Although it could get a little lonely at times in the rambling Country House Pauline would obviously get those children/grandchildren visits, although Hugo less so – I mean he ensconced himself in the Big Apple.

John left her that snowy Christmas a few hours before Miranda & Keith came over from France for their Xmas visit/stay!

Family Historically only son Hugo felt unable/incapable to take over his father's banking arms and took his kitchen table doodlings to a higher most profitable arena: his mini creations even made it onto exclusively rich female bags.

In that select arena it is a case of the Rich buying/selling with other Rich pricing the ordinary hoi-polloi out of their select market!

And so you could pick up a couple or more of Keith's creations for the price of one of these apparently well sought after (by the Rich only?) Hugo inscribed *Coach hand held bags!*

Additionally, again you as likely find Hugo sells so many more of his creations than Keith, simply that his Litho Reprints he could easily churn out by the plenty, whereas you only got one of Keith's at a time!

NB His name was fully, **Hugo Arthur Rundell Guinness** – *the Arthur Rundell after his Grandfather – the Rundell designated the Banking Arm. (Geneality Chart at back of Book).*

But I do Hugo a disservice, he did still retain a sales link with a local Notting Hill Area Art/Antique Store plus his original simple creations developed into full blown/grown TV/Cinema ingredients/scores... Here a *BBC Storyville documentary Hi Society – The Wonderful World of Nicky Haslam (2012)*. Back in the USA, unknown as the voice of Nathan Bunce in *Fantastic Mr. Fox* (2009).

But, for me his greatest work was with his friend Wes Anderson on the story for The Grand Budapest Hotel (2014), which gave him a shared nomination for the Academy Award for Best Original Screenplay. For all his post UK accomplishments his father would have been impressed, even his Eton Educated did not take up the Bankers Work Baton!

And here I leave the following credit to last as it links in a certain friend to connect brother Hugo[1], sister Miranda[2] & Sabrina[3] together:- (Hugo's)[1] *The Royal Tenenbaums (2001)* starred a certain *Anjelica Houston*.

The Old and the New...

Many flickr thanks to 'photo by Alan Light' 26mar90 - 255273566_9587c28ed0_c

Many wiki thanks to Mingle Media TV - httpswww.flickr.comphotosminglemediatv13334157143 - Anjelica_Huston at the UCLA Institute of the Environment and Sustainability's An Evening of Environmental Excellence. March 21, 2014(cropped) This file is licensed under the Creative Commons Attribution-Share Alike 2.0 Generic license

Yes, she of Coastal Galway, John Houston *Plain Jane Guinness & I Once... West Galway* Beach Fame –

Author Copyright

She is a Sabirna[3] long time friend and also starred in *Ever After,* which took place in the French Dordogne, so beautiful' Valley as she called it and she built it up to influence Miranda[2] to visit/stay there with her painter hubby[4] and open up their farm home to guests – then about £125 p/wk (you even had a swimming pool to yourself!) (But needed a car to get anywhere as the bus only seemed to run to suit only the school kids!)(↑↑)

And the reason to bring in Hugo here is simply one of Aristocratic Inheritance: The Patriarch James Guinness had passed away in 2006, his wife Pauline in 2017 and guess who would end inheriting the Farm etc? Yes it seems female emancipation rights don't run into the Gentry's Male Inheritance First way of thinking & doing!

But now back to the less favoured artist...Strangely Keith[4] couldn't get the Burren out of his system and it again featured in his life 2018 with his *Burren Collection* at The Gallery, Burren College of Art, Newtown Castle, Ballyvaughan, Co. Clare.

But, even for this *ordinary* subject, being married to the sister of a then potential future Queen, although it didn't materialise, the Royal Connections were not totally severed and, as such, existed in the background: her hubby being an experienced wheelwright and so (the now late) Duke of Edinburgh knew where to get his (?racing?) carriage serviced!

Quiet Miranda, in the limelight background, contentedly tends their home/barn/gallery at the top of a hilly coast road – enjoying the freedom the area affords her!

And just another Historical Payne Creation Note:-

1990 The Pink Floyd Pig Balloon –

- ✓ This was one of the many creations from Bungay-based artist Rob Harries.
- ✓ Whose *inflatables* reputation just ballooned there-on-after
- ✓ And the job requests for Rob and his team,
- ✓ Including seamstress Shirley Russell *and painter Keith Payne*,
- ✓ Poured in from inflated ego idea copying/demanding megastar clients!

....

PART 9: HELLO JASMINE (+ HOLLY) – THE ORDINARY #

Jasmine:-

She is the great-granddaughter of Diana Mitford (later Lady Mosley), who was one of the Mitford sisters, and her first husband Bryan Guinness, later the 2nd Lord Moyne. Her paternal grandfather, the Hon. Desmond Guinness, was a conservationist specialising in Georgian and classical architecture, while her paternal grandmother, Mariga Guinness, was born Marie-Gabrielle, Princess of Urach.

But here #, Jasmine Guinness & Her Grand-Parents' Chequered Past:-

WWII again the main startling source –

Lady Diana Mosley

COPY.

loane 8291.

10, GROSVENO[R]
S.W.1

Confidential

June 25th,

My dear Philip

It has been on my conscience for some time to [write?] that the Authorities concerned are aware of the ext[reme] dangerous character of my former daughter-in-law, [Lady] Mosley. As the matter was mentioned in the Secre[t?] other day, I have no doubt that those concerned a[re aware of?] public comment on the arrest of Mrs. Joe Beckett a[nd the] impunity of Lady Mosley and there are many who ar[rive at?] the conclusion that there is one law for the infl[uential] and another for the friendless poor.

It has been suggested to me that the Author[ities] may have no detailed evidence as to the opinions freely expressed by Lady Mosley so I enclose her[ewith a note] of conversations which my grandson's governess ha[s had?] when taking him on visits to his mother.

It is widely believed by those who are aware [of Lady] Mosley's movements that her frequent visits to Ger[many are] concerned with bringing over funds from the Nazi Go[vernment. I] therefore also enclose a list of the dates on which Lady M[osl]ey went to Germany which the governess has extracted from her diary. Owing to the governess being absent for many months in 1939 on account of a serious operation, she has no dates entered in her diary during the last year before the war.

I feel it rather embarrassing to write you this letter and am sure you will understand that it would be very hard on the governess to call on her for any evidence on the subject which would lead the Mosley family to know of the information which she is giving. For this reason I have not mentioned the governess's name though it will of course be readily supplied if required.

I am not clear as to the activities of your Committee but if this matter is outside your scope perhaps you could have the letter passed on to whoever is responsible.

Yours ever

Walter

Archive Document reference: KV 2/1363-1364

Lady Diana Mosley (1910-2003) was one of the daughters of Lord Redesdale, and had the reputation of being the most beautiful and dazzling of the 'Mitford girls'.

She married the heir to the Guinness company, Brian (later Lord Moyne), at the age of 18, but subsequently left him and then married the British fascist, Oswald Mosley.
She was introduced to Hitler by her sister, Unity, and maintained a life-long admiration for him and his political beliefs.

KV 2/1363 commences with the Security Service taking an interest in Diana Guinness (as she then was) when her association with Oswald Mosley first came to its attention in 1934. The file includes reports of her frequent movements to and from Germany by air, a report of her secret marriage to Mosley in the presence of Hitler and Ribbentrop in 1936, and various pieces of intercepted mail and phone conversations. Her baggage was inspected at (The same airport where Sam had his Italian Connection run in with MI5!)> Heston Airport in August 1938 on her return from a visit to Germany, and the suspicious contents (including a new autographed photo of Hitler) were reported to the Service.

Diana Mosley was not interned on the outbreak of war, and remained at liberty for some time. There is a Home Office letter of May 1940 explaining the Home Secretary's decision not to intern her at that time, and then correspondence from her former father-in-law, Lord Moyne, (from above) which seems to have resulted in her detention the following month.
A copy of the form requesting her detention is on the file.
She was interned in Holloway prison, and there are reports of her visitors there, and also a transcript of her appeal hearing against her detention.

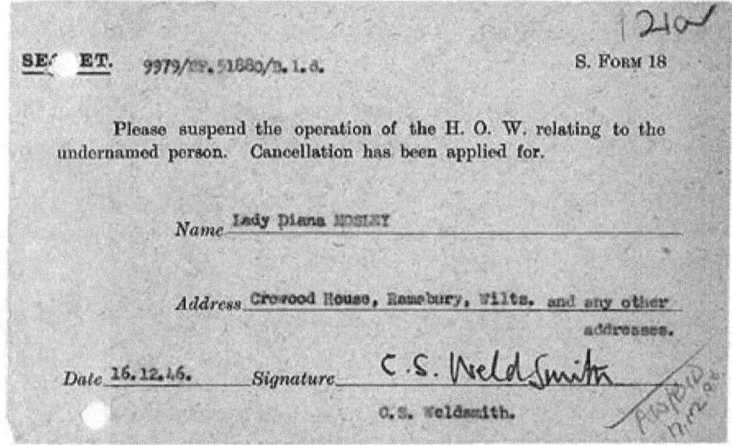

KV 2/1364 continues the story, with further reports of Diana Mosley's visitors at Holloway from 1941 until her release from detention in 1943.

The Home Office warrant on her was eventually suspended in December 1946.

After this, the Security Service decided that there was no further justification for maintaining a separate file on Diana Mosley, and later correspondence relating to her can be found on the joint files with her husband already released (KV 2/884-897). Both files contain reported comments and correspondence from members of Diana Mosley's family.

....

Diana, Lady Mosley (*née* **Freeman-Mitford**; 17 June 1910 – 11 August 2003) was one of the Mitford sisters. In 1929 she married Bryan Walter Guinness, heir to the Barony of Moyne, with whom she was part of the Bright Young Things (see Jasmine later) * social group of Bohemian young aristocrats and socialites in 1920s London.

Her marriage ended in divorce as she was pursuing a relationship with Oswald Mosley, leader of the British Union of Fascists. In 1936, she married Mosley at the home of the propaganda minister for Nazi Germany, Joseph Goebbels, with Adolf Hitler as guest of honour.

Her involvement with fascist political causes resulted in three years' internment during the Second World War, when Britain was at war with the fascist regime of Nazi Germany.

She later moved to Paris *(Where Edward & Wallis ended up also- discussed earlier)* and enjoyed some success as a writer. In the 1950s, she contributed diaries to *Tatler* and edited the magazine *The European*. In 1977, she published her autobiography, *A Life of Contrasts*, and two more biographies in the 1980s.

She was described as "unrepentant" about her previous political associations by obituary writers such as the historian Andrew Roberts.

Her co-fascist antisemitic, Hitler loving sister Unity did not follow Diana into incarceration, as earlier choosing at the inception of the War to put a bullet into her brain, thus **again** highlighting + perpetuating that being Rich cannot prevent Family Tragedy & is no barrier to a catastrophic early death.

Unlike dear old Uncle Samuel Guinness' son who *accidentally* lost his life to the gun at an early age, Unity's aim was not that precise and so she did not succeed in taking her own life.

But the short-lived legacy was extensive brain damage and a protracted passage to certain (*meningitis*) death half a dozen years later!

Mosley's 1989 appearance on BBC Radio 4's Desert Island Discs was controversial due to her Holocaust denial and admiration of Hitler. She was also a regular book reviewer for Books & Bookmen and later at The Evening Standard in the 1990s.

A family friend, James Lees-Milne, wrote of her beauty, "She was the nearest thing to Botticelli's Venus's Venus that I have ever seen".

Well I think not?! And you?   (see Below)

Here as an example on the right is Unity in London in 1938, wearing a Nazi party badge (*Anonymous - National Archief, Public Domain, https://commons.wikimedia.org/w/index.php?curid=62956658*). (**U** ↓)

(**D** ↓) And Diana's picture, on the left a year earlier…1937 at the Swan Inn in Swinbrook (Author William Acton Dec'd 1945 during WW11 active service).

(Apparently both classed as beauties of their day!?

Or just Plain Janes?) Eh Charlie Boy?

But, John puts us straight >>> the trouble with all this type of adoringly putting a specific female on such a high beauteous pedestal, after many decades on this earth it has been heard to be said of thousands of other adored females – so as Charles Spencer once suggested about an especially renown Devonshire Duchess Ancestor of his, it should all be taken with a piece of personal pinch of salt!

Here a portrait of her in her pomp –

Although her big toe was a beauteous let down!

BUT it was the profligate losing gambling which did for her >>>

AND so someone took her place as the new Duke's bed warmer, although some say it was an early example of An Aristocratic 'Menage a trois!'

So welcome here the even more stunning (?) replacement >

The ever so sexy Lady Elizabeth Foster - the rival who would take over all!

↑ But back to those Mitfords:- perhaps one of the other 6 sisters deserves a special mention?

First may I point out they were somewhat outspoken and being so well off felt they could say/do what they *whimmed*!

But, Diana discovered that she was not above the UK World War Law!

Unity preferred taking her own life than facing up to consequences of metaphorically sleeping with the Enemy's Chief & Close Confidante Cohorts.

The others in the Clan had their own brand of conflicting Political leanings – each to their own! And might have favoured their own choice with monetary support.

But one of the six went one rebellious step further than any of the other 5 by opposing Daddy and with unprecedented gall denounce his ultra-Conservative Fascist stance and incredibly renounced her inheritance even before she had left her teens! *(**She was the daughter of David Freeman-Mitford, 2nd Baron Redesdale**)*

This coupled with her limited scholastic achievements – no GCEs for her: even our People's Princess and her Love Rival got at least 2 GCSEs between them!

But like our dear departed Queen she too married a cousin – hers a second which might show how limited her gene pool change choices were?

They moved to London and lived in the East End, then mostly a **poor** industrial area. Mitford gave birth at home to a daughter, Julia Decca Romilly, on 20 December 1937. The baby died in a measles epidemic the following May – the disease didn't distinguish between status!

Fortunately they had a second daughter, *Donk* in 1941, but then, in the same year, unfortunately, the War then took dear Esmond away after a successful bombing run!

Civil Rights Activists' Lawyer Treuhaft took over the spouse mantle in 1943 and both idealists *(she ultimately k/a the family's red sheep!?)* went with the US officialdom loathed (?) leftie Communist Party, from which they resigned in 1958, before they later having refused to testify the House Un-American Activities Committee. **

As far as kids go she was cursed, whether an ex rich woman, or now a new less poor than before one, one of her 2 boys died young – a immature 9-year-old hit by a bus!

The sad part was that she retained her Rich/Royal Nobility Stiff Upper Lip Character Upbringing, which in other parts of this Book and others it has been shown that such engage in marriage just to ensure a male Heir was produced and then the interest in the female/male dies off! Reminiscent of a certain Diana Family or two now internally separated!? Where upbringing love & affection was SUB-contracted to the latest Nanny!

So, it will come as no surprise that she was not a money short, lower class touchy-feely mum!

Hoover via his personal executioner's tool, **COINTELPRO** *(See the introduction to my Book,* ***The Rich Don't Give a Shit****)* continually had them on their/his Radar ** after her joining up with Martin Luther King & Co in 1961 and spending the night with him/them barricaded in a Montgomery Church from the Ku Klux Klan, awaiting rescue from the Alabama National Guard.

So, she dodged a bullet then, but not ultimately that Big C which distinguishes not between Rich & Poor, as lung cancer took her away in 1996 !

But what for me was exceptionally remarkable after her Civil Rights Activity etc was that, in spite of her poor educational upbringing, she ended up a Prize Winning Author: her list below, for me personally, puts mine into sharp incomparable relief!

Works

- *Hons and Rebels (U.S.: Daughters and Rebels), 1960*
- *The American Way of Death, 1963*
- *The Trial of Dr. Spock, the Rev. William Sloane Coffin, Jr., Michael Ferber, Mitchell Goodman, and Marcus Raskin, Macdonald, 1969*
- *Kind and Usual Punishment: The Prison Business, Alfred A. Knopf, 1973*
- *A Fine Old Conflict, London: Michael Joseph, 1977*
- *The Making of a Muckraker, London: Michael Joseph, 1979*
- *Poison Penmanship: The Gentle Art of Muckraking, 1979*
- *Grace Had an English Heart: The Story of Grace Darling, Heroine and Victorian Superstar, E. P. Dutton & Co., 1988, ISBN 0-525-24672-X*
- *The American Way of Birth, 1992*
- *The American Way of Death Revisited, 1998*
- *Decca: The Letters of Jessica Mitford, edited by journalist Peter Y. Sussman. Alfred A. Knopf, 2006. ISBN 0-375-41032-5*

....

Jasmine –

Her great great great great great grandfather was Arthur Guinness, founder of the Guinness brewery. Her parents Patrick Guinness & Liz Casey split up when she was 12.

But, from all above before, that I'd like to select... **Bright Young Things**...(from above) * I'd point out that Jasmine was no stranger to celeb types from an early age, as so many stopped over at her parents' Leixlip Irish Castle. <> Plus the Rolling Stones connection with Sabrina & Miranda Guinness, coupled with her God-Mother being Marianne Faithful!

So, her 2006 **'Hello' Wedding Photos/Invitees** would have been quite natural for her to promenade.

So, it would be no surprise to see range of celebs from older Lulu Guinness to younger Princess Eugenie and presumably her illustrious cousin attend plus her long-time friend, Angelica Houston, whose father, a long time friend of the Grand Father, Desmond, had his own Irish getaway on the Western Lettermullen, Galway Coast., just over the beach hill from mine!

Author Copyright

Scenic in so many ways with its famous loughs, Corrib is to the south & Mask is to the north, with the awesome Connemara Mountains to the west. Northern Connemara is notable, if not for just its wondrous sights, then more so, as it is Eire's most predominantly Irish speaking region, more commonly (locally) known as the Gaeltacht *(Well known to **Miranda**'s canvass covering Beau!)(**Ante** = **Before**)*

It was overlooking one of its many region's lakes that bore John's wife and within *over the neighbouring hill* baby-crying distance from Houston's beach pad – you'll see one of her family places in the distance where they introduced/welcomed *him* to local Irish food, even the local seaweed delicacies AND their specially brewed clear drink (*poteen*) hospitality!

....

Now back to a *'Honeyjam' sort of intro...*

When is the time most people relax, imagine 'Lazy Sunday' *by* The Small Faces *and yes, it is the ideal time for nodding off and dreaming: that time set aside for rest & relaxation – a time to start holidaying for most of us, but for John it had significant connotations down, away off Portobello Road way.*

His dream materialised that day of rest, though she would be there again working, although maybe he wished she had been **on** one of her many times off *holidaying*! But, the twins welcomed being the recipients of the related *featured* personal invitation, although no photo opportunity was allowed – as is in keeping with her continuing privacy *'enforcement'*!

So, to end, as **in** *'Dreamer'*, the song where the *dreaming* gauntlet challenge to achieve the most extraordinary had been thrown down, but, she had no need of such a song, as her own *dream* Ladbroke challenge was, **in** reality, set by herself.

Well, could she do something out of this world?
Some might say she did.
A clue?
...distant cousin's shop
(As once seen in an 'Adulthood' scene!)

(The Old Premises)

Once of Portobello Road, but subsequently moved around the corner to Blenheim Crescent.

The old days you might find some Eastern Latvian Bloc type female worker there, but when going around the corner the 2 Partners took shifts and you weren't sure who'd be there when?

A Model & Painter Duo – a quick detour visit to...

And, as we all mothers know, work can be such a juggling act...especially if you have kids..*...!

At a previous Show John noticed she was many months gone and so... .....*
Emails were exchanged primarily about little Ruby...and the business ..and one of her designed dresses...
Jasmine O'Dare Rainey07 July 2010 at 02:18
(Rainey was her married name)
>>>>>>
(Once and perhaps still a model...?) Jasmine's other forte was as a clothes & interior designer..
She once had a range sell out at a famous High Street Shop: her matching lines contained duvet cover/quilt/cushion. Although the sales revenue received did not match the effort expended creating/manufacturing the lines. ᴹ&ˢ
Her dress line also did well elsewhere – John even considered getting one for his wife...
(The stores in question were M & S + Selfridges)
>>>>>>
Honey * also had kids – 4 boys – a right handful – but she managed to cope with all the Admin complexities of a high street shop...emails were exchanged and she ended in her own style.**.
And she signed off in her own inimitable style...

Thank- you ....
Honey Ha**biba** Bowdrey**

(NB (No relation) ** Biba *was a London fashion store of the 1960s and 1970s. Biba was started and primarily run by the Polish-born Barbara Hulanicki with help of her husband Stephen Fitz-Simon.)*
(?Lady) Honey HaBiba Bowdrey & Jasmine (nicknamed Jam) Leonora O'Dare Rainey >>>

At the time I seem to recollect she lived with her family in a large flat overlooking the Kings Road; Jasmine was just north of Notting Hill...

M&S (......*M&S – didn't make the money Jasmine hoped for, in view of all the hard work she put into that labour!*)

<u>PS Although it seems lately that a certain Willoughby TV presenter slotted in quite easily & became the new fashion designer extraordinaire to M & S follow, 5 times over since!</u>

John continues... Honey was the mainstay of the Admin side and took on roles no matter how daunting to some? Caught her one day doggedly trying to unravel the set up procedure to install a new credit card payment system.

She succeeded, but frivolously I might add not all was a success on a specific kiddie's book reading side.

She'd ask Children Book Authors to guest read their latest publication – this gent was due from way off Devon, I promised to bring the Grand Kids, but couldn't as one went sick.

The next time I popped in Honey said that I hadn't missed much: The Local Power Grid failed in the Ladbroke/Notting Hill Area and so being a Winter afternoon, the darkness would have set in and so the event had to cancelled at the last moment as there would be no Lights/Camera & so definitely no Action! The now poorer Author smiled it off!

But the future Shop Seas got Choppy and I noticed something on their Accounts which raised my Financial Mind's Ringing/Warning Bells: things might not being going so well.

So I wrote to suggest a few thousand £ Loan Injection!

I was rejected!   Well, I wasn't that well known to them?

My Financial Rejection was Fortunate actually, but not for Directors like Jasmine who had already ploughed so much of her cash into her Business Baby, only to lose so much of it!

Not long later...but much before Covid took so many other businesses!

2017: *Their Company,* <u>Honey Jam Limited</u> *Company Number 05775368 went into Creditors* [C] *Voluntary Liquidation.* **(*Finalised 2020*) (*Finally got Covid killed off!*)**

(https://find-and-update.company-information.service.gov.uk/company/05775368/filing-history)   **And the** then perhaps poorer Jasmine might have then lost a pretty packet?

Only a view of the final accounts could supply the answer!?

And Portobello Road perhaps lost its *Old Worldy* Toy Treasure Trove

Only a visit and chat to the locals could supply the answer!?

[C] *A Creditors' Voluntary Liquidation is a process which enables Directors to formally close an insolvent company voluntarily. It's often chosen by directors as a means of taking control in the face of continued creditor pressure and the imminence of a Winding up Petition.*

But a Company Trawl threw up that in certain intervening years a lady with the surname <u>*'Ross'*</u> *(?) was part of the Honeyjam Company Scene – However* it was the address shown which threw up its **Jointly** Owned Lands Registry Oddity:

RESTRICTION: No disposition by a sole proprietor of the land (<u>not being a trust corporation</u>**) under which capital money arises is to be registered except under an order of the registrar or of the Court!?**

So, what was that all about? Old Sam's <u>*Trust Stuff*</u> rearing its head?

I leave that to you all! (A Mya Aside-*(Needless to say John knows!)*

For me the end was inevitable, not just for the Accounts foreboding, but simply like her illustrious Ladbroke Grove Cousin who too discovered technology is a great innovator, but a great destroyer of already well-established businesses who cannot embrace the new ways/methodology: hers the handheld recorder, with Honeyjam, the I-Pad which crushed old style building blocks/wooden toys materials etc which lay in its devouring path!

One shareholder lost a packet; another bought the toy stock for a song!

Yet, strangely, another got away owing a similar packet! ? But not a case of (toy) 'swings & roundabouts! However, the Ever Inventive Guinness Girl, once the face of Goya now apparently counting for nothing, but undeterred was already trying to reinvent herself in the Modelling & other known to her fields of activity as her photo would pop up in the (? Now defunct?) Evening Standard, although the cynics amongst you might say (if you knew?) her illustrious Cousin worked for its owner, a certain Mr Ledbedev, who, like his employee, links up Royally back to our Historic Kings & Queens: his good mate Mikhail Gorbachev (D. 2022) used to Annually Celebrate his wife (D.1999 – Leukaemia), Raisa's Cancer Charity Foundation, at times in his next door neighbour's garden space!?

Where?

Below, none other than in Hampton Court Palace!

 Author Copyright

Author Copyright

A regular attendee, apart from Ledbedev and his Guinness Employee, is a certain actor of some renown?

Hello Hugh (Author Copyright)

Honey went back to her first love, painting, and the accomplished artist in her can be demonstrated at **homegirlhoney**.

Another Connected Addendum:- *Evgeny and another friend, once in high places, but now the media cameras are not so friendly.*

Pity his stay in power was so dramatically curtailed!

But not before (in his Prime Minister role) bestowing a Special Title upon his friend!

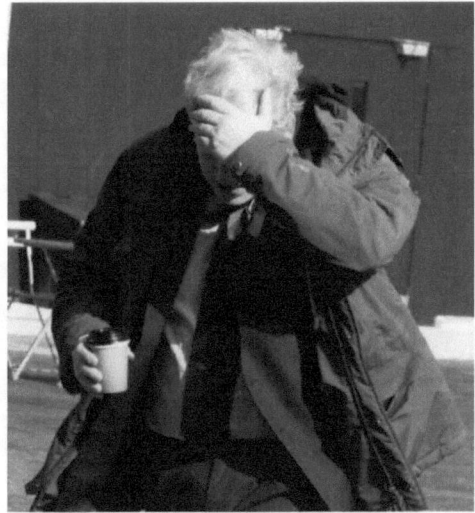

Author Copyright

2010 Evgeny Lebedev at the 10th anniversary Wikipedia party, London – Many Creative Commons Thanks to Author Allan Warren. His full title is Baron Lebedev, of Hampton in the London Borough of Richmond upon Thames and of Siberia in the Russian Federation!

His father >>>

<u>Alexander in 2019 <></u>
<u>Many thanks to **duma.gov.ru**.(CC Attribution 4.0 international licence)</u>

Evgeny's 'mother-in-law' is ONLY seven years his junior! ↓↓↓

<u>NB</u> *His father 'Alexander' apparently a Russian KGB Colonel and future Oligarch(?) married a Russian teen many years ago, many years his junior of 27 years.*

BUT After some 20 years & children later his 'Model' 'Elana' seems to be calling it quits?

AND perhaps some slight salt in a rejected breakup wound her latest 'beau' is Serbian!?

AND for those not in the know Alex publicly supported the Russian (?war mongering) annexation of Crimea!?

Lena can be seen in Vogue as perhaps her (younger!) fella Taras Romanov another model!

Alex, using his KGB (?) or Parliamentary position saved Lena from a drug related prison term when arrested at the tender age of 16 – they married when she was 18.

PART 10: POOR MICHELLE BUT NOT THE PROPERTY

Many think of the Guinness Dynasty as one with a never-ending pot of gold for all with that Surname?

But you cannot be further from the reality of things: Jasmine also mentioned such, that not all are inundated, only the select few.

Hence there is a poor side!

Well, poorer....

One such exemplifying this is a lady called Michelle Guinness.

It's oddly coincidental that Michelle said not all Guinness Named Family Members were wealth off, the same I found applied to certain Goldsmiths.

I mean Kate's Mère was a Goldsmith, but fortunately wealth ultimately found her, although through marriage & that union also spawned her own profitable party-catering side-line.

And coincidentally Kate's Husband's Mother's, one time proclaimed, best friend had a similar one going on many years ago. (Also another Kate – explained Chapters Back!)

So, let's encroach upon their <u>Dynastic Domain</u>.

The family has many strands, even a poor Religious linked one: ask Michelle and she will let you know, *although we disagreed about the English Arm's London properties, as to which had the biggest garden!*

These might just be couples of couples

of small open◇larger◇secluded◇grander, or more so

(*Including a couple linked &/or related!*) cited/sighted examples:

(All Author Copyright)

More to follow in later Chapters...

... *although we disagreed about the English Arm's London properties, as to which had the biggest garden...*
For her it was <u>*More*</u> <u>*Phill's*</u> <u>*Hill-Topped Place*</u>; for me it was the <u>*Chained River Walk Home*</u> and certainly not the <u>*Squared Cumberland One*</u>, to name a third in town; ignoring the fourth smaller flat ledged type, as <u>*Town Flat's*</u> don't figure high enough here! (See Book Last Part).
The third & fourth, the great-nieces'; the first, the nephew's; the second the Great-Uncle's, or just like the Americans, known to me as *Great Uncle Sam!*
Or from another prospect, not aspect, daughters, father and <u>his</u> uncle!

Well, what do you think?
I leave it to you.

PS The Leasehold one's Freehold was Rothschild's, (that family again) who purchased it to keep it within the *Carouselled* Family (later).

....

Michele has spoken at New Wine, Greenbelt and Spring Harvest as well as for the WI, Rotary, and Inner Wheel. She has even appeared at luncheons for flower arrangers - without ever having arranged a flower.

Michele Guinness was brought up to love and live out her family's Jewish heritage.

However, in her teens, she felt something lacking.

Searching for answers would eventually lead her to a destination she never could have imagined: marriage to Peter Guinness (the great-great-grandson of the famous brewer), who--to her family's shock--would opt for another kind of spirit and become an Anglican minister!)

Peter is now retired - The couple have a grown up son and daughter, and six grandchildren.

But to me, the Jewel in her Crown is her writing skill whose prolific catalogue puts my feeble efforts to my great shame!

So who needs Wealth?

And so it is one wife to another >>>

....

PART 11A: JULIA THE SAGE BEAUTY

Sabrina's youngest female sibling's love life took a hundred and eighty degree turn compared with Michelle, where Wealth and all its gilt trappings fell neatly into her welcoming arms.

True love at 18?

But the parents had more than a hand in arranging the liaison with her future millionaire beau over the next County.

Although Michael would as likely find it very hard to resist the beauty she was then, before him!?

From the resulting Union there came 4 children, the eldest of which she continued with her mother's tradition of giving her a name ending in 'a' – hence Natasha. (LATER)

But, here forget the Money/Fame/Royal Links (*previously best friends with Diana and recently one of the seven godparents of her Grand-Son Prince George*) and all those associated trappings – she put herself to very good Community use for those less fortunate than she.

And so, this lass, as I had shown in earlier Chapters with others, had two other commendable strings to her Educated/Supportive Bow.

A visit to Hammersmith Hospital might have shown you her office space.

And so, you'll discover her well accomplished medical first forté encompasses her second (LATER).

After initially working in publishing, she trained as a counsellor.

Her first counselling job was as a volunteer for Westminster Bereavement Service and then she began to experience traumatic loss first hand when she had to do personal visits to the bereaved – her own personal traumatic experiences would occur much later e.g. her friend Princess Diana; her Sister's grief when her husband had apparently committed suicide; and most recently possibly when one of her daughters was diagnosed with cancer!? (LATER)

She also did stints in a drop in centre for MIND.

In 1994 she helped launch and establish Child Bereavement UK with Jenni Thomas as Founder (Another prolific author!), I worked as Founder Patron to establish and launch Child Bereavement UK (*via The Anna Freud Centre*), which is now the leading national charity that supports families and trains professionals when a child dies or when a child is bereaved. (LATER)

And amongst her other varied Charity roles, she was Chairman of the fundraising arm of the charity Wellbeing (formerly Birthright) – *which is dedicated to improving women's and birthing people's experiences of pregnancy and childbirth by promoting respect for human rights. It believes that all women and birthing people are entitled to respectful maternity care that protects their fundamental rights to dignity, autonomy, privacy and equality.*

A psychotherapist specialising in grief and then worked as a bereavement counsellor in the NHS paediatrics department of St Mary's Hospital, Paddington, where she pioneered the role of maternity and paediatric psychotherapy.

She has said that a trauma is a psychic wound that has not been processed, and is stored in the fight/flight/freeze part of the brain, the amygdala, and that EMDR [E] is the best evidence-based treatment for trauma.

[E] *Eye movement desensitization and reprocessing (EMDR) therapy is a mental health treatment technique. This method involves moving your eyes a specific way while you process traumatic memories. EMDR's goal is to help you heal from trauma or other distressing life experiences. EMDR works by helping people move past trauma, anxiety, or certain other mental health disorders. But if you have a condition you were born with or was passed down through your family, or you're dealing with complications from a brain injury, EMDR may not be appropriate or helpful.*

NB1 Because stability must come first, you don't use EMDR to process trauma when a patient is actively abusively using alcohol, drugs, or something to help them feel less. You can't effectively practice EMDR phases 3 – 8 with someone who has yet to experience a safe, trusting relationship.

It is a trauma therapy that has helped many people heal from the psychological wounds of trauma. The therapy is safe and effective, but there are some side effects associated with it. And it is controversial because of these **potential risks and supposed lack of research**, *but the controversy may be unwarranted.*

(It is interesting, that word controversy, since her Guinness Family were schooled in the Montessori Fashion (Natasha's inner London 6 bed house was a stone's throw from such a school!) = The Montessori method of education is a type of educational method that involves children's natural interests and activities rather than formal teaching methods. A Montessori classroom places an emphasis on hands-on learning and developing real-world skills.

The EMDR also had a statistically significant superiority over CBT (p = 0.005) in alleviating anxiety. Although EMDR was observed to be better than CBT in reducing depression, this difference was not statistically significant.

NB2 Cognitive Behaviour Therapy (CBT) not to be confused with Mentalization-Based Therapy (MBT) is a type of long-term psychotherapy, which the Anna Freud Clinic run courses for and based on ↓ Peter Fonagy's Books on the subject. (BELOW & LATER)

They are also mentioned/recommended in Book 4, Chapter 2 of my Legal Sanctity of Marriage Series > - Emasculated Virility - The Eunuch Syndrome

Hello Peter...

 Author Copyright

In 2021 she announced the launch of Grief Works App, a mobile application for iOS and Android to help the bereaved navigate their grief.
She was appointed Member of the Order of the British Empire (MBE) in the 2016 New Year Honours for services to bereaved parents of babies.
She is a vice president of British Association for Counselling and Psychotherapy and is an Honorary Doctor of Middlesex University.

And like Michelle before, a resounding author in her field:

1. *Grief Works: Stories of Life, Death and Surviving, was published in 2017.*
2. *This Too Shall Pass: Stories of Change, Crisis and Hopeful Beginnings is published on 5 March 2020. ##*
3. *Every Family Has A Story: How we inherit love and loss was published by Penguin Life on 17 March 2022.*

Written when she stepped back and went into Private Practice: the Book is similarly structured like its predecessor, Grief Works!

HER BOOKS HAVE BEEN PUBLISHED IN 17 FOREIGN TERRITORIES.

(I feel so small in comparison!) (At least the Professional that she is, she cannot be accused of having her Book(s) Ghost-written, like the Guitarist Member of the Group her two oldest sisters palled about with over so many past decades – Keith knows about the Autobiography Fox I'm alluding to!)

(All Author Copyright Below)↓

Author Copyright

....

Author Copyright

....

Author Copyright

So, encompassing the next which is to follow, as plaudits go **she is head and shoulders above all the rest!?**

And so, Diana's (now/then squabbling?) Children knew where to come for advice, or Kate & Wills with their Anna Freud visits and comments, which was her husband's own pet project ## (LATER).
In 1994 she *helped* launch and establish # **Child Bereavement UK**, and. as founder patron, continued to play an active role in the charity.

He husband was already a Trustee in the Anna Freud Society, 1993 ##

And here is your introduction:-

The old original seemingly ram-shackled office of old, situated in an out of the way location.
The office staff then numbering less than 15, were situated on 2 floors, with the brunt of the work done upstairs; the lower the rest area and where photos recalling great events/achievements were posted.

The most memorable getting the newly arrived Australian Men's Cricket team to take part in their Charity Golf match!

Author Copyright

Just outside, along the road was an expansive park area where Easter featured in communal children's activities like egg hunts or rolling down the hill etc. with plenty of hikes in the great country outdoors, which her daughter would be the first to advocate.

Author Copyright

To get you an idea where it was situated off the Oxford Road

Hell Fire Caves close by and Bledlow Ridge a few miles away from that hidden away in a quiet road, the High Wycombe HQ.

NB Registered office address changed from Clare Charity Centre Wycombe Road Saunderton High Wycombe Buckinghamshire HP14 4BF to Unit B Knaves Beech Way Loudwater High Wycombe HP10 9QY on 20 August 2019

When their Patroness & Hubby lived quite close by in London, in their Connaught Square abode, which they sold at a tidy million or so £ profit, a time she used to pop down to see her staff.
This home ^{See} is where her daughter dipped her toes into being a Secretary for the Country Landowners Association – she has come a long way from there (To Follow). ^{See} Part 12...
(An example of the type of House you get for your several millions)>

(Author Copyright)

The car and external renovation work is optional.
But you do get a Garden Square reserved for residents' use!
Tony Blair # and # Wife Cherie moved in down just down the road – <u>plus then at least four on duty Metropolitan Police Service Diplomatic Protection Group Diplomatic Protection Group officers.</u>

And here another Regal Link:-

Connaught Square is mainly a series of four-storey terraced houses surrounding a private communal garden planted with mature trees, shrubs and flower beds, for sole use of the residents!.
It was the first square of city houses to be built in Bayswater. It is named after a royal, the Earl of Connaught * who was from 1805 until death in 1834 the second and last Duke of Gloucester and Edinburgh, and who maintained his fringe-of-London house and grounds on the land of this square and Gloucester Square.
* Prince William Frederick, Duke of Gloucester and Edinburgh (15Jan1776-30Nov1834) was a great-grandson of King George II ** & nephew + son in law of King George III. ** He was the grandson of both Frederick, Prince of Wales (George II's eldest son), and Edward Walpole. Prince William married 1st Cousin Princess Mary***, the fourth daughter of George III. Queen Victoria was her niece!

Editor's Note: * It is interesting to know of yet another centuries old Royal who managed to become owner of such Prime London Land! (the Dukes of Westminster & Northumberland were similarly endowed! = Guinness friends). Also note the use of the favoured William name which is currently used by our Prince.
As was the also favoured George ** which further muddies the Regal memory recollection, adding to the two Greek ones earlier!
And lastly that dear Mary *** name which further muddies the Regal memory recollection, with the Marys named before!

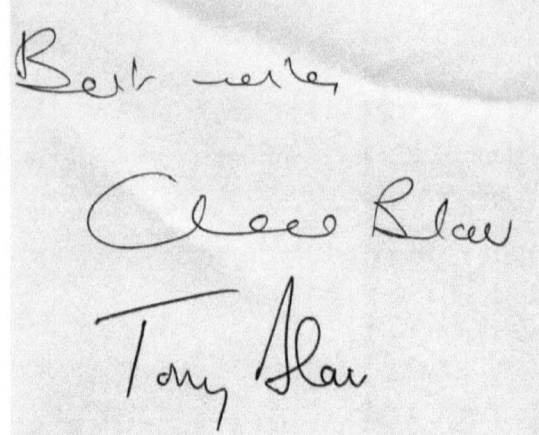 ↑ # **But that story is not for here**!

Although Tone's Organisation's Russian Dissociation will be – much later...

So, you've had an idea why I called Julia a sage: obviously the brainbox of the siblings and blessed to have married one her equal and business shrewd with it – so it is no shock to see their daughter, Nat who's inherited so much of the talent: University Degree + plus the all-important Imperial College Business School Diploma and future Experience. (Later)

PART 11b: ANITA THE BEAUTY THAT IS RICH

Having been close to Diana and her boys it was no surprise that she was there with all her Mental Health grounding and Bereavement Advice Experience, she was the one for that particularly painful job.

Their mother's death really kicked in hard and the pain stayed thereafter!

But her special organisation helped/helps so many ordinary others, as the pain felt is exactly the same – Rich or Poor!

Just like it helped me when my first husband was taken from me by the Big C, followed by our depressed, missed him so, daughter who in her scanty party clothes froze to death as the car heater packed up when, with too much booze + a touch of something else, she lost control on that isolated snow filled hill bend!

If you can recall Part 4 above I mentioned >

"Nor, Anita, her 1st from the noose!"

This Anita was/is her middle sister who too suffered tragic heartfelt/painful though perhaps not unexpected (?) loss when her husband, Amschel Rothschild, millionaire heir to the banking dynasty, in 1996 hanged himself in a Paris hotel room while suffering from depression brought on by his mother's death.

And ever the professional and close sister, Julia was there no matter how long it took!

It took Anita 6 years to move on and marry her James Wigan.

But, more sadly she was needed again some years later as Anita's 15 year old Grand-Daughter, Iris, who lost her life in a quad accident at the family farm on 8 July 2019, Rushbrooke, near Bury St Edmunds, I seem to recall?.

NB Anita named her second child after her older sister, Miranda.

And here I will lighten the mood...

Her new (Wigan) husband's father was a Major in the Coldstream Guards and their motto is, *"Nulli Secundus" (Latin); "Second to None"*

James reared horses and had 2 stud farms one in the West of the Country, the other which Anita helped run, East, Suffolk way.

But occasionally they'd run their mares at southern courses. And so it was to Sandown (?) as I recall went the Horse Box et al, as did John, the betting man that he was...

He was given the nod by one part of Anita's crew and backed this first-time-outer @ 5/2 and was rewarded with a *Monkey!*

At the Winner's Enclosure, he rewarded Anita with a triumphant, smiling *Thumbs Up!*

(For those not acquainted with the term, a Monkey = £500!) (Not Bad Eh?)

There again just a monetary pin prick in their/her fortune laden collection(s).

For those who like the simple quite life, their marriage connection is far from it!

Perhaps it is just with the limited (rich!?) numbers who they pal with, but it then it must be inevitable that the local beau tradesman would never get a look in!?

Anita's first husband would set scores or more up on a path to an indolent future life with no more financial woes: I mean 'Amschel Rothschild' was worth a literal 'mint'!

Great wealth seems to follow their paths in relationships, as had Divorce!

Her first son James married Nicky Hilton, who was previously married 2004 to businessman Todd Meister. BUT That marriage was annulled less than three months later: so much for marrying on a whim!?

She married James in 2015.

Anita's current partner was also a divorcee:- the Fitzpatrick Rose he married in 1977; he divorced in 1991 – Eton Educated (as so many in this Book were) he married Anita in 2002.

As far as the 2 daughters go, they had a complex relationship(s):- the twist here is that Sisters Kate and Alice married brothers Ben & Zac Goldsmith, although Ben married in 2003, but divorced Kate in 2013 – adultery was apparently cited!

And in the same year, Anita married the now free Zac! But, no fairy tale ending as apparently for our ex-Etonian Zac & Anita divorce was on the cards, 10 years later!? But no strange thing for Zac for already having been divorced in 2010!

Other coincidentals his love of playing cricket and his outside endeavours:- he received the, already mentioned, Mikhail Gorbachev, (See Part 9) founded, Green Cross International Global Green Award! Mikhail friends with Evgeny Lebedev, who like Zac was given a Peerage by old mate (See Part 9) Boris Johnson!

But one significant aspect of so many of the above is their Philanthropy: well who couldn't be that with all that idle wealth surrounding them!

But Anita is meant to be also a kind and considerate person – wealth ignored.

This other significant aspect as with sister, Julia, is her demeanour – she 'apparently' is equally at home with the Rich/Royal & famous, just as Julia is with those ordinary folk who respect her opinion and advice in loss suffering circumstances, the Doctor Professional, she is.

But there are times when the Rich & Ordinary Others don't easily mix: simply put it would be a matter of funds.

John once complained of the price of *special* tickets when he went to see the Faces in Surrey, at the Drummer's Polo Park...

The ordinary ticket price was around the £50 mark, but to get in the Groups Privileged tent would <u>cost 10 times that</u>!

And so it is like the last Child Bereavement Annual Fund Raiser attended by me, (The motivational speaker/guest of honour was Baroness Tanni Grey-Thompson) the ordinary going price would be far less.

But, as in other more select *money talks* pecking order only the select would get first dibs at attending **such as**

- the *1st April 2006 Child Bereavement Charity, at the Sladmore Gallery, Bruton Place, with sister Sabrina, niece Nat & Ben Goldsmith's ^{MM} (yet to be ex* model overthrown) Missus,*
- *(* crazy really while he was being divorced his ex-wife's sister married his older brother!)*
- *^{MM} (Hence advertising that Jewish Intermarried Rich Families Triumvirate plus the Samuels make 4 >< Guinness/Rothschild & Guinness. (AND then Goldsmiths making an Excessively Rich Nap Hand!)*
- *Just as those Next Over the Page Nat Carousels try to depict.*
- **Definitely a John's craw in the throat:-** <u>**it's who you know**</u>**!**!!!
- *Just seemingly like the Spencers + Churchills + Washingtons interdependency mentioned before))*
  More guests included Samuel & Jamie Wroath, Prince William (see ante), Sahar Hashemi, Gerry Farrell, Olivier & Esme Lane-Fox and Lady Jane Fellowes to mention - <u>***a select few***</u>.

But no matter to her, at whichever she is still the gracious, magnanimous Hostess, switching from table to table...

Her daughter is gracious & magnanimous too, like her parents with the Children foremost to her concerned/caring mind. (Later)

<u>Footnote:</u>
There is also an offshoot in that each Christmas Time the Bereaved <u>*for any*</u> & all are recalled in a Special Service at **St Martin-in-the-Fields** the Church of England Parish Church at the north-east corner of Trafalgar Square in the City of Westminster, London.
It is dedicated to Saint Martin of Tours.

It is also a service which certain Police & other bereavement liaison officers recommend to those who lost a young one dear to them to attend, like a family known to me, whose daughter was murdered (shot in the back)! (But that story is not for here!)

The painful memory has never left her sister ever since!

The Charity has gone from strength to strength with satellite offices in so many parts of the UK <> Glasgow, Leeds, Cheshire, Cumbria, Buckinghamshire, East + West London.

But, hubby Michael is up there with her making his own great impact!

But first it is their eldest daughter's stage....

PART 12a: NATASHA THE SAGE FAILED NOT THE WORK

Rich's Love's Carousel of *Rich Love* ↓↓↓ revealed >>> (her husband is called Rich)

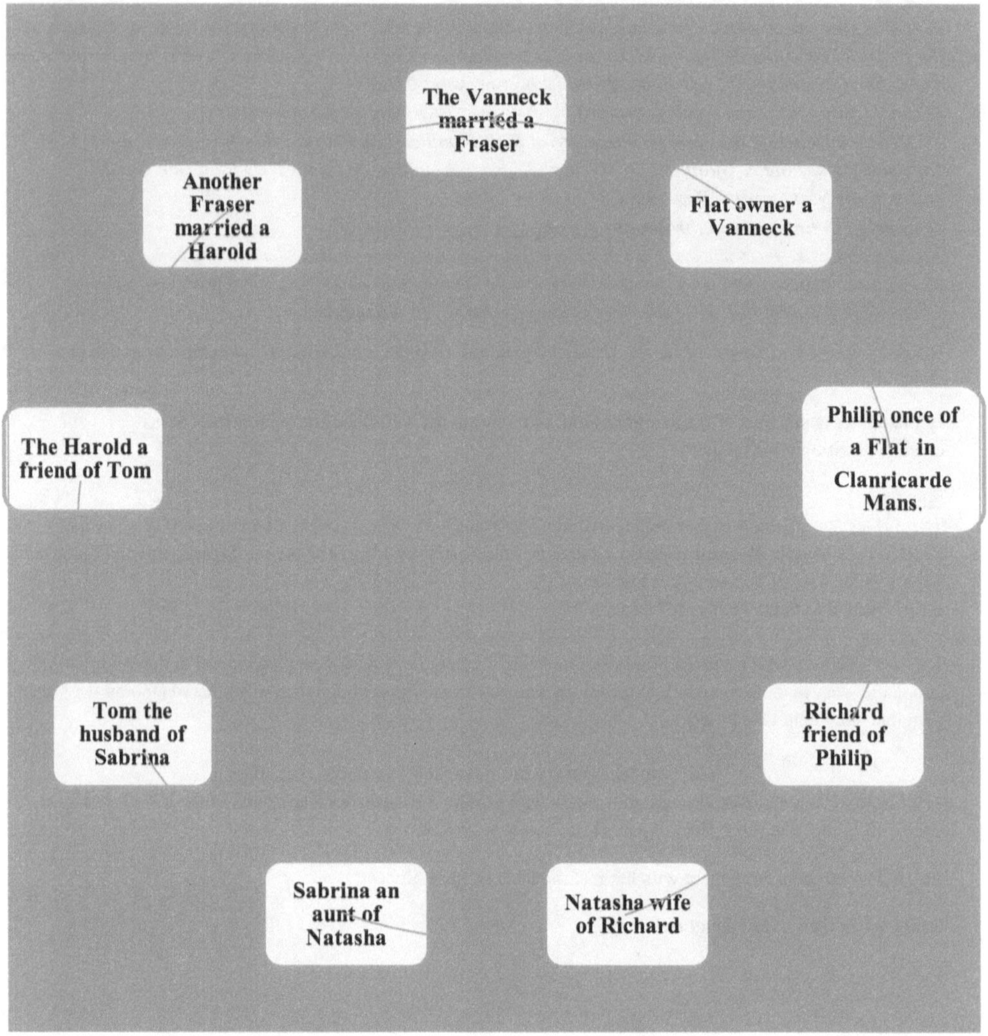

- The Vanneck ~~married a~~ Fraser
- Flat owner a Vanneck
- Another Fraser married a Harold
- Philip once of a Flat in Clanricarde Mans.
- The Harold a friend of Tom
- Tom the husband of Sabrina
- Richard friend of Philip
- Sabrina an aunt of Natasha
- Natasha wife of Richard

Author Copyright  (Yes, a distant memory, too!

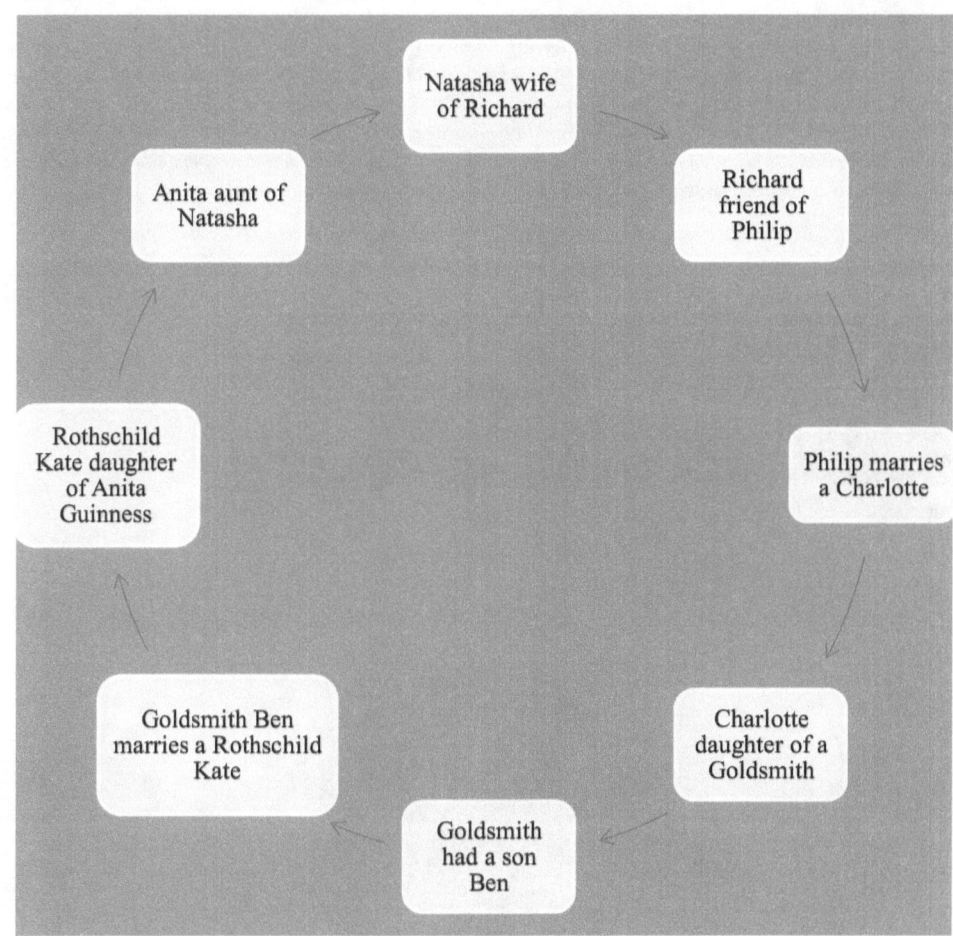

↑↑↑ - *And there's possibly more?*

- Fraser's Wikipedia was Edited by a Brewery Guinness lass
- Another Brewery Guinness was put up by a Channon
- Channon's pad at one end of Cheyne Walk
- Sam Guinness at the other end
- Mick Jagger's in the Middle
- Mick Jagger's PA was once a Guinness Miranda
- Miranda used to make 'Doc' Jagger's outside appointments
- But the Belfast news had their Brewery one dying some years back
- But his PA was actually the Banking Arm's one
- And she too is another of Nat's Aunts
- And so now Nat's *Puddles* are no longer *Muddy*
- And the two circles are now neatly sorta joined!

......Silly Linkages Over .....

But she was just another ordinary off the Cale Road Family Woman Inhabitee, in spite of her one time young playmate being none other than Prince William!?

Funny, you know how I like my coincidences and it was so with old Laszlo, one who married into the Guinness Dynasty: his prison incarceration site was in Cornwallis Road, not far from her new place. His would be the second if you recall Mitford's? Hers to the right in Holloway prison,. Although the nearest to her is the famous Pentonville Prison. So many in such a small Islington location: seemed needed to accommodate all those, too many, crooked elements! But it has gone well up market in certain parts since then!

If a lucky 'Muddy Puddles' follower, you could have crossed her path at one of the Muddle Puddles open days: here is one such example down St Albans Park way...

Her little son who joined her later on the testing obstacle course!

(Author Copyright)

NB1 The Boy/Child's face is covered according to standard privacy procedure, but her children may have been freely used in her own advertisements in the past!

NB2 After the event this one tough cookie just flipped him on her back and off they went!

Actually, John would *'muddy the water'* still further that Sunday afternoon. If it weren't for the fact he wanted a certain confusion resolved, their paths would never have crossed.

Today he would meet the sixth generation of the family, the fifth opposite, the sixth, little Wilkie, her youngest (son).

And there could be some strange beings invited by her there too
↓

 *Author Copyright*

Dan <> Available for Kids Parties but he needs a lot of Space!

The Big Man He Is!

And here a sample of her *Muddy* Wares!

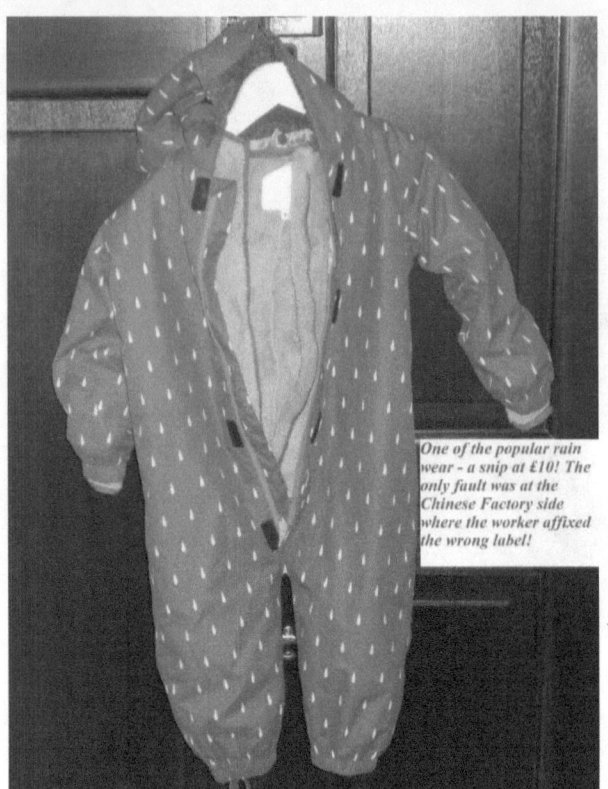

One of the popular rain wear - a snip at £10! The only fault was at the Chinese Factory side where the worker affixed the wrong label!

Author Copyright

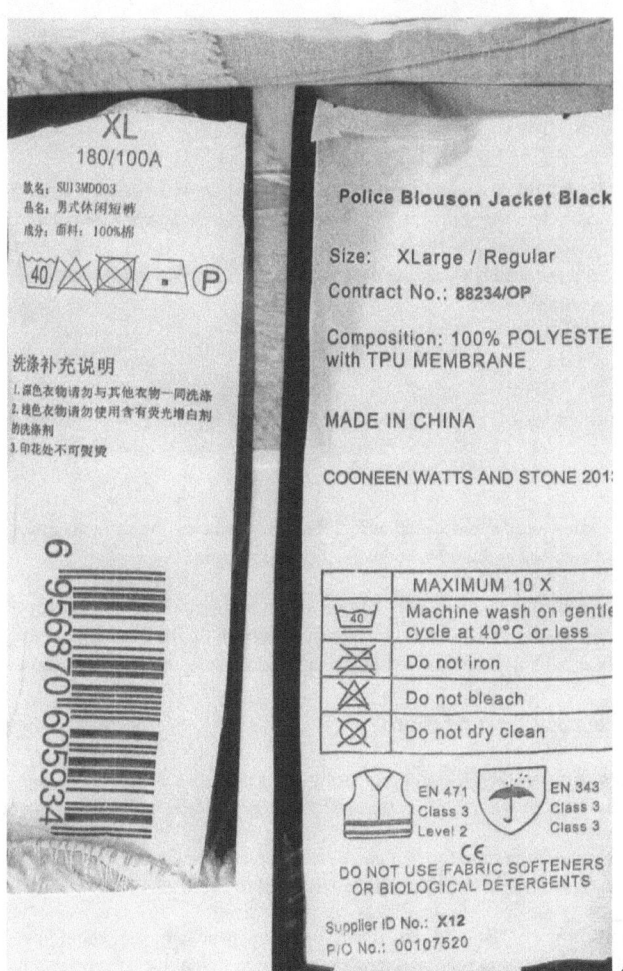
Author Copyright

Got a signed receipt just in case there was a serious fault inside.
There wasn't!
Great Bargain!

Interesting enough her signature is slanted to one side – the right.

And that would make her the only left handed Guinness Gal I ever encountered e.g. Sabrina & twin Miranda are both right handed etc. *(As I recall I think her hubby is left handed also!?)*

<u>For John, Somerset would come northwards to him unexpectedly and with it a sort of accommodating treatment he didn't expect? Was she different?</u>
Actually, John would *'muddy the water'* still further that Sunday afternoon. If it weren't for the fact he wanted a certain confusion resolved, their paths would never have crossed.

Today he would meet the sixth generation of the family, the fifth opposite, the sixth, little Wilkie, her youngest (son).

Though, first a fashion/attire coincidental comment, "*She had on her favoured pearl earrings – pearls – favoured just like Mrs Annan!*

Then it was those shoes… "*Oddly enough her aunt wore something similar in white at her wedding; she wasn't one ever for high heels; perhaps they gave her corns, or she had knee problems like her late mum?*"

"Or that she *plainly* finds them so comfortable?" My eyes lowered to his choice… "OK, you've got me there: open toed sandals mean I don't get sweaty feet!"
"So, you're a fellow flat heel lover, too?"
No response as John got back on track.

"I read up on the company before setting off to quiz the attending staff and on arrival was amazed she was there in person (There was no hint on the web pages she, the managing director, would come, but a staff member had hinted at it)!

When I approached I admitted I knew who she was and asked, while she was sorting through goods & paperwork, if we could chat – she agreed and the *first* conversation then ensued:

I asked about the company; enquired as to its formation, current set up & future plans; the networking links, then left, but she might have known more just by the hints I dropped especially the question about <u>*Dad's*</u> estate bookings, from which she freely divulged she now lived in North London, so could attend these outings more easily.
<u>I didn't press the point and left to watch the event unfold.</u>

Dan was whipping up the kids into an obstacle climbing/crossing fever pitch, it was free to be enjoyed and they did, but not as many as expected as there was a chill in the air, though John, later, had to point out other factors.

Then came the time to clear up and go; the time for *that* enquiry: the episode had gone just as that first time with <u>her</u>; there was a slight coldness in the air, but he expected the *real* chill to come when …"

As a Psychology degree holder & lover of the outdoors, if she shared his penchant, she would have recognised the *male spider* approach: he knew <u>she</u> another female, too, had the power; would she exercise it now, or **in the future**?
Would his rapprochement be met with rebuff, and show of fangs???

"The event had drawn to its close and packing up was the order of the day – it was then or never … I approached with the half price factory reject clothing I bought for the grand-kids; money in hand, proffered with a <u>*signed*</u> receipt request, although the <u>*real request*</u> was to follow and the *second* conversation then ensued:

'I've met Royals & celebs and they felt the same about the Press how they misrepresent, even fabricate, things about them, so…<u>Can I ask a personal question about a certain article?</u>'

Her back was half to me as she turned to hand me her change & signed receipt and then we were truly face on for the first time despite our having conversed earlier – I expected the Too Bothered Acid Tongued Rich Retort *'who are you, do I know you, or wish to know you?*
<u>Yet, she indulged my question, without reproach!!!</u>

"*OK.***"**

'I read an article about your <u>Aunt</u> where it was claimed she was 'hacked', but she was neither blackmailed as expected, nor the foreign perpetrators caught <u>(As expected, I thought to myself)</u>. Was it true?'

'Yes and it was a very difficult time for her, but it is now in the past, a distant memory; I don't think anybody was caught.'

She thought again and re-iterated,

'No, I don't think so.'

I thanked her and left, never intending our paths would cross thereafter. I unsubscribed myself from the firm's web site: I had got what I was after, but felt the need to explain – again I couldn't resist the temptation to put my oar in #, as I wrote about the company & its personnel's performance on the day where I felt they missed several tricks to boost sales and the # mislabelling!?.
I did this for her with an attachment, then it dawned on me how her Aunt's hackers had tried it on me those many years prior and any sensible PC user would not open an attachment from an unknown sender!

So I would never know if she did and saw my explanation…..?
Or, in particular my sympathetic response to that distant memory,

The problem as I saw it was that everyone seems to lie, or fabricate, not just the press; doubts crept in as to whether what **all** the Police told me in the interview room of her statement was ever **all** what she stated, but just made up to see my reaction?!

Then I rec**all**ed the Notting Hill Station Officer's e-mail comment on the article which I had conveyed to him:-

> July 2011 Don't believe all you read in the press. Have a good weekend. DS … @met.police.uk.

………………

The full Guinness Hacker Case Details will be revealed in The YCTV story later on – where the Evil Alex will make his debut!

………………

It is coincidental that she married a fella called, *'Rich'*, but guess who holds the golden purse strings? Perhaps, if you knew where she/they lived you might just find in whose name the title was in?!

The same perhaps might apply to her also richly connected cousin's place, who married Rich's best mate, Philip, but it might be that they all just have so many properties!?

NB Nat/Rich/Phil all went to St Andrews! Coincidentally Speaking.

The lads then spawned their (avant-garde?) sales ideas there.

But that aside, *Rich after their joint venturing,* went down a more richly connected career path representing such as that luxury jewellery brand, *Vashi!* Nothing more need be said? Eh?

But his lady love continued in the same Charitable Vein as her parents: the Child Connection was Continued to so many's benefit, although indirectly.

So how did it all start, apart from those inherited brainy genes?

Well, in Part 6 I did mention her (ordinary) teaching stint...

But where did her Business aptitude/talent begin to blossom?

Well her Business Degree did help, but there is nothing like first-hand experience – so her Dad started her off slowly helping him along in his Family Business(es) Office in London [See], until 2013. These simplified down consisted of 3 strands:

To manage and develop start-up projects in her father's investment portfolio – in the main these were:

1. *Murex Energy (See also Part 14): renewable start up launched in 2010 to identify, develop, finance, construct and operates medium scale renewable projects in the South West of England. (Murex is fully explained & figures more extensively later...)*

2. *Full Fact: was the UK's independent factchecking charity, start-up launched 2009 - established to hold politicians and political journalists to account. (Still ongoing)*

3. *Phoines Estates – the main family interest as it includes & covers their 3 vast Country Estates: in the Highlands [Tay], North East Somerset and Exmoor. Harping back to and continuing the old Gentry Traditional Pastimes <> These being the commercial shoots, but also included a commercial property portfolio, plus farming, renewable energy projects which will be expanded upon in her father's illustrious later Part.*

[Tay] Not that far from the Menzies Estate – Kate (See End of Book) being one of Diana's good friends; additionally, just North of my husband's own celebrated birthplace – below ↓

Taymouth Castle Perth Scotland

Author Copyright

John's first encounter was at Mells where he made enquiries for some on the possibility of hiring out some guns for a local shoot at their place.

<u>Ever the professional she replied with all the detail</u>

I am afraid we only let a limited number of nights' accommodation attached to a shoot booking for a team of eight guns. I am sorry we are not able to help. Best wishes Natasha.

<u>Here's John's Cynical after thought</u> - I considered it but my *Enfield* 3.3 rifle & **12** gauge, 2 bore [xx], shooting days are over.
The bouncing & bobbing rabbits were real hard long-range targets to cut down in my French Uncle's Dordogne Farmland, over the hill from a small neighbouring *Lot* Village.

Whereas the glorious **12**th Fowl targets dead easy to splatter at such close range – although the game wardens will make out some shoots are really challenging to down your game with a single report!!

Unfortunately for the birds, if the first one doesn't get you, then the second, or third, or fourth deadly will!

[xx] *Apologies to the experts amongst you, John, yet again, is wrong, 2 bore is/was used to down Elephants, not Rabbits!*

The appearance John gave was that he didn't go?
He may have tried to mislead me, but came clean the next session...

"When you arrive at the front gate

Author Copyright

you're welcomed by a specially specific bell/intercom code system...

MELLS PARK	
ADDRESS	CODE
House	B0001
Stable Block	B0002
Gardeners Cottage	B0003
Park Lodge	B0004
Berry Hill	B0005
Michael	B0006
Julia	B0007
Gill	B0008
Theresa	B0009
Clare	B0010

Author Copyright

And you'd wait there to be collected, or whatever...for me it was their Head Gamekeeper/Farm manager...and so onward & upward the Tor Rock Hilly Drive to be astounded by a 13-window frontage!

The inside is truly magnificent – their Marble Arch Home had a wonderful square tiled floor entrance hall >

- candelabra lighting above;
- a extremely large 5 x 4 feet painting to your left;

- on the right the hallway takes you to steps leading to the lower levels;
- oddly for such a large place, the slightly sloping staircase from the ground floor only had 12 treaders?!
- but a stunning 1/2 window at the top, where the staircase went right angled to the 1st floor landing, although the window had security bars across it, for the obvious reasons!
- The Blairs got around this small detail by simply buying the premises which backed onto theirs!
- Under the half window is another painting with display lighting above it;
- and when the sun hits the glass at the right angle the effect was dazzling sparkling –
- but that had nothing on the Mells Entrance Area!

NB Nat's room was upstairs and overlooking the garden so closely that the trees early morning rustling branches brushed up against her bedroom window pane!

But Back to Mells:

- Expensive Antique furniture sofa/stools etc fill the area;
- Ceiling to Floor true velvet/silk curtains -as in her aunts' shelf (see end Chapters);
- the light mahogany staircase carpeted from bottom to top;
- wondrous paintings greet your eye as you ascend;
- the very slowly inclining 9 treader staircase wide enough to fit three so no moving furniture in any cramped positions!
- The bedrooms really special to the onlooker/occupier, but the best is the one at the end of the first-floor corridor!

You certainly get your pampering money's worth:

- an in-house Chef, so your stomach is well sated;
- a skilled masseuse to ease your aches and pains
- even before the next day's shoot;
- thereafter the Chef takes pride and place
- cooking your downed fowl to your own special requirements!

And the table you are seated at is a rival for Uncle Sam's, here accommodating at least 20 at a pinch, but far less for those paying their hunting way!

- The white ornate cornice ceilings something to behold,
- matching the white (working) marble fireplace
- guarded on the mantlepiece by two bronze warriors on horseback,
- flanked by two double candle lights
- and capped off with a simple, though famous, Constable Country Scene Painting.

NB This is one of their three sites you can go Hunting within...

<u>(You'll take a trip around the Estate with John later)</u>

And the budding entrepreneur Natasha was, she knew the procedure inside & out!

And for this young woman ever onward & upward.

Although she didn't forget her first love, the great outdoors: and so it would be Daily Hilly Fields private instructor keep fit sessions and other such physical activities such as walking about &/or rowing around her parents Estate Lakes – no wonder back carrying her 6 year old caused her strong frame, no strain! –

Although *'let's go cycling'* might now raise an internal eyebrow between spouses as Rich's latest Chief Marketing Officer Job is with **Cowboy** a Foreign Company based in Belgium, manufacturing electric bikes for urban riders!

Rich Ascott + stubble as I met him

And how do they get the time to be together with his working with a foreign based company? Silly, like half the Western Commercial World it is obviously that his work all done on his home PC! Well, suppose so? Maybe not? (See their business success compared below..)

But seriously, in spite of her active life, life would shortly deal her a sickly blow! ᶜᴬᴺ

John then recalls the next time their paths crossed where things had developed for her as her Dad's confidence in her grew: he let her run one of his companies, although he retained all the shares via another company...

And so eventually *Muddy Puddles* became her sole Domain!
And a great expansive job she did...achieving top Children's Brand retailer in her first year, 2013 (further accolades in 2021+2022!).

And there's even more to this Natasha inspired/driven Company Arm:

We support Farms for City Children, providing full sets of waterproofs for children visiting the farms, so they can work hard and reap all the rewards from their week on the farm while staying warm and dry.
We also support a local charity, urban wild places who work to get inner-city children outdoors.
We are helping their cause by providing them with outdoor kit, raising funds with your help from sales of our puddle pac-a-macs, and running some outdoor workshops for them too.

But her star started at her Wycombe Abbey School, whose motto is *in fide vade = go thy way in the faith*
And that self-belief got her to where she is today, but along the way a serious hic-cup: ᶜᴬᴺ cancer was diagnosed in 2019 before she HAD reached 40! –

Then pre covid, but now 2022 in remission – thankfully, but whatever her drive was unimpaired as her work direction focus became more expansive mid-time in 2021 where she founded, **Muddy Puddles Nurseries** – her new full-time occupation, ᴺᴮ¹ having left others whom she can trust at the **Muddy Puddles Clothes Sales Helm!** (EG Anna Sara Riger) and with *a handy £750k in the Company's Bank!*

And for interest's sake the clothes shop distribution factory/shop can be found at *Bridge House River Side North, Bewdley, Worcestershire UK*

So, it's from one illustrious daughter, Mrs Natasha Vivien Rebecca Ascott, her married name, to one even more so, to *her Daddy*...and his favoured grateful interests!

Keeping it down the Family Way...

231

[NB1] *At the end of November 2022, Christie & Co, announced the sale of the Sunshine Montessori Nursery situated in Wheeler End, Buckinghamshire.* [NB2]

*Established by Virginia Roden in 2008, (**See Part 2 info**) Sunshine Montessori is a reputable, Ofsted rated 'Outstanding' day nursery that can accommodate up to 45 children aged between three months and eight years.*

[NB2] *Children can also enjoy access to a forest school which compliments their* [NB3] *Montessori ethos.*

Following a confidential sales process with Christie & Co, it has been purchased by Muddy Nurseries which was established by the founder of children's outerwear company, Muddy Puddles, Natasha Ascott. This is the company's second day nursery setting.

[NB2] *Wheeler's End is just Northeast of the once head Office of her mother's Charity,*

One of her ever-expanding company portfolio: her MUDDY SUNSHINE LTD k/a The Chargor/Mortgagor leased the property known as the Old School, Bullocks Farm Lane, Wheeler end, High Wycombe, [NB1] *Buckinghamshire, HP14 3NH on 4 august 2022 and made between the scout association trust corporation (1) and Virginia Roden (2) ## and assigned to the Chargor on 31 October 2022.*
NB Her parents initial domain was in High Wycombe before their move south, but so many Charity links remain there. E.g. >>>
Addendum Update:-

 *Author Copyright*

[NB3] *Nat's expansion has continued onward & upward in spite of her Covid Time cancer Scare!*

And here I'll leave you with...
A Right Royal Rich Puddle Muddle Connection!
...an *adapted* personal Early Hour (Mya) contribution insight aside:-
...*she provides coats for refugee children in the UK and Calais – all their seconds, ...put back into the refugee drop-in she works at...*
I can certainly vouch for the quality of the product, though I never knew she was so versatile, athletic, creative, caring and giving especially as she was one of those privileged born into money and connections, although nannies are quite commonplace now.
Yet when speaking to her she is quite down to earth and practical and easy to talk to – perhaps that was helpful in her teaching years. – but her creativity in her designs was one thing I was amazed at, really would put my book to (YCTV) shame, which she even helped with the ending, now, 'a distant memory', but that's another story.
PS Dad's place (one of 3 large estates) Mells Park, is a great place to visit if you like horse riding &/or hunting pheasants, grouse etc...they even used to let you stay over in their wonderful surroundings! (See before…)
>>>>>>>>>>>>>>>>

BUT, AND IT IS AGAIN THAT BIG SIBLING BUT:-

THERE ARE FOUR OF THEM.....

PART 12b: COMING & GOING WITH THE OTHER THREE SIBLINGS

One can say that none of the four had a poor base like John to start their foray into the great wide world outside: John's parents were post war immigrants who had everything they owned destroyed by Hitler/Stalin – so they were literally bases apart.
And with Rich parentage their Individual Trust Funds were more than most of us earn in a Lifetime......John ascertained!

Here is story from my,
Plain Jane Guinness & I Once...Chapter Thirty Six: Where There's a <u>Will</u>, There's a Way (Out) – <u>Trust</u> me?
Part 2.

Reminded me of the time I was with a certain Brewery Investment Manager who was quite amenable until I mentioned my connection and he, too, **evaporated** *before my eyes!*

Ah well, it was interesting how some can make a million, then lose it, only to make it again! And get, then lose, then get it again + a dolly bit of much younger skirt – oh you women have so much love to give – to all those (Much?)(Older?) **money** men, whose eyes you attract – <u>specifically</u>!?

This particular investment portfolio, *I was led to*, particularly with Nat's help, freely broadcasting her family history to all & sundry, was of interest, so it was an easy transition from those Energy etc. Directorships... primarily as it was the vehicle for the Trust(s) created for the kids' financially fraught free future – <u>*possibly*</u>? 10, or 20, or 30+ million plus £ split amongst 4 (maybe more) can't be bad for no effort by the beneficiaries – but... "But, I bet you know the exact figure down to the last penny?"

"Well, to the pound, but it was that *Stout* Money Man, I *palled* about with for a while, who <u>also</u>, unbeknowingly, had a hand pointing me in the right direction: it's amazing there is so much in the Public Domain, if you know where to look! The Guernsey Account(s) more problematic, but the Virgins Islands stuff, couldn't get my head around that door, so to speak. Even Cherie's lot couldn't help me there, or perhaps, just didn't know/ not up to it? ... **Do you know of anyone in the know**?"

"<u>**Well, no**</u>." *(I did, but I didn't want him to know, as it might raise his curiosity into my life, <u>even more</u>! We all have our own special secrets and mine were not ready for <u>my</u> Ray* sharing (*though later?).*"

"OK, but one thing bugged me, where does one find a *Bear's (skin?), or, Bear's head, or is it a Burst Head Settlement? Perhaps a commune in Kent's own Horse Guard's Parade?*"

Then the answer materialised:- **Coat of arms of Viscount Bearsted**

? The Historical Family Crest!

Shield of arms of The Viscount Creative Commons Bearsted Author Robin S Taylor.

John paused and smiled, "Amazing, 10, or 20, or 30+ million £ plus, but still small enough to be an exempt company, set up here around the turn of the century, but treated like a <u>Non-European Economic Area,</u> (EEA) with all that goes with a LP, or is it a LLP?! Ne'er mind. Yet governed by UK Trust Law? Ah well ... all above board **&** *so many heads*!

So what might they do with their money – property investment for one, or two, or more; there again one might have a large family so needs must look elsewhere; seems they all did and left their parents *honeying* around in *Apple* County.

So, *cash in pocket,* where did the four young'uns go:

Chelsea? Notting Hill? Mayfair? No!? Because these are the new upwardly mobile, debt free, young trend setters of the day, but not all flew the adult home area nests!?

- Well one preferred W10, within good old Kensal Rise, at around half a million, a snippet if ever there were one, those years back! Just a stone's throw from auntie's old, mortgaged place. But, in the poorer northerly part, a shorter stone's throw from distant auntie's *Castle-girl* cousin. Though this 2 bed, open-planned house is ideal for letting too!

The others, incredibly, incredulously, not there again!

- Well one, just adjoining my plain old Kings X hunting playground, bounded by Somers Town, Highbury and Islington, plus the Kingsland High & Hackney Road.

"Brings back some fond(ling) memories no doubt?"

He nodded approvingly, "And, not *skirting* the subject, you too?"

My gaze met his, but not my blush. Little did I know what *skirting* he'd get up ... **too**, in my future, in **his plain old** *(secluded)* **Kings X** *(hunting)* **playground** (such/the *appropriate words* there – you'll understand when we arrive there)?   He continued regardless...

"So, more *cash in pocket* was well spent, but they had still to expect more in Company as voluntary dissolution called it to an end.

Oh, those well-known *grisly* haunts close to so many memories: never walked at night alone near/through the Barnsbury Estate in my days without a knife in the back pocket, to stop a knife in the back!

- Well one, a Highbury (flat) way > Like sis, but a year later, not as good for around half a million, as lease extension due soon – thank goodness to have a share of the freehold, (like auntie did) to negotiate with self & partner owners.

- Well one, *off* the *'Calee'* (pronounced *Kal-ee*) Road, then < Only, £900k, a mother needs to find a bargain big one; so one less than the parents old 6/7 bed town house family home overlooking that well known Arch: made a £3m+ killing sale there, a few doors away from Tone's extended place. Oh and the use of those private gardens, kiddie's swings included (Oddly, these gardens are not free, but attract a Local tax!).

- Well one, interestingly enough, this, Lizzy's best friend, just like her partner's ex-partner's new Office place close to Hackney's East-End (a stone's throw from her friend's husband's office HQ, adjacent to Hoxton, a couple of blocks from a close to her heart Colbert Street *(Colbert? An odd name, but here so friend coincidental – Rich(ly) speaking!)* and on the way to trendy, expensive Shoreditch, but strangely enough surrounded by Hackney Estate Housing, *(See↓End↓)* so perhaps was better suited to her creative sculptural, artistic, canvas, photo work?) is also owned by her, the wife (Another Trust beneficiary? Well, she was *all-Golden* before!) I suppose £700k+ cash is pocket change for her? As with hubby's garish design excursions – Andy Warhol he's not. More of a 15 minute ** man and prize x?x?x?x than I'll ever be, though his you-tube duet *with a Rich fella* comes close to his * dress sense! Co-incidentally, a *RichMix* is just around the corner from them! But, do they care, with all that wifey money to sustain their whims and where that might take them? But, take care, the house is also in wifey's name ONLY! Sister's hit a black ice skid patch!? Although one wifey's said it's all tight between them, *so far*?"

"Ever the pessimist again John?" "No, not really, as you know my relationship philosophy that it's the woman who determines when any relationship has been determined." He chuckled, "But, if there is a family history of lengthy solid partnerships, then, like hers, then no doubt about its longevity: the literal, until death do us part!

Yet, did he sell a lot of * it, and so much more! (Rich, Brainy & Creative – what a triumvirate, that hubby, eh!)
 But, ** where is he now? ** *An Electric Belgium Bike Man? (See Part 2)*

....

A Rich Girl's Park Paradise?

Author Copyright

I included this picture to show it's not all Castles and Regal Abodes with them: The place above is in upgraded Hackney, London, with nothing Regal within miles.

The aspect of trying to go it alone and make a splash in the Commercial Fields *(No Muddy Puddle pun intended!)* means to come in contact and befriend the 'Ordinary' and not the Personage! *(The latter actually means someone of importance/elevated status).*

And for them the ordinary man/woman become the persons of importance in their business and social spheres.

And as mentioned well back I'll give you an insight into the Rich & Natasha ventures!

But first, like their Royal William friend, the marriage match started out by being at University together...And a shared Psychology Course brought them closer together *(How Freudian!? A reference to Natasha's Parents' Charity Link!) The Anna Freud Clinic).*

Although only Natasha seemingly wears that gold band on her finger – although this is nothing new to me, in this era.

Oddly enough both are left handers, well we nowadays no longer beat kids who use that hand in preference to the favoured right! More likely than something seeped in superstition?

Sinister in Latin = on the left, nowadays sinister = harmful/evil:- in days of old you kept your enemies there so you could smite them with your sword arm = the right!

Both, with nothing Regal about them, being the clever/industrious/inventive persons they are, they go from strength to strength in their Respective Commercial Fields! – Well up to a current point!?

THE CLEVER MALE v	THE CLEVER FEMALE
Univ. of St Andrews – MA in History of Art Minor in Chemistry & Psychology* *1999 – 2003 Love Blossomed! As did friendship – Phil Colbert also went to the same Uni and too studied Psychology!	Univ. of St Andrews – MA in Psychology* *1999 – 2003 Love Blossomed! Teach First – Qualified Teacher 2004/05 + Distinction Mini Business MBA 2005/06
Post Uni with Phil started Rodnik Ltd which operated wef until dissolution 2021-	2008 Strategic Business Director of father's Samual family Office <> Phoines Estates & Murex + various start up programmes.
NB To keep it in the Rich Family: Phil married another artist, Charlotte Goldsmith, whose * half sibling is Jemima Goldsmith (Khan) lived in New York, like Rich's Wife's Uncle. *Half sibling because she born whilst her father was still married to another woman! She has a long list of credits and shows to her name, as does Phil!	
As part of Rodnik we are not a Rock Brand, (2007/08)Rich on drums, Phil on vocals along with Peaches Geldof & Jamie Winstone on keyboards + Riley Keogh ? whose mother was Lisa Marie Presley (died of cardiac arrest Jan 2023) + Daphne Guinness ?whose father is the 3rd Baron Moyne (see ante re Moyne) **	At the time of resigning from Daddy's Company set up, took over Muddy Puddles Ltd (Child wear) wef 2013 which went from strength to strength even shortlisted Brand of the Year – Drapers Sustainable Fashion Awards. Then she expanded into another child related field >>>
** Just to show the circles they frequent(ed?) ** But the people they work with/deal with # now are more your normal Jack & Jill (?)	
Apart from the time when Rich and Ami, Director of Comms, were invited to Downing St. #	
Senior Positions:- Alfred Dunhill until 2013 All Saints (not the Pop Group) > 2013/14 Just So 2014/19; Vishivashi 2019/22 – then Chief Marketing Officer Cowboy (Premium Range of Electric Bikes) Based in Brussels, with partner store in Amsterdam.	2021 Founder/MD Muddy Puddles Nurseries of which she and Father Michael were Directors to this year 2024 – NB not to be confused with Muddy Puddle Nursery **12864324.**
Coincidentally, after her cancer scare, Natasha (with Dad) has gone from one Company strength to another: now involved in 4 more = Muddy Sunshine, Muddy Nurseries Group, Muddy Puddles Property, Muddy Puddles Online - Brains and Business Sense Exemplified, BUT Dad has his (? Overlooking) Director finger in virtually all of the above!	
*** Like Wife, like Husband, the Bike Business expands successfully (?) with 2024 Paris Olympics partnership with Adidas:- offering their athletes and guests in Paris a modern way about town fitted with Google Maps Navigation, Share My Ride, and Crash Detection!	
*** Hence perhaps his profit soon optimism: saw him speaking at 'Love Tomorrow' 2024 show under the banner 'Impact Entrepreneurship' from which we discovered that it was (5000+ individuals) crowdfunded, but unfortunately it was around-post 'covid time' so times were hard! He said that in 2023 they had ** £8 millions loss less than 2022, but by later in 2024, but claimed 2025 s/b profitable. He left then * But what grabs you is how erudite and free flowing a speaker he is! Co-incidentally ** Euan Blair's fanfared App Company can outstrip Rich's as it too has succeeded in consistent losses into double figured millions + even associated layoffs. ** (See next pages) Who makes a profit for two consecutive years is anybody's guess!? NB * Rich left Cowboy bikes June 2025 then joined LYMA ## -(much nearer home, NW1 5QT - apparent breakout pioneer of world-leading anti-aging innovation, **elite** waiting list for its $6000 device! And so John ** it is not always Hunky Dory in Elitist Connected Society Circles!	
Although He (Rich) + She (Natasha) = An Enterprising Business Brain Match Made in Heaven!	

LYMA:-

Puts me in mind of a Shakespeare Quote,

> 'Thou art a lady;
> If only to go warm were gorgeous,
> Why, nature needs not what thou gorgeous wear'st,
> Which scarcely keeps thee warm!'

HERE

King Lear, Act 2, Scene 4. Lear tells Regan (one of two conceited daughters) (Cordelia being the goody two shoers) that she is a fashionable lady. If she dressed only to stay warm (what "nature needs"), she wouldn't need the gorgeous clothes she is wearing, as they barely keep her warm.

So to all those who want to spend thousands of pounds to maintain/improve their skin tones etc – it can certainly be achieved in more simple, consistent skin day care routines?
There again those who buy such equipment can certainly afford it, so who am I to poo-poo it?!
Well you do get a free Globe Trotter Vanity Case, apparently worth just a fiver short of a thousand pounds!

Again perhaps an elitist piece of replenishable equipment?
And refills start at over £150!

BUT all this outward appearance concentration overlooks the most important aspect which needs maintaining properly and that being what's beneath the skin <> the inners!

Treat that with disrespect and all the outer skin laser treatment won't contain any Big 'C' attack:- there are many instances in this book as to how many died painful internal body ravaged deaths!

So the correct diet and a sensible everything in moderation should be the approach from adulthood day one!

Your laser thingy won't compensate for any alcohol, drug or smoking abuse – just tell your failed kidneys, nicotine destroyed lungs, internal digestive etc systems and you men out there and your cancer riddled prostates!

BUT regrettably everything is now how well you can display yourself!
Multimedia outlets are proliferated with such!

Enough suggested as I go back to my meat and two veg dinner!

>>>>>>>>>>>>

FROM COUPLE PAGES BEFORE

2022 Euan   Performance: Reports from early ** 2026 indicated losses widened to over £60 million, despite rising sales, following a push into the US market.
Walmart eat your investing heart out!
Photo Author = Village Global Source
https://www.flickr.com/photos/villageglobal/52530780781/

……….

Euan Blair started his internship at Morgan Stanley Bank in 2007; his start up company, Multiverse matches school leavers with more than 300 employers including Google, Facebook, Morgan Stanley and Depop, and provides on-the-job training tailored to the needs of employees, as well as personal coaching and extracurricular activities and societies akin to those at university.

It is interesting for any new employee to note that all have at one time or another been fined for various 'infractions'! So what nefarious/unscrupulous ways of working can one learn there!?

>>>

GOOGLE (ALPHABET INC.) has been fined multiple times, primarily by the European Union for antitrust violations, totalling billions of euros.

Key penalties include a

€2.95 billion ($3.5 billion) fine in September 2025 for abusing its dominance in adtech, a €4.34 billion fine in 2018 regarding Android, and a €2.4 billion fine in 2017 regarding search results.

September 2025 (Adtech): The European Commission fined Google €2.95 billion for favouring its own online display advertising technology services.

2018 (Android): A €4.34 billion fine was issued for restricting Android device manufacturers.

2017 (Shopping): A €2.4 billion fine was imposed for promoting its own comparison-shopping service.

Other Penalties: Additional fines have been issued by French regulators (e.g., €325 million for privacy/cookie violations in 2025) and various other jurisdictions.

Google frequently appeals these decisions, arguing that their services help businesses and consumers.

>>>

FACEBOOK (NOW META) has been fined multiple times, totaling billions of dollars for privacy violations, data mishandling, and regulatory breaches. Key penalties include a record $5 billion
FTC fine in 2019, a €1.2 billion GDPR fine in 2023, and various UK penalties, such as a £50.5 million fine for violating competition rules.
Major fines and penalties against Facebook include:

$5 Billion (2019): The Federal Trade Commission (FTC) imposed a record-breaking $5 billion penalty for data privacy violations following the Cambridge Analytica scandal.

€1.2 Billion (2023): Ireland's Data Protection Commission fined Meta €1.2 billion for violating GDPR by transferring user data from the EU to the US.

£50.5 Million (2021): The UK's Competition and Markets Authority (CMA) fined Facebook £50.5 million for breaching an order during the investigation into its purchase of Giphy.

£500,000 (2018): The UK's Information Commissioner's Office (ICO) issued the maximum possible fine at the time for failing to protect user data during the Cambridge Analytica scandal.

€265 Million (2022): Data Protection Commission fined Meta €265 million for data scraping issues.

>>>

Based on search results, there is no evidence that Depop has been formally fined by regulatory authorities. However, the platform faces ongoing scrutiny regarding scams, counterfeit goods, and user safety.
Key details:

Counterfeit Concerns: While users have noted that the platform is "rife" with scams and counterfeit items, there are no records of government-issued fines against the company itself. Although the company claims it bans users for violating terms of service, including selling prohibited items, counterfeits, or conducting off-platform transactions.

User Action: In one case, a user mentioned suing Depop to recover funds from a banned account, resulting in a resolution.

Regulatory Compliance: Depop, which is owned by Etsy *, must comply with trade restrictions and sanctions, such as those from OFSI in the UK and OFAC in the US.

*Etsy itself has undergone a major transformation from being a site for artists to ply their hard grafted trade to a wider audience with initial success, especially during covid, then found its site under false traders and AI attack as the ease at which they could make an easy fast buck copying original works and claiming them as their own! And as a consequence the real artists found themselves under a two pronged attack:- 1st = the algorithm Etsy set up to weed out all the falsies ended up scooping up the 'realies' who had to spend ages proving their authenticity! The bogus ones just recreated themselves under another false name, as likely based in the far east! 2nd Admitting AI defeat Etsy allowed so much as acceptable trade, but seeing a money-making opportunity started changes terms of operating, doing such as 'join our free postage' for goods over a certain amount, or you real creators find yourselves on such as the not promoted list/category, thereby putting so many out of business! (It gets much worse ** see later)*

This followed the need to make more money like the Amazons of this world as their profit making was becoming greatly eroded over time, such that mass layoffs occurred! (Like experienced by Euan's company, not so long ago, which I only mentioned as Depop is Etsy* owned and might experience the 'losing money' pinch ripple effect?! Such that the placement opportunities might wane!?) BUT there again the AI mass produced stuff + all the fraudie copies being circulated as true originals might still sustain rocky Etsy?! The picture as of now from both perspectives:

Well, many long-term, creative, and handmade-focused sellers feel that Etsy has made operating on the platform significantly more difficult in recent years. While it remains a major, accessible, and user-friendly marketplace for beginners, the platform has undergone a strategic shift that has created, according to many, a "hostile" environment for genuine artisans.

Here is a breakdown of why many creative sellers feel alienated: **
1. The Proliferation of Mass-Produced Items
 AliExpress/Temuification: A common complaint is that Etsy has become flooded with factory-produced, non-handmade goods, allowing resellers to undercut genuine artists who make their own products.
 Weak Policy Enforcement: While reselling is technically prohibited (outside of vintage/supplies), sellers complain that Etsy is slow to act against obvious drop-shippers, forcing authentic crafters to compete with cheap mass-produced items.
2. Rising Costs and Fees
 High Transaction Fees: Sellers have reported increasing fees that eat into thin profit margins.
 Forced Advertising: Etsy's mandatory "offsite ads" program, which takes a significant cut of sales for sellers with over $10,000 in annual revenue, is a major point of frustration.
 Pressure to Offer Free Shipping: Etsy's algorithm heavily favors shops that offer free shipping, forcing sellers to either raise prices—making them less competitive—or absorb the costs.
3. Algorithm Shifts and "Copycat" Culture
 Reduced Visibility: The algorithm is perceived to prioritize high-volume sellers and those who pay for ads, making it difficult for new or small creative shops to be found.
 Protection of Intellectual Property: Many creators find that when they post a unique item, it is quickly copied by others, and reporting these infringements to Etsy is often a slow, ineffective process.
 AI Saturation: The rise of AI-generated content has made certain categories, such as print-on-demand (POD) and digital products, extremely crowded and difficult to stand out in.
4. Limited Seller Control and Support
 "Renting" Space: Sellers have limited customization for their shops, and, more importantly, they are subject to sudden, unilateral policy changes by Etsy.
 Account Suspensions: There are numerous reports of shops being suspended with little to no explanation, or for mistakenly being flagged as "resellers" when they are not, causing massive disruptions in income.
 Protection Programs: The "Purchase Protection Program," while good for buyers, is reported by some sellers to have increased the number of scammers attempting to get refunds while keeping the item.

The Other Pro-Perspective
Despite these issues, some sellers still find success. Supporters of the current Etsy model argue that:
 It is still the best platform to access a large, buying audience.
 Success requires adapting to new, more rigorous marketing strategies, rather than relying on old, organic search methods.
 The platform can still work for those who find a specific, niche, high-quality market.

Ultimately, for many artists and crafters, Etsy has shifted from a supportive community for handmade goods to a high-pressure, competitive retail environment that favors volume over quality. (See link >>>)
https://www.google.com/search?q=youtube+etsy+letting+down+sellers&client=firefox-b-d&hs=xZnU&udm=7&uact=5&oq=youtube+etsy+letting+down+sellers#ip=1
BUT especially see Chloe Rose Art = https://www.youtube.com/watch?v=rmkQ6xGBTXw AND the upshot is perhaps the creatives might feel like trying out such as:- *MakerPlace by Michaels is a handmade marketplace where we treat buyers AND sellers with respect. Shop unique gifts now...*

<u>Post Script</u>…Depop is experiencing a transitional phase in its business trajectory
. While it remains a dominant, high-growth, Gen-Z focused resale app with roughly 30 to 42 million registered users, its valuation has decreased, and it is being sold by Etsy to eBay for $1.2 billion in 2026, a drop from the $1.6 billion purchase price in 2021.
NB The downsides to Depop include high fees, significant buyer/seller scams (like non-delivery claims or counterfeit goods), intense competition, the burden of shipping management, and a lack of strong protections, with many users reporting issues with unreliable offers and inconsistent customer service, making it tough to profit without effort, especially for beginners.

>>>

PART 12c: THE SIBLING SPOTLIGHT NOW FOCUSES UPON

The 'Child' seems to play an inter-connecting role between so many of those inter-related:- From above and later >

1. Birthright
2. Child Bereavement Trust
3. Anna Freud Children's Mental Health
4. Sponsorship and Trusteeship in any such as the above
5. Then the Royal Patronage (Willian & Kate) of such as the above via the Samuel (&/or Diana) Link #   #
But that simple name dropping you know they are in a different stratosphere form us all lower lives – the nail gets hammered home when Julia & Michael celebrate their 40th Wedding Anniversary with guests invited such as Ex PM David Cameron & Spouse!   There again the daughter was a playmate of the Current Prince William (soon to be King?)
6. The Muddy Puddles Children's Clothing Company
7. Followed by the branching out by Natasha into Nurseries
8. Then we're back to Child Mental Health as two sisters follow in their illustrious mother's footsteps!
9. Say hello to **Sophie & Emily – another brainy psychotherapist pair!**

Sophie

- She is a UKCP and EAP accredited psychotherapist with years of experience.
- With an MSc in the person-centred approach from the Metanoia Institute (UK) – with whom her mother also had a tutorial role.
- An MSc in Experimental Psychology from the University of Cambridge.
- Amongst others has been a therapist in the UK and Ireland, in the NHS, in schools, in an eating disorder clinic and for the domestic violence charity Woman's Trust.
- Additionally, for the award-winning criminal justice charity Switchback, which supports young prison-leavers to build a stable, rewarding life. Something (Home Office) John would be aware of as it is a perennial problem for the various Government Bodies concerned, especially the (re?) education of recidivists!
- Her office based is/was ? in Islington, London N1, just around the corner from one of John's theatre haunts, the Almeida and not far from another, the Donald Pleasance Theatre! And just down the Cale Road from her sister's large London pad! Although she also does work at her other sister's offices situated in central Bath, just opposite another John favourite, the Jane Austen Museum!

Emily

- She is UKCP accredited integrative Child Psychotherapist (An integrative counsellor believes there isn't just one therapeutic approach that can help a client in all situations. Instead, they consider you as an individual and your circumstances and use elements of different approaches to help you explore and cope with your problems.)
- Possesses an MA in Child Psychotherapy, with years of experience.
- Amongst others has worked for 7 years as a clinician at the Yale Child Study Center Outpatient Psychiatric Clinic for Children.
- Additionally, also teaches the Infant Observation seminar at the Institute of Arts and Therapeutic Education in London.
- As stated above her office is based in Bath, north of her Somerset home when young – Mells Park, Somerset – which area is also covered in this Book.

And what of Michael's Male Heir, Benjamin Peter Marcus Samuel, like dad his is a very different work route from his sisters:- you can find him at Egerton Capital (UK) LLP! (His Charitable Trust features with his father's as one of the financial supporters for the new Kantor Centre of Excellence.)↓ **(Later)**

1. And on the frivolous subject of men: One missing piece to my puzzle: who is Emily's beau? And if this were some afternoon romance movie the question posed would be , 'Why did she leave Yale USA after so many years and come back here?'

2. But, and it is a very serious But to end on: but why should such a rare disease assail one certain female member, not a few years after the eldest daughter had her cancer scare: the matriarch of the family has suddenly been afflicted with a serious rare disease, although Justin Bieber was affected by the self-same <> _**Julia Samuel, 64, has been assailed by Ramsay Hunt Syndrome, which is a rare neurological disorder that typically affects adults over 60 years of age. The disorder is characterized by facial weakness or paralysis of the facial nerve (facial palsy) and a rash affecting the ear or mouth. Symptoms are usually on one side of the face (unilateral).**_ When seen, she looks like a pirate with her one eye patch, but with a severely distorted facial expression! Not a pleasant sight!

3. But problems compound here with Julia's deceased best friend's husband, Prince Charle 3rd catching his male form of cancer

4. Then, that big whammo, Julia's God-Son's mother & daughter's childhood playmate's wife, Princess Kate has an even worse progressed stomach form of the same disease and as likely would appreciate Julia's Counselling expertise in this matter, only to find Julia herself has her own serious affliction!

5. NB Mother and two daughters ended up joining force under the Samul Therapy Practice Limited umbrella, concentrating on On-Line Therapy…. A true TRIUM FEMINARUM <> =our first special group of three <> here women <> another special 3 (See Chap 14f) then the family threesome (part 11b)(Which became a married unified foursome <>   *Alternative Terms: Depending on the context, a group of three powerful women can be k/a trinity, or three graces.*

BUT then the real deal outstanding special male three = Chap 16b)

Email Addendum (**Before Kate's Big Bad News Hit**) > Emily & Sophie >
Sorry to hear about your mother contracting that horrid Ramsay Hunt Syndrome, my thoughts go with her and her family.

And it is only a few years back your dear Natasha had that Cancer Scare!

But she's over that I hear – thank goodness.

Keep up the good work   Mya

PS I was very fortunate to attend your father's Anna Freud/Kantor Centre opening – a magnificent establishment.

I always imagined either of you would have ended up doing a stint there.

Then on Kate's announcement:- Sorry yet again!   It just isn't fair!
I just saw Kate's cancer treatment announcement.   I know how close your families are.
I hope you all pull through.   Mya

6. <u>**But all this shows the ordinary guy/girl in the street that wealth, fame and power do not buy you any extra time from disease when it decides it is your time!** (Expanded upon in my 'The Rich & Powerful' Book.)</u>
7. <u>**For all the above all we outsiders can do is just await the Guardian (?) publicised outcome!**</u>

NB 1:- Julia update February 2025 so better with no facial abnormality showing!
You can find her Podcast on You Tube AND if you want an insight into Charlie Spencer's Sexual Abuse - Look there Also!
NB 2:- Her daughter Natasha Ascott update got over her cancer infection also! And her Muddy Puddles Nurseries are going on at a pace!

BUT HERE ANOTHER GUINNESS PERSONAL LINK....NOT ALL THAT WELL KNOWN >>>

The twins were students there for a time & the first time John saw this comic, she was at a **Y.C.T.V.** (Sabrina Guinness Patron) show appearance.
(She would many years later also do a stint on Sabrina's younger sister's show! # below)
Ruby wrote the scripts with Dawn and Jennifer and later became script editor on their biggest hit Absolutely Fabulous. Her career changed direction again when BBC bosses decided she should present documentaries. Some time thereafter she changed tack and went on to gain her mental Health Qualification.
She is a prominent mental-health advocate and was awarded her OBE in 2015 for services to mental health – OF WHICH SHE TOO WAS A SUFFERER! *

She gained master's degree in mindfulness based cognitive therapy from Oxford University:- also Professorial & other links with such as the Mental Health Nursing at the University of Surrey + an Honorary Doctorate from the School of Psychology from The Universities of East London & Staffordshire. She was recently appointed Chancellor of Southampton University.
It is plain to see why Ruby ended up in conversation on Julia Samuel's Podcast, another known Psychotherapist!. #

Under psychiatric supervision * Wax underwent a course of something called RTMs *** (repetitive transcranial magnetic stimulation) and <u>went on new medication</u> and became a lot better.
In May 2023, Wax released her new book and accompanying audiobook I'm Not As Well As I Thought I Was, which details her recent life including further time spent receiving psychiatric treatment and battles against depression.

NB As a sole child growing up she admitted in an interview she did not really know her parents nor love them in the true sense, rather in a primal way, suggesting a connection to what is most essential and primitive, rather than something that is learned or developed. It is strange in an odd way to me, in that her mother spoke 9 languages yet could not effectively (?), or should that be maternally(?) converse/communicate with her only child!?

(***Repetitive transcranial magnetic stimulation (rTMS) is a non-invasive brain stimulation technique that uses magnetic pulses to target specific brain regions. It's primarily used to treat conditions like depression, OCD, and migraines, especially when other treatments haven't been effective. rTMS works by modulating brain activity in areas linked to the condition, potentially improving mood and reducing symptoms.)

Coincidental Addendum:- In 2013 Ruby Wax and the Centre's Chief Executive Professor Peter Fonagy discussed whether we can prevent ourselves from losing our minds:- Ruby Wax, comedian, psychotherapist, neuroscientist and one of the one in four people in the UK with a mental health problem, and Peter Fonagy discussed the many methods of mind-taming, from the "talking cure" and self-help to drugs and neuroscience. Peter as you will have been told, in this book, is the Chief of the Anna Freud Centre (below) – Prince William ## & Kate are its Patrons and a through a twist (?) of fate Ruby accidentally met the Royals on a retreat in the Scottish Island of Iona in 2025! Although, a coincidence, (?) well it would have been no surprise their bumping into each other as their paths have crossed several times in the past!<

(> Just showing how the Wax, Guinness, certain Mental Health Charites & Royal families remain inter-connected over the years!) (Keeping in a Family so to speak!) Especially when Sabrina above had a boyfriend called Prince Charles, who only happened to be the future father of Prince William ##!

PART 13: ANNA TAKES OVER FROM DADDY FREUD

The Prelude to Michael Samuel's (Next) Part in all of this!

(#)Oh it's Ann-oth-a Freudian Centre, this, with its innovative Family School Unit, concentrating on kids' Mental Health, which coincidentally, conveniently dovetails the other two, relative led, mentioned above...
(#)Just **Ann**-oth-**a** purposeful John misquote, but not of the Sigmund variety, otherwise they'd have had him visiting as a patient, not as a visiting guest!

Sigm. Freud
                                Later...

∷∷∷∷∷∷∷

Sigmund Freud was an Jewish Austrian neurologist and the founder of psychoanalysis, a clinical method for treating psychopathology *(the scientific study of mental disorders)* through dialogue between a patient and a psychoanalyst.

Freud's Sculpture inHampstead   *Sigmund's & Anna's Plaques*   *Sigmund at 16*
by Oscar Nemon   *on Hampstead Museum Outer Wall* *with his mother*

His place of birth, Pribor in Czechoslavia, and the year he died, 1939, had special significance here...

Anna, his youngest child, born in Vienna, Austria, which she and her family left in 1938 and moved to (?safer?) London's Maresfield Gardens, as Hitler's fervently whipped up war against the Jews was literally being increasingly heated up; the year of departure and her own life had special significance here...

Wherever the family stayed, be it the Czech Republic, or Austria, the result would have been the same... as, below, the iconic plaque in Auschwitz [dth] depicts: the camp = the magnet; the Jews = just insignificant iron filings!

But, and it is another of those Famous Person's Big Connected Buts, there were individuals in important places (One extremely Rich – Needless to say?), who were there to help get him out of Germany: Ernest Jones, the IPA leader [y], obtaining the many permits Sigmund & Family needed to get them into London; the Rich [x] Benefactress Princess to get them out of Germany. (Perhaps replicating Tom Stoppard's own childhood experience (see Part 16b).
Even then he/his daughter had to first undergo serious SS questioning, before they were allowed to leave! Not all were so fortunate: his sisters ended up in Treblinka and their remains became ashes-to-ashes history!

[x] *See also further below – (Item 20);*

[y] *Ernest Jones, another psychologist, who wrote the definitive Sigmund Freud biography, covering three volumes, from Freud's vast array of correspondence and the documentation provided by Anna: that so much of it was in German was not a barrier, as Ernest's wife, Katherine Jokl, another Jew, who also went to school with Freud's daughters, so was one of Anna's friends, spoke the language and was on hand to interpret, and is likely the one we should thank most for so many of those 'translated' quotes we bandy about now.*

[dth] *Auschwitz accounted for some one million deaths, about ⅙th of the total, but, and it is a Big Historical Factual Note But, it is significant for all those who choose/chose not to believe, or were born & indoctrinated after the event and are now part of, or willing to join the current Nazi/Hitler Movement, there is <u>No Official Written Order in existence between Hitler</u> ← → <u>Himmler</u> ← → <u>and the German Army Hierarchy</u> ordering the extermination of... And so, one can quite understand (**<u>Or, really, can we</u>**?) why they wish to believe that the Genocide(s) never took place! Although, tell that to the millions of Poles/ Russians, whose families were decimated!*

<u>***I suppose you really had to be there to believe***</u>

<u>***Man's inhumanity to his fellow Man/Woman/Child!!!***</u>

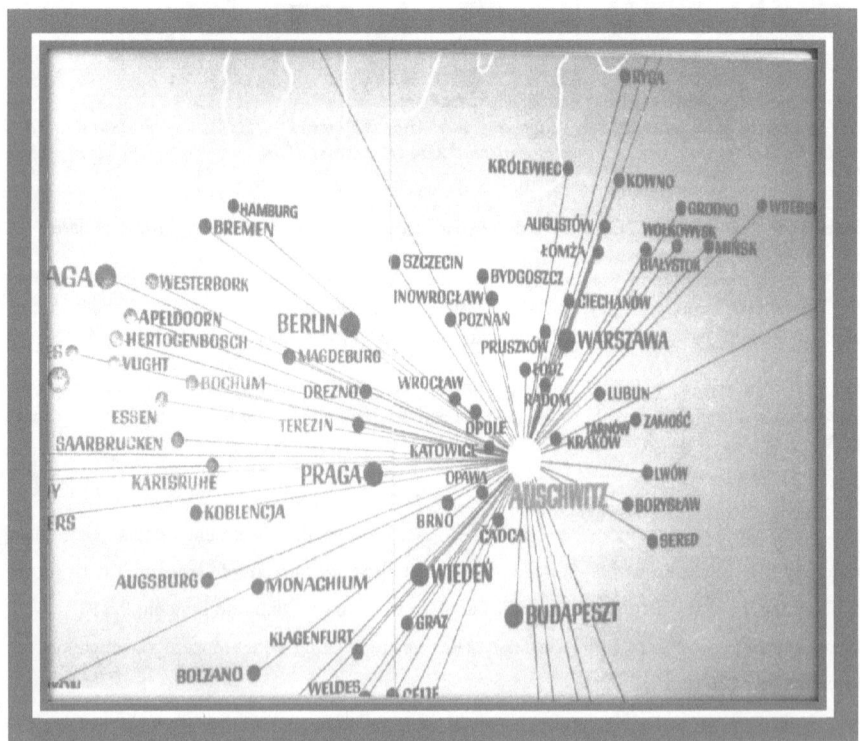

:::::::::::::::::::

1947 – Sigmund had died by then, but his daughter's bitter # comment on people was reflected in his, own *bitter*: *I have found little that is 'good' about human beings on the whole. In my experience most of them are 'trash', no matter whether they publicly subscribe to this or that ethical doctrine or to none at all. That is something that you cannot say aloud, or perhaps even think..* [22]

>>> *In one of many letters sent to Oskar Pfister, his friend, a Pastor.*

To this and Anna's, on the same subject, John surely, hauntingly, subscribed!

But, strangely, unsympathetically, this bitter attitude seems to run through other Freud members: cruel, spoilt Lucian also seems to have little good to say about people whose paths he crossed in his life!

But, then there is also the muter, more restrained:

"Men are more moral than they think and far more immoral than they can imagine." Though, John might have misinterpreted the immoral aspect, with his usual sex-on-the-brain thought process, but that is not to say that little did either of us imagine, as we discussed his and his daughter's quotes that afternoon, that, much later on, they were not going to allow us respite...
....

The daughter had a lot to say and write for herself: her educating imagination knew no bounds and on that subject she eruditely pointed out about imaginings, that they can be 'esculently' [E] *(Stoppard eat your heart out! John might say here!) served up any which way, but you'll never be able to sink your teeth into them! (Nor, (**John**) can they ever tell you something new, you knew nothing about, before! Only, reality can teach you, in experiences learned, sometimes, too often, the hard/hurting/unhappy way!)* [E] *=Edible as in Latin Esca* = Food

Coincidentally, she like Diana had unhappiness during her life causing each to seek the safe eating disorders solution to their externally inflicted, personal pain. Anna, too, like John, was no stranger to discussing Daydreaming and Masturbation. Actually, she and John shared this incessant, though let's not forget, **natural** *urge, at differing stages of their life, and she made no secret as to how much she enjoyed it (Nor* **John***, come to it!)! Hence the/her desire to write of such 'imaginings', in her, 'Beating Fantasies and Daydreams' (1922), but I'd disagree as to her assertions & conclusions. Her urge to was, like John's, at many times taking her over, perhaps as there was no man in her life, as there too was no girl in John's, or, an alternative# to satisfy her passionate cravings, (Perhaps she needed* **BJ**# *– my own Big Black John Vibrator!).*

Her passions were, in (her) the main, single digitally wet, satisfyingly centred on more Medieval Chivalry, *the kind where* John Gere's Lancelot *seems to be constantly arriving in time to save his* Julia Ormond's Guinevere, *but whatever, it was cause for father to investigate at length and he was not averse to quoting about it...*

And here you'll be in for literally an education into the Freuds!

And my own Professional Asides

Sigmund Freud Quotes *I imagined* applicable to the many...my auxiliary thoughts are **bold** in the brackets, as might be found John's behavioural links) - (But certain of them might apply specifically certain of this Book's *Female* Players one of whom tried to dip her toes into that pool of Love & Relationships and got Drowned by the Dismay?) Other comments show how the bounds between Doctor & Patient (mine John, remember him?) can become blurred and crossed with perilous consequences...

1. *(Just like I feel!)* "The creative writer does the same as the child at play; he creates a world of fantasy which he takes very seriously." (+ **Somewhere to escape to.**)
2. Dreams are often most profound when they seem the most crazy. (**But invariably so hard to unravel or comprehend?**)
3. The doctor should be opaque to his patients and, like a mirror, should show them nothing, but what is shown to her. (**But images can get blurred and misconstrued!**)
4. We choose not randomly each other. We meet only those who already exist in our subconscious. (**Or consciously in our day-dreams?**)
5. He that has eyes to see and ears to hear may convince himself that no mortal can keep a secret. If his lips are silent, he chatters with his fingertips; betrayal oozes out of him at every pore. (**And from his/her/the eyes!**)
6. We are never so defenceless against suffering, as when we love. (**But, revenge is sweet(er?)! – Later**)
7. A man should not strive to eliminate his complexes, but to get into accord with them: they are, legitimately, what directs his conduct in the world.
8. Illusions commend themselves to us because they save us pain and allow us to enjoy pleasure instead. We must therefore accept it without complaint when they sometimes collide with a bit of reality against which they are dashed to pieces. (***Akin to a person's Dreamworld Personification***)
9. (Poor John led to?) The goal towards which the pleasure principle impels us – of becoming happy – is not attainable: yet, we may not, nay, cannot, give up the efforts to come nearer to realization of it by some means or other. (**Perhaps another example of the *Positivity Effect?***)
10. In the theory of psycho-analysis we have no hesitation in assuming that the course taken by mental events is automatically regulated by the pleasure principle. We believe, that is to say, that the course of those events is invariably set in motion by an un-pleasurable tension, and that it takes a direction such that its final outcome coincides with a lowering of that tension that is, with an avoidance of un-pleasure or a production of pleasure. (***The serotine suppressor's suppression?***)
11. Words have a magical power. They can bring either the greatest happiness or deepest despair; they can transfer knowledge from teacher to student... (**With me the fear was that he would learn/deduce more of my private life/experiences, or lack of them?**) ... words enable the orator to sway his audience and dictate its decisions. Words are capable of arousing the strongest emotions and prompting all men's actions. (**But, with John & others, it's the music/beat!**)
12. If you want your wife to listen to you, then talk to another woman; she will be all ears. (**But, be careful what she hears you saying!**)
13. Where they love they do not desire and where they desire they do not love. (**So, no hope for the lecherous led Johns of this world! Presumably, also, not a sound base for any lasting relationship?**)
14. (**Between us, could John/I distinguish**): The ego represents what we call reason and sanity, in contrast to the id which contains the passions.
15. (**That's why patients like John retreats to fantasy land?**) The madman is a dreamer awake!
16. The only unnatural sexual behaviour is none at all.
17. (**As John and all other in such situations exemplified & exhibited**): How bold one gets when one is sure of being loved.
18. (**To explain John's and others in similar predicaments, their future acts?**) Let us consider the polarity of love and hate....·... Now, clinical observation shows not only that love is with unexpected regularity, accompanied by hate (ambivalence), and not only that in human relationships hate is frequently a forerunner of love, but also that in many circumstances hate changes into love and love into hate. (**<?> Best reflected in *Enigma's 'I love you – I'll kill you!'***)

19. Illusions commend themselves to us because they save us pain and allow us to enjoy pleasure instead. **(Another essential escape to individual Dreamworld!)**

20. In a film entitled *'What a Woman Wants'* Mel Gibson had his own special insight, which no other had: that of being able to read his female counterpart's mind. But, Sigmund's one special <u>self</u>-indictment was that as a respected person in his particular field he claimed (<u>in writing</u>) to have had no idea! So, added to the fact he was a male, then, should we, <u>let alone his daughter, Anna and confidante, Princess Marie Bonaparte</u> [20] [X], <u>whom he both studied AND advised</u>, take with a pinch of salt his ideas/essays on the female form: their self-satisfying acts [20]; their <u>vaginal</u> v <u>clitoral</u> [z] orgasm; Are the *natural* connections, less fulfilling?

This dire (<u>*desperate/urgent*</u>) emphasis on the sexual side is reminiscent of John's <u>1%</u>, (the expected though not maintained percentage of time indulging in love making) though as envisaged, likely, as not, the norm for most is one decimal point to the left *, not the all-encompassing thing it is made out to be by Freud and his cohorts!

If nature is to believed and not Sigmund's/Anna's/Marie's misleading ramblings, you will perceive that that apparent be all AND end all coupling, usually quite short, is suddenly erased from the needy memory banks and not to resurface for much longer * than we are prepared to admit to others (and ourselves), as the other 99%+ essentials take the full focus of our, now, uncluttered mind, as the climactic orgasms etc are placed far back into the *'fulfilled'* memory banks, until the next urge resurfaces, which falls within a different time frame * for so many different couples, as well as the different (*timeframe*?) emphasis * placed upon it, by men * & women *!

Dr. Mya Xavier

....

With Anna it was quite basic that others, around her, should think highly of her, but did not go as far as mentioning that emotion, love, although, most of her adult life, London apartment neighbouring doting Dot might have been, hers!?
Which leads us back to her protective father and his *loving*, but not *ephebophilial* thoughts...

21. " Human beings are ~~funny~~ ? s/b strange (as it is no laughing matter!). They long to be with the person they love but refuse to admit openly. Some are afraid to show even the slightest sign of affection because of fear. Fear that their feelings may not be recognized, or even worst, returned. But one thing about human beings puzzles me the most is their conscious effort to be connected with the object of their affection even if it kills * them slowly within." **(But, <u>not akin</u> to dying in one's self-made <u>*Gladys Knight, Bed of Thorns*</u>?)**

[1]*Creative Writers & Day Dreaming (1908);*

[2]*The Interpretation of Dreams (1899);*

[3]*Recommendations to Physicians (1912);*

[5] *Fragment of an Analysis of a case Hysteria (1905) Ch2. The First Dream: Ref Dora (Her Masturbation!)* – *Fragments 7*

6-8); [6]*Civilization & its Discontents;* [7]*To Ferenczi (1911);* [8]<u>*Reflections on War and Death*</u> *1918);*

[9]*Civilization & its Discontents;*

[10] *Beyond the Pleasure Principle;*

[14] *The Ego and the Id (1923);*

[15] *A Metaphysical Supplement to the Theory of Dreams (1917);*

[17] *Letter to his Fiancée (1882);*

[18] *The Ego & the Id (1923);*

[20] *AKA the self-penned téléclitorienne with her Theory of Female Sexuality: Fantasy & Biology;*

[4, 11, 12, 13, 16, 19, 21] *Attribution doubted by Freudian Society; (Does anyone know the actual original source?)*

[22] It could be said Freud and Pinter were so much similar with their churlish, surly snaps at people & society? Pinter, one of the original angry young men of the 60s, but Sigmund was his more famous predecessor in that field, where he was especially caustic and scathing on the subject of religion: you just need read what he had to say on this in his many publications > Group Psychology And The Analysis Of The Ego (1921), The Future of an Illusion (1927), Civilization and its Discontents (1931), Moses and Monotheism (1939), Obsessive Actions and Religious Practices & New Introductory Lectures on Psychoanalysis).

<u>*Whether you agree is another matter!*</u>

....

All of which leads me to ask what you think of my analysis in the matter?
Would you all *agree*?
Does it show I even have the right credentials to be a psychologist, or <u>***just his***</u> psychologist?
Perhaps, even *Patient John* might have considered this at times?
But, again **fantastically**, <u>Anna</u> set him straight,

as in that, *'Dear John......................'* letter, she wrote...

....

Anna died in 1982.
But her Mental Health legacy did not!
Eh Michael?

....

<u>*The Dead PPS:*</u>
It seems the dead will have the last say here AND later.
But, and here it is just another encased Ashes scene which needs playing out.
So, we must revisit the Freud Family Golders Greens Urns' Seclusion.
But, and here comes that Big 'B' distant relative But:

Then, as it was after it was smashed by an over-zealous, kidnapping fan?
Now, surrounded by well-wishers and gifted memorial books.
And, flowers, which are actually out of place,
as rocks are the Jewish de-riguer!

I made a reference a few pages back about people denying the Holocaust's Existence, and it is sad when at the Cemetery one can still see/hear that archetypal ignorant, young fat white male yob chanting Anti-Jewish comments! Sadly, it is still World-Wide! Why?

BUT I AM ENDING ON A GO/ADS CONTROVERSIAL NOTE

(And as likely to put me at loggerheads with the Anna Freud Type Child Mental Health Welfare Establishments!?)

*** *If we, in a strangely linked way, combine Porn & Children's Mental Health we can go down a certain Transgender Route, where the two nowadays apparently overlap, but they are not the same thing. And it was spawned by something John said another time.*

It doesn't take any effort to view those sites where you observe certain depraved ? men, with certain ? ½ man ½ woman? giving of their particular gender and so we get large breasted & large membered individuals engaging from all sides to those perverted enough to consider this a normal acceptable engagement!?

But, and here is the Big But, what is normal to one is the opposite to another. Which brings me to the recent modern Psychological trend of 'affirming a young person's chosen gender', which as we have seen with Adult prisoners can actually manipulatively lead to Rape being occasioned where it should NOT occur as the wool is once more pulled over those in Authority's eyes, as those conniving enough are well aware of which story to tell to get them their desired end(up!)!

As with children's diagnosis, is it really a reliable practice?

Years back such Gender Dysphoria Diagnosis was never on anybody's mainstream Psycho-Analytical consideration. Just like the modern trend to consider overactive children having some sort of attention deficient syndrome!

So it is with this playing with Gender Orientation and creating an epidemical surge in numbers which do not really reflect Society's actual mix!

Autism is likely the actual problem and should be treated as such, so not reliant on the ill-informed/experienced adolescent patient's view, nor pressurised by the latest media driven campaign diagnosis!

Dr Mya Xavier

BUT NOT FORGETTING MARIE'S LINKED EXPERIENCES >>>>

ANNA v MARIE

I have added this as an additional piece of information as to the trials and tribulations and perhaps inherited characteristic traits, which Philip's side of the Hereditary Lineage brought to the future table which he and his own future ancestors would be part of and might explain, there again might have no relevance, as to the difficulty some of his children had in making the right marriage choice, for whatever reason which might have replicated so much of which happened in the Historic past!

Marie is the final piece in my convoluted regal explanatory puzzle!

Perhaps one might use the Psychologist's well use diagnosis:- OCD – well Marie was certainly one sufferer, again perhaps hers was an *'inverted' 'frigid fetish'*?

There again I might introduce you to another term I have coined to aptly describe Marie's sexual contradictions i.e. so many lovers but with so little sexual satisfaction – which situation I would entitle:- **Emotional Orgasm**!

The Romantic Ideal/Notion often overshadowed the Physical Ideal/Notion such that the Euphoria of again being with the one craved coupled with the apparent Ecstasy of his presence gave her the soaring Climactic buzz the penile intercourse could not ever attain!

And this emotional orgasm is replicated millions of times over throughout the world, by both sexes; it exists at the time one partner cannot achieve, nor even wants to sometimes, as the pleasure fulfilment of their spouse is paramount & the other experiences it vicariously when the other 'cums' and the achievement of making it happen for the other is utterly self-satisfying in itself!

I'll let you ponder my new diagnosis as I elaborate.

Her birth was extremely difficult and traumatising for both mother and infant - she had barely escaped death, but her mother didn't and the child in later life blamed herself for this tragic consequence!
This coupled with another near death pulmonary illness convince Marie that she had inherited her late mother's constant (?) dicing with death frailty!

Her early life experiences contributed to her hypochondria, but more so to her phobias!
Her apparent easily infected frailty meant she had no outside contact in her infancy, and this coupled with her Father's parental frigidity to her affected her outlook on life on the outside, particularly with the opposite sex!

Hence her childhood without peer companionship coupled with her own father's **(emotional)** frigidity towards her, which some suggest was the basis for her failure in relationships with the many men she let into her bedroom life: and there that word *'frigidity'* should now be considered in its **sexual** context!

Apart from her upbringing experiences, the aspect of imaginings &/or dreamings have a part to play, just as they did in Sigmund Freud's daughter, whom he also studied:

- For the daughter the aspect of a knight in shining armour saving the day, but without ever seemingly 'fully' (!)(?) engaging with a male – so in her own way *'frigid' (!)(?)*
- But she was able to satisfy herself digitally, whereas...
- Marie's frigidity was somewhat a *self-insinuated notion* as her total focus was on the Vaginal Orgasm!?
- But also in biographical writings of her AND her own diary entries, the alternative digital alternative experience seemed descriptively absent!?
- This was strange to me as her Grand-Mother was not against this aspect and female (lesbian) coupling! Whereas the male on male was frowned upon in many Countries where it was against the law! For me their religious

thinking, amongst others, then may have thought as such, because the male on male totally mimicked many many animals' way of impregnation – but not for the Humans!

- Whether this was due to the then current mores where such stimulation was taboo, or she didn't consider such a *'properly achieved orgasm!?*
- Additionally, no mention of men coming down on her to perform *'cunninglingus'*, perhaps again the types she went with again may have considered it against the nature of things, procreationally!?
- And (successful?) foreplay was never mentioned also.
- So I am back to my, *'emotional orgasm!'*

Anna:-

In the context of her intimate friendships with Lou Andreas-Salome and in particular with Dorothy Burlingham, with whom she formed a life-long partnership, questions have been raised in relation to Anna Freud's sexuality, notwithstanding the absence of any evidence of, and her denials of, any sexual relationships. ^{Young-Bruehl – Anna Freud Biography}. The historian of French psychoanalysis Élisabeth Roudinesco ^{Freud: In His Time and Ours} argues that it was repression of her homoerotic sexuality that influenced her in the pathologizing of homosexuality in her clinical work as well as in her prominent advocacy of the policy of the International Psychoanalytical Association which debarred homosexuals as candidates for training as psychoanalysts!?

That poor little rich girl, Marie Bonaparte Diary Book EXPOSED!

And I am not really going to touch upon the endless correspondence exchange with that renown Sigmund Freud, who was partially responsible for one of her female relatives being committed to a Sanatorium!
No.
Neither that, being wealthy **, she was BOTH Beneficial & Benefactress to BOTH Sigmund and his daughter, Anna, during those (Jewish) simmering Pre-WWII warring days & nights! (Expanded upon in a later *Parts 13 & 14f*) **

BUT
It is her Book portrayal and quote copies regurgitated from thereon and its Diary/Rambling Sources, coupled with my own previous running commentaries:-

1. The first is this that this innocent (? phobia conscience?) was very quick on the male manipulative uptake to be able very swiftly to interpose herself between her Gay Husband and his Homosexual Lover of old!
2. There again one might class both the males as Bi-Sexual as they seemed to have no difficulty siring children via the supposed unattractive (to each of them) female spouses!
3. However, sweet Marie was able to quickly 'Cuckold' her husband George, in a way not mentioned, nor envisaged in my Book on the subject:- *'The Legal Sanctity of Marriage, Part 7 – The Cuckold!'* She would

engage in passionate kissing (and more ? *) on a Chaise Long with her husband's gay avuncular over attentive lover, Prince Waldemar, in full view of her non-participating husband, Prince George!

4. The build up to this situation was their promenades-à-trois in the Woods, where she would kiss each alternately:- the indoor chaise made it a more comfortable setting with room to take full advantage of their intimate proximity! *

5. I labelled each with an * as it appears she declined the opportunity to allow another man within her:- all her male loving husband did was the minimal *'Wham Bang Thankyou Ma-am'* a couple of times to ensure a Male heir production, which was a Nobleman's wife's main task! (The second child was a daughter). And her future dalliances were in the main of a romantic notion level - perhaps akin to an adolescent pair exploring first base and no more, only words! Well until she got into the real swing of things – but she never went into physical detail, so perhaps it was all in her 'romanticising' mind?!

6. But an important caveat here was that body/brain shattering orgasms were important things lacking:- hence her genital operation(s) and nagging books on the subject and what she considered related & merited discussion! And this is where Sigmund Freud entered the picture and ultimately saved his life! (See ** above)

7. What is not really covered is the apparent lack of guilt and/or remorse neither Marie, nor her Uncle-in-Law felt towards each of their spouses – to confuse matters Waldemar's wife's name was also Marie!

8. When fully accomplished George's Marie took it to the Cuckold extreme with her French Prime Minister, Briand, having his way in the bedroom, whilst her scorned hubby listened at the door -OUTSIDE!

9. She had a long string of lovers, but when writing her recollections of such in her, *'The Men I Have Loved*, it seems she preferred the letters written her: so it was for her the verbal intercourse she favoured over the physical intercourse!

10. This would not come as a surprise to those around her, if they only knew what her particular pleasure attainment problem she suffered from! In the below *** it is explained how certain African Tribes got around such a female problem!

11. Additionally the wealth was such an added bonus to achieve the desired:- to save the above **, but on a more personal note to buy a mansion in which to entertain her lover, Briand:- the lucky so & so had the best of both worlds, as his rich female actress mistress also bought a place for their coupling times!

12. But what I also find strange, anatomically, is that how come wham bang thankyou ma'am George scored his 2 pregnancy goals with minimal INTERaction, yet her string of lovers failed to?

And I will end where I started:- Marie's Compulsive Under Achieving Fixation

In 1935 she met the future President of Kenya, Jomo Kenyatta ## (He also stayed with her, the following year, at her son's home).

*Their discussion apparently centred on female 'circumcision' ***, a hot potato subject in East Africa *** and in Great Britain among British colonialists and reformers and Kenyan cultural nationalists. Kenyatta became a key figure in the controversy.*

.........Marie's interest in the matter came from her explorations of female sexuality: were all women bisexual as the two sites of the source of erotic pleasure – clitoris and vagina – seemed to indicate?

There again a false conclusion because she didn't have the capability the natural female about her had and had successfully experienced!

She had 3 operations to attempt to cure her 'faulty workings'! But the Africans were ahead of the Europeans on this aspect:-

NB On the lurid for some, subject of the female genitalia [z], there is a serious sexual educational Butt point to be raised here for the triumvirate above: on the subject of the 'inner labia' in Africa they practice 'Kudenga', where it is stretched to optimize sexual intercourse. There again if the female form enjoying herself with no viewing strings allowed the web is still unbeatable, even if most is stage ~~massaged~~ managed!***

And whichever conclusions were drawn and future legal enactment changes etc. it made no odds as Kenyan Africa didn't change, like other retrograde cultures and FGM continued unabated.
Just as did the male attitude to the (lowly and vulnerable female) and as it does <u>NOW</u> where the female is just the standard malevolent male indiscriminate 'rape fodder!'

↑ *(I covered both *** (African) Clitoridectomy & Vasectomy, in my Book, Book 2 of 2*
The No-Change-Here Sex Anthropology of Homo Sapiens -Whatever The Penis Wants, The Penis Gets
(Into) in Chapter 12 - F & M Genital Surgical/Mutilation!
NB Kenyatta published an anthropological study of Kikuyu life. ##

.:::::::::::::::::::::::::::::::

Well now you've had a taster as to what our late departed Prince Philip's not-so-distant relatives were about! And one can only surmise which characteristic trait or phobia Philip and/or any of his own children could have inherited!?

Ha Ha – I jest? ~~Off~~ Of Course!
I mean naturally!

PART 14: MICHAEL ETHICAL COMPANY CHARITY MAN

a) Nat -ural Rich pre-thoughts.

"NATURE LOVER – NATURAL BORN KILLER'S AIDE?
John butts in...
I don't understand how she, a countryside walking nature lover, one who freely advocates taking kids to view it rambling amongst woodlands; encouraging the discovery of all the different flora, fauna & insect life; being totally soft and maternal with it all, should have been such a keen supporter of her elders' anachronistic country killing indulgent lifestyle, being their supportive secretary and all that?

It killed Sam's innocent gun cleaning Son and paralysed his hunt loving horse bucking Dad, but he ended up saving and expanding their ever so profitable banking business, so great *emotional* consolation there?

Stranger, I put it to her to encourage the young lads to catch flies (or bring a box of maggots) so they could feed the many different species of spiders; a sort of countryside killing on a much lower scale, yet so natural and no guns blazing away, just silent awe viewing the arachnid in action.

But, she baulked at such a suggestion and wouldn't condone the natural killing way, which not all children see as enjoyment!

Yet not so for the Gentrified types, with that unnatural pellet powered sadistic carnage.

But, she's since moved inner urban and perhaps has now left that *specific gentry fowl/fox mad man pleasing* sport (if that is what it is to them) and can now Country walk the nearby Regent's Canal stretches without the sound of a gun report echoing in the distance with the squeal of another of nature's gifts being brought to ground and to a dog's barking, fetching to heel!

Ah, well, I suppose they, one-sidedly, blinkeredly, see it as another example of the gregarious need, just like the stag/fox hunt: I wonder how they'd feel if chased by a pack of dogs with no gun to protect them then?

Perhaps, with all their excess smoking &/or drinking, their heart might give up before the first bite tears their skin/flesh/bone apart? There again the dogs might even be greeted with a lovely smelling, **bloody**, appetising mess of a broken man's heart as the ever-accelerated pumping palpitations forced it to explode within!"
And so started another related *richly entertaining* John-type session!?"
"*Rich* was brainy & creative, but I wonder if he would have come so far, especially if he hadn't been a fellow psychology minor?
St Andrews is their own Scottish rich *(partner-pairing off)* playground! Ah, well, *Rich* another case of who you get to know, not what you ..."
John's hobby horse had once again thrown him towards rock bottom, but he didn't dwell on it and got back in the saddle!
"He officially dissolved his *partnered* #Rodnik Band in 2009 – they'd split up 2008), *(# not to be confused with the similarly named UK Company run by Kenneth (from his Edmonton home?) – though apparently nothing to do with The Band, as its work is listed under category 86900, which relates to 'Other Human Health Activities' – who'd've guessed?)*.
Their next best thing came & went, as did the main protagonists their separate ways – strange although a new *solo* Band was formed.
#Perhaps their style went as far as it could go? Although, post their 2008 split and that end of their line 2009, one *Band* continued to parade with **New Rich Goldsmith Wifey**-in-tow, while the other tried something new: the UP market Dunhill, then to All Saints –

No, not the girls I went on that Charity March with –

the diminutive Mel & Shaz) and *just so* as you know, the latest a managering directorship** like his missus.

NB: That Amnesty International Non-Marching Part of the Band below

Author Copyright

(Rich, Brainy & Creative – what another triumvirate!)(Nat/Rich/Phil).
St Andrews Uni, also, seems to churn out the best around!
Daddy-in-Law's neighbour's ^{LL} son Mark also went there – keep it in the neighbouring *titled* family way! Nice place there & yours *truly* had tea & cake on their ^{LL} lawn there, ↓ too! ^{LL} =*Lord & Lady* As*qui*th

(Author Copyright)

Like the trust above, the names people use can be fascinating: why would you name something after a genus of medium, to large sized <u>predatory</u> tropical sea snails, which are carnivorous, commonly called rock snails. For one as naïve as I, I could only surmise the answer lay in the word underlined? Some sort of take-over company, I suppose. ***↓

Some seem Ok, but borrowing is a theme; others not so, with so many more, new fledglings, spreading wider and wider, as their numbers grow.
Well, maybe not, they're not birds? Tentacles?
No.
What bests describes a growing threat from a snaily shellfish?
Just a gooey, sticky slime?
Well, not really ... well what do the names imply ...
John looked somewhat bored by it all; I awaited the list which he clutched in hand – lists were becoming more of a feature; our sessions beginning to follow (his) an orchestrated patter(n); he obviously wanted to get some sort of bogey off his back – it wasn't long in coming – He stated the strange name, again from his *favourite* Latin.
 ??????
 Yes, it's not your usual common company nomenclature."
 "Nor is your *clature*?"
 That brought back his smile and impetus was regained ...
"Like rabbits these shell-fish breed, <u>and some</u>; from one birth to another, although some died by the wayside, others needed *loaned* aid >>>

258

And so from an historical introduction to Nat's Hubby, followed by a bit of a confused John moany, moany ramble, but he was unaware of the Samuel's generational history and a certain sea-slug but which Nat was aware of and introduced us to some pages back –   **The Famous Murex!**

<<<>>>

b) Sam's Historical Murex Past

Marcus Samuel, 1st Viscount Bearsted, JP born on fireworks day, 5 November 1853 – Died 17 January 1927), known as Sir Marcus Samuel between 1898 and 1921 and subsequently as The Lord Bearsted until 1925, was a Lord Mayor of London and the founder of the Shell Transport and Trading Company, which was later restructured including a Holland-based company commonly referred to as Royal Dutch Shell.

Samuel was born into an Iraqi Jewish * family from western Europe in Whitechapel, London.
His father, also named Marcus Samuel, ran a successful import-export business, M. Samuel & Co., trading with the coalition in the Far East, which Marcus carried on with his brother, Samuel Samuel.
Samuel realised the potential of the oil market during a prospecting trip to the Caucasus in 1890.
*In 1891, he secured a nine year exclusive deal with the * **Rothschilds**, to sell Bnito's kerosene east of Suez.*
*Samuel had commissioned the design and construction of a safer generation of **tanker**, safe enough to transit the Suez Canal.*
*The first of which was **Murex**, that set sail from West Hartlepool for Batum on 22 July 1892, where it acquired its load of kerosene.*
*Samuel then built ten additional ships, also named for **seashells**.*
And now we all know about the Samuel's penchant for seashells!

*And you can see how far back the Samuels & Rothschilds go!

<<<>>>

c) <u>And now for an extensive John Led Tour of that Famous Mells Park Place.</u>

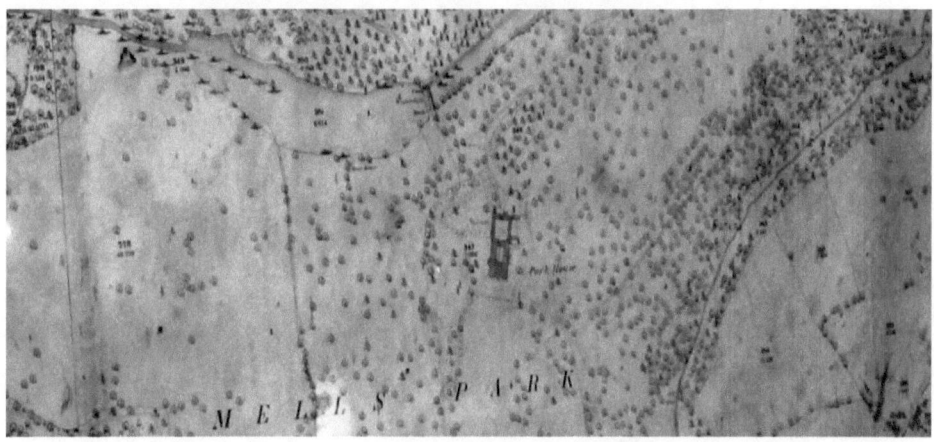

Mells Park expanse - of old – pre-fire! And pre-rebuild – to new! ↓
(NB It is interesting that so many above connected Rich Types settle Somerset/Dorset Way?)
I had always wanted to see/get inside there, her brother's <u>inherited</u> farm ** and the <u>special</u> one of the brother-in-law's 3 parklands[†],
And, here a preview of the **<u>Mells Phoines</u>** sights in store to marvel at if you visit.... # Outside, *a Keeper Dick, a Duckery, a Serpentine, an Arboretum, a Lake, a Tor Rock....Inside, a wonderfully ornate Staircase to the many 1st Floor bedrooms – John will apprise you with the best in the house, later!* **

But, I always thought the Legal Definition of a Park was that it was dedicated in perpetuity for the free and unrestricted use of the Public? But, definitely, not this one!

(# Note those strange names – there are so many more, later!)

But, first that initial invitation to...

"Joan, being one of the Committee, kept me aware of the situation on the *levels,* but remarkably what swayed it was the Fayre Committee Chair, Jake, pulling up alongside, in his sport's car, and insisting I promise to come. Enough said and he added the privileged couple overlooking us from their own hill-top palace (et al) were nice people.
So, how could I refuse?
But, they weren't really keen on the whole she-bang ^{Below}, as opposed to their-bang, bang, bang, you're dead fowl!!!!

But, he would say that wouldn't he? And disbelieving John carried on unabashed...It's easy for those *'high & mighty'*, who look down on us from their exalted, well-connected position in life to be considered so magnanimous – especially as the limited time they appear from on high they seem to be doing it for our benefit.

And all those underlings clamouring to be under their spell; ingratiating themselves to those who apparently were the sole deserving of their personalised silver spoon mouthful."

(John was to change his tune as he got to know some of them better and what they did for the ordinary behind the Media Driven Scenes!)

"John, be fair, didn't you too have the same opinion of the *Old Girl* (as you call(ed) her) during those early Palace days? And she had the literal golden (table)spoonful?"
The response showed the playful Johnny had come out to play,
"Your good memory can be a right Royal *Reginal* pain ... but yes, I suppose I did then."
"And now?"
Well, at the Garden Parties & at Bernardo's, I could see for myself, but not approach as close as I could those meeting-in-the-corridor days, gone bye-bye."

A special smile recalled...

(Author Copyright)

"And he did say they were nice, perhaps they really are?"

"OK, I grant you the Samuels occasionally let the young riders circuit gallop over their lower fields, or one of the three local hunt groups have a *trail hunt* over a selected path, and might even sight a solitary fox, before they turned out of the lower estate: although, they never allow their **Park** land to be a car park overspill ^{Below}, during the Annual Village Daffodil Fair Day.

(This was perhaps more of a sign that he got fed up queuing to get into the Easter Daffodil Fayre via the Farm beyond Mells, further on the right, up the hill road which bounds the Park!)

Living in the country (*Apart from the tales you're told*...) you can come across so many different, grin inducing, names as you walk in & around estates.

Let *Mells* take you round: *a Snatch Bottom, a Beech Grove Bottom, a Duckery, a Lake Covered Wraggs Mill, a Lily Batch (not a patch), a Berry Hill, a Berry lodge, a Vobster Plantation, a Tor Rock and its Artificial Cave, a Gothic Finger Lodge with a Finger Gate pointing to a Finger Valley, a Hare Warren, a Cobby Wood leading Northwards to a* **Grand Park House**.

Around the House are formal Gardens on two terraces retained by freestone walls with stone steps connecting the levels.
To the south & east you'll find sunken lawns & gardens, a stone pool & fountain; yew trees abound and through one particular Eastward gap you can view the park, where the stables are approached from the east also.
There was also once *a Temple* and abounding, Northward, a Waterfall/Sluice & Weir, plus, Southward, a bit of *the Serpentine* around.
But, getting back on track, what's most grin worthy are the name links which everybody knows of: a bit of old 18th century *Strangeways,* a relative of Little Jack *Horner* [Later], some 20th century *Jekyll, but, no Hyde* and then *the* **Trotter** *family,* who resided there and sold it on: now we know where *Del Boy & Co.* lived before their own *'high & mighty'* Nelson Mandela House!*"*
Inevitably, John paused here for his own special grin, added something from distant archives...where [Later] the *Original* Horner will be found in those MELLS HISTORICAL HAPPENINGS:

- Little Jack's Little sister was about then: ... Francis's attendance at a meeting of the Cambridge Camden Society, 1 Oct 1845. (35) Lizzie Horner (at *Mells Park*, Frome) concerning a donation and the death of Mr Pinney, 22 Sep 1845.
- Even Jack's father got in the *'madcap'* act: ... F Horner at *Mells Park*, concerning a reference for Charles Candy, 7 Mar 1881. (102) William Hewson at Wells, concerning the position of bailiff at Wells Asylum, 5 Mar 1881. (103) James Adams...
- Once one could walk across but in 1788 came an Order for the diversion of a footpath in *Mells* and Leigh on Mendip, which runs from Leigh on Mendip village to Drums bridge across *Mells Park*, to be diverted to follow the roadway to the south...
- Strange John? The names which abounded in the early 1800s: ... Hobhouse of Hadspen, Sir Richard Colt Hoare of Bruton Abbey, bart., Sir Thomas Swymer Champneys of Orchard Leigh, bart., Thomas Strangeways (?Uncle?) Horner of *Mells Park*, John Phelips of Montacute, William Dickinson...
- And, in 1986, secret peace talks began between the South African government and the African National Congress. Some of these talks were held at *Mells Park....Hope they could hear themselves above the din of the Game Bagging outside! (Or not side-tracked by the idea! Well one of the topics must have been the killing on their lands?)*

After which *characteristic* sarcastic comment, he, then, continued.
"But, despite all their royal connections, they are not the Lord & Lady Muck to whom all the village look up to: this exalted position remains with their Lordly Landlord As*qui*th & his Wife (although the kids know each other well – Facebooking/Googling etc and *that* Scottish Uni)."
Lady As*qui*th, not a *qui*tter, who really *mucks in,* is the Community Spirit driving force and responsible for placing *her* Little Village in the **RDPE** eye. (*Rural Development Programme for England)*
Oddly enough a kindly lady who didn't mind my walking about her back garden, though I didn't get a free meal as I did with the late departed mistress of Muncaster Castle.
Mind you I could get served hand & foot at the *Local* Park owner's table if I could make up a team of 8 *, though, not to 12, gun toters!

Funny, **12** attendees also applied to Pauline's cousin, who, in spite of being another Lord's Lady of all he/she surveyed, has to convert so much on his **M**(e)**ander**(ing) land to holiday building lets."

"And where does the **dozen** apply here?"

"Well, his Lady-wife does the cooking – <u>as women should</u> …"

I saw the glint in his eye so did not rise to the bait …

"But, she is a selective chef, as, to evening dine, you need that as a minimum number, anything less she seems to consider unworthy of her time & talents!" *(More likely, economical, John!)*

So, sarcastic John was definitely also out at play …

"But, as palatial surroundings go, surpassing her husband's cousin's, but *not a patch* on her husband's cousin's son-in-law's!

The key is the point"

As was his riddler-self …

"The key?"

"In each, it's the personal view…"

"But,"

"The estate manager …"

"Talking nonsense again, are we John?"

"Sorry, mind overload, let's settle on five years past and go from there."

I had no idea, nor would you, but it all emerged from the Somerset Country mists …

"The key is the Estate/Farm Manager: if you recall one escorted me out, the other in; this one knows Patricia# too!

Though I never got to know the *Phoines fully!*"

He saw my head slope to one side as my eyes glared, but I couldn't stop the grin – his devious mind was at work: a strange man one moment down, then up, if the circumstances were his to control, or rather manipulate.

"It started when the Village Pub# underwent a complete overhaul and had to close down for several months – the neighbouring Nunney Castle Village Hotel saw this as the ideal opportunity to go a *Melliferous-Person-Poaching;* so I'm not talking eggs, but the best staff, especially kitchen –

Oh <u>*Tanya*</u> could really dish up the best dessert!

But, <u>*Trish*</u>, that special serving wench, had the connection!?   ……

The Parkland is cut off from the public by an auto-gated entrance – the keypad has the usual combinations and <u>her</u> date of birth doesn't get you entrance, but pre<u>fixed</u> B00 etc *potentially* does. (To which Nat has already introduced us to).

And, once inside, you are greeted by the first of many imposing sights:

The manager apparently doesn't live on the premises, rather up around the *Hilly Berry* corner; you might even recognise him through the small car he drives.

Ridiculously enough, his and his colleague's car are also used, not to drive around, but on a special day to stop all the other pleb/non-aristocratic car owned cars, especially at Fayre Days when the younger Estate Manager & Staff stand astride their parked older saloon and even smaller hatched car to stop visitors to the Village illegally [Above] parking across their property boundary & egress etc. (Although, for so many, the Main Entrance is via Berry/Mells Lodge to the North!).

Hence, the Owners dislike of the Annual Village Daffodil Fayre Day Event! [Above]

Yet, on those quiet non-Fayre days all that obstructs you is the low front wall.

So, *following the Local Riders*...
Keeping to the right, along one of the Hare Warren Wood Tracks hugging the Hill Road wall, you can then make your way along Finger Valley, as you do so the house disappears from view, onwards towards the lower surrounding area where you find you've *picked up the grassy* covered slopes of Cobby Wood, and hope you avoid being *(Althorp) picked up and turfed out!*
The outside view denies you the full extent of the Estate, [NB Below] but the lower area, away from the buildings perched above, is a great scenic walk, where the water drain flows to your right, which takes you, via Snatch Bottom, to the northern-most part, where it meets the River.
Along here you'll come across sluices, a weir; a waterfall, which in turn invites you to the Duckery."
"Or, just a vivid imagination?"   He smiled, as always ...
"Walking the Estate yes, but part of the Hunt, I don't ride, just as I don't know any shooters, so my access would be otherwise *un-securable.*"
I smiled, back, as was now usual ...
"Creating new words again, John; or a feeble attempt at another double-entendre?"
Smiles broadened, eyes met, dilation on one, or perhaps two?
"And if I got caught?"
"You didn't, cos you're here to relive the short, tall, tale! Go on..."
He broke off for a few seconds, then ...

"Strangely enough when you speak to the keeper-in-the-know they even breed the special Kami-kaze type whose flightpath, with a bit of lift to it, is best suited to the killing thereof: I understood that the Michigan Blueback / Chinese Ringneck crosses are the pick of the self-destruct breeds!

Getting yourself on one of the beater's crews, you can view *how adept those fowl are* at **'*suicidally'*** presenting themselves to the gun broadsides.
Thankfully, the hunter/killers were well adept at their 'sport' unlike their 'nouveau riche' Slovak [BK] counterparts, who can on occasion mistake the back of a beater for a Pheasant – a simple mistake to make, but you'd notice that the screams of pain are somewhat different!

[BK] *It happens even in France: The President of the Goudelin-Bringolo Hunt shot/killed his partner/wife whom he mistook (?) for a Boar rummaging in a Corn Silage Field!*
"See – always be positioned behind the gun barrels or some stray pellet, or worse, a bullet could hit you in your unsuspecting, unprotected back – so as a beater **Duck** as soon as the targeted Birds take to the air...!"

NB *The closest you can get to a good view is via paths along Melcombe Wood (see Park(s) diagram below... But, you'll have to strain your neck over the Walls-In-Your-Way!*

The Monstrous **Mells** Head *engulfing* its innocuous neighbour!

To the West That *Greater* Mells Park Mouth Engorging upon →→→ That *Smaller* Melcombe Wood		Whilst To the East That *smaller/lesser* known ←←← Mells Park Face Looking away ignoring its Rich Bigger Brother devouring That *Lesser* Melcombe Wood Fowl n' all!

You need to go hill climbing towards Vobster to reach Soho and its similarly named farm to gain access to the best Melcombe Wood path to view its bigger gobbling neighbour – although the walker's signpost was far from prominent!
Your walk would be just a third of the true length of Mells Park and, as such, from the outside you don't get the real idea how big the grounds really are; I thought one place within to murder the pheasants, but there are more and even some lakes to break the pheasants' death plunge.
And, apparently, there can't be anything more gratifying watching the dogs on a far bank dipping (*as the fowls' bloods-a-dripping*) in & out as they fetch the birds at the end of a hard-working day (*the guns must be so heavy (You Judge Below↓) for old men to carry so long during those sporadic pellet splatterings!?!*

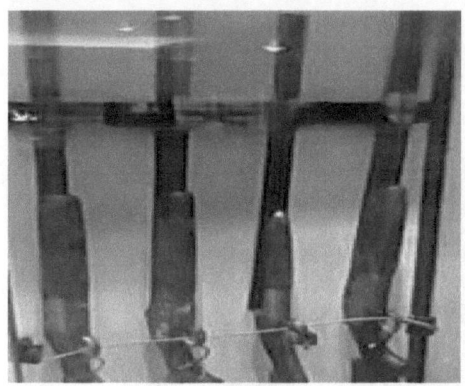

Comically looking, male, middle-aged spread shotgunners are the norm, all jacketed and *wellied up* (Suppose she got her penchant for *these* at an early age and so knew how to cope with *Muddy Puddles?!*)
And after all that male dominated limb-killing exertion one might expect a female on call to sort out all their aches & pains, a *masseuse* obviously and plying her *manual, muscle relaxant* trade in the privacy of his own bedroom (the maximum * bedded is 8)!
Confusingly however the masseuse can only be booked for the evening before the shoot: seemed silly to me, but Dick & Co are experts in the field so who am I to argue with the tradition?
I expected this to be the total family's home yet *she* had also lived in the Devon estate, but you can't keep them apart for long as some years all the family and crew spent Christmas at their main Country Estate Seat."

Oddly enough in all the 3 shooting estates, there was a marked difference to *Princharliemer's* Scottish one, where if you know his architect, you'll discover the barns all potentially *obsolete* awaiting conversion to living accommodation – so much more profit in that and once again more wealth falls into the Regal Rich's kilted lap, unlike their shot grouse, which is *dog-fetched* to them!"
"Seems you are not in favour of this sport, so how would this play out with Phyllida and Patrick, (Muncaster Castle Fame) especially as he told you he was speaking at the House of Lords, pro-hunt, albeit Stags, which predominated at their Ardverikie Estate?"
"Doing even more homework, yet again – I must stop letting you know in advance of future session thoughts! It's another sad tale, like old Sam's, yet here it was the wife to pass away first – a family stalwart with an equally determined passion for her UK Stately Home Restoration. Ah well life goes on, regardless of sentiment."
He paused; morbidity left him and back came his perkiness.
"Funny how close the three places are: take a left from General Wade's and you get to Phyllida's Scottish ancestral home. It is said Queen Victoria stayed there, she did the same at my birth castle; the Big Yin starred in Mrs Brown being filmed there, Sean Connery did likewise at mine with his.
But, to be serious for a while, (a very short while for John!) Patrick enjoyed it there. Perhaps more than their Cumbrian retreat as something dear to his heart existed there – **stalking** of course! (See, I told you so – all will be revealed...) Only the English Language could have a single word whose connotations could be so different, **no sex** here, but beatings abound! (John, still playing with his words!)
Red Dear were the prey here, but you'd only get a few thousand pounds change out of your 10,000 on the day!!!"

 *Patrick At Home When We Visited Him & With Us Having Tea In Days Gone By*

"So, why favour him over M & J's Domains?"
Again I didn't see it coming, but it was something jointly <u>*dear*</u> to us both…
"I thought it would be obvious: the lunch, tea AND <u>cake</u>, Phyllida and Patrick shared with us in addition to their Lord & Lady Guided Tour, family tales like one reminding me of the Houston beach retreat *poteen* days, where she caught her youngest two daughters trying to make whiskey out of the cattle's barley in the cellar at Tynron, when she lived in Dumfriesshire – but thankfully for the girls, no Excise man came calling that day, too busy like Anjelica's Eire-way having a small dram in the local boozer; <u>plus</u> the Castle ghost stories <u>also thrown in for free</u> – Do you think I'd get the same *melli-fluous* treatment Somerset way, more a ↓ *mell-of-a-hess*?!"

He finished there, but I'm sure the 32g of No 5s gunshot powder s*mell* would *spark* & explode into life, if they only knew!

<<<>>>

d) <u>And now to the John Led *Renewables* Money Nitty Gritty ></u>

(He recited a list of around 2 dozen Company names >>>
I had awaited the list(s) which he clutched in hand) –
(Included at the end of his list there was a WyndellhamMix!?)

For those interested ↓↓↓ - Incomplete List 1

That wonderful (Cement?)
WyndellhamMix!?
And >>>
- Lower Webbery
  - BH Solar
  - Babbington
  - Rifton
- Western Bullaford
  - Bake
  - Wilton
  - Energy

- Woodford
- Trevozah Barton
  - Solar
  - Solar B
  - Solar C
- Lower Newham
- Manns Newton
  - Fursdon
  - Ramsdown
  - Martin Solar
  - Frizenham
  - Trerule Solar
  - Quarry
- Primrose Solar
  - Bennacott
- Energy Wind

"And, so we come back to that something called the <u>WyndellhamMix</u>!?" Which bugged John.
(Definitely nothing to do with cake making!)(Cement?)

Well, it actually refers to one of those fellow Directors Michael had a Business relationship with <> Mr Harry Hugh Patrick Wyndham; in addition to Harry, there were three other individuals and each were mutually involved in over 2 dozen projects with him. Who are they?
They're not for today!

Amongst his Company Workings one **since 1999** stood out: number 03819888, which was none other than The Anna Freud Centre! Its Official Classification is, *'Other Human Health Activities (86900).*

It is actually classed as a large Company as it employs more than the legal qualifying lower limit of 250: actually, at the last knockings it was 328!
The healthy balance sheet shines proud before him with £32million net assets; the cash at the bank of over £5million must be the envy of all other Charitable organisations!

And now for his Active Murex prefixed, Sea Slug...Linkages >>>
In no particular order...

- *Energy Solar*
  - *Power*
- *Martin Solar*
  - *Power B*
  - *Fursdon*
  - *Bake*
  - *Wilton*
- *Babbington*
- *Energy Wind*
  - *Energy*

And like his daughter said many pages back, **Murex** '...renewable start up launched in 2010 to identify, develop, finance, construct and operates medium scale renewable projects in the Southwest of England. *((Ethical Investment Types)*

John carries on...

"Suppose I got it ***↑ wrong (again!). Perhaps with a view to energy conservation and all those Government grants, or some other tax advantage? Although these sometimes don't last."

"Ever the critic/cynic, yet again John?"

"No, not really, as you know my view on those who have money, they know how to make more, like they say, that the rich get richer and the poor get poorer ... but your husband's namesake had his head screwed on well when it comes to finance and the rosy red cheeked apple doesn't fall far from the daddy tree (no naïve country bumpkin there under his shooting cap) – how else could one so sweet hold so many high level, important decision making Directorships &/or Appointments (with Daddy, ever there, in supporting control? ◇ *'with his secretary, she was his assistant, did whatever, # or anything he needed with his philanthropic dealings/start-ups etc...'*).

And, then, there were the kids to look after, likely, as she's such a caring attentive mother, not at boarding school, like their aunties/uncles; then there's hubby, then travel here & there... wow how does she cope?

Even regular dawn runs around some local hilly fields! A nanny helps, of course! Summer respite in the Scottish Highlands also affords relief and, so handy, Daddy has another Estate up there!"

"So, she's **sweet** and her opinion of you, **sour**(ed) no doubt and not appetising as a good **Chinese**?"
"But, they do include lemon & lime?"
"We're being silly now aren't we?"
"You mean me?"
"Naturally, who else?"
His bright *puer*-eyes settled on my face, as his smile followed and *kissed* mine, reciprocatively: another seed was sown.

And it was from her open meeting admissions that give John the key to so much more – *he didn't even have to pick any locks* – *all it took was a simple key word search and all about her/them was revealed/revealing!* And, keeping it in the family, Nat's Mum's words set me along the right path: directed me to stroll down dye/bib Mayborn Way!

....

"2006 was another vintage year, I think, by then, the Brewery Arm had already settled 25% of their wealth for (?Was it some Alchemy?) cash invested wisely in return ... but for a certain gamer it was a time for contemplative resignation:

NB But No [MM] Muddy Puddle Wear Just Yet...Their Times were yet to arrive..

- Process Improvements (1989)
    - Jackel International
- Jackel International (U.K.)
    - Acacia Chemicals
        - Haditos
    - The Maws Group
        - Maws Suncare
    - Sangenic International
        - Ravina
        - Edizol
    - Technomould
    - Niche Plastics
- GE Romney (Bama)
    - Spotless Punch

- Kindertec (#)
- Activity Toys (#)
- TP Activity Toys (#)
- Steri-Bottle (#)
- Tommy Tippee (#)(←*apparently somewhat famous-Nat had boasted to John when they talked.*)
  - Cotton Bottoms (#)
  - Mayborn Florists Sundries
  - Mayborn
  - The Mayborn Group

>all < apparently died en masse?
But, with it, came a *Jesus/Jewish* rebirth!

>>>>> And, so, *two Millennia* later, this is where 3i came a'calling … well, there was about €8m at stake and, with it, a *Newco* (not apparently the TP one) private equity deal was struck…"

(#) I flagged these up as they, to John, sounded *kiddy-type* names: The type of businesses he had ventured into, but only 2 stood the test of company time, although one, ^{MM} not named in the list above, is withstanding the acid China make 'em cheapest clothing test of time – *with a young woman at the helm!*

Then, John returned to *coincidentally* time …

"Strange what coincidence throws up as you get an insight as to his scope; these merit special attention:
- Poison Diaries whose registered office is 17 Walkergate
Berwick Upon Tweed, Northumberland TD15 IDJ + IJP *coincidentally* lead you to Northumberland's Alwick Castle. The Poison Diaries seem now dormant and Michael has no further interest there, but with the following he still does...
- Full Fact, a registered charity, limited by guarantee, which is an admirable *ethical* investment, but not sure if one which highlighted his sister-in-law's Press Plight(s)? Although this was his clever, resourceful daughter's co-created baby. *Coincidentally,* hung out just around from *ma chère's* old Gray's Inn judgement corner!

 *(Author Copyright) (John at her side? I & The Mail only know!)??*

John broke of, as he sometimes does...

"Poison, just like Camilla's relative Gus's *Middleton House Asylum*!" He giggled.

And so here is your introduction to another of the Samuel's (Greater?) Wealth Connection, but on a Massive Scale – k/a Northumberland Estates.

And here we must recall Tara & Anita's eventful life events:-

People imagine the likes of multi-millionaire families that how their excess cash is spent is unimportant to them?
Well Tara even at 30 too much money would only have led to her ultimate earlier demise.

So with this carefree, laissez faire attitude being one to be curtailed, or with the Duke & Duchess of Northumberland postponed, we can find them taking a Court Case against their 18 year old son >>>
In 1999

The Duke and Duchess of Northumberland won a court battle to delay their teenage son inheriting £1m when he turned 18 - because he could be vulnerable to "vices".

The High Court agreed to alter the terms of a will so that the inheritance - which also includes a £250,000 annual income - will now pass to Earl Percy when he turns 25.

What happened since? Is not my Guess!

Their Ancestral seat being Alnwick Castle, but the rest of the world now know it as the place they filmed parts of Harry Potter!

John adds

"And if you look at the different stamp denominations you'll see Alnwick again is put in a privileged position over and above the ordinary: no second-class internal mail sender/carrier, but only overseas USA & all Air Mail points West!"

We laughed.

One of the oldest, grandest and richest in the country – worth more than £800 million.
Its land includes 100,000 acres of Northumberland, an estate in Scotland and 2,000 lucrative acres of prime Surrey Business Park: for individual properties/premises have a look at Northumberland Estates advertising – you can even stay in their gardener's cottage!
#Londoners need look no further than Kew Gardens neighbouring Park Owner, whose Estate is just about a third its size, but no public strolling there?

I love how you read about all that nonsense about love at first sight, but at 16, you must be leading some sort of sad, sheltered life, so it must have been the money and title – well, he was a Lord in waiting.
But, I know it wasn't that then, as she came from money* too AND legendary athletic prowess – I know she could skate a bit, but her Great Uncle was Max *Whotsisnam* (*look him up*) – making my sporting sorties so miniscule ...
*he/she only became worth over £300 million on his inheritance, after they had married.
And the current Duke's door to such elevated Status only came about (recalling Anita's pain) again with the suicide of the First Incumbent, his brother, due to his inability to cope suicide!

Then suddenly John was back down, south...to praise his financial idol wizard, Michael
Recalling his Company lists...
- I hadn't mentioned all the companies he has/had a **finger** in, but, his **finger** extends from NW3 5SU # to Bangladesh, Ethiopia & Burma, making *my African entry* expeditions so miniscule ...

"You *nearly had me* there John!"
His eyes lit up at the unwitting innuendo, but no verbal response, just you're being that *naughty girl* look ...
I had to wait a long time again for the session's theme to be revisited – the first sign of the depressive (envy) at last.
"Yes, at first, but it turned into admiration with the last, and the best, on the list, coincidentally the one he has had the oldest connection with.
Why, not sure, but (#) might give a clue and as coincidences go, there are more: this help for mental health school sufferers (his sister-in-law's for disaffected, though some likely also mentally unbalanced juveniles); his

wife's psychoanalyst's experiences) and there was I looking over their shoulders from *my Maudsley type personality disordered* Unit!

(#)*Oh it's Ann-oth-a Freudian Centre, this, with its innovative Family School Unit, concentrating on kids' Mental Health, which coincidentally, conveniently dovetails the other two, relative led, mentioned above...* (#)Just **Ann**-*oth-***a*** *purposeful John misquote, but not of the Sigmund variety, otherwise they'd have had him visiting as a patient, not as a* **visiting** *guest!*

Sigm. Freud

*(Already been **visited**)...*

So, *the **Lady's*** expensive re-location ᴴᴹ to its adjoining Rodney Street ᴷᴬᴺ seems resoundingly, financially sourced, if *she* gets the Royal nod of visiting support approval! (....and lead free building grounds)"

ᴷᴬᴺ The Kantor Centre of Excellence picture fronts this Book.

ᴴᴹ *Not from the Hampstead's Mares-Field Building which actually houses the Anna Freud Memorial Stuff and is distinct from the Operational Mental Health Organisation).*

He continued down Company Way & got his *'ethical confirmation!*

"There ᴷᴬᴺ, late last July, I *garner*ed more info about *that Murex-Man* from *that Somerset-Man, that Smart-Gym donor Man* – apparently ethically charitable, something like Triodos, but here you only get an annual dividend and can only sell your shares for what you paid for them!"

"So, no get rich quick scheme **here**!"

"But, **there**, *Champagne & Pymmes on the roof terrace,* **anyone**?"

In spite of the dark portending clouds, John's beamer lit up his face – again no despair, but cheerfulness… but, there's always a *but*, or a why, or … from John, today near the end there was no exception, as his misspelt word came back to the fore.
"**Querky**, how oodles of cash allow you to do so much; but with those without, the world is not your oyster – no pearls for them! Me, a non –swimmer, wouldn't/couldn't get close: oh, to have & be able to swim in their cosy, cushioned, millions of pounds abounding, esoteric pools!"

"Come on, John, snap out of it!"
His reply, one might suggest, indignance, but with John you need to look further for the humour-man within.
"Oh, another specialist CB elastic band T treatment? One hard pull and it's all better – ouch – don't think so!"

"Be honest, you have everything a man would want/need/wish for?"
He rubbed his lower lip against his upper, moistening as he did.
The mouth opened slowly and his tongue took over the strokes, left to right, right to left; then he bit his lower lip –

"You might have, **I don't**."
I avoided the personal inquiry response.
"But, honestly, from what you've led me to believe over the months, there isn't anything really missing; so why always the return to misery?"

"I probably will tell you, but not today."

The session ended, left hanging, the missing part to his puzzle was yet to be slotted in – but really I could guess, as he might have guessed mine.

No, I think I know; **he's only guessing**!

I went home that evening and reviewed my state of affairs, or lack of them, as Mary would point out: my *initial outing affair* had yet to materialise…

"I probably will tell you, but not today."

e) Trusting to Trusts but not the Sam Way

Arguing with an Investment Broker, on a comical note…As his misspelt word came back to the fore <>
'**Q**_uerky_'.
The Latin word was actually, ***Quercus*** = *Oak*.
John, with his Classics Education, suggested the Investment Trust Fund name should have been **Glans** = '*Acorn*'.
'*So, from that the Investments would be seen metaphorically to grow into big oaks!*' as what the Fund would have wanted to achieve!
They laughed and went their separate Tube ways home.

But John had one last Inheritance card up his sleeve for me:-

"If you're fortunate to socialise with one of the many Guinness Investment Brokers/Advisors you can glean where the big & smaller monies are."
One he admired was one of the Guinness' Investment Portfolio Trust Managers who personally replicated Adam Faith's ability to make then lose then remake his own millions but keep them + grabbing the future wife-to-be attention of his 20-year-old younger spouse! (Who says Money doesn't Trump Love when it comes to Pairing Off Choices?)

But it doesn't take any insider information to figure out that The Northumberland Estate Inheritance/Trust Fund Amounts far exceed the Samuel's?"
"But John it has been well publicised/documented, so no guessing would be needed, would it?"
"OK, but in reality seeing what the Duchess had to contend with and go to Court for, one can really argue how much does any individual really needs to feel secure?
So, perhaps on a lower more (Parental Chosen) practical scale, with just your *few* allocated millions with which you first buy your house, preferably near those you know, say here Notting Hill/Ladbroke Grove Way and then have enough large change to go merrily on with your life!"   …

John was not ignorant of Inheritance facts & figures, like those apparent Media Inflated Sabrina Funds, upon which he would pour scorn. She had made a public declaration sometime in the 1990s ◇ at a YCTV Charity Auction that she was not Rich and had to go to work etc, had a mortgage etc., so he felt safe in his assumption of her gross asset wealth! Jasmine highlighted the same misconceived fact.
But, unlike Sam's he didn't have total access to James's full Trust detail – he died some 10 years later ◇.
And between those times, ◇ the YCTV financial bail outs never came from her, rather via Clive? (See Later)

But apparently all the Gossip Columnists seem to have some inside information as to the Trust Detail and are claiming how she will be hundreds of million dollars richer come 2025 AND five years later, on top of the $100 she already apparently has!?
"Where do they get such nonsense from? She'll be 70 in 2025!
John poured vitriolic scorn on such sites:
"These yankee doodle types just seem to randomly pick numbers out of their mist laden, uninformed clouds!"

Suffice it to say **NOW**, none of that concerned him, (And, using Nat's words to John, **NOW a distant memory**).

But back with the Samuelites with some simple investment account/public property record checking, he did note within which property areas he understood they made their *astute* purchases to suit their individual needs & preferences, **which are not for disclosure!!!**
And no mention of such ridiculous Trust figures like above of a $200 million here & there to toss around between them!
Ah well, 'C'est la Vie!'
Needless to say Nat with 3 kids in tow, would be expected to have the biggest house (in the area etc she had mentioned when they met) – similar in size to her parents' old Marble Arch situated one, where she cut her teeth on Business Secretaryship – but a snip at less than a ¼ of the price!
Area mattered there more as it could have aided Rich's daily tube &/or train travel toil to & from his then Old Street workplace.
But as we know he has *'cycled'* away across the Channel since then!

And then there was old Daddy who could pop in and put his feet up after some serious *'Anna Freud Funding [RJ] Discussions'* ½ a mile across the road from her. But the New Build Financing might start to ring some *alarmist* (?) bells!

And so on the Rodney Street Eastern Bloc Horizon, Bigger than All the above Funds put together, [RJ] a certain Billionaire Hitter had appeared – in the form of a Shining Black Knight in Cash Funding Rescuing Armour! Leaving his visible legacy on the front of Michael's new Centre of Excellence!

<u>*So why worry?*</u>

But, and there is always a Big But with John: And here it is all the Way from the Great US of A!

CAATSA Section 241(a)(2)-(5) requires a report on Russian parastatal entities, including an assessment of their role in the economy of the Russian Federation; an overview of key U.S. economic sectors' exposure to Russian persons and entities; an analysis of the potential effects of imposing additional debt and equity restrictions on parastatal entities; and the possible impact of
additional sanctions against oligarchs, senior political figures, and parastatals on the U. S. and Russian economies.
Russian parastatals have origins in the Soviet Union's command economy. After the dissolution of the Soviet Union, the Russian government conducted large-scale privatization of these entities; in the early 2000s, it began to renationalize large companies.
The Russian government has responded to economic shocks, including the financial crisis in 2008 and the imposition of sanctions in 2014, by increasing its role in the economy and ownership of parastatals.

As of 2016, Russian parastatals accounted for one-third of all jobs in Russia and 70 percent of Russia's GDP. For purposes of this requirement, Russian parastatals ˣ are defined as companies in which state ownership is at least 25 percent and that had 2016 revenues of approximately $2 billion or more.
A list of such parastatals and the required analysis specified in Section 24 1(a)(2)-(5) are included in the classified annex of this report.

And here *Embarrassingly (?) for so many* - **situated in Appendix B, Oligarchs @ No 35 is > Vyacheslav Kantor...Who?**   **Read on and Discover >**

But Kings X calls us for our first port of call >

f) <u>Anna's Complete Overhaul Courtesy of some Very Special Fellow Jewish (Etceteri) Patronages</u>

So you'll note this constitutes the Front Cover – Can you read the name at the front of the Grandiose Building?   **(NB 3 pages on >)**

Well, what happens now? Apparently Nothing? Apparently!

But, and here is another John Big But:

April 2022 <> King Solomon High School in Redbridge has dropped the name of its benefactor, Viatcheslav Moshe Kantor, after the oligarch was sanctioned by the UK government earlier this month over his ties to Russian president Vladimir Putin.

April 2022 <> A Hampstead private school is 'reviewing' the name of its sports pavilion after a Russian billionaire was sanctioned by the UK government in response to the invasion of Ukraine.
University College School (UCS) named its new sports pavilion The Kantor Centre after the businessman and philanthropist Viatcheslav (Moshe) Kantor.
Dr Kantor donated to UCS through his charitable foundation. The Kantor Centre officially opened at the school's playing fields in West Hampstead in autumn 2019.

April 2022 <> Viatcheslav Moshe Kantor's Charity, which donated £9m. to the Private (Royal) Marylebone Hospital and a Charity set up by the Prince of Wales used and supported by the then Queen and the Royal family, has been made the subject of an inquiry following sanctions.
And even old Tone got in the rejection act:-
October 2022 <> His Tony Blair Institute, that not-for-profit organisation, has announced its severing of links/funding relationship with Billionaire, Moshe Kantor!

And as likely there might be more in the offing?

Apart from being EXTREMELY WEALTHY this man, a Russian Jew, actually maintains an impressive array of *philanthropic* credentials, which are as follows <> President of the European Jewish Congress (EJC), co-founder and President of the International Luxembourg Forum on Preventing Nuclear Catastrophe, co-founder and President of the European Council on Tolerance and Reconciliation (ECTR), and founder and Chairman of the European Jewish Fund (EJF). Kantor also serves in leadership positions with the World Holocaust Forum Federation (WHFF), World Jewish Congress (WJC), where his is Chairman of the Policy Council and Jewish Leadership Council (JLC).

But he still suffers from those Associated Russian Sanctions!
And for how long?
But Michael, Anna & Co Welcomed him with readily open grateful arms
<> Want a Peek inside?

Yes <>

So let's retrace to its Grand Opening –

Yours Truly Attended!

From: Anna Freud National Centre for Children and Families [mailto:no-reply@annafreud.org]
Sent: 24 April

Subject: Booking Receipt - Booking-SIM13-37913

Tel: +44 (0)20 7794 2313
12 Maresfield Gardens, London
NW3 5SU
www.annafreud.org

Doctor M Xavier
Banish Anguish Clinic, Harley Street,
London, United Kingdom

24th April

Booking-SIM13-37913

Dear Doctor Xavier

This email confirms that payment has been received for the booking below.

Schools in Mind: Centre of Excellence Celebration Event (London)

scheduled for 18 June

Participants: Doctor M Xavier

A separate email has been sent confirming your course booking. If you have any questions, or wish to make a change to your booking please contact jamila.yeboah@annafreud.org with your Booking Reference Number Booking-SIM13-37913.

Thank you for booking at the Anna Freud National Centre for Children and Families.

Anna Freud National Centre for Children and Families is a company limited by guarantee.
Registered in England number 03819888
Registered office 12 Maresfield Gardens, London, NW3 5SU
Registered charity number 1077106

NB from 3 pages back >

2023 UPDATE

I suppose the pressure was just too much, or the potential adverse publicity and possible overspill affecting their own Young Royal Supporters on High?

<u>NOTICE THE DIFFERENCE? NO MORE KANTOR!</u>

<u>*Now Back to...*</u> Anna had started it from those humble offices down Hampstead Way...

Whose related Mental Health Offices were in a location in Rodney Street – they were becoming too small to deal with all the ever increasing work, advice & teaching on their specialised subject they attracted, it was decided by the Trustees – The Board's head being none other than our Philanthropic Michael - with Bold Expansive Plans that a new larger adjoining building be built.
And knew our Russian/Jewish Billionaire? Need you ask?
And so we ended up with such a Magnificent (Expensive?) Edifice!

**Whose Patrons/Supporters/Financers were Many in Number >
But, First Pride and Place to**

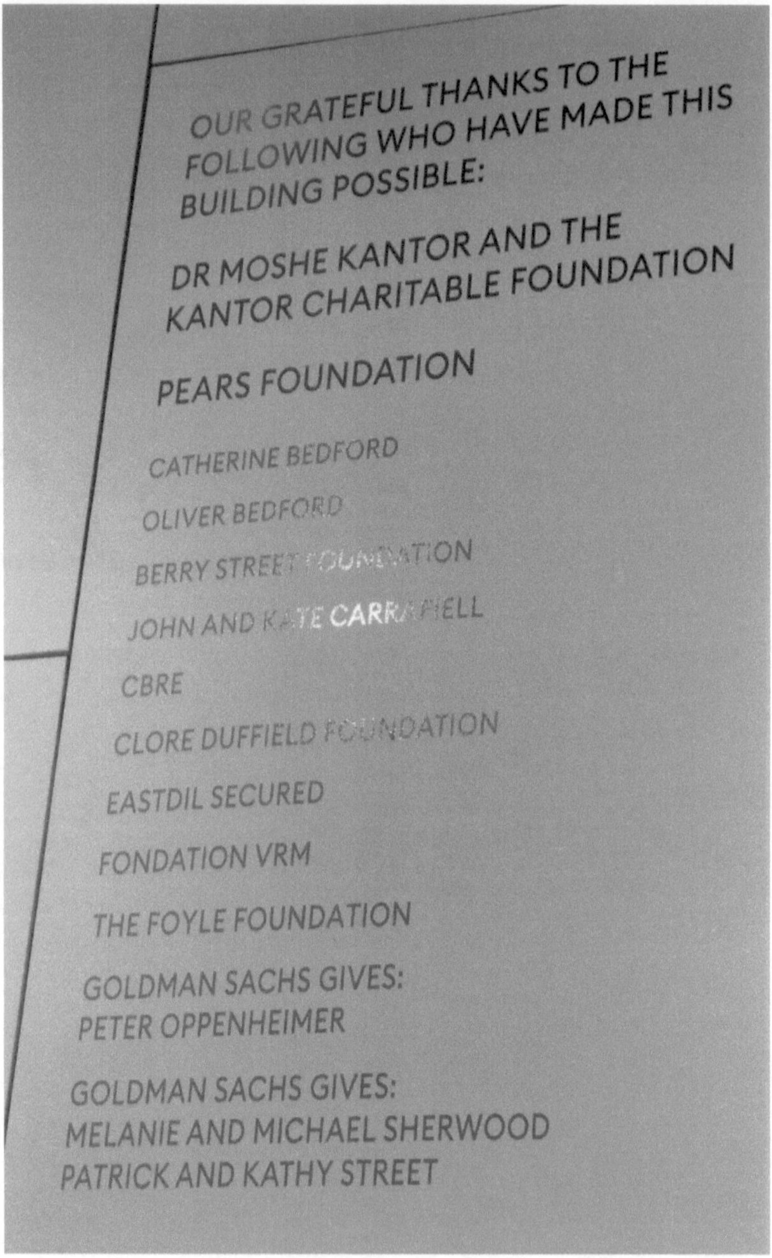

OUR GRATEFUL THANKS TO THE FOLLOWING WHO HAVE MADE THIS BUILDING POSSIBLE:

DR MOSHE KANTOR AND THE KANTOR CHARITABLE FOUNDATION

PEARS FOUNDATION

CATHERINE BEDFORD
OLIVER BEDFORD
BERRY STREET FOUNDATION
JOHN AND KATE CARRAFIELL

CBRE
CLORE DUFFIELD FOUNDATION

EASTDIL SECURED

FONDATION VRM

THE FOYLE FOUNDATION

GOLDMAN SACHS GIVES:
PETER OPPENHEIMER

GOLDMAN SACHS GIVES:
MELANIE AND MICHAEL SHERWOOD
PATRICK AND KATHY STREET

10 Lines Down: And the next also shows Michael & Son Trusts Charitably Donating ↓↓

> GREENOAK
> THE HANDS FAMILY TRUST
> LARS AND ANNICK HUBER
> THE LORD LEVY
> MARIAMARINA FOUNDATION
> THE MONUMENT TRUST
> ELIZABETH AND DANIEL PELTZ OBE
> LEE POLISANO, CARROL MCCUTCHEN AND FAMILY
> THE MICHAEL SAMUEL CHARITABLE TRUST
> THE PETER SAMUEL CHARITABLE TRUST
> ---
> THE SEGELMAN TRUST
> DOMINIC SHORTHOUSE
> THE SIR JULES THORN CHARITABLE TRUST
> THE UTLEY FOUNDATION
> GARFIELD WESTON FOUNDATION
> THE CHARLES WOLFSON CHARITABLE TRUST
> THE WOLFSON FOUNDATION
> RANDY AND JEANNE WORK

All the above greet you as you leave the Lobby Area and continue into the Building's Inners.

"And you just a Humble Balliol Fellow/Friend Supporter!?" **His glare said it all!**

Now for the Tutorials >>>

15:30 – 16:00	Registration, Networking & Refreshments
16:00 – 16:15	Welcome and overview of Schools in Mind and Mental Health and Wellbeing in Schools Programme Jaime Smith, Director of Mental Health and Wellbeing in Schools (AFC)
16:15 – 16:35	Therapeutic work in schools: Schools Outreach Team Cyra Neave, Senior Clinician, Schools Outreach Team (AFC)
16:35 – 16:55	Peer Mentoring at Firs Primary School Rachel Blurton, Deputy Headteacher, Linda Talbot, Learning Mentor and pupils (Firs Primary School)
16:55 – 17:05	Discussion / Break
17:05 – 17:25	The Pears Family School Brenda McHugh, Consultant psychotherapist, Co-Director of the Family School & Co-Director of The Family School Programme, Pears Family School
	Learning from school-based mental health research: links between mental health and academic outcomes Dr. Jess Deighton, Co-Director (Evidence...)
	Q&A
	Networking

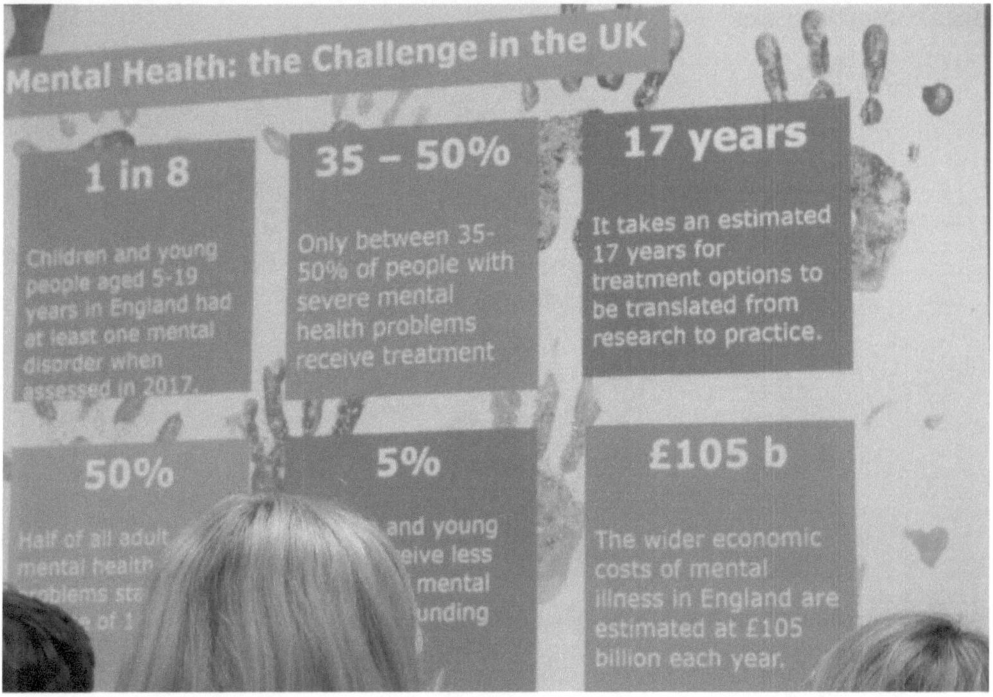

Mental Health: the Challenge in the UK

1 in 8
Children and young people aged 5-19 years in England had at least one mental disorder when assessed in 2017.

35 – 50%
Only between 35-50% of people with severe mental health problems receive treatment

17 years
It takes an estimated 17 years for treatment options to be translated from research to practice.

50%
Half of all adult mental health problems sta... of 1...

5%
...and young ...eive less ...mental ...unding

£105 b
The wider economic costs of mental illness in England are estimated at £105 billion each year.

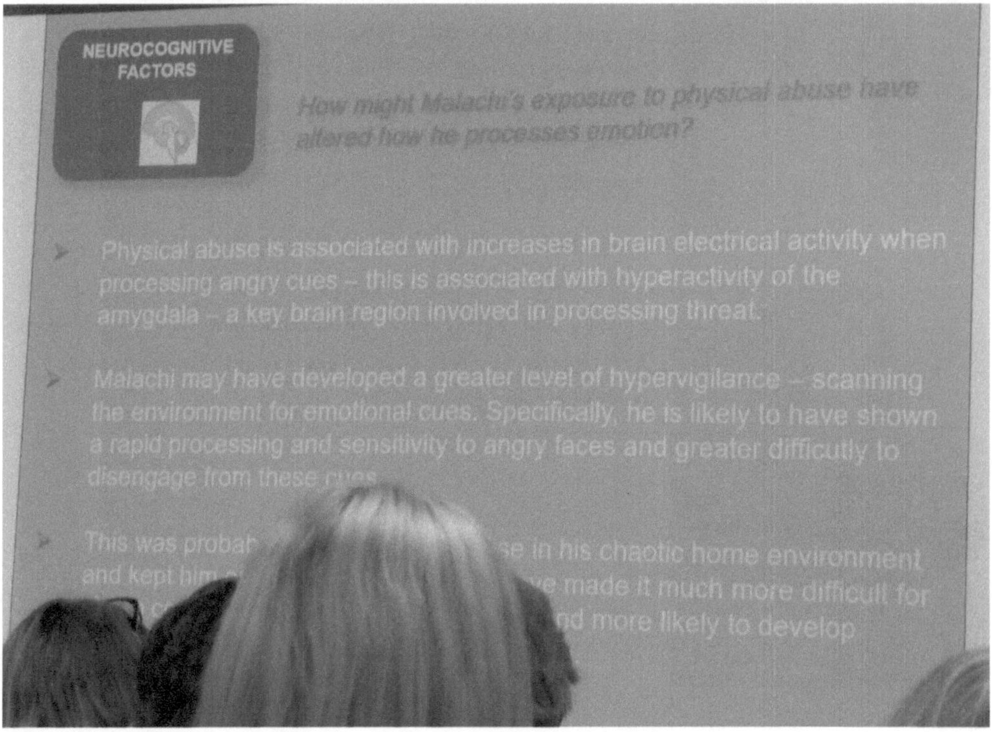

NEUROCOGNITIVE FACTORS

How might Malachi's exposure to physical abuse have altered how he processes emotion?

- Physical abuse is associated with increases in brain electrical activity when processing angry cues – this is associated with hyperactivity of the amygdala – a key brain region involved in processing threat.

- Malachi may have developed a greater level of hypervigilance – scanning the environment for emotional cues. Specifically, he is likely to have shown a rapid processing and sensitivity to angry faces and greater difficulty to disengage from these cues.

- This was probab... ...se in his chaotic home environment and kept him ... ...ve made it much more difficult for ... ...nd more likely to develop

And one special Peter more

Author Copyright ◇ **Peter Fonagy** is the Chief Executive of the Centre.

I THINK THAT ABOUT SUMS IT ALL UP....

Footnote: Michael has seemingly supported this particular special to his heart Charity the longest of all his other Charitable projects.
But, and it is a Big Royal Patronage But, one Big Hitter is HRH The Duchess of Cambridge (Now Princess of Wales) is a Patron of the Anna Freud National Centre for Children and Families.
Michael's Wife Julia is Kate's Son's God-Mother. What a Regal Co-incidence!?

In May 2019 HRH The Duchess of Cambridge opened the Anna Freud Centre. During the visit Her Royal Highness also met with families attending Pears Family School, an alternative provision school for pupils aged 5-14 who have been excluded or are at risk of exclusion from mainstream education.

**ANNA FREUD TRUSTEES THIS LIST ILLUSTRATES
<u>A REAL POWERHOUSE OF NOTABLES</u>:-**

Michael Samuel MBE Chair

Catherine Bedford

Tori Cadogan

Antonia Cowdry

Andrew Evans

Pamela Hutchinson OBE

Anne-Marie Huby

Namrata Kamdar

Professor Linda Mayes

Peter Oppenheimer

Daniel Peltz OBE

Professor Steve Pilling

Dominic Shorthouse

Sarah Wood OBE

PART 15: SABRINA – YOU CAN TRY VALIANTLY – BUT?

THE

(Hello Sabrina!)

YCTV STORY

BASICALLY PUT

....

John's Personal (YCTV Intro)

"So, that old lady said life & relationships; you've said health & relationships. I have another for you – dreaming!"

He looked up at me in his *familiar* way, with his *familiar* grin, with his *familiar* eyes, in that *familiar* cognizant way.

"I shouldn't be letting you know what I might talk about in future sessions, as there won't be any surprise."

"Well, don't you concur?"

"And with a bit of that high-brow lingo!"

I could have taken over then, but, here, it wasn't my time to say: here, it was his time to say, when. He recognised this, although no word was spoken, he knew where he had to go and when was now!

"Yes, it is not only those who are without who **dream** of getting it. Just cos you're either rich &/or famous, or, from this, well-connected, **you can dream** of achievements, which apparently are out of your compass, even out of your comfort zone, but you can still give it a try! *She did*. But new technology **within her dream bubble** eventually caught up & burst it! Or, was it just those *beneath her*, who just didn't cut the mustard for those *above her*, either rich &/or famous, or, from this, well-connected, whom she wanted to *financially* attract? Or had the edge just gone from her resolve?"

....

<u>Y</u>ou <u>C</u>an <u>T</u>ry <u>V</u>aliantly (The beginning of?)

<u>In John's personally experienced words hereon...</u>

Hi, Nice to meet you ...I am happy for you to speak of The Citykids Foundation as we are honored for you to use my quote ...Best, Laurie...

"We believe if you bring young people together from different racial, cultural, and socioeconomic backgrounds and challenge them to develop their own solutions, they will respond with energy, imagination, commitment and action.

Our Mission & Vision are accomplished through employing four basic, but, powerful principles: Safe Space, Youth-to-Youth Communication, Multi-Cultural Bridge Building & Leadership Development."

So, said cultural activist Laurie Meadoff, who founded CityKids, as a non-profit, multicultural youth organization located in New York City.

The seed was there, then, and someone, here, then, planted her own.

And so it began to grow.

In just over three years, almost single-handedly she had raised half a million pounds to fund the project – though not her money, as she was not as rich as all thought so - she was still literally only a working girl, she confessed!

Here would be as good a place as any.

Hard to imagine it was once a disused car factory.

Some compared it to, was it *Kids & Co, or CityKids*, whatever, the links were there in New York and Los Angeles and perhaps that's where the satellite idea was also fledged? And in 1992 (she had been for the past years working in the film business at the time with just 2 limited credits I could find) the latter city suffered riots, similar to those here many years later. Their solution lay in focusing idle hands & minds into something constructive giving the youths a sense of ownership. It is a moot point if we have actually well handled the aftermath in the UK and compared the respective aftermaths.

Hers concentrated on the kids feeling of self-worth and that they too could be creative and it gave them their means to their self-created ends, whether through scripted stories, music &/or dance outlets. Later, some would get a chance to draft Children's TV scripts and get acting opportunities – young age being no barrier.

Youth Community TV

It first broadcast 1/10/95… launched after the 'Challenge Anneka' team converted a community hall in North Kensington into a television studio in 24 hours. After the initial finding their way process, programmes went out on cable three times a day.

"One thing, not made a mention of, was the, perhaps, Charles Levison's assistance afforded to her? Anyway:

Anyone, aged between 11/19, could join and gain training in all aspects of television production. There were daily workshops incorporated into a structured educating process.

As a member (noticeably over three quarters were ethnic minorities) you could move up through the level system making Programmes for their transmission. Ultimately you could get the chance to make Programmes for digital TV channels and get valuable work placement within the media industry.

There was In-house training support at all levels & it involved working on varied productions. All training was by practical experience, with NO lectures or essays. Whether you were interested in learning technical, creative or performing skills, they offered training to suit your needs and desires.

When you joined you would do a brief induction course, where you would meet staff and assist making a TV programme. After this you became a level 1 member, rising to level 3 as you gained more experience and knowledge – all at your own individual pace.

Once at level 3, you would have the necessary experience to go for a job in the media industry.

The first chairman was Greg Dyke; the BBC and Channel 4 were also supporters.

Literally, in those early years the kids going through its doors nearly averaged 200/annum! Success was not guaranteed, but was achievable if one persevered: one 'graduate' joined YCTV, aged 13, went on to obtain a John Lyon Bursary at LAMDA and went on to be with the RSC... YCTV helped so many escape their ever so real troubles at home and around them; enlarging and developing ever so raw talent, it gave them that first tentative step into the media industry...

The keypad entrance would introduce you to a receptionist who made you sign in *(like I had to each time)* and then it was upwards and onwards to the first floor to a left, right angled balcony, which overlooked the stage area. Then you would make your way to the offices. Getting back out was one of two ways: one the front door and the other a large dimly lit concrete staircase, which could feature in spooky or murderous plot lines!

The back door led into a possible garden space (regrettably on some occasions a dumping ground), but an outdoor area which too could be used to practise/develop scripts/scenes. Budding film makers trying to succeed in something they began to enjoy *working* at.

And there were so many successes. Well for so many there was only one way from rock bottom – so this gave them an upwardly mobile feel, and the camaraderie helped at so many levels, but all great things must come to an end sometime!

Although, there was no sadness at the farewell party which she promised to attend, joviality and photo exchanges abounded, free spirits at play – perhaps the final venue had some *pub* to do with it?

But, that was their last hurrah …But, ***history*** was to show there was so much which came before...But, ***history*** taught people another lesson: *If the Press has no* real *news to report upon, a simple expedient for fleshing out, say the rear sports pages, as the front, is with a source/friend says, or whatever, suggests/might imply etc. then is critically dissected from all angles and, hey presto, an apparent news worthy article, even though it is something old and exhausted, just rehashed in a different fashion. So, that the source, I handed her, quoted in that Sunday Supplement, Ladbroke Hall article,* **was not a friend of hers!!!***)*

This was typical of her abhorrence of what people write/say of her, nearly all made up, or wrong, or ignoring truth, just done for the sensationalising of her life, which wasn't as such, just to sell newspapers! With photos a definite, no, no!

She would say never to believe what the press write about her – that *Winged Beat***Hell** connection was a later perfect example. Simply put, it was kinda like, '*One should never believe anything that was written and only 50% of what was said!*'

So, it's now back to...
The Charity, such a fantastic and rare thing where the early years' credits go to her for the vision and the drive to make it happen- it really took something incredible to start a charity and keep it going all those years! It certainly wasn't easy.
But, it wasn't a solo effort and thanks too, go to everyone involved with the organization and for their acts of generosity, with their time and money.
And it initially had big ideas/plans: one of which was to have satellite stations around the country and a possible annual Hollywood Scholarship, although she ultimately discounted both as they weren't to happen, interestingly enough some time later she told someone that there was still a hope of creating such a satellite station in LA & New York and had applied for the necessary tax status in the US, but nothing more seemed to arisen: likely then it fell at this first hurdle, or the funding couldn't be found. Funding was always the critical factor in all planning decisions, selling to a broadcast Company was so much more profitable than anything else, but the custom hard to come by.

The creative teenagers were encouraged to take ownership for their creations. But, from ownership comes responsibility and they then realised why schedules need to be maintained and targets met, the Cable TV, Videotron, outlet demands also highlighted this. Television, at one time boring, or unfulfilling, now took on a different meaning and became more personally relevant. The creativity content was student driven; all seemed to get a role whether at the front or behind the camera, with the staff, in the main, advisors, supporters and stimulators. In 2000 there were 10 full time staff, not that many more than when I last visited and pay not bad (In the late nineties the Office manager was on around £20k/annum). On the last named subject, employment, it offered a way to improve skills to get jobs.

<u>In 2001, things began to expand,</u> with over a thousand on their database, the Charity was attracting specific and all too welcome support both financially, administratively, educationally; with those internal facility improvements; skills training development was not forgotten (*it was still a problem for the older students whose potential & industry were not in question, but whose knowledge and experience needed broadening &/or increasing somewhat to bridge the gap with external competition*) – to this end GLALDA injected a massive £200k, for which her Changing Faces project was the beneficiary!

And then the mooted TV Mentoring scheme …

The earlier years were great times and had many stories to relay: that David Bowie attendance, her greatest achievement?

Or, was it that innovative passing the *Mic?*

Additionally, London was not the Charity's only oyster: being richly connected her relatives had their Estates to use as settings, her brother-in-law's down Somerset Way, a typical location experience example. There, for example, is quite expansive, hilly, woody, & lends itself well to outdoor film scenes, even abounds with several streams/rivers thrown in for good effect.

290

It was admirable, her involving the kids & staff inviting them to that/those Estate(s), or her place - so many Patrons ignore those who keep the Charity afloat.

Her involvement, all hands to the pump so to speak, although, as Charitable acts go, within the (female?) family, such acts are no stranger to them: *As shown earlier/ante*.

....

*Y*ou *C*an *T*ry *V*aliantly (Hunky-Dory?!)

The *disaffected* youth she was trying to attract in accordance to the Mission Statement was not always according to any strict definition and so the door was opened to others who just sought somewhere to express their skills/ideas, within appreciative common circles. Perhaps Luky was one, who with his friend, Ant, shone above the others for a while: both from impeccably middle class homes, though were perhaps authority challenging tearaways of sorts at one time. They went on to a better life in sunny California, although only Luky figured on **her** face book pages, albeit his more public page, not the personal – there again he was the one who started passing *Mike* about and **she** provided the celebs to use *him* and then hand *him* to another – even *Tones* our ex PM (P170)!

But, not all was peachy behind those key-padded doors, as with all organisations there are those satisfied and others *disaffected,* even within, by the goings on: did mother make some of her babies cry!?

It is common that a *celebrity founder* is dependent and reliant on the advice and activities of the CEO/Manager in charge on the shop/stage floor; this sometimes adversely affected those who joined hoping for support and direction, which did not always present itself as aspired.

But, first the contentious issue, the other types who came through the door and were fêted for a while: some were given money, invited to *that flat* etc. unfortunately some with Mental Health Issues who, some might have claimed needed proper professional support, *(The Julia Sister/Michael Brother-in-Law Anna Freud Type)* not patronising.

No matter what, these, perhaps, might have been dropped, or substituted as soon as selected and used – there were so many more who could take their place!

There again later there were some clear victories for those less physically & mentally able; so there are always two sides to this *lad's broken* coined tale!

But, if simply put, working with young people, so many **with so much serious psychological baggage**, is not a simple process and it needs to be done as professionally as any other work should be and with hers, like thousands of other organisations, it might not have been so in a few cases. This is not a criticism just a fact of that type of organisation's life: kids from broken homes/lives are a challenge which 100% successful transition guarantees cannot be given – but they gave it their best shot!

There again who could blame the staff or this *god-sent* benefactress whose only concern was the well-being and lot improvement for the many she saw living about her with no prospects, nor change in sight, for their disillusioned life.

So many did benefit, the dissenters were the minority; so many had the fairy godmother beside them, some showed off to all the celebrity friends when taken on tours around the facility, encouraged to tell their individual sob stories to cameras, sometimes embellished, like so any others, to play upon the heartstrings of potential funders. But, in the main, when there, <u>she</u> was always proffering advice & heartfelt encouragement to each and every social/economic group – black was white and white was black to her ie no natural bias - and offering hope for the future: the pumpkin expansion evolution came with its own big bang, although not short-lived if compared to similar others, as the full development would be curtailed as certain, predictable problems started to make their presence felt and forced changes and detours, which would lead to the inevitable cliff edge demise.

There again, here is another two-sided tale where student and school tried to get the??? out of each other, which suited each of them most.

Sad, this comment on life plays itself out daily in all walks of life!

Well, yes, but some always imagine the goings on through rosy tinted glasses without problems as all were striving for a shared goal, but it was how <u>some</u> tried to go about it, that saddened. Although, one special, exceptional employee went the extra hundreds of miles defending the weaker against bully boys trying to break in – *the only things broken were her ribs, or was it her arm?* She deserved the highest praise, but her name (later) could have been lost to ignorance posterity.

Speaking of bully-boy tactics, on rare occasions one, or two of the working students might have been subjected to some heavy-handed management treatment, affecting some individuals financially & more importantly emotionally, where their workload burden was increased more & more, not the remuneration … but regrettably all one could say at the time was *'welcome to the real world'* where everything is not hunky-dory!

Though, the salutary lesson learned by those who upset those perceived as higher up the Forbes list – annoy he/she/them at your peril and (welcome to) the *be-blanked-also* at any future media function staged meeting venue!?

There again were they not well praised for their good work & sterling effort, afterwards, or did *She?* There again, perhaps, the rebellious ones (<u>*like in all other walks of life*</u>) were not liked for their being such, so it would be the cold shoulder treatment outside! *Funny how that lack of eye contact is such a giveaway!* Not really funny, but sad, really.

Conversely speaking, putting the boot in on the other foot, then you got the scenario where, like quite a few certain people were easily as capable of using <u>her</u> for their own needs/ends, as she possibly might have been at using them to massage her own ego, or look good in front of people she wanted to impress with her philanthropy, or do-gooding.

There again *no change here in the outside real world*, but philanthropy implies financial clout, yet not possible as by the lady's own admission, bucket loads she had none (though there was no mention of the existence, or future receipt, of/from any possible Trust Funds then?!), but, then, there again wasn't there also, as well as the first floor flat, a Country Cottage?

She might have got angry at times when discovering *her exploitation by pupils et cetera,* as she was unaware most times until it was brought to her attention. Contradictively speaking, having the Charity's experience on one's CV did not seem to carry any future weight outside?

Whether it really did/did not does not tarnish the memory of all the successful ventures & partnerships with so many: support over the years had been by a wide range of Trusts & Foundations, Central & Local Government, Individuals & an increasing number of Private Companies.

But, several of the staff were also guilty of such actions of trying to get into the industry, or rubbing up with the celebrities <u>she</u> introduced to the group. With such happenings the atmosphere might have become, on certain few occasions, a tad strained.

But, getting back on track with some facts & figures...

Aspirations at the start were great, with a scholarship to the best student and possible satellite expansion, but things had to be scaled back when NTL TV Channel folded and after about 3 years the *dyke* needed a finger insertion to stem the flow and it wasn't for her want of trying as she always tried to be in the office as much as possible.

But the Board brought in some BBC type storm trooper(s) and the balance of power might have shifted at the turn of the century when a former BBC News Business Manager was brought in to run the Charity and the BBC maintained their committed administrative support; Carlton & Granada were to finance training & offer placements; Channel 4 supplying a studio & editing suite.

Then, in 2004/05[X], there also came a process of re-organisation, continuing through into 2006 – a certain advisor/benefactor type Charles Levison died that same year.

[X] *Sometimes in 2004/05 her students (and <u>herself</u>?) were introduced to* **a Tom Stoppard Masterclass** *– if so,* **she left an impression** *whose fond recall was to make its real matrimonial mark much later?*

Hereafter, activities seemed to have taken a broader scope: in addition to their already successful in-house Individual Learning Plans, a bridging programme with Ravensbourne College having been accredited by the London Open College Network.

<> Here are those easy to recall >>>

Julian Temple	Martin Hughes (Comedy Producer)	Michael Ford (Double Oscar Set Designer)
London Philharmonic Orchestra	Gate Theatre	Theresa Russell
Anjelica Houston	Tony Blair > Mic <	< Self-effacing Peter (*moving* > *house*) Mandelson
Harrison Ford >	David Bowie >	< Iman
Bill Clinton	George Lucas	Bill Murray
Jeremy Irons (*also for her youngest sister's Trust*)	David Frost	Dan Ackroyd
Prince Nazeem	Bob Geldof Et Al!	Michael Figgis
Perhaps a Beatle, or, not, but definitely a Model Hall + Her *Jaggering* NE Packhorse Leading Rolling Stone too!		

Then, there is also a variety of shows they produced, from the simple Political Party Events and Pop Star Gigs & behind the scenes stuff, which were not the ultimate revenue streams (Later):-

Jump Start (Documentary on Entrepreneurs)	A special *'Round Table'* BAFTA work on the state of kids	West End promotion reel for the play, Journey's End
Kids n Art project – young people engaging with theatre	Cycle Safety films for *Notting Hill Police (Someone we know knows the latter, all too well!)*	Studio Showcase of Young Talent for Black History Month
British Airways	Underground Soundz	Cinemania
Skills Workshops across all Craft Skills with further education & BBC training advancement in mind	Programmes aired on not just on NTL, but also the Community Channel, Sky, Home Choice & Video Networks	The famous £250k BBC commission, yet so short lived, Pass the Mic *(2000's main attraction)*
Newsdays, their successful studio magazine	School Group Productions	Dramas such as Moonlight and Half Full
Community based films like Dalgarno	Special under 14s documentary about life on their estates	Membership of Creative London's C-Hub
Cinema Shorts for Channel 4	London wide *Taster Days* covering animation & location video training	The legacy of their LDA Changing Faces 4 Program
LDA Steps Partnership with Paddington Arts & Video College	YCTV Radio Treats and Channel 4's Citizen Power	And one of its more notable *spawn* the Toxteth TV Project

But, by 2007, student numbers began dwindling as there weren't enough projects to engage them.

It never recovered them/then.

But, there were some surprising successes: one, who came with nothing, but, strove above the crowd. No wonder he was the only ex on her Facebook page: he certainly was an innovative achiever of his times.

His 2006 Dubplate Drama, which gave viewers the chance to use text messages to dictate storylines. At its peak, the drama attracted 400,000 viewers on C4; PlayStation dealt with 5000 downloads and on occasion servers crashed!

He did so much more; presumably somewhat of a posthumous piece of reflected, *Jewelled* glory in YCTV's Crown?

But, that's not doing justice to all those getting on in the industry both in front and behind the camera – there are still so many on different trade and professional publications"

....

You Can Try Valiantly (At work & Play)

"*When we did speak freely* (No photo, thank you!) it was interesting that she had all the financial side well buttoned down, whether it was advice from her CEO, or Facilities Manager, or Board Members, or the family Solicitors she retained to represent the Charity.

And so it was, money came from all available sources, even EU grants for staff etc.

I did mention from my own experience the draining effect of the rent* on such a big place and the TV Channel fees, let alone the wage bill, (**the purchase of the Freehold was suggested, but it went no further*) but she seemed unfazed, the staff levels actually increased thereafter, but that's what comes with success – expansion, but then the real juggling act monster is created – there is only so far it can go without consequences ...

There were to be two significant factors, really outside her control the first would be the hermaphroditic, ever so swiftly, reproductive barnacles attaching to and eating away at her wooden hull, known as the ever expansive hand held camcorder; the second the market, where the good programme capability of the students and the set up were called into question by those willing to pay for TV/Media exposure, (*Perhaps as soon as they got any good they felt they could go their own way? - I don't know, but I guess so?*), so it was left to grant aid and commissioned, less profitable, based work.

With *handed* access to the figures you, like me, could not fail to notice there was a significant disparity between *'restricted' & 'unrestricted funds'*: the former were subject to specific conditions imposed by the donor as to the purpose for which the income might be used; with the latter the funds could be used for any purpose within the charity's objectives.

An example of the stranglehold of the former can be shown over the last half a dozen years and should/could/would have hindered expansion:

Year Ended	Unrestricted	Restricted *	Total
30/6/2002	→	→	803 *
30/6/2003	79	742	821 **
30/6/2004	192	900	1092 ***
30/6/2005	137	760	897
30/6/2006	98	470	568
30/6/2007	0	548	548

Tabulated these - rounded up/down, in 000s.
So much simpler on the eye.

*It is sad in one respect, that in 2001 the Board had BBC put their own person in charge and at the same time the Changing Faces project coffers were boosted by the * GLA's massive grant programmed injection, yet within a short while certain cracks began to show.

Despite assurances a couple of years prior, Channel 4's financial commitment was significantly *gut-wrenched* from the Charity's coffers.

➢ The * GLALDA funding, inadvertently, or not, became the major restricted grant source and buoyed the organisation against the financial pressu**rising** waves and over 5 years the amounts were staggering:
2002/03   £200,000

2003/04 295,000

2004/05 408,000

2005/06 174,000

2006/07 257,000

The transition from 2002 to 2003 was not seamless, with so much stitching coming loose in a significantly large quantity with Channel 4 reducing their funding from £137500 to a paltry £12500!

Also, it didn't help at critical negotionary stages with large Charity ** donors to argue with their own God, or Goddess, who could/would indignantly pull the plug to the tune of another £95000, although there were always those imagined multi-millionaire pop star friends to fall back upon, but, incredibly, they never supplied a well-padded cash pillow to cushion the landing. That must've grated her and it had to be another Charity which finally bailed out the sinking ship, their mothercare*de Haan*ds out bearing gifts benefactor, but it came at a price as YCTV *ideas were tapped out.*

Although, Peter's has banged on to greater things.

Squaring the Circle, though *not in* (her now) *Stoppard terms*: if we imagine the founder's public impression is one of wealth, then *that* Charity's bank account did not reflect any patronly large deposits, it was left to other devices and people of certain means – many's-a-time in the latter struggling years did the **'*Jones*'** Chair keep the end of the month wage bills paid – he, it was, at the final takeover, who was £20k, or so, out of pocket, not so apparently any of the founder's!

So much for any rich, famous, heiress tag – no large sums seemingly emanating from there and from another noteworthy source – an old friend of some of the family: I would have thought *NE horse power* penis envy would have made such people flaunt it as compensation? Ah, well, wrong again!

Such famous people with limitless pockets would have easily kept the Charity afloat, but it sank without a (now) trace!

But, if a tiny todger didn't do it for her (monetarily, of course!), Gregory did.

People, like him, were a boon to her initial Charity success: his Channel 5 & BBC position a god send, financially and pupil educationally speaking – pity 2004 came and he went *resignedly* on his way. Meantime, quietly, behind the scenes, she was achieving expert status and with it invites to Committees, including Teenage, or Children School linked Governmental – perhaps being also funded by Y.O.U. helped in their own way, by word of mouth perhaps. Strangely enough, her littlest sister's organisation was invited to train some of them to cope years after big sister's grant receiving days were over!

Without any massive celebrity cash injections there were still those annual, *special* (*not for les pauvres Plebs*) auctions, which were one of the Charity's lifelines, like her sister's and so many others, would not then have been necessary – some friends, eh? But, there again *one* wouldn't have been able to compliment **her and her twin** shyly refusing the audience's plaudits, if *one* hadn't attended – eh?

So spurned on, it was onward & upward for the Charity: significantly in 2003, by which time there were about 20 staff & a dozen-or-so tutors, the local membership had increased 30%, plus more regular attendances; 300 had achieved the basic course standard, half of whom moved into making the Charity's Programmes for TV viewing; the ethos had expanded into something of an extra curricula school and vocational trainer. But, as academia goes, the standard was still low with 2 achieving HNC & HND qualification (The next year there would be 8 hopefuls).

To really get on the first run of the media work ladder e.g. BBC, because there are so many after so few places, the minimum requirement was a degree, which was so far out of a vast majority of these *pupils'* achievement reach!

Anyway, as far as the Charity went, in spite of the funding losses, post 2003 outlook was looking good and I was to eat my words (2004/05) when so many made their entrance into the BBC, MTV & Channel 4 TV world! Not forgetting those into Further & Higher Education – it was no wonder people thought of it more of a competing school!

There were also some memorable tales from those who enjoyed their times: all were complimentary & one went as far to say:

'YCTV was such a fantastic and rare thing. When I described it to people they couldn't believe it - it sounded so cool.

But, let's focus on a certain IzzyWizzy Let's Get Bizzy Girly & here we go <> from this little lass >>>

'It's all been incredibly hectic the last few weeks leaving Uni and moving out etc. I really enjoyed my week at YCTV. I really enjoyed working with a new group of people and brainstorming ideas to make our own individual piece. The people running it were lovely and really supportive, giving us creative control and letting our imaginations run wild. I also enjoyed that there were different areas which we could explore and help out with, script writing, acting, camera work, editing etc. All in all it was something which I am extremely glad I did and given the opportunity would love to do again.'

And the parents got involved too!

'I also attended as a workshop helper and I used my writing to help workshop ideas for a script. An Indian guy whose name I can't quite remember ran the workshop. He was great too. We work-shopped an idea about a girl falling amongst thieves and becoming a prostitute and drug addict; really cheery stuff but that's what came out of the kids.

But, what horrible themes seem to permeate their mind and life, such a sorry tale and it's the <u>woman who suffers yet again</u>, perhaps there were more guys at the workshop than gals?

I could see what he had said triggered a memory, truly bad at that and one I apologise for relating, but it had a bearing on life as it was then – it was no wonder so many of them sought a refuge from the *respect thug/gang culture* which prevailed thereabouts.

If only is a repeated *theme-thought* in selective, recollective, upsetting memory driven life, but here it played out fatally, so skip the next couple of paragraphs **in red in the original,** unless you want to feel sick!

Many newspapers during 2007/08 depicted how dangerous the local streets could be, but regretfully, mirrored throughout the UK where in so many, many, many areas base savagery predominates!

It ended up a fatal irony that where parents trying to do best for their kids, thinking the grass is greener over there, flee a Country to one considered <u>so much safer</u> and within it move to the *better school districts,* here the move was from London's South to North Kensington, the Country they fled from was the Tyrannical oppressed, or Rebel Killing fields known as the Democratic Republic of Congo – and you know my views on that Country – from there *to the cultured and law abiding* English shores, well that's what the rose tinted/colour*ed boat-*brochures state!"

One who John knew trying to make a difference for Women there!   (Author Copyright)

Here is his (John's abridged) version of all what was Press reported; what was said at Court; or just the plain talk on the streets as it was relayed via him, both in his capacity as a *Governmental* representative, or ex Charity pupils' parent – the choice of **BOLD** font is intentional: (It appears in RED in Colour Copies!)

- In 2007, they had previously chased his friend through Shepherd's Bush market and cornered him in a shop, where they set upon him: punching, kicking and stamping him to a pulp.
- Then one <u>brave-boy</u> emptied boiling water over his face and body. Amazingly, they didn't do a <u>good-enough job</u> on him as (?Miraculously?) Seun survived!
- His sister had also been attacked in school by a boy with a knife and CS gas, and one of his friends was struck with bricks.
- He had been challenged to a 'one on one' fight, only to be set upon by a group made up of <u>three</u> of the same youths (isn't this now such a sign of the bully times!?) who now confronted his Amiable <u>Ami</u> , a young <u>Bloomer</u>, who was soon to become <u>Toast!</u> As, about more than half a dozen more <u>brave thugs</u> arrived, killer dog in tow (isn't this now such a sign of the bully times!?).
- The dog is set upon the defenceless, greatly outnumbered (law abiding) youth (<u>the kindly bastards even have dogs doing their dirty business for them!</u>)
- The Court heard how CCTV records show the bit part player, Kodjo, backing away from the <u>star players and their co-starring biting pet</u> (off the lead) as they move in on him.(John's interpretation of how they must have felt – high on their own self-made stage/show?) So, reminiscent of Lord of the Flies, where Piggy was to be spear-pushed over the cliff edge.

- There again here they came with knives, so this now became a slasher movie, where the <u>lead</u> striker revelled in the gore, just as did the <u>Tribe</u>.
- There again here they came with baseball bats which broke bones: where <u>all the Crew</u> revelled in the crunching noises, which were indistinguishable from each other, whether the protecting arms/leg/hands/ribs or the fatal head Caving by these young Neanderthals: this now became a Kodjo snuff(ed) out movie – wasted, but such a waste: those welcoming escape YCTV boards would never be trodden again!!!
- In May 2008, five <u>boys</u> (so now reminiscent of those <u>small kids</u> in Mexico who kill indiscriminately for <u>small change</u> –Oh, how life is so cheap?) (Now? No, just as it always has been!) they were convicted at the Old Bailey of crimes relating to Kodjo Yenga's murder:
- Two <u>big men</u> aged 13, another was 15.
- They were jailed for life and ordered to serve a minimum of 15 years.
- Three others were found guilty of manslaughter, and were sentenced to 10 years, with five years licence on release: those two <u>big men</u>, aged 13 & 14!
- And the most significant elder (in John's eyes/mind), then 16, who had been released on bail # on the morning of the attack (in a separate case involving the intimidation of a witness).

From the above **our bail/parole system has a lot to answer for** # and how can children as young as those just turned 12/13 consider this a future **normal** way of life for themselves?

There again, after 5 years our system will (Feltham?) licence some of them to repeat their *head smashing* favour on some other unsuspecting, innocent **s-o-l-e!**

(The spelling is meant, <u>*not soul*</u>, as it always seems to be the *lone-oner,* who is set upon by a group (all frenzied up!)!"

- It was one of a spate of teenage murders in the capital: twenty seven teenagers were murdered in London in 2007 (18 were stabbed, eight shot, and one beaten to death) (And the school Kodjo attended had two of them!). It was the worst year on record for fatal teenage violence - **until ...** Regrettably, it all now seems to happen everywhere again & again & again, ad infinitum, as the knife way of life, Countrywide @ a thousand a week, is becoming a rampant killer plague contaminating our Society's Streets!

And so, connectively, <u>back to the *fictitious* prostitution & drug addiction story</u>!"

... 'I sort of outreached it and scripted what they came up with. I ended up playing an old slapper; this always seems to happen to me, who helped lead this innocent young girl down the path to doom. It was all quite good fun and we filmed the whole thing in a day. It all happened in a week.'

....

*** (from way above↑) <u>She, too, cut it short resigning from the Board of Trustees 1/12/04; the year ending 30/6/05 continued albeit under now ever increasing severe financial restraints and the funds started, year-on-year, to diminish, until that fateful day 24/10/08.</u>

NB For all those who thought that because she claimed she was not rich, she didn't draw a salary from the Charity: As during her Trustee days, she would not be allowed by the Charity Commission Rules. To obviate these she'd have needed their permission, which I understand she **never** sought!

....

<u>Y</u>ou <u>C</u>an <u>T</u>ry <u>V</u>aliantly (Money *Matters*)

*This was about the time Jenny made me aware things were not so good near Portobello Way. A year later, one of the Racial Equality Contact Units painted an even more **ceasing to trade** sombre picture as to the future.*

....

When you begin to talk to Ex Students/Workers/Board Members, Grant Payers/Contributors et Cetera, you get given/handed all sorts of information verbal & written. (part 1)

...I think this broadly covered their Mission Statement...>>>

The Board of Trustees, which can have up to 30 members, administers the Charity (only up to11 in 2003).

The Board meets on average four times a year to set and review strategies and policies. Other than the Directors, the founder gives her time freely to attend meetings and visits on behalf of the Charity...

<u>Although she resigned as a Trustee 1st December 2004, perhaps the start of self-severing of the YCTV umbilical cord?</u>

There were two distinct, but intertwined strands, the YCTV Foundation and YCTV proper. Their closely connected vision can be easily seen, when their key objectives are compared:

1. The YCTV Foundation to
   a. provide a positive alternative to the risk of street culture. To build a sense of Achievement by encouraging young people to manage and complete their own projects
   b. provide young people with the opportunity to engage with the educational process through the medium of media
   c. offer access to higher education to students without the necessary academic qualifications
   d. provide vocational advice.
   e. encourage young people to build networked for the future.

2. YCTV itself to
   a. promote life skills such as communication, teamwork, confidence and self-expression.
   b. give young people a platform so that they can be heard.
   c. re-engage young people by releasing their creative talents
   d. excite and re-engage young people into the learning process
   e. create television for young people by young people

The strategy for achieving its objectives was thus:

By the engagement and retention of young people between the ages of 12 to 25, through a formal program of media training, which covers video production, drama, music, animation and studio, by offering a formal and non-formal internal structured progression ranging from basic induction though to advanced level: Levels 1 – 3 > where Level <u>three</u> is an industry standard level of professional skills.

Despite the re-organisation, there was production activity every month using the ideas of, and research by the young people, productions by school groups and a summer program of specific dramas; a number of <u>their Community</u> based films; in addition a series of short films which was devised, written, directed and crewed by a team of 15 to 17 year olds which were screened at Channel 4.

Then there was the introduction of menu driven training, covering animation, location video training which enabled them to reach far more young people than previously: primarily through one off "taster days", outreach which covered all London regions.

Further funding for the LDA Steps program was achieved by developing partnerships with other voluntary organisations: this included Paddington Arts and Video College and would enable 70 young people to access training across the three west London charity bases through to 2008.

There was a mix of trepidation & anticipation then about the future, as they were expanding their studios offering the Community greater access to involve themselves in the filming and production of live, studio programmes.

The process of re-organisation of YCTV started in 2004/5 continued through into 2006 ... Targeted external partnerships & collaborations would direct the fundraising strategy, the objective being to move to a model of _sustainability_ .

This aspect would prove the sticking point!

The statement ended with a sort of kids' forecast future expectancy.

The core objective for YCTV remains the long-term retention of excluded and marginalised young people using the pull of production and other media skills to keep them off the streets and constructively engaged in enhancing and developing their own life skills and self- worth.

Very impressive and no show of any internal strain, but, monetarily, things were showing their financial strain...

Financial Review

The Charity made a net loss of £76k as compared to a surplus of £95k in 2005.

Gross income for the year at £649 thousand was down £375 thousand on the previous year largely due to a significant reduction in grant income from government funded bodies, down from £500 thousand to £295 thousand, coupled with the decision to reduce the number of projects undertaken for third parties, which required the buying in of external specialists.
Perhaps, reflective of the workings of the Civil Service, at least YCTV was a fledgling, not a well-established, well oiled, supposedly, well managed machine, but both found to buy-in the best, **costs**!###

These latter projects while generating high gross income, because of their dependency on buying external expertise, ### were very expensive to undertake and made minimal contributions towards the underlying core costs of the Charity.

In addition because of the specialist expertise needed for their completion the direct involvement of the members of the Charity was limited and it was felt did not justify the high investment in staff time and energy.

A not so simple trade-off and it was against the perceived way forward when first created: were the kids now not perceived as good enough?

Expenditure at £725 thousand was down £215 thousand reflecting the reduced activity referred to above.

However the reduction in costs was not as high as the reduction in income due to additional costs arising from the restructuring, the benefits of which were forecast as not to be realised until future years and the need to deliver a few residual projects entered into in 2004/5, which still required the buying in of external expertise.

Investment powers and policy:

The Charity held no investments & it was also not dependent on any single class or form of donation. All funds received were used to further the direct charitable expenditure of the Charity."

Then three years later # the Company's Removal Men Moved In!
Not before the archives were plundered by all and sundry there.
Some computers crumbled under the downloading strain – hers too!

1039218 -
WET RIVER RESOURCES became a **Removed Charity**
Other names
YOUNG PEOPLE'S COMMUNITY TRAINING FOUNDATION (Old Name)
YOUTH CULTURE TELEVISION (Working Name)
Charitable objects
(1) The Advancement Of Education And Vocational Training Of Young People In Need
(2) Such Other Purposes Being Exclusively Charitable According To The Law Of England And Wales As May From Time To Time Be Determined
Lifespan 05 July 1994 until 08 October 2008.
It officially ceased to exist 16 September 2009

Fourteen years. Not bad for an *apparent* rich, famous, heiress founder, who put her heart (not her *apparent* wealth) where her mouth was! And what came out of it was <u>now</u> more important as more *Bodies* wanted to listen, not just locally, but the broader Charitable field and also the Governmental from the Home Office to the Department for Children, Schools and families et al.

The money came from so many listed sources.

But the Big Ones Missing were those Super Rich Pop Stars &/or those with so much money they didn't know what to do with it!

Strangely nothing is shown of any vast donations from those sources!

So how good a friend were any of them really?

But those ever well established *(Part of the inter-related family Triumvirate)* **Family links (incl. by marriages) Goldsmiths & Rothschilds were there with their bucket loads until...????**

YCTV donators list of so many of the benefactors, commissioners and funders, who contributed to the continuance of such a well-intentioned *projected* dream (*pun intended*!)

(Some may be of assistance to so many well-intentioned Charitable Organisations, or just Start-Ups)

Incredibly these are just the tip of the immense iceberg out there awaiting you, though unlike the Titanic's, these are here to save, not sink, your vision!

But, how long you keep afloat
is down to your directional choice
& the type of other well laden ships,
which you can attract
to your own project, establishing port?

<u>But the list of names is quite impressive:</u>

BBC
MTV
NFTE
BME TV
Channel 4

Arts Council England
Garfield Weston
Goldsmiths) _a family link_
Rothschilds) _a family link_
Cavendish
Sigwood
Duffield
Niarchos's
Weinberg
Woo Foundation
Newbury Trust
Nottinghill Trust
Peabody Trust
Kensington & Chelsea *(Where Rickman's YCTV Trustee wife was a Councillor)*
(Or, your local Council)
British Board of Film Classification
Barclays Bank
(Including their Media Team)
Paul Hamlyn Foundation
Chrysalis
Granada TV
Carlton TV
Camden Charities
Heritage Lottery Fund
London Development Association
Home Office e.g. YJB/YOU
(Or, applicable Government Dept.)
HLF/Young Roots
First Light
European Social (Staffing) Fund
Rayne Foundation
Calouste Guilbenkian Foundation
BBC Children in Need
War Child Charity
Rose Foundation
Esmee Fairbaim Foundation
Deutsche Bank
V Charity
Rathbones Trust
Wates Foundation
Turner Broadcasting
Shine Trust
Woodward Charitable Trust
ATS Chasing Dreams
Orange
Ravensbourne College
Bootstrap Enterprises
John Lyon (One of the original YCTV backers) (Note 1)

Bloomberg (**Note 2 i**)

Eranda Foundation (**Note 2 ii**)

And lastly, not leastly, the (God) life raft k/a the Peter de Haan Charitable Trust, which resurrected/re-incarnated YCTV as Ideas Tap!

And these don't include the Rich & Famous contributors whom your own Patron Saint Founder can bring into your outstretched hand coffer fold.

Note 1: There is plenty philanthropic money around, you just need to discover where – perhaps here is an example of what you know and not who?

JOHN LYON'S CHARITY - TOP 20 GRANTS PAID 2004/05 LD
Harrow Development Trust 340,000
Specialist Schools Trust 172,500
Unicorn Theatre for Children 150,000
City Literary Institute 125,000
London Diocesan Board for Schools 100,000
The Peter Beckwith Harrow Trust 76,204
Kilburn Youth Centre 70,000
Rugby Portobello Trust 50,000
West London Sports Trust 50,000
Roundhouse 50,000
Brent Youth Service 40,000
YCTV 40,000 (£90,000 over three years towards salary costs). #
National Theatre 35,000
Holland Park School 35,000
Endeavour Training 35,000
Kentish Town City Farm 33,000
Hammersmith & Fulham Dance Residencies 32,000
ACAVA 32,000
Brent Centre for Young People, Harrow 30,000
Anna Freud Centre 30,000 (# A certain **rich** brother-in-law's pet project support <> they're moving on Up! <> **many pages _prior_**.)

Note 2 i: The £35000 Grant, in 2002, was suddenly withdrawn and the accountancy year 2003 showed as Nil.
Note 2 ii: More critically this £60000 Grant was also suddenly withdrawn around 2002/03, but not shown in the period ended 30/6/03. (John heard possibly why, but the basis of the argumentative cat fight will remain your mystery.)

In spite of these unexpected losses, the annual budget 2003/04 had increased to an astounding £1 million!

....

*Y*ou *C*an *T*ry *V*aliantly (The End)

"When you begin to talk to Ex Students/Workers/Board Members, Grant Payers/Contributors et cetera, you get given/handed all sorts of information verbal & written.   (part 2)

Not all was generated by any YCTV source...

It was a perfect example how she had come from her *chosen* obscurity and became so sought after by so many public & charitable bodies; requests for Board attendance, her opinion, knowledge & expertise sought (a simple case of now not who you know, but what!).

Nothing exemplified this more half a dozen years into her tenure: she found herself shortlisted with five others for the prestigious Creative Britons 2000 arts prize of £100k for life-transforming work – acknowledging those able to best motivate others and be a catalyst for future talent!

It was Britain's biggest cultural prize, whether won or not each of the 6 nominees received £20k for the organisation of their choice.

Sadly, she got her piece of the cake, but not the cherry on top, coming in joint second to Barrie Rutter (Later to be an OBE, his wife a WATE –Mrs Clive Jones would know what I mean re her teaching Alma Mater Awards System.) whose supporters (National Youth Theatre?) praised the way he made a *non-sense of elitism!*"

(*Some might cynically suggest, part of such a group, was one of those also up for the award, sitting just on the next table to him*!?)
Maybe her upper-class background did for her....?

But the point should not be laboured as there are also more worthy of our/her praise!

ROLL CALL OF HONOURABLE WORTHY MENTION:

- First call for the lady & her friend, but mostly herself;
- Thanks to all the Production Supervisors like Jess, Beverly, Kebba, *Jessica*, Gawain, Rafs, Alex and many more;
- The many fun time members like the early Luke, Antony, Leon, Leyton, Ricky, Sean, Alex, Geraldine, Hannan, Christina, Vannessa, Tharan, Isha, Pamela, Lama, Lee, Nana, Phoebe, Rachel, Damian, Jenna and Javone;
- Those later likes of Steven, Amber, Mani, Lucy and Melita.
- Poor **Kodjo** & The RFL team and his *fortunate a*live friends;
- Other worthy latecomers Asli, Nana, Lucy, Gillian, Jess & Isabel;
- Some of the boss types old & new, Mary, Salim, Andy (the scar), Neil, Joan UN, Katherine, Erin, Amber and those other CEOs, facilities managers & production managers too many to recount;
- Helpful Greg and his Corporative Assistance;
- Those unsung and those who want to remain nameless;
- Special mention to UK Online & its 2001 massive computer supply support
- Above & beyond the fractured ribs call just part of the job, the special likes of *Jessica*;
- Kind old philanthropic Clive, at the beginning, without whose financial sponsorship certain students would not have progressed & much later, nearer the end, without whom the likes of staff would have gone wage wanting at ends of months during the final throes and he, who felt no regret at his five figure loss at takeover time – *but oh how he hates those 80 odd,* **infernally protected** *elm trees down on his Bucks Country Estate.*
- All the kids the likes of whom are happy to call themselves ex YCTV &/or its Facebook friends;
- And then those handed over to, who kept the ideas tapping along after the fall like Gwyn (gwansbrough@....) and her benefactor boss *pdehaan@ ...* & his Halo trust... **.....creating** *'the new concept rather than the 'old' broken formulae'*
- (*But, all this too would fade away some years later.*)
- A simple response then, but now?

"Well Peter, it seems you consider that YCTV was the old broken formula, but it had a lot to commend it:

- not just a grant dispensing machine
- ideas tap seemed to lack personality
- the old YCTV brand was well known & respected
- it became a model for other similar projects around the UK
- it was something special to have its founder get shortlisted as charity businessperson of the year
- it engendered a Community spirit
- the feeling of belonging
- being part of a gang/group where you didn't have to look over your shoulder
- a refuge where familiar problems could be aired and discussed without fear, with special(ist) help afforded
- it attracted those types of youths who didn't find a fit anywhere else
- they had a special affinity & respect for the staff & especially its founder
- it catered for the disadvantaged and scholastic outcasts who had nowhere else to go
- learning became fun
- so many friendships made & maintained thereafter
- despite so much competition the stories of so many ex YCTV making it into Media work placements abound with some really special success stories making their name & mark in the Industry
- Its demise has left a large hole in Labroke Grove's Young Hearts!
BUT
- admittedly it was too parochial & had limited appeal (even with the Changing Faces 3 project which partnered it with Raw Material, Bootstrap & The Harrington Scheme)

- the funding set up did not seem to persist as hopefully yours will
- maybe near the end the founder might have lost heart and perhaps the Trustee vote
- funds/fundraising initiatives may not have not dried up (you have a bottomless pit no doubt)
- maybe the same people got fed up being asked?
- the aspect of restricted funded projects somewhat stifled its growth
- the public conception that the founder had easy/constant access to multi-millionaire pop star pockets was misplaced
- rule by a large batch of trustees seemed to be a case of too many cooks
- directional changes did not achieve desired results and created internal conflict
- another lesson: '*Don't argue or upset your rich sponsors!*'
- maybe also having been just a PA with limited film experience was not enough to cope with all the problems financing, setting up and maintaining such a considerable business (albeit philanthropic) enterprise - or perhaps ultimately being a Russian Oligarch's Social Secretary is, such a better bet, less fraught with stress & strain?
- And if a *hands-on* founder and original backer were to suddenly find themself asked to take time away from the office, perhaps, ultimately, it does not pay to replace them at the helm!

But then continuing a certain *eulogy* ..."Perhaps, the best praise one could give to her is that her vision-made reality, at the time, became the longest ** surviving AND successful Charity of its type to continue providing a safe haven where marginalised youngsters chose to go to enjoy themselves AND indirectly learn & develop through the innovative training it provided, perhaps better termed as **an Educational & Media Revolution**.

But I think she (***the Social Entrepreneur*** ## and not the Rich, Famous, Heiress) deserves the last words *in response to John's YCTV info request* >

>

....   **Sabrina Guinness**April 3, 2010 at 7:55pm   (???↓↓)

Re: ex yctv students comments about you and YCTV

(She expressed her sadness at its demise! But with a final wish for John..)
xx

'**She missed it also!**'

<u>**Gone but not forgotten – thanks luv and a Happy Easter to you two xx**</u>

(Author Trademark Copyright)

A POST YCTV PERSONAL CALAMITY!

But, and it was such a Big But of a Shock: Within three months her computer was hacked and her most valued possession, her privacy, was greatly compromised; her inner-most electronic thoughts were now in someone else's possession!

Alex and Co. had her under their thumb, somebody unknown to her would reign; her connections compromised and blackmail threats could now be given *free rein!*

Phone numbers# changed to no avail – the hell of not knowing what would come next; the least of her worries was that her Facebook identity was later hijacked/recreated: three being## in existence luring others to click on the link to see what would come next – malware no doubt!

....

** YCTV Post & Now IdeasTap (Tapped out around the summer of 2015, but a Hiive of *Busy-Bees* helped it *fund* into 2016)

One put it in a nut shell:

"Working with IdeasTap is an incredible opportunity for us – albeit one tinged with sadness as it's come about as they wind down. These guys are the industry leaders, the go-to guys when it comes to helping people in the cultural sector get the best start in their careers, and are an organisation we've been inspired and influenced by hugely ..."

As with the many roll calls within YCTV, who remembers any of them?
So, with IdeasTap and its final throw of its funding dice, who will remember any of these budding young directors: will any of the 12 chosen few have cut the mustard and made their unforgettable *'Vic'* mark in the future – and what of those cast aside?

Annie-Lunnette Deakin-Foster Chris Cuming Elizabeth Williams
James Berkery Jenny Ogilvie Joanna Clare Lama Anine
Mark Conway Maxine Yell Natasha Harrison
Rachel Nanyonjo Rachel Drazek Samantha Pardes
Simeon John-Wake Simon Pittman Tara D'Arquian
Thea Stanton Vivienne West Wayne Parsons Yarit Dor

I leave it to you to review years hence.

....

*Y*ou *C*an *T*ry *V*aliantly (At work & Play)
(Deceased (*Spidered$_x$*) Bowie & Kodjo revisited)

Post Script: One thing I had not divulged/discussed was John's fascination with Spiders and their webs; perhaps with him you'd say his webs of deceit, or deviousness, so the web reference could be construed as allegorical?

I leave it to you.

"Not everyone is crazy about spiders, but they need introducing here. It is interesting to note that one song, which had poignant significance, was *'Glass Spider by David Bowie'*, although some might say it is not an arachnidan song at all, but is, in part, a (tortured) metaphor about growing up, of being abandoned by your parents and learning to live on your own.

"You always think your mother's there. [help]
But, of course, she never really is," [help]

So, David Bowie said in '87.

*But, with much regret, this boy's mother was there, having made the change choice, which so painfully for her and equally so painfully for him, become just another lost **soul** statistic.*

[help] *This reference/introduction to parental presence, or lack of it, is no coincidence **here**, as **here**, we revisit areas/arenas w**here**, perhaps, 'If Only' they were t**here**, then **their child** would still be **here** and not there, in **their** blood-died **memory**!!!*
But, and it always that Big But, the killing will never stop, no matter where you live!!!

....

*But, all this victim related sadness is to be reserved for so much later, where the blood will **again** & **again** & **again** flow **unabated**!!!*

(As it always has!) ◇ *(And so it always will be!)*

....

And so,

-------------------------*Here also,*

YCTV's end will be!

//

YCTV ADDENDA

But, now returning to the nooks & crannies of a certain Hall, where reality for John kicked in:- *Remember he was a Patient of mine! So had his many Demons to shed...*

"Getting back out was one of two ways: one the front door and the other a large dimly lit staircase, which could feature in spooky or murderous plot lines…"

A large exhalation, then he was back on *script*.

"I tried valiantly and failed – even offered myself up as a driver – rejected again, no foot in the door for me as it was unceremoniously chopped from under me and another door closed in my face."

"No change there then?"

"Even more dismally this time!"

"You seem more philosophical than sad though?"

"Well, when you kicked in the teeth so many times, there comes a time when you begin to expect it as the norm and in that way it softens, perhaps, deflects the blow.

Anyway, it's all *nat*ural *muddy water* beneath my rotten rotting bridge …………………..………….…."

"Come on John snap out of it, give me another *history* lesson."

So, it's now back to there & her..."

He relented, took a breath and sailed into it.

At that first meeting, she was naturally shocked to see *'an outsider'* ensconced in her domain, so it was natural for the *'suspicious'* in her to enquire what brought me to her.

I showed her the article from that Sunday Supplement – the soured a friend of hers... *"No friend of mine contributed to the article you've shown me!"*

But, I dared not ask about her previous princely connection, although my times at the Palace and my below stairs *(photographed)* contacts gave opportunity to learn more than was ever reported!

(Here his favourite – The Chef/Kitchen Staff AND Cake makers!)

John and his family were not allowed to take photos at the Garden Party Event!

But for those who know the layout, this is John's back steps to the Garden Memento!

So, I introduced her Great Uncle Sam into the conversation, although my poor name dyslexic/memory recollections led her to think I was speaking of another? But, no matter, the link had been made. I later confirmed in writing exactly whom I'd been talking about and Cheyne Walk with its massive dwellings were no strangers to her: the Stones & their manager having one each along there! Oddly though, I heard an interview [Inter] by Sam's daughter, **Marit**, made and there was no mention of mixing with Sabrina's bunch? [Inter]

????????????

[Inter] *https://www.bl.uk/projects/national-life-stories* *1999*

(NB But, one story won't be there and it actually was thought to hasten her demise:- **It's significantly placed at the end of this Book**

But now back to the seemingly mundane in comparison...

<<<◇>>>

The subject then led to my talking up the twins' abilities and stage experience, both on the boards and as behind the scenes managers: she said they should come and visit – we arranged the following Sunday and the rest is (later) history...they were accepted, but Daddy <u>couldn't</u> tag along!

But YCTV carried on regardless as did John: "And then there was that mooted TV Mentoring scheme …"

John paused, "Not sure how it went, though not business oriented like ChèreB's Foundation, perhaps though still one-to-one, anyway, whatever, <u>she</u> & a friend had conceived the youthful idea in the USA: it was born here and the times I saw her in action I thought it <u>her</u> baby as <u>she</u> was there from birth until slow constricted death.

It had its PHOENIX rise but perhaps the *ideas tapped out?*

311

The bailor coincidentally was an ex-male *'mother'* who *'care*d', and with his about £20 million to <u>legit<i>imate</i>ly</u> keep from the Tax Office with one of the many well *tap*ped *ideas,* the Charity creation.

The twins had joined and had great times … and had many stories to relay: David Bowie, her greatest achievement, for me, then, there was Tony passing *Mic* over to *he-who-makes-her-admiring-smile* – (I too later was to be Tony's beneficiary, kind person that he is, as is his ~~Sherry~~ Cherry Baby, Tony Valli speaking) – I don't know what happened to *Mic* after that episode, but <u>her</u> night out with Peter soon followed.

By the way, *it* wasn't <u>her</u> idea: her Facebook link had the answer (if you weren't there at the time) – to his public page, not private one – amazing I didn't think kids from well off middle class parents qualified – as mine didn't really, but still were invited and attended?

They had to pass <u>her</u> place on the way to the studios: some *privileged* students had at times been invited there, although just an ordinary, normal 2 bed unit, like others down that way.

Normal & ordinary, as was <u>her</u> brother's expansive Hillhooked **inherited** farm. The *sporting rights* were also a short drive away. (*Again it's the fella who always inherits in their exalted landed* **gent***rified way of life!*)*.

The latter for example, is quite expansive, hilly, woody, & lends itself well to a film location, even abounds with hens, sheep & horses, with a trout stream thrown in for good effect (for those wanting a lesson, the angling expert/tutor frequents the local pub down the road): the same <u>expansiveness</u> could be applied to her brother-in-law's large Estate, Somerset Way.

I always admired her involving the kids & staff inviting them to that/those Estate(s), or her place [SH] - so many Patrons ignore those who keep the Charity afloat.

[SH] *The Shelf explained at the back end of this Book with a special Kate!?*

Her involvement, all hands to the pump so to speak...

I was amazed at her naivety in that article long after the Blackmail, Hacking scandal *'I never knew people could do such things?'* – Let's say the gossip source quoted her verbatim then the rest follows: Although my Notting Hill police contact also told me not to have blind faith in the article?
Sometime later, he would revisit this aspect with another personal, probing question, but not here – a notable, *no-belle* niece would fill in his blank of doubt.

"John, looks like your vivid imagination has gone into serious overdrive here?"
"No, I told you a few moments ago that I was asked to make a statement!
I could say so much more as the Police read her statement to me, but … And to think I asked all her ex-students and employees known to me to write giving her support during those difficult times!?"

<u>*"And the outcome?"*</u>
"Seemed a waste of time and effort –But, it did give me access to so many and their mostly fond recollections of it & its co-founder – I could never trace the other after."

"You mentioned the press > as the press reported it < How did you feel about that?"

Like I said before, I once wrote a note of complaint with my phone number included and for a first time discovered what being a celebrity's life was like: I found out through this and a future foray how bad the press could be, the Royal Correspondents in particular, not the one currently being prosecuted, but another tabloid one, made mine intrusion small fry – sex was always the slanted selling point and I was unexpectedly phoned up & asked if knew of anything salacious! Me – the nobody, the nondescript?

Funny really what I <u>then</u> thought of such people, the irony being that any of them might be named White, or Good!

Misnomers if ever I saw them!

312

Things have really quietened down, now there is no *private sucking* to publicly report upon.
It was interesting that the second time I was, **_personally_**, pre-warned that not to believe anything the press wrote about her: then came her *celebrated* liaison night out that wasn't in reality and it took some time and her personal effort to get the Press to apologise and print their retractions.

But, the scariest episode was yet to come and perhaps naivety was the common factor, or was it me – well it had to be?

"So even nondescripts have their day?"

"Yes, pity though it's only a day –

I really needed something long term!"

"Long term?"

"I suppose I'll get there in due course, if we're still in session."

"Back to Court parlance now John?

I can't wait till your trial begins."

"Touché, again!"

....

*Y*ou *C*an *T*ry *V*aliantly (Hunky-Dory?!)

… The twins had joined and had great times … but all was not rosy-red on the **Lads/Lasses Broken Hall of Dream Mirrors** Horizon!

With me out of the picture, the twins got on like a house on fire: well she did personally invite them in, even if they were not anything like the disaffected youth she was trying to attract in accordance to the Mission Statement.

There again, here is another two sided tale where student and school tried to get the !!!! of each other, which suited each of them most.

Sad, this comment on life plays itself out daily in all walks of life!"

"Sad, John, for you also? You've been devious and manipulated people in your own way: we're all apparently cast from the same cloth, aren't we?"

"What about strained?"
"What like tea through a sieve?"
"I think you mean strainer, but I understand the reference."
"OK, let's get back on track with some facts & figures.

....

*Y*ou *C*an *T*ry *V*aliantly (At Work & Play)

Surely, John, there were many good times before the volcano erupted on this mini Pompeii?

It can't have all been doom and gloom, or is that the half empty John for you again? Where's the half full perky-up fella I've come to smile with?

It's sad …"

"What is, John?"

John paused and **I expected** the comment on the life the teenagers featured, "What horrible themes seem to permeate their mind and life, such a sorry tale and it's the <u>woman who suffers yet again</u>, perhaps there were more guys at the workshop than gals?"

He broke off here, breathed in heavily and let out a long sigh, I could see what he had said triggered a memory, truly bad at that and one I apologise for relating, but it had a bearing on life as it was then – it was no wonder so many of them sought a refuge from the *respect thug/gang culture* which prevailed thereabouts.

<u>**If only**</u> is a repeated *theme-thought* in John's selective, recollective, upsetting memory driven life, but here it would have been played out fatally, as it did in the earlier historical/factual CHAPTER of the same name as this. But, and it is that murderous <u>red</u> filled Big But, do we really need reminding of such a heart rending <u>red</u> blot on Ordinary Society?

We are already reminded of it on a daily basis, highlighting how modern life has reverted to basement level revenge kill at any cost antics.

So I have skipped the killing, but, by all means, feel free to relive **it** all over again 30 pages back! But, in deference to the remaining relatives & friends that very *Big Blood-Bath* I have omitted them here, thankfully some of you might say? As...

(The rest would have made for tearful reading for those hurt most!)

But, the rest begged repeating...

John had his own opinionated views on the matter, which will no doubt replicate itself… "From the above **our bail/parole system has a lot to answer for** # and how can children as young as those just turned 12/13 consider this a future **normal** way of life for themselves? There again, after 5 years our system will (Feltham?) licence some of them to repeat their *head smashing* favour on some other unsuspecting innocent **s-o-l-e** (John meant the spelling, not **soul**, as it always seems to be the *lone-oner,* who is set upon by a group, all frenzied up!"

He paused
"I think we should get back to something cheerful now, don't you think?"

"Yes, John, <u>back to the prostitution & drug addiction story</u>!"

"Unfortunately, like the twins whose education came first, before graduating to one of the top six Universities *(I told you the twins were supra-different)*, the lady's daughter couldn't continue, her other further studies took her centre stage; there was also, like the twins, the aspect of lengthy travel time; and lastly not a disaffected youth either.

Although, personally I always dreaded their trips to their film course sessions: from sniffer dog patrols at the Ladbroke Grove tube station entrance/exit; and only a few blocks away an assortment of *base life lived featuring* drug clinics, a battered wives Church soup kitchen haven, an aids addicts clinic cum shelter/advice centre (Suppose, <u>she</u> never had that walking in fear problem, as she drove to/from all venues)."

He paused yet again and a grin lit up his face – his knowing bright eyes fell upon me – his grin became a broad smile ... "Back to work and, whilst on my networking duties visiting the Race Unit, I met & told them about the episodes such as this: Jenny overheard and she seemed to know much about the Charity:

"I know Johnny –My Unit gives it an annual grant!"

I viewed the file and saw the degree of support.

In later years it would concentrate more on using the Charity facilities to educate the indigenous Youth Prison Population and coincidentally use her youngest sister's *(West Wycombe's)* CBC for the Unit to learn more about coping with death –

CBC-

I could've done that for them, just relating my **family's** experience having one of theirs get a **fatal** bullet in the back – some cope, but not those closest who never **forget**, for whom it takes the slightest *trigger* to start the cascading tears!"

Sadness etched his face!

"Ah well, only another thirty, or forty years left to ... Can we *cut it short* here, please."

*(Those **words** sent a chill through me!*
*Why I didn't know then!! But, I certainly know **now**)*

....

*Y*ou *C*an *T*ry *V*aliantly (Money *Matters*)

John broke off to allow himself a little dig... "Reminds me of the Civil Service, at least YCTV was a fledgling, not a well-established, well oiled, supposedly, well managed machine, but both found to buy-in the best, costs!"###

"I see sarcasm has popped in again!"

He chuckled and continued, but not totally in a YCTV vein!

"If you want some sarcasm, how about early 2006 the front of their offices being the backdrop for another Prime Minister attracted to their door steps. Cameron used them to introduce his new youth initiative to the Country, a sort of Labour Party re-hash of the previous year, his trumpeted Community Service Plan for Young People.

Whatever happened to that?

Neither apparently a new idea, more of something from the USA, k/a The Corporation for National and Community Service set up in 1993.

But, on a _more_ serious matter, the venue is just a stone's throw from his Primary Residence and not his House of Commons Second Home, so he wouldn't claim any travel expenses then! "
John chuckled some more,
Whatever happened to that?
And then back on the same course...
"Funny about Cameron, me like millions others thought he just sprang out of the woodwork and took Conservative Control, but, and it is always a Big But, these apparent suddenly rising to the top from nowhere types, have usually been around years.

Do you recall 1992 when Lamont was Chancellor and interest rates were going through the roof?

Well who was with his PS in the background, advising?

Well, how to keep a lid on the extent of the real figure of how much of our foreign currency had to be sold and ultimately how much the attack from foreign speculators cost – actually seems it was 50% more than what was originally touted.

But, and it is a Big But, what's a Billion between UK tax PAYErs etc? Well perhaps our future PM knew the answer to that one, but wasn't letting that cat out of his boss's Red Box.

So, was that the standard price of Conservative financial Stewardship and Economic Competence.

Oddly enough, Mridul, he?/she? might have questioned the figures then, but, then, who remembers him?/her? ~~that well~~ at all?

Ah well, all water under our History's many broken bridges needing mending!"

(SO OUT NOW WITH THE OLD – IN WITH THE NEW – _REP<u>AIR</u>MA<u>N</u>_)

↓

Author Copyright

& then back on YCTV's history track >>>

....

CHAPTER Fifty Three (v): *Y*ou *C*an *T*ry *V*aliantly (The End)

Sabrina Guinness April 3, 2010 at 7:55pm   *(???↓↓↓)*

Re: ex yctv students comments about you and YCTV

I raised my eyes and met his somewhat meek, enquiring smile –
"Nothing need be said; it speaks for itself, doesn't it?"
But, I sensed he was hiding something?! …..

(???↑↑↑) I had my photo doubts, as perhaps you might too? # ↓ 2010
                    *Her's could have just been a cut and paste copy from any of those
paintshopped false image manufactured bogus sites* – <u>or was it</u>? *(Well there were at least two more when I did
my own search! But Why? How Come* **(Later!)**

"A year after that apparent, now, distant memory of 2010, you'd think her close relative would be wary of giving out her personal detail, but who am I to say, but, then, those Thornhill Ladies could have joined Nat at the crack of dawn in Highbury *Hilly* Fields with her/theirs-to-be personal trainer and she even gave them both her personal g-mail address & her 07834 ……. mobile number!
And some time later publicly informing readers where she & the family spend summer; her + husband work hours; the work of the Nanny + the kids picking up/dropping off school running arrangements!
John interposed**...** *"It was easy from there and other detail she made publicly available + our meeting discussion to work out all that other stuff..."* (As you have all been introduced earlier...)...
"She & Her Dad's Company dealings were even relayed by her!
Ah well, if she has no qualms, why should we?   ##
She is the Mistress of her own, most likely, fortunate, lucrative, successful, supported destiny!
PS She still maintains her dawn jog before she gets into her creativity *Puddling* designing mode – quite remarkable!" ###

(### Another hint as to John's confessed envy, this time of the daughter, not the father – where industry seems to run through that line of the family!) Though he <u>just had</u> to add,
                    "By-the-way where is hubby during all these jogging exertions?"

↑ 210 - When John related all this to me I was puzzled that, she, who could have been Queen; she, who had held all the misrepresentative Press to account, had not had these cruel & invidious sites closed – don't suppose Facebook even knew of the theft?

Ah well, they weren't John's doing; nor should he be their undoing!
Poor password protection and privacy settings have caused many a downfall, and the fall was hard to take: she was now just part of the crowd, no longer a **_Queen-in-waiting_** – Civis to Plebs* with just one (remote) keyboard click!

<u>**Her movements became *restricted*, as did her case!**</u>

Yet, after all his experiences, John felt sad for her: she, who had tried to touch so many younger, less privileged hearts!?

317

There again, that was then and this is now and he didn't dwell on it –
'A distant memory, as her niece Nat would, St Albans later, relate to him!?
(Although her * **_Lady-like_** Matrimonial **_Royal_** Resurrection)
(Which John mooted a few CHAPTERs back)
(Had yet to come!)

....

<u>Y</u>ou <u>C</u>an <u>T</u>ry <u>V</u>aliantly (Extra curricula) Revisited...

↓↓↓

TO ALL YOU YCTV LOVERS

I was there the year after it started - full of donated PCs - the room on the 1st floor where budding film makers practiced story writing - the dingy basement. Well I now fancy writing about YCTV's history: its successes, – failures, the effort; the rewards etc. witty comments about the founder and examples of innovations like 'pass the mike'...how it mushroomed - how it is now sorely missed & why. And what's the view on IDEASTAP, just as good? Freely circulate this to anyone who had an interest/experience at Ladbroke Hall – I'd like to hear from them. Thanks John

↑↑↑↑

<u>"So, it didn't come to pass</u> – the book writing I mean?"

"Well, no, well not nearly as long as I would have liked, <u>*as you've just been shown*</u>, but I suppose you get the drift and like the comic said there's more, but it veered towards family homes & personalities, wealth, power and connections made, or required to be made.
(Hence, the perhaps ponderous split & doubling up of CHAPTERs!)

The problem here is no matter what you discover there is more, but on the way you encounter stone-walling and so the only way forward is to infiltrate & inveigle, but the stumbling block is that not being either rich, famous, or an heir apparent(ly), you have to provide the closed circle with something else to whet their interest & feed their *interest appetite*, but being just a **_plain John_** it would be futile effort and would just get me mocked like I have so many other times.

Plainly, being <u>plain</u>, doesn't get you noticed.

A simple fact of this modern technological life/age is that if you're rich/famous with connections, all you produce, whether literally deserving or not, you'll always get to the head of the profitable queue.

Look at the daughter-friends, Chelsea & Ivanka, of the battling Clinton & Trump Presidential Dynasties, their individual, *'It's Your World'* & *'Governing Global Health'* AND *'The #**Trump Card**'* & *Women Who Work'* will always get top billing –

I'd just get a publisher/printer's bill!

I gave it a spin to 4 who I thought might be interested.

<u>They said nothing</u>!"

So it ended there!

But it was what happened in between that threw up a famous Chair of YCTV Trustees name:-

And so it was of Muswell Hill here John come I!

....

John,
A Question was posed

Clive Jones CBE
Tel no: 0208 xxx xxxx
Mob no:078xx xxxxx
e-mail: clivexxxx@xxxx

Reply....

I was there the year after it started - full of donated PCs - the room on the 1st floor where budding film makers practiced story writing - the dingy basement. Well I now fancy writing about YCTV's history: its successes, – failures, the effort; the rewards etc. witty comments about the founder and examples of innovations like 'pass the mike'...how it mushroomed - how it is now sorely missed & why. And what's the view on IDEASTAP, just as good? THEN

All questions at his neighbouring Alexandra Park pad John posed were answered and certain secrets revealed – but not for here! As also later did a certain ex CEO & Staff + Students!

....

IN Between YCTV Times

"It's a long list, so?"

"I suppose it was only fair with all that effort & energy expended making the Charity a viable, reputable prospect, that there would have to be quite a bit of early years' socialised bonding with so many connected representatives and other *fonctionnaires* to promote her own fledgling corner: specialised events, media & TV Channels kept her a busy party bee and so many of those connected with hers (present/past) might also be there.

You cannot be in the office all the time, as the CEO & other workers might have to be: we all need a bit of R & R sometimes, whether it be a sudden trip to Mustique, or is it spelled Mistique, or is it Mystique?"

John, paused for a little giggle to himself: he was having fun in his own inimitable styled way.

"Or the Barbadian Caribbean for the hot sandy slopes, or the family's Austrian homed escape for the cold snowy slopes, but, whatever, she deserved the breaks.

And, so, the self-imposed nightlife must go on."

John recounted earlier comments,

'In 2001, things began to expand ... but it is sad in one respect, that in 2001 the Board had BBC put their own person in charge and...'

"Perhaps the latter was a relief in some way, or a kick in the teeth, I cannot tell. I heard stories, but it leads me into her private fun life. Private in the sense, *By Invitation Only,* where the special elitist (some **ranked** by the poor, others **ranked** by the social page followers) people attend. There were many, though some had more significance and interest, than so many others.

But, first let's go out for the night with her and revisit some notable people & events where the-she again was a toga adorned Civis & not a tunic attired Pleb, **the bringing down to earth hacker had yet to enter her life!**

So let's see some examples of what kept her in her own sought out private spotlight – some, outside the certain sacred inner-circles, about so many names would ask, WHO? Judge for yourself > Coincidentally, all took place within London (*like another Niece's*). Travelling can be a bore!

And high heels nearly always out, as flats favoured throughout most of these laborious days standing about, tough on the old pins – especially if you might have an inherited knee problem *(like her current beau?)* - taking in all the free company & ambience, wine & food etc. – although can't imagine the clothing came free/cheap: nearly always wearing something new/different!

But, in spite of the BBC enforced/suggested change 2001 where her pet project began to lose its hue, her social side never faded ...

And so, back to that *paparazzi photographed* & *memoired* Social Calendar, or perhaps, not so? >>>>>>>>>>

- 6 April 2001 She and her (*that yet to be perhaps (in)famous*) niece played Host to two of the Rolling Stones, as Bill Wyman & His Band the Rhythm Kings played at the Roundhouse in Covent Garden & Charlie Watts with His Jazz Projects.
- 10 July 2001 attended another reception in London.
- 21 November 2001 at her ex-boyfriend's [1]opening of the New British Galleries at the Victoria & Albert Museum ([1] *Poor?!* Regal guy stuck it out in spite of a notable sore eye!) Other notables there included Jasper Conran, the Culture Secretary perhaps on another Official representative freebie and over 100 members of the Jain community, Mehool Sanghrajka Director of the IoJ and the JAINpedia Project as well as stakeholders from the British Library, the Wellcome Trust and the Bodleian Library and finally by Wesley Kerr, Chairman of the Heritage Lottery Fund London Committee. *Strange where she gets invited*, but more notable followed.
- 25 July 2002 On the other side of London for her at the "Lost in LA Mancha" Screening at the Screen on the Green in Islington, London.

There it ends, although john had produced all the event visits/invites in between, but that would just bore you, n'est-ce pas

But, and it is a Big But, we need leap on ~~~10 years > for a particular love-angled reason...they 2 both were there at the same times...

- 29 March 2012 also there **Tom Stoppard** with Felicity K. at thanksgiving service for the Queen Mother and Princess Margaret at St George's Chapel in Windsor, England.
- 15 May 2012 at The ASAP (African Solutions to African Problems) Lunch held at the Louise T Blouin Foundation, 3 Olaf Street, London W11 also there Sue Crewe, Tara Agace, Ozwald Boateng And Bodil Blain Lynn Rothman, The Hon.Lavinia Bolton and Lady Mary-Gaye Curzon Priscilla Higham, Jane Ormsby Gore and Tiggy Kennedy Lucinda Garland Widow Of Joe Strummer And Erin Morris Saffron Aldridge Violet Neylor-Leyland, Charlie Day and Lynne Franks Priscilla Higham And Dame Janet Suzman Melia Mcenery wife of Eric Clapton Maryam D'abo India Windsor-Clive and The Marchioness Of Worcester (mainly all white female & only a handful of Blacks again though!)
- 13 June 2012 at Juliet Nicolson's Abdication book launch party in Mayfair. Also there were Sir **Tom Stoppard** and Maurice Saatchi, Flora Macmillan-Scott and Hugh Harris, Lord Hutchinson QC, Carol Victor, Gerald Scarfe, Jane Asher, Ed Victor and Maurice Saatchi, Fiona Shackleton, Galen Weston and Hilary Weston, Galen Weston, Henry Wyndham, Ian Hislop, Trish Garcia, David Dimbleby.
- 26 September 2012 cheek-to-cheek photo with boss Evgeny Lebedev + amongst others Ben Goldsmith Nick Mason, Tracy Worcester and Bryan Adams attend the Pig Business Fundraiser at Sake No Hana in London,
- 3rd October 2012 at a party to celebrate the launch of the new gallery Pace at 6 Burlington Gardens, London, and Ed Victor
- 8th October 2012 at the First Night of Poetry Week at The Arts Theatre, Leicester Square plus Lord Maurice Saatchi.

- 18th October 2012 at the Crossfire Hurricane Premiere after party held at Quaglino's during the 56th BFI London Film Festival. Here, also there Will Stoppard with his wife Linzi Stoppard & Sir **Tom Stoppard**.
- 29 November 2012 at the Fayre of St. James Christmas Carol Service organised by the Quintessentially Foundation in aid of War Child held St.James's Piccadilly, London Ben Elliot, Ruth Wilson etc.
- 26 February 2013 at the private view of Bill Wyman's new exhibit 'Reworked' at Rook & Raven Gallery, Rathbone Place London. Also attended by Annabel Brooks Roy Hodgson with his wife, Loraine Ashton, Reg Traviss & Mitch Winehouse with wife Jane, Debbie von Bismarck, Tiger Lily Taylor & her Mother Deborah Leng, Mike Hucknall with his wife Gabriella Wesberry.

'From here on with her new plus One - So now her creaky knight in shining armour has come with his own entourage carousel & she, not one to sit in the back room of her country cottage knitting, or in the front room reading, with no inherited genetic knee problems to concern herself with, so in the fairground of her own life making, it's now a case of jumping from one carousel to another as the moment and inclination takes her.

So here we have one of _his_ famous events:

- 2nd December 2013 St James's Christmas just isn't Christmas without Sir **Tom Stoppard** 's annual literary party at The London Library with Helen McCrory & hubby Damian Lewis, walking stick Andrew Marr, Claire Tomalin, Emily Doherty and Joanna Mollo, Hannah Bronwen Snow and Alexander Armstrong, Nura Khan, Thierry Heathcoat Amory and Jasmine Dunne, Rachel Heslop and Nicky Dunne Sir Tim Rice and Lady Sarah Chatto

Compare this with one of _his_:

- 30 November 2014 with Sophie Hunter, *Evgeny Lebedev*, Anna Wintour, Victoria Beckham, Christopher Bailey and David Beckham attend a champagne reception at the 60th London Evening Standard Theatre Awards at the London Palladium

But, sandwiched in between one fella needs a special mention:
- 11 September 2014 at Mark Shand's Memorial Service (he, 62, died when he tripped while trying to light a cigarette and hit his head outside the Rose Bar of the Gramercy Park Hotel in April. He was a passionate conservationist and founded the charity Elephant Family after saving one Indian elephant, Tara (pictured) from a life of misery before riding her on a thousand-mile trip) with an interesting selection, some of whom have appeared before but let's start with the obvious: his sister Camilla, **Prince of Wales, Prince Michael of Kent and Princess Beatrice, Prince and Princess Michael of Kent,** Lady Gabriella Windsor **and then the non-royals like Stephen Fry** Arpad Busson Ayesha Shand, *Mark Shand's daughter*, with her cousin Katie Elliot Lady Annabel Goldsmith Zac Goldsmith and Jemima Khan, both cousins of Mr Shand's former wife, Clio, Ben Goldsmith and fiancée Jemima (Anita mum link?) Edward Fox, Rula Lenska and Tim McInnerny Yasmin Le Bon, her daughter Amber, Bianca Jagger and Trudie Styler, Sir Nicholas Soames and Lady Astor, mother of Samantha Cameron, the prime minister's wife. Kirstie Allsopp Bella Freud, Charlotte Dellal, Mario Testino, Lord William Astor with his Daughter Flora Astor, Marie Helvin, Sir Jackie Stewart, Duke of Marlborough and Sir David Tang.

(NB > All that McCartney press nonsense he/she/they had to suffer, it seemed quite clear to John that their paths rarely publicly crossed >
- 1 July 2010 at The Old Vic 192 Summer Party supported by W Doha at Battersea Power station in London also Stephen Fry, and Robert Lindsay, Deputy Prime Minister Nick Clegg, Jimmy LaHoud and Kevin Spacey, **Mary McCartney Sir Paul McCartney** # and Sir Peter Blake, James McCartney and Rose Blake, Saffron Burrows,

Evgeny Lebedev and Joely (another head smashing rich sport) Richardson, Sally Greene, Polly Morgan and Mat Collishaw, Jann Haworth, Sir Harvey Goldsmith and Lady Goldsmith, Stephen Daldry, Malin Jeffries (prev Swedish model Malin Johansson), Rupert Adams and Nadja Swarovski, Dylan Jones, James Corden and Julia Carey, Emma Pilkington, Georgina Cohen, Ronnie Corbett and Bernie Ecclestone, >>>>>>

Only time they seemed to appear together at any function since that infamous episode March 2007 – *from my vantage point*, I could notice that she sat on the adjoining table, No 17, though back-to-back with **Mary & Paul**, she/he/they could easily engage etc.)

<u>If you were PARTY to the Whole List</u>
<u>You'd have noticed all those other repeat Invitees.</u>
<u>The repeats, beaten hands down by her,</u>
<u>the perennial invitee / attendee and that's why</u>
<u>it is so important</u>
<u>to settle in the capital!</u>

<u>(So I wonder what the comparative wilds of Dorset Offer as Replacements to that Filled Social Calendar?)</u>

"John, you're being somewhat too critical, so many of the others might have been enjoying their own *by-invite only* event (I have had many and no doubt you, to a *much lesser extent*?) where she didn't attend, which you haven't bothered to record."

"OK, point taken, although the *lesser* dig was uncalled for, but that detail would have got a bit un-wieldy?"
"And this list isn't?"

But

I suppose the natural questioned posed by you all is *'How does he know all this and more importantly all the ~~~ missing intervening 10 years?'* The simple answer was above >

(~~~*His original source material would simply be the photo opps she gave wherever she made her public visits, but not that the public were invited, only the privileged* paparazzi *photographers -* and their *Getty for Sale* photo records on so many files…Go exhaust yourselves…*)*

(~~~*His original down the years list ran for some 20+ pages!)*
(What you have/had here before you is where it started, then, more importantly, the jump to the more recent **Stoppard** *Love Story Growth and ultimate wed destination! The first inklings, according to John, could have been conceived at a Seminal YCTV Seminar Meeting: From Above >*

X *Sometime in 2004/05 her students (and herself?) were introduced to a* **Tom Stoppard** *Masterclass – if so, she left an impression whose fond recall was to make its real matrimonial mark much later?)*

"Second point taken, but despite its slightly expansive nature, it's odd that I only noticed one boyfriend photo – so perhaps all those suggested/press pronounced dalliances were groundless? And the nearest to any touchy-feely was with Ronnie, arm around the waist, slurping her gleeful cheek!

Although on a rather sickly that Evil Savile used to go up Diana's arm with wet kisses as his mouth went onwards & upwards, until it was pulled from him.

She didn't like it, obviously, but he still managed to wangle his way passed the Kensington palace Gate Security Staff, in spite of orders to the contrary!

So, regards her *circle of male admirers, this is a closed circle and could be a much smaller one at that?*"

"John, you should know her better than that and the *'sleeping with whom lies,'* she constantly had to refute/defend – she openly told you not to believe what is wrote about her purported *dalliances,* although one might have been true: didn't Wyman's writing suggest that the Group thought even at her then tender age, the key to her *heart et al,* she apparently left that special place open for *that* Prince[1], who then could enjoy all he surveyed!"
Or, should that have been, surveyed all he enjoyed?" <>

*Apologies for John's characteristic crude comments...Just highlighting **the London Commoner's way of** articulating his over active thoughts!)* <>

"Wyman's *true* depiction, or a ghost writer's, or not? Not like his award winning friend Richards, who received the award & accolades for something apparently written by another!
Maybe he covered her too in his?
Maybe not? I never read it. Nor you, I presume: if you've read one, you've read them all, type of thing.
But, anyhow, they only give away what they feel salivates, but not ultimately satisfies enquiring minds – *Steve Strange's another sleeping with whom? Never Elaborated upon Example*!"
"Well John, whatever you read, or those you tried to speak to, you have to concede her privacy is paramount and all that side of things would be out of the public eye and behind closed doors and drawn curtains, no doubt."

"Long velvet type ones at that? (Like @ mells...) Suppose that's more correct and that explains what the police read out to me what the hacker & prospective blackmailer said on the phone to her. Perhaps, **that Alex** knows more than us all?

But SG said that there was no blackmailing her!?!

So it's all the more confusing, that the police also told me not to put faith in that newspaper article!

I needed that sorting out in my mind and her relative n<u>ice</u> n<u>iece</u> has put me straight."

"There again, John, those who had e-mailed and possibly face-booked her were the ultimate targets – perhaps she didn't have the money people say she has?
Remember that (years) earlier article you quoted."
"Yeh, the one she claimed to be just a working girl; the one where she forgot to mention her other W10 *flat* asset, albeit it mortgaged, (? + possibly, a Hants Country cottage?)

Ah, well... but there again so many of the events above were fundraisers, in the company of real wealth, where all prices were inflated considerably, so once again I'm confused! Although ...what Clive told me about her *richness*...???
                        (He left me hanging as to what he meant?)
Yet again another reflective John pause...
The old Trust Income[2] cycle where the trickle becomes a deluge, as when a certain age/milestone is attained/reached?
That side intrigued me ever since the day that old *Sam* showed me a copy of his will after we joked as to why he wanted me to do his tax appeal stuff for him: *'You cost me nothing!'*

[2]*Perhaps, John had a point, as has already been pointed out, another apparently rich famous heiress, Tara Palmer-Tomkinson, like others mentioned before here, had to work until she attained 30, then the Trust Fund became hers to drug fritter away whenever her crumbling nose cravenly felt she wanted more!*

"Since, YCTV's departure from the Charity scene, the founder found (paid?) employment with the Evening Standard Limited & Independent Print Limited owner, as his diary/social secretary.

From that, her social highlights would *principally* be linked to *(Look what I'm doing, today)* Lebedev and his friend's public event announcements: say old Gorbachev and his Foundation &/or his wife's Raisa Charity (his being #Mikhail, not ##Evgeni, who's the handsome (*prince-like*) son, forever upright **&** outstanding...

And, not surprisingly, rich godfather material – but which AND whose would surprise all those not in the know! But, that is another closed circle of richly connected friends!
A clue: The godson's parents are a musically *Eltonian, not Etonian,* gayly richly married couple?

....

But now back to another musician...

....

<u>Y</u>ou <u>C</u>an <u>T</u>ry <u>V</u>aliantly (At work & Play)
(Deceased (*Spidered*) Bowie & Kodjo **revisited**)

"You always think your mother's there. ^{help}
But, of course, she never really is," ^{help}

Bowie said in '87 – he, who was later to be, another superstar visitor, **she** attracted to the <u>YCTV Ladbroke Hallowed Hall of Famous Visitations</u>!

Forewarned is Forearmed?
You can still try valiantly,
BUT,
You can still get stabbed -
Any place you go!
What comes next is not a pretty picture!

Thanks to Toa55 at FreeDigitalPhotos-100280042

'Oh it's so sad, yet in all this there are winners, albeit a few', though the losers maintain the murderous momentum, as more from Ladbroke die and it was foretold by me after the first mob killing above – I hated to be right again!

- 25th March 2010, just as YCTV departed, so did another sole soul: A 15 year old Sofyen Belamouadden, from a Fulham based school, so wasn't studying at St Charles College Ladbroke Grove, like so many of his eventual killers supposedly were. Victoria Station, where Sofyen was killed was an area well known to conflict where St Charles & Henry Compton pupils, the latter where around half of pupils speak English as a second language; refugees, gypsies & children from care form a significant part of the intake – overall, perhaps, an argument against too much immigration (and *uncontrolled* integration?), but let's leave that to the Brexiteers – these schools would engage in conflict, though the Comptonites were far more notorious with the amount of people their current & ex-pupils had killed before – Kodjo Yenga the best known to YCTV.

And then, thankfully, an apparent lull in hostilities, but no apparent coming together of rival factions at Christmas for a friendly football match. But, lulls are usually reasonably short, as this too was one!

- 3rd July, 2016 Fola Orebiyi, leave Nigeria at your unperceived peril, a perhaps obvious candidate for YCTV if he were about that time: just finishing his GCSE at the local Holland Park Secondary, a trainee actor at the Academy of Live & Recorded Arts in London, had written & performed in plays about violence among younger people – but it didn't really prepare him for the real, killing experience; **again alone** with no chance against a baying hoard, so reminiscent of the Lithuanian Jew _public_ killing spree of the 2nd World War! Notting Hill, the scene of black humoured irony where rehearsed love blossomed near that famous Portobello Road blue doored bookshop, that it should also become an unrehearsed life destroying location – it was because of such gang killings that the effective legal principle of _'Joint Venture'_ was introduced. **But, that seems to have disappeared in later cases! Why?**
- 2017 and still no change as another 15 year old pupil (from the Capital City Academy NW London) gets stabbed to death # in Kensal Green! ###
- **The drilling paragraphs just highlight the killing just won't go away!**

After all that **goes around** Ladbroke Hall I can appreciate why his, now _her_ Wimborne **comes around** as such a _different_ attractive **SAFE** proposal! = Not Safer Anaesthesia from Education, an African Charity, but African Solutions to African Problems, which the late Alan Rickman introduced her to. His wife was on the Royal Borough of Kensington & Chelsea Grant Committee to which Sabrina's YCTV Charity used to make application to, for Local Funding.)

Thankfully, # not everybody dies: apparently in a recent _couple_ of years there have ONLY been thousands+ **p.a.**, non-fatal stabbings in our Touristy Frequented Capital: well, perhaps the Tourists don't actually frequent those areas, nor are encouraged to, too?! And if aware would skirt around such drug filled and crime ridden events like the Notting Hill Carnival can descend into?

Yet, again, doesn't every Capital have its own, renowned, no-go areas?!

Drilling-Killing in 2:4 You Time.... I leave it to you.
As you now just _Drill_-Decipher $^{DR\downarrow}$ another of his list hitting series! ##

Another _Honour(able) (?) Killing_ Roll Call=Another Kill Proclaimed!
1011 (That Portobello/Ladbroke (YCTV) _Disaffected_ Link Survives! As did their singing members, Digga D & Sav'O, their Prison stint – Who, thereafter, continued their unifying chant with CBO approval!
Hits (All Social Media has now gone out of control!)
Hits (All Social Media has now so much to answer for!)
Hits (But Facebooked, not on the person!)
Hits (But GRM Dailyed, not on the person!)
Hits (But Linked Up, not on the person!)

Hits (But Press Played, not on the person!)		
Hits (But Snapchatted, not on the person!)		
Hits (But Twittered, not on the person!)		
Hits (But You-Tubed, not on the person!)		
Beefs (But no cattle in sight?)		
Capping (But no hat in sight?)		
Drill Music (But no Army Sargent in sight?)		
Shells (But no beach in sight?)		
Splashing (But no water in sight?)		
An ASBO (Simply overcome with a simple artistic mask cover!) – or go *'Incognito'*, but that is no guarantee of not being *'Chef-fed'* to death – no *Cook*ery instruction needed here as to how/where to insert the blade(s)! Gangsta Rap=Where actions taken now speak louder than any words!) Kennington, Peckham, Brixton Crews (No Boat Racing here though!) ???↓↓↓???		
12 World	A.M.	Blow Smoke
410	AB	BSide
67/SJ67/LD67	Anticz	C Biz
Chef	Dip	Giggs
Ching	Fry	Going Cunch
Crash	GB	Harlem Spartans
Headie One	Lynch	M-Trap
HitSquad	MDot	Odunyi
K	Moscow 17	Poke
Psycho Members	Showkey	Splash Addict
S1	Silwood Nation	Teewhiz
Scribz	Skengdo	TizzyT
Wiley	Young Dizz	And, elsewhere,
YB	Zone2	So many more?

Here I must take my leave of my *Drilling Brethren* and suggest you read *Noisey's* piece, https://noisey.vice.com/en_uk/article/ne94yx/uk-drill-music-london-knife-crime-austerity-government-2018, whilst I return to...

As History would have it, the next year there would be no *murderous discriminating of young males, as the knife (then gun)* would take no age discrimination prisoners, sorry, dead bodies, as the death toll passed 50*, as the year welcomed a bloodied Spring! (*Soon though to top 60*!*)

But and *it* is always a Big But, *it* was nice to see that the death toll was much more evenly distributed amongst the age/sex groups, with a *couple* of females and even a baby thrown in/on life's ~~scrap~~ death (*dead bodied*) **heap** for good measure.

A break down, including many black *males*, shows:

25 under 25s, 7 25-35s, 22 35 & overs!

Females seem to get off lightly, *again*, with just that *couple* making the total.

But and it is always a Big But, statistically they are <u>far</u> (away) *better off* to be living in India, where just a *couple* made the headlines during the same period, albeit that they were **only** gang raped and then used as <u>kindle</u>!

There again within those ignorant Patriarchal Muslim Communities, you can get married off, with Daddy's consent, <u>not yours</u>, at the sexually ripe *old* age of 16. Not to your liking? Then run away before the big day.

Isn't to be wedded, **without consent**, <u>forbidden</u> in Islam?
Tell that to so many (purposely?) base ignorant (Sudanese and so many other) men, who will ignore such, just as they will ignore the newly entered child's painful screams on a night, which the Western Women look pleasurably forward to - their Wedding Night of Sexual Bliss – but the Sudanese Et Co.? (?so many already FGM sufferers?) certainly <u>do not</u>, as so much blood flows from their innocent mutilated sexual orifice! But and it is always a Big But, who will stop such, <u>still practiced</u>, Child marriages, if the Males do not?
? I thought John would end it there, but there was more and from where, well the link threw me!

"Poor Cow/Poor Cows those Rich/Elite Royals, just their lot to be considered **brood mares** by their *superior* Stallion Hubbies to *AC/DC Sink their Pink* into!

Then, so many treated badly afterwards: yes we had Diana and before her, her Mum, who actually put the knife in her daughter during those despicable divorce proceedings!?

But it just seems to run through their family/families.

We make so much about their being so much? *above* ? us, but historically they have been like those Sudanese!"

He paused, screwed his lips, then bit his lower; stared at me intensely, without a trace of a smile.

"Look at Charlie-boy, he didn't really have inter-personal skill role models, perhaps the opposite, the unfeeling type. Just look at his Dad's childhood experience, whose father took his mother away: *asylumed*, castrated, with a large dose of their own secretly practised FGM, ensuring she had no further kids, nor enjoyed the company of men within, to encourage the self-same outcome!

<u>What kind of People can they call themselves?!"</u>

....

Certainly, not the end to a session I would have ever forecast!

....

BUT THE END OF THE DRILLING STORY

I HAVE LEFT TO THE END

As so many of you will not want reminding

The criminal is Winning the Bad v Good Battle

And we with just one finger in the Crime Deluge Dyke

Are Policingly Powerless to Stem the Ultimate Flood!

Dr Mya Xavier 2022

....

But and it is always a Big But, John would be John the next time, where smiles and beaming eyes would be exchanged, with a little more than a suggestive little remark here and there.

....

*Y*ou *C*an *T*ry *V*aliantly (Extra Curricula) Pt 2

"So, it didn't come to pass – the book writing I mean?"
"Well, no, well not nearly as long as I would have liked, <u>as you've just been shown</u>, but I suppose you get the drift and like the comic said there's more ...

THE YCTV STORY IS NOW COMPLETE.

<u>WITH HIS FINAL ADDITION:-</u>

The Demise: 2008
Although, there was no sadness at the farewell party which <u>she</u> promised to attend, joviality and photo exchanges abounded, free spirits at play – perhaps the final venue had some *pub* to do with it? "
But then there came an Anniversary PS...

The Revival: 2018

There is a big reunion planned and very big Whatsapp group has just been created.
<u>And, would she, again, promise to attend?</u>

<u>I don't know</u>

<u>I never went.</u>

::

<u>PART 16a: STOPPARD HUBBY</u>

<u>From before...</u>

Sometime in 2004/05 her students (and <u>herself</u>?) were introduced to a Tom Stoppard Masterclass – if so, she left an impression whose fond recall was to make its real matrimonial mark much later?)

So let's visit those other path crossing memory retained functions:

- 24 August 2007 at Woodfest, Ronnie Wood's gypsy themed 60ᵗʰ birthday party, Kingston-upon-Thames, & also there *(And was it then the dye was cast)* the old **Sir Tom Stoppard** <who stood out like a sore thumb amongst the rest, mainly the same old Cockney crowd, don't matter>.
- 6 June 2009 (And that awful unflattering red gala dress & flyaway hair) at the Raisa Gorbachev Foundation Annual Fundraising Gala Dinner, at the Stud House, Hampton Court Palace upon Thames, London, England, - *an international fund fighting child cancer.* Alexander Lebedev, (an intellectual, he is happy to spend time with the mega-rich but would rather hang out with **Tom Stoppard** –
- 13 June 2012 at Juliet Nicolson's Abdication book launch party in Mayfair. Also there were **Sir Tom Stoppard**
- 18th October 2012 at the Crossfire Hurricane Premiere after party held at Quaglino's during the 56th BFI London Film Festival. Here, also there Will Stoppard with his wife Linzi Stoppard & **Tom Stoppard.**

AND THE REST IS MATRIMONIAL HISTORY >>>>>>>>>>>*with a hundred + year old*
¹ *Turbo Tagging along, enjoying their mutual garden company!*

PART 16b: STOPPARD AND CRICKETTING PINTER

John thought old wicket-keeping hard stop would soon become a full stop! BUT he passed John's imaginary death by 80 goal post, which became a winning post until 29 November 2025, when at 88 not out, demon bowler death finally smashed his life wicket, bails, stumps and all!!! (So what now Dear 'Dorset' Again Single Sabrina???)

- Wicket-keeping suited him as his *pins* were on the decline and the sprinting outfield was potentially no field for his smoker's * lungs & his *doddery legs,* aka his **cronky knees**!
- Dear now older Sabrina would be totally familiar with such complaints back up Hilly Farm where her mother's knees gave way to operations at an early older age and so there in days past, you'd be greeted by that installed sweeping stair lift.
- And as the title of this Book implied: Sabrina now has to always be there to lend her arm to her chosen literary husband, at times very verbose, elder statesman, which is a far cry from those perhaps less demanding YCTV days, looking after the young writers of the future. (PS Thank goodness so many of those bigger mansions now have ground floor en-suite bedrooms).
- Contrary to John's forecast, Tom has actually made it to 80+ in spite of his ## contemporaries' shared interests: the standard being fags & booze, but he had another which excited John's & my interest that of a literally sweet tooth!
- From his early writing days to now, he'd have a jar of sweets before him. So perhaps it might not be a booze imbibing, or smoke inhaling related death for him like ## Harold & Vaclav, although he apparently has a smoker's breathlessness *.

- Harold contributed to his own demise (? stubbornness again?) as his own writing habit was to smoke whilst in his Wife's Divorce settle Home in the basement, with the windows closed! <> His lady Wife would have her open up in the *eyrie loft* room!
- And irony of ironies in 2013 after Harold's demise, Tom was awarded the PEN Pinter Prize for his work opposing abuses of human rights.
- NB Tom first met Vaclav (Havel) in 1977 where oppressed human rights were to end up triumphant.
- It was about this time Tom rattled off his, *'Professional Foul',* which, as his followers know, had no connection whatsoever with any sport – surprisingly enough!?
- And the cause of his stroke? Will he have another? And let's not forget Covid is still on its hunt for those with underlying problems!?
- But his Type-2 ** diabetes might have its say, but until then he'd have envied My/John's sweet-toothed wedding spread >>

i. ** Type 2 diabetes is a common condition that causes the level of sugar (glucose) in the blood to become too high.
ii. It can cause symptoms like excessive thirst, needing to pee a lot and tiredness. It can also increase your risk of getting serious problems with your eyes, heart and nerves.
iii. It's a lifelong condition that can affect your everyday life. You may need to change your diet, take medicines and have regular check-ups.
iv. It's caused by problems with a chemical in the body (hormone) called insulin. It's often linked to being overweight or inactive, or having a family history of type 2 diabetes. (Consistent with all those sedentary writer types daily lifestyle!?)

- And from his special sweet tooth, one could deduce/appreciate Felicity's own personal style of enticing baking!
- But, tooth implants could be the result of constant sweet attacks, or perhaps also some related to the constant smoking &/or drinking?
- I leave that to you all to ponder that and the laser eye treatment, which is just matter of fact now for the elderly, while I concentrate more upon this Book's title word(s)!
- 'The Legal Sanctity of Marriage' can mean so much to so many, but the word sanctity here means so much more than people fully appreciate: **ultimate importance and inviolability.**

- If you compare/contrast so many famous artists' way of living within the sanctity, so many are control freaks so how does that wear/wash with the wives of their marriage(s)?
- Those *'artist'* types are likely feelingless and have admitted as such, say at other's funerals they don't cry!
- Perhaps being self-centredly focused on what they do/want to do/achieve is to the memory loss of all others?
- Tom admittedly ignorant of so much of his Jewish Heritage -Celebratory Date/Event meanings e.g. The Passover Seder, when preparing/researching/reliving his *Leopoldstadt?*
- But not being aware of those little insignificant things which go on around, best exemplified when, a year or two back, it was pointed out to him that his old lovable *Turbo* stalwart[1] had attained that landmark year age of 100!
- ([1]Again apologies for the possible incorrect/inapplicable use of the word? My erudition is light years behind his, metaphorically writing!)
- But laying the flippancy aside: If you compare/contrast so many famous artists' *bohemian* [x] way of living within the sanctity, so many are adulterous (some to the extreme) so how does that wear/wash with the wives of their marriage(s)?
- [x] *A socially unconventional person, especially one who is involved in the arts; mid 19th century from the French bohémien 'Romani, Gypsy' (because the Romani were thought to come from Bohemia (now part of the Czech Republic), the latter is coincidentally where Tom was born!*
- But, so many artists, due to their fame & fortune can attract any female even one 50 years the younger with just a compliment and wink with a promise of so much more if the female does as he wishes – Picasso & Roth spring to mind.
- So, so many females have a skewed interpretation of *'love'!?* Much to the chagrin of those lesser/poorer lights who fail to attract them as they have nothing *spectacular* (And Secure?) to offer!? (Love also seemingly does not figure in this *coupling* equation)!
- So was it the case with so many whose first marriage failed having had a wife whose instability apparently caused the split.
- But, hey it is likely it is that type who stuck it out through the thin lean early times and observed the *ultimate importance & inviolability!*
- But, it seems that type of man, *old* [L] *Tom obviously was not always seemingly of that sticking it out ilk*, and at times perhaps even in a small *man* way typical of certain of those within >>> the 2 books contained in

'The No Change Here Sex Anthropology of Homo Sapiens'!

- The Books compare/contrast 200 years ago with the present, somewhat, but dissimilar to Tom's *'Arcadia'* as there is no cross over, just a reinforcement of the lack of change: the anthropological study shows man (vir) was/is/will never change no matter what any *'Legal Sanctity'* propounds, if that is the correct terminology? But, I'm sure Tom would know if I asked him!?
  - 'Arcadia' here has the hint of one of the Book's Carousels: The film was produced by Mick Jagger's Company; he apparently being a very close friend of Sabrina, who is now Tom's wife!
  - Moreover it is about The Enigma Machine at Bletchley and it is there you'll see Tom's Plaque contribution # to the fallen Polish Fighters – the Poles were also then the leading cryptologists.
  - (NB Hermione Lee's immensely long [L] (992 Page) *Tom Stoppard: A Life Biography* - *she* speaks of his having 'a roving eye'. [L] *Oddly when John perused this title on Amazon's Look Inside facility, he noticed that someone may not have noticed, or attempted to, but the preview had on show to the interested reader, all the Book's First Part, and on its way into Part 2!)*

And the man himself in his Prime?!

(PART OF A VERY SPECIAL PEACE-LOVING TRIUMVIRATE)!

	This file is licensed under the Creative Commons Attribution-Share Alike 3.0 Unported license.
Description	Русский: Том Стоппард на приёме в честь российской премьеры «Берега утопии»
	English: Tom Stoppard on a reception in honour of the premiere of "The Coast of Utopia" in Russia
Date	4 октября 2007 года modified by: emerson7 20:29, 9 October 2008 (UTC)
Source	Русский: Загружено по просьбе автора
	English: Uploaded according to the author's request cropped from: Image:Tom Stoppard 1.jpg
Author	Кондрашкин Б. Е. (ru:Участник:KDeltaE)

He & his Jewish family (born Tomáš Sträussler), just like Sigmund Freud & daughter Anna had a well-off benefactor to save them from Nazi obliteration:- Just before the German occupation of Czechoslovakia, the town's patron, Jan Antonin Bata, transferred his Jewish employees, mostly physicians, to branches of his firm outside Europe. On 15 March 1939, the day the Nazis invaded Czechoslovakia, the Sträussler family fled to Singapore, where Bata had a factory.

....

And not forgetting his dear (naturally) departed friends >

Screenshot from Harold Pinter's Nobel Prize lecture, 27 December 2005	*Vaclav_HavelThis file is licensed under the Creative Commons Attribution-Share Alike 2.0 Generic license.*

NB His wife's Wiki Pages has in the past been edited by a Guinness!

....

But now for some *Red Slazenger* Stoppard Sporting History et Al.

Harold Pinter called it the best game in the world, John didn't view it with such acclamation, and said such in that Sunday, August 4th 2002 * Gaieties Game v Hornsey #, for whom **John** guested, but he always maintained it was great for the camaraderie and bringing different, even conflicting, cultures together: an episode with a group of West Indians exemplified this later on. # (Info: *Hornsey was just a part of Islington, which **John** had* *previously Captained*.) And age ensured there was no Stoppard with his red Slazenger wicket-keeper's gloves in sight! Perhaps by then his pins were not such a rock solid base as they were in his agile youth?

But this Cricket Captain History lesson is for all...

A Shorter Pinter Brief:- Irascible at times when his word and attitude was questioned on the field and off it by spectators – it was no place to have noisy kids playing within his earshot whilst he was on the field of play – play? It was a religion with him! As the kids found to their embarrassed and upset verbal broadside cost!

Unlike John, he never scored a half century, or carried his opening bat, although wasn't without doggedness and some of his innings were long but not literally run strewn. And, to his heart-felt shame, his early innings days were littered with duck's eggs!

He'd made his own debut in 1969 after taking his son Daniel to Alf Gover's legendary indoor cricket school for some coaching. The club was captained by his son Lauri Lupino Lane, who was succeeded in 1972 by Harold Pinter.

But his insistence as Captain, a right stickler for the Rules of the game etc., ultimately did for the stubborn him?

Never a believer to give an inch and expected such from the opposition, when he didn't really need to!

It was a match v Guy's Hospital, but his team Complement made up only **seven players.**
Friendly game convention would be that the Team short would ask to borrow the required number of extra players needed from the Opposition, so they would at least have 11 in the field.
Although they would normally have to make do with the number they came with to be their Batting Complement.
John went one step further, below: both were fierce competitors, but one *shrewd, conniving* Skipper knew when to stretch the rules a bit; the *stoical* other just let his elastic hang there unused, so to speak!
Pinter was adamant they start playing with only their seven!
Now if they were to bat first there might have been a chance the rest of the team, stranded in a traffic jam/pile up many miles away, but he won the Toss and to the ultimate chagrin of his fellow teammates said they were to field first, with only 7!
Some Big Mistake which went down like a lead balloon and made their feelings show very early on!
HP being of the *old school* would not accept dissention in the lower ranks, but the caustic comments would hit a chord within him.
But, they were being hammered!
When the final jibe straw came whilst fielding, he resigned on the spot!
Perhaps being a rather spoilt person expecting all to rally round, he was not voted back in & when his replacement at a subsequent match asked for a piece of advice, HP gave him short shift; HP then also dropped 2 sitters; ran out his Team's best batsman, just runs short of the winning total!
....

John had no such stiff upper lip scruples...
His Team was short by 5, due to a Flu epidemic and the Match was against the team who had knocked them out of the Cup previously and the league title was on the line.
Others would have surrendered the Match, but John had no such intention – this was his grudge *revenge* match.
He knew some of the Islington West Indian Colts, the 2 of whom also played in the Sunday Football league with him and he knew they would be in that same park, that same afternoon.
So, it was no effort, nor risk, on his as he asked Ossie & *Nellie* (his name being *Nelson*) to get 3 others + them to play.
John's only stipulations were that he was Skipper and he opened the Batting; they could be whatever they pleased.
The opposition were never made known of the subterfuge, nor had any inkling as John, his team & the West Indian Lads kept their lips sealed.

Needless to say, John Won/They won – the title was theirs and, unlike his oversensitive illustrious fellow Captain above, John took charge for another season before Inner London promotion took him away.

And that Gaieties Match v Hornsey?
It was a Draw as that perennial game spoiler, the rainstorms called an abrupt early end to it all!
Tea-Time with cake & sandwiches anybody?
John never did meet Tom.

....

PS If you hadn't noticed Turbo earlier:-

There is an even older resident at his home, now past 100 and counting is his favourite back garden roamer: his tortoise!

....

PART 17: A POST SCRIPTED FANS-TASTICAL MALE FEMALE FINALE!

^{SH} *The Shelf explained at the back end of this Book with a special Kate!?*

DONFEATURES.COM

Kate Menzies DON_ONT_53_SLATER

And why is she here, little devil Diana?

Front pages = little devil queen!

↓

So why is she here?

She's no Guinness? But there is a link later & in Chapter 41 of *Plain Jane Guinness & I Once*...And

Let's take you back to a scenario where you were always interested in those she palled about with in her younger days.

Well, here is this apparent Party planner Worker, who in her bygone days only netted about £20k pa, but not that much in the scheme of things.

The Middletons were **apparently** far better and **apparently** more profitable than she then.

Apparently until their Company Numbered 12191766, Party Pieces Holdings Limited went belly up owing some £2.5 million! (Notice the largest Creditor again was HMRC!).

The Administrators sold the business, BUT, guess how many of the non-secured Creditors got paid?

And could one from the past argue that this why the Royals of old would never advocate *'Morganic Marriages?'* Where such would never happen? Kate is from a Non-Royal Family.

But for that other Kate above, why should she care, she had Wealthy Daddy to fall back on.

Later I think she got her business feet firmly grounded having a business partner as **Camilla Leigh Pemberton** – and if memory serves, her Daddy was daughter-in-law of a one Bank of England Governor!?

Her Queen's Gate 2 bed 1st floor flat was testimony to that fact.

And here is a comparable – Sabrina's Ladbroke Grove 1st Floor Flat was also 2 Bedded.

From the front you could see the right curtained bedroom, while the left the usual dining room leading to the kitchen etc behind.

Although as size goes the lower flat was 3 bedded and extended further back than hers.

And so if you are viewing from SG's above at the back you will see the protrusion below for some feet and this shape gave rise to the term *'the shelf'*.

The additional benefit was that the area could become an enclosed large patio setting with a railings surround – somewhere to sit at a table and go all entertaining al fresco!

Sun bathing?

Well unfortunately the sun wasn't that all accommodating with its heat rays, as the back of the flat area was starved for most part of the Summer Afternoon days!

So back to Kate's flat.

The <u>joint</u> front entrance would be at the bottom of stone steps and your entrance barred by a large imposing iron railed gate!

But as luck would have it, John found this no barrier that eventful day.

He passed that way one day on his way to The Albert Hall – he could have taken the No10 bus from Kingsway opposite Harrods, as the 2 love birds did in my **'Legal Sanctity of Marriage'**.

But he knew all the back doubles and the Queen's Gate Area was on his Tax Officer's Patch.

He was close by and wandered closer to the partying sound emanating from her place.

Drawn by the gaiety he saw the Iron gate was invitingly open and that was just the *unsolicited* invitation he just couldn't resist!

Up the stairs and amongst the throng she & Di were there this the first time they met, but not the last.

The area they were on was similar to Sabrina's, but smaller as Kate's place shared this area with the neighbour's Flat A – Hers Flat B – both Flats narrow Frontages greeted you as you made the top of the stairs.

<u>**"Sorry to intrude but I am lost – I am trying to get to the Albert Hall."**</u>

Kate the ever-enchanting hostess then took his arm, led him downstairs with her irrepressible smile and pointed the way to go.

'So that's what's at the top of those stairs', he said to himself as he went on his contented, but photo less way. Although there is one by someone else somewhere else in this Book….

……….

She and Di were close pals like Di + Julia they were photo-shot everywhere they went, but not on this other special occasion?

Imagine these two plus one other well off female out on a special event, that of say a Charity Challenge: no easy challenge as say in the Alpine Area?

So, Diana's Charity stint was to slum it in one of those Mountain Cabins?

Or if that doesn't grab you say in one of those Centre point's homeless beds etc.

The point I am making is that it would be well outside of her comfort zone.

And so when the coast was clear she skedaddled to the nearest plush hotel, the other in tow.

And so the outside world, *knowing no different truth*, were deceived *by her personal default*!

So this little **Devil**, like the Queen could have been in private, was not the little **Angel** she was always portrayed to be!

....

Kate's Hubby's Restaurant was just across the way from The National Geographic Society Building where John met Di again...

↓

With a Special Author's Tribute to One Ex-Soldier

who went the Extra Mile! _ _ _ _ _ wow

You are invited to

A ONE-DAY SEMINAR

RESPONDING TO LANDMINES
A MODERN TRAGEDY AND ITS SOLUTIONS

Royal Geographical Society
Kensington Gore, London

Thursday 12th June 1997

Arranged & Hosted by
The Mines Advisory Group
&
The Landmine Survivors Network

Guest Speaker: Diana, Princess of Wales

In partnership with the Co-operative Bank plc

1600-1745   Perspectives, Closing Panel:

Rt. Hon. Clare Short MP
Secretary of State, Department For International Development

Jill Sinclair
Director, Non-Proliferation & Arms Control Division,
Canadian Department for Foreign Affairs & International Trade

Shorty was there also...

But so was another special co-speaker with our Princess...

ʷᵒʷ And he merits the special attention and praise which is only reserved for the most brave!?

His speech highlight he was once a paraplegic in one leg beneath the knee: the rest of his lower leg had been shattered from him by an UID!

(Well Landmines and their destructive effect was the theme of the Event!)

But what put this future American University professor was that he actually revealed he had had both legs below the knee operated upon and replaced by artificial legs!

Why?

The second was for him passable, but not always pain free and immobilising at times.

And it was this special time that he needed unfaltering speed immediately as on this day to his horror his 3-year-old daughter had opened the front gate to the busy road below.

He had to stop the possible end to her innocent life to the unfeeling vagaries of the relentless, remorseless traffic flow.

He failed spectacularly as he fell trying, but his child lived on thanks to a quick witter passer-by.

He then perceived his other leg as totally unreliable and dreaded a recurrence of that day's heart-rending episode – so had this other leg knee high amputated willingly so he knew his movement would be utterly reliable!

....

 As far as reliability went the Media made out Di was haemorrhaging friends by the dozen when her breakup/divorce problems were rife and one of the supposed victims of her contacts carnage was Kate!

But Di reassured John, just like Sabrina put him right, that he should not believe them as she had only recently seen Kate's Baby Flora in Hospital around the same time as she saw Jemima Khan's first!

....

And so their strong bond remained – I mean why not Di had introduced her to her future Beau, restauranteur Simon.

Di's choice was spot on, the beautiful smiling couple are Simon & <u>Kate</u> Slater <u>(Née Menzies)</u> Her Dad figured many pages back...

Unlike Di's parents whose princely choice turned out ghastly!

And when it all went sour did not her mother then put the knife in her distraught daughter's back.

Ah well the Nobility with its strange standards is not all it is *media* cracked up to be!

....

And so their strong bond remained – (From Above...) Here I would mention 2 additional: her Mental Health Expert, **Julia** and her South American Ambassador, **Lucia**.

Julia has her own featured <u>*Chaptering*</u> – The Sage in Part 11 (ante) – but Lucia needs her own featuring here, if not, just to dispel a *persistent press possible misrepresentation, or at least a lack of clarity as there are actually 2 Lucias who gained prominence and proximity, each in her own way to the originally married couple – Charles & Diana.*

The first woman to apparently have it away with our current King # was Lucia Santa Cruz.

She was the daughter of the Chilean ambassador in London, Victor Santa Cruz, during the term of President Ricardo Froilan Lagos Escobar. Lucia also lived a successful life, becoming a University Professor and writing several books before being made the director of Chilean national TV. Marrying Juan Luis Ossa, she also had three children and remained friends with both Charles and Camilla **until her death in 2019 aged 77**.

The two had met during Charles' time studying for his undergraduate at Trinity College, Cambridge.

Lucia by profession was a linguist who spoke four languages and had degrees from multiple famed Universities, including Cambridge's main rival, Oxford.

Their first meeting was at a dinner party in 1969 and apparently it was love at first sight, and apparently (per his Biography) sex with the older (experienced?) soon followed! #

Although my dear late departed John in Chapter Fifty Four: Hello, Your Majesty (ies) – Part 2 *always suggested he apparently knew of more (Willing Country Wenches ?) who might have also been arranged/lined up (at possibly an earlier age?) – but Lucia was happy to bear the older woman 1st time mantle, so who am I to dispute the claimed licit liaison? Unless what John told me was true!?*

Similarly, who am I to dispute the claim she was the first to introduce Charles to Camilla in 1971?

And so now to the other Lucia - **Lucia Flecha de Lima:** She had became a trusted & loyal friend of Diana in the early 1990s when her husband, Paulo Tarso Flecha de Lima, was Brazilian Ambassador to the UK. She also acted as Secretary of Tourism of the Federal District.

She claimed that of the three significant men in Diana's life, she was 'not in love with Dodi Fayed', she may have had a 'passion' for heart surgeon Hasnat Khan but against all the post marital odds, 'the love of her life' was Prince Charles! (But we all know how that would turn out!)

Interestingly if you read articles you might be shocked, or confused, that both Lucias became friendly with both Charles and one, or both, of his Lady Loves!? His **Chilean** Cherry Popper with him & Camilla And Diana (!?); the other **Brazilian** (loyal friend), with him & Diana, even with hubby Paolo going on holiday to Brazil with them!

Here I would point to a problem with the Chilean mooted friendship: if Diana knew she had originally introduced Charles to Camilla, I doubt there could have been anything akin to a friendship between them!

And she had also opened her legs to her future hubby would have killed off any possibility stone dead – as divorcing Charles would ultimately be to her!?

NB Apart from the age difference, Charlie boy could not have married his first (**older**) love as she was a Roman Catholic (RC) and that was a Royal marriage no-no!

And as likely not a Virgin, so another Royal marriage no-no!

So I now pose the question who first popped her cherry?

And how many before Charles had known her (RC) Biblically!

....

NOW

That promised update follows >>>>

Marit **Guinness Aschan** (b. 28 January 1919, d. 27 September 2004) gained an international reputation for her contemporary enamel work, especially for the exacting plique-a-jour technique used in the missing jewellery.

She redefined the craft of enamelwork, developing the traditional and pioneering the new in an extraordinary career encompassing wall panels, freestanding miniatures and sculptures, most recently turning to jewellery - all of her work is infused with profound originality and stunning beauty. In the opinion of many she was unquestionably one of the true greats of her craft.

Born, Marit Victoria Guinness, she was the daughter of Henry Samuel Howard Guinness and Alfhild Holter. She married Carl Nils Wilhelm Gunnar Aschan, son of Nils Aschan and Baroness Elsa Djurklov, on 21 July 1937. She and Carl Nils Wilhelm Gunnar Aschan were divorced in 1963.

Coincidentally, like her mother & father she did her WWII War effort: working in the Ministry of Information.

She was educated an enamellist and wrote extensively on such subjects: . She wrote the book Modern Jewellers, The Art of Jewellery, published 1968; Enamels, published 1985.

Her main (*working*) home was 25 Chelsea Park Gardens, London, just around the corner from her parents' Cheyne Walk address! But her address had added significance as the place was bought for her by her father to support her work/life jewellery making/designing passion: he even installed a kiln therein (like you see in glass making workshops) for her to continue her creativity, unabashed/undistracted by outside interferences!

In October 1998 Marit brought a large collection of jewellery to Johan Galtung in Oslo, Norway for a retrospective exhibition - with many additional new pieces, too. Afterwards, *Elfad Bodiskhanov*, known in the trade and husband of the Norwegian TV personality **Marit** *Christensen*, offered to sell the entire collection, together with some gold boxes owned by the gallery's proprietor and others. He announced plans to visit three clients in the Middle East. The collection was last seen all together at the Oslo Norway Jewellers in 1999, shortly before Mr Bodiskhanov disappeared.

While he was away, he telephoned Marit Guinness Aschan, claiming to be in Switzerland. When he reappeared, he had neither jewellery nor payment. Even his passport had disappeared (he claimed it was stolen), so it was difficult to establish where he had been. He may well have never left Norway. **He served three and a half years in prison for this and other crimes.** His wife **Marit** Christensen claimed that he had been in Russia. She also came under investigation. He however apparently suggested that he had the pieces melted down for the gold and precious stones - a tragedy if true, because the value of the materials is a fraction of the whole collection, in terms both of art and of money - but this may well have been a bluff to try and put off the investigation of his wife.

One or two of the major pieces were quickly recovered; an alert police officer spotted a necklace and one of the gold boxes in a pawnbroker's window in Norway, but the bulk of the collection remains lost. A Norwegian jeweller also reported seeing some pieces when they were brought into his shop, lending support to the idea that they may never have left Norway.

An Additional Oddity? > Strangely coincidental that his wife should also be named, Marit!?

Marit Guinness Aschan died in 2004, having never fully recovered her health after the loss of so many masterworks, (John exchanged correspondence with her daughter just a short while before she passed, having been made aware how sick she was!) and her dented spirit faltered thereafter, but with one extraordinarily, out of the blue, ***phoenix-like*** brief extravaganza type sortie into family related party-land:

July 2001, she hosted a party at (expensive?) Claridge's (where else!) for 500 people and designed a tiara especially for the occasion, to celebrate the 60th birthday of her ex-husband Randle Brooks [R], the 21st birthday of the couple's son and the 17th of their daughter, who was <u>coming out</u> that summer.

[R] Randle Brooks was born 1941. He married Juliet Marit Gabriel Aschan, daughter of Carl Nils Wilhelm Gunnar Aschan and Marit Victoria Guinness, in 1980. He and Juliet Marit Gabriel Aschan were divorced in 1990. He died on 11 November 2020.

Here one might say, 'a possible classic case of a Guinness Cougar?' Well, I mean to say he was 22 years her younger!

But whatever the difference in age, the other significance was she again like so many of her predecessors AND peers married into even more money:

Just like the Northumberland link(s) I mentioned much earlier, although a couple of hundred miles further north, here is another worth getting to be financially part of?!

When Randle, a conservatist and one of the North West's largest landowners in the decades since his father purchased the Tatton Estate in 1958, died at his Peover Hall home [P], he left his 5,000-acre estate and other holdings to his family.

He with his wife, like Muncaster Castle Phyllida and Patrick (And others similarly inherited) Randle Brooks, who was 79, and his wife Juliet devoted years to the restoration of their other land holding, the grade two-listed [P] Peover Hall, and its gardens and park, in Knutsford. The family's holdings also included Knutsford Heath, which has hosted large public events over the years.

Continued from above <> To my knowledge Marit never created another piece again.

A site was created by steelpillow.com to highlight the theft – an example of a sample item below

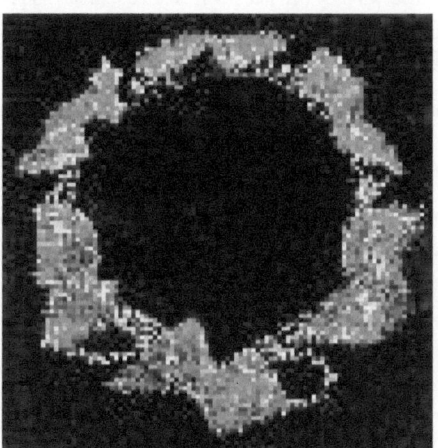

!!!!!!!!!!!!!!!!!!!!!!!!!!!!!!!!

<u>Regrettably the Site was only updated until 2008 when it all ended up as a possibly fruitless effort as the jewels seemed deemed to be lost for all posterity!</u>

Although there is no official statute of limitations for criminal cases in the UK (unlike many other EU countries and America), limitation periods do apply to many aspects of business and consumer litigation, including debt recovery.

But here in the Uk only 6 years for Fraud!

Hence the futility of continuing...

And in her mother's Norway...

Federal law says that the general **5-year** statute of limitations applies in every case unless there is a specific code section that extends the statute of limitations for that particular offence.

Pity they didn't have that here for all those futile *lost* Yewtree cases!

....

And As *Drillingly* Promised

Certainly, not the end to a session I would have ever forecast!

....

'But the Drilling Might Stop There'.

Then, his tack changed to a lighter, brighter side.. "Funny, the Power of Song, I think **she** *and her staff missed a trick here, when it was all about the disaffected Youth: if only they had welcomed &/or encouraged/directed their Local Thugs' malcontent energies through song, rap, then, for the more extremely felt,* drill *itself, ultimately?*

There again one girl staff member already had had her ribs broken (ante) so perhaps the thug element was painted/tainted/branded as such that they (barred) were thought as just local predatory leopards unlikely to change their violent black spots.
But History has proved that concept groundless?"
Or has it? As just the contrary obvious continues to proliferate?

As he took out another folded paper.

He always, constantly maintained that everything bad that comes here, comes from the US – this I gather emanated from Chicago...Bad?

Editor's Note: ^{DR↑} THINGS ARE *perhaps* SLOWLY CHANGING ↓

- UK police are monitoring more than 2,000 "drill" rap videos on YouTube in their war against London street gangs.
- YouTube has deleted some/only a couple of hundred at the request of police of the thousands identified because of their links to crime.
- The gangs use YouTube to threaten rivals and boast about their attacks. And the police have used YouTube videos as evidence against gangs in court.
- The stakes are high: More than 4,000 people a year are stabbed in London, mostly in gang conflict.
- At least four rap groups and rising are now banned by court order from performing or publishing their music.

- Drill rappers are angry. "This is a threat to freedom of speech. Nobody in a free society should be imprisoned for words," one group says.
- So, what do you say to that claim?
- As more names are placed in the Met Police's Prosecution Sights Frame...who claim that they had 'identified a direct correlation between drill videos which glorified violence and subsequent shootings and stabbings on the streets.
- Here are just a few names of recent note/repute:-

Isaac Donkoh, a Rapper Leader of the Beckton E6 Gang – now all imprisoned for serious crimes.
The 1011 Gang (Notting Hill see table above) – some of whom have recently been released.
The W12 Gang
The 410 gang in Brixton
Jordan Bedeau
Digga D
Krept and Konan & their *Change.org* petition
Skengdo x AM

For further information updates view the Metropolitan's *'Operation Domain'* Investigation Results <> *The scale of London's gang wars is terrifying: In the 2018-2019 year ending in March — there were 4,277 stabbings. The previous year there were 4,732. There were 122 homicides of all types in the most recent year, an indicator that stabbings tend to leave their victims alive.*

In total, 21,484 offences from knives and other offensive weapons including knuckle dusters, sharpened screwdrivers and deliberately broken bottles were recorded = 59 per day according to the Ministry of Justice!

Notting Hill was mentioned above and its Carnival still throws up its regular homicide etc – the irony being that another young Rapper Takayo, aka TKorStretch found his life curtailed under the Westway Overpass, outside Ladbroke Tube Station, the same station John used for his YCTV days and under the same Flyover he did his Charitable Work Stints beneath – the wealthy Quarter being only a couple of hundred yards North of all this violent commotion!

And can you wonder?

With over 200 Carnival Time arrests, including 30+ for carrying offensive weaponry; including less than a mere 9 sexual assaults; including nearly 4 dozen other assaults!

A carefree, I don't give a dam if I'm arrested #, Criminal Type within his Crowd Protected/Camouflaged Operational Paradise!

But, as we leave the carnival to its own de-*vices* and drive South you can find other Rappers down Streatham way.

But is singing their chosen career path, or otherwise?

Whatever you wish to think, apparently [R] another Rapper (Madix also k/a Mad Itch 67 - *part of the MOBO-nominated group 67*) real name Chris Kaba was shot, but not by a member of a Rival Gang etc but by The Police! [R] *Although apparently not so according to his future mother-in-law who claimed he was just a (non-violent peace loving?) apprentice architect?*

There again *apparently* trying to evade them (the police had tried to stop him after the activation of an automatic number plate recognition camera (ANPR), believing that the car he was driving was linked to a firearms incident days before) causing them to ram his car to stop is not a good driving move, as the bullet(s) fired his way proved.

But, and it is that Perennial Big But, what was this Rapper &/or Architect supposed to be guilty of that warranted his shooting?

No gun found again scenario?

As John puts it many times: *That all bad, shoot first ask questions later, if the suspect is still alive (?!) comes from the USA – just view their news!*

But, Did They Here? Why not the tyres first?

Perhaps, yet again another Review Investigation will answer the most fundamental questions which the Community and Family pose – but what of the feelings of his mother?

Just to another soon to be forgotten case of *'It hurts Mummy!'*

And what of the USA where John had always maintained is the source of so many of our Crime Ways, especially which attract and indoctrinate the violent gullible young, who are not the Constructive base of our up-and-coming Society!

This Year 2022 the New York PD had their own equivalent called 'Operation Drilly' which resulted in arrests: the need to brag online/You Tube **on both sides** *of the Pond has made evidence finding for the Authorities a Piece of Cake until the Boasting Drillers figure out how to use creative (secret coded) derogatory nicknames instead?!*

But, and it is that Perennial Police Numbers But, if they are already struggling against the tide then the tide is becoming a tsunami flow as those *'Immigrant Boats'* containing 40% Albanians, whose violent upbringing past see us a very soft Police Political Correctness Touch and their Channel crossing forays are bringing over more foot soldiers to continue the violent onslaught on all (good &/or bad) as first it is drugs – cocaine then UK cannabis mass production – then these criminal evil types crossing over from drug trafficking, to people smuggling, document fraud, modern slavery, money laundering and ultimately the last and most feared that of arms trafficking!

Hence the increase of shooting/killing incidents! Reminiscent of their own Country Based Mafia where violence dictates and determines what stands before them, in their profit-making way (turf wars?).

What adds salt to their catch-us-if-you can stance is their own openly advertised, blatant/flagrant Albanian Drilling Scene and from that how many more drill rap videos can the Met's Manpower effectively monitor, before they collapse under the numerical superiority of those Albanian Criminal Elements wanting to sing their own praises?

And if you say what Albanian Drillers? Well the ordinary law abiding citizen would be ignorant of such as *'Stealth'* – well not to those in the business as he attracts millions of views for his Videos!

And other names not known to the General Public, but feared in the Underworld Circles – *the 'Hellbanlanz' gang operating in East London, but just a tip of the possible monstrous gang family mountain of 2 dozen and rising(?); criminal names like Fation Dauti, Kastriot Ahmati, Biedar Doka, Erion Mehmetaj Ferbeen Hoxha, and so many more as the numbers are frightening.*

But as luck and Juris Prudence so many of the above have *apparently* been deported back to Albania, but and it is always that Big Corrupt But, how many will slip back under our hand tied Radar and how soon - ? Bribery to get results is now so common in that Country as regrettably it will only be a short time that it will be rife in nearly the whole world!

We will be fighting a losing battle unless we arm <u>ourselves that/our front enforcement line</u> – to the teeth.

And no it is no pun or whatever, because these individuals and their respective gangs have no respect for human life, because they keep theirs in this Country should they take others – a real case of come back hanging as this is the only way to reduce their numerical superiority and willingness to operate in a tolerant free society, where death could look them in the Gallows eye if caught and found guilty?!

The great fear for all parents should be that they never get near any of the above and get drawn into their unforgiving network: there the parent will not have to worry about their Mental Health Well-Being, as a bullet or knife will rid them of that fear and the life of their kid!

But is there any escape?

So far one only hears of problems in North England, London, the Midlands, the East...

But it is likely a Big Sorry But that if it is not an Albanian Mobster, then there is the British Equivalent, the Serbian Equivalent, the South American Cartel Equivalent reps equivalent here just down the unsuspecting road from you behind some closed curtains beavering away producing drugs to either kill or addict us!

But spill the beans on them and they will as likely spill your inners across your kitchen floor – IN Broad Daylight!

European Membership has opened up our Borders to so much of world's Dross & Dregs, it won't be long before the Authorities will have to raise their White Administrative Flag for their overworked, undermanned and under weaponised/protected front liners whose own life is on the line all too often! But Governments constantly want to cut back on front line officer numbers!

Already we have only a 5% Prosecution rate; too many on Bail before the Hearing and just drift away into the UK Ether and resurrect themselves under another foreign name; prosecution timetables being unmet as the Min of Justice doesn't attract enough Barristers for the Court Work as it is a pittance for the effort/work/sacrifices they have had to make to get qualified; not enough Courts built to speed up the backlog:
Courts have been closing for at least 30 years now here!

Nottingham, which has always had a High Crime Rate, as does Yorkshire, wherein Leeds there is open warfare on the streets by Rival gangs weaponised to the hilt with whichever killing weapon they can lay their hand # upon, to lay their opponents into their early grave!

The foreign criminal trade has no fear of the puny, unarmed, over educated/qualified Street Bobby – if you can see him there that is!

But, yet again, their numbers have been drastically cut and their effective way of going about their business stymied by their politically correct boss's limiting confrontation instructions!

No wonder the younger criminal's way of doing business is violence first, as there is little likelihood of being arrested &/or effectively sentenced!

But poor ***It Hurts Mummy*** at home is continually waiting for that death knell knocking at her door to tell her poor impressionable gang joiner is no longer with her as a machete has cut his body in two! (His gang lost the fight!)

And in Liverpool you just have to be a constant <u>media highlighted</u> innocent child bystander to be killed by the rival gang employed hitman, whose stray bullet doesn't hit its prescribed target!

Then strangely all the stops are pulled out!

But nowadays can you/we rely on the Police generally *'fighting'* our victim's corner?

The answer is that simple ***'solitary figure in the crime wave dyke'!***

So NO is the answer, whether enforced or by choice, so many feel let down:

- One bereaved wife had to fight and investigate against the CPS & Police Negative Tide who would prosecute the driver who did an illegal three point turn on a three-way dual carriageway and killed her husband in the Process! Through all her efforts she got justice. And no surprise here, her local Bedfordshire, Cambridgeshire & Hertfordshire Police Forces were already under investigation themselves for failings in investigations!
- One certain celebrity personage, Noel Edmonds came up against the same *'unaccommodating'* enemy of his Legal Rights Due Juris Prudence Justice – here like so many he was defrauded by the HBoS Reading fraudsters – he had to struggle to be heard and as the Police were not about doing anything he made a nuisance of himself at the (New Owners) Lloyds bank AGM – whether there he got more to go along with him (perhaps in a later Class Action?). Through all his efforts he got justice. And no surprise here, his local Police Force, Thames Valley Polices Force have been on more than one occasion subject to investigation themselves for failings in investigations amongst other things!
- The Bank Board Members were castigated for failing to act, rather than cover up, the Fraud when it was pointed out to them!
- A statement by the APPG also makes reference to a report entitled 'Project Lord Turnbull' compiled by Whistleblower Sally Masterton. Masterton, a former employee in Lloyds high-risk division, authored the report in 2013 claiming certain executives at HBOS 'concealed' a fraud at their branch in Reading before the bank's takeover by Lloyds at the height of the crisis.
- And we now know what happens to Whistleblowers in all walks of Life – A Sacking! Or take the payoff and keep stumm! But here the whistle blower was made redundant, was not properly compensated, and the FCA has done nothing to support or protect her. She was not the first whistle-blower on major banking fraud to be let down by the FCA.
- Astonishingly the Financial Reporting Council (FRC) gave a clean bill of health to the HBOS audit that year. The conflicts of interest over this within both the FRC and FCA still need to be looked into.
- *The cynic might think that the senior civil servants within the Treasury are too interested in their future <u>lucrative</u> employment within the banking system to want to disrupt the cosy relationship with the banking system they currently have.*
- But, and it has been a Very Big We The Criminals Know But: Neither the Serious Fraud Office nor Financial Conduct Authority (FCA) has the capacity to take on major banking fraud.
- Another great death producing scandal was that of The Royal Mail Powers not acknowledging their <u>**New**</u> **IT Programme was not Bug Free – hence all those malicious prosecutions – much later overturned, but too late for some life self-takers!**
- And so which high & might personage within the echelons of the above were brought to Criminal Charge Book?
- BUGGA ALL!

And so, back to *"It Hurts Mummy!"* as that Book Title States, but, and it is a Big Questionable But...

- Is it because your lad is Drilling?
- Is it because he is a Drilling Gang Member?
- Is it because he is a Violent Gang Member?
- Is it because he is a Murdering Gang Member?
- Is it because he got Caught?
- Is it because he got Convicted?
- Perhaps, none of the above, but more likely, that he was injured.
- Or worse still!
- Then, *"**It Hurts Mummy**!"*

But, and it is a somewhat Big Perennial But, did *'it hurt a Daddy also?'*

As it is not uncommon for there to be no Father-Figure in the Picture.

Some might say it is because so many feel they have the God Given Right to sow their seed and then *'blow the consequences, as they take their uncommitted leave...? But do the females accept this?* ^{x}

Co-incidentally as John would say about everything bad coming our way comes from the USA!

Well, a simple example then was when a local practitioner reported that *12 pregnant black women came for consultations. Some bring their children or their mothers.* **Only one brings a husband.**

But it is more worrying that so many of them had no intention of getting married! $^{EH?}$

^{x} So apparently they don't view their own as marrying material!?

And here in the Uk it was similarly in 2010 we were highlighting a really high disproportionate % of Black Single Mothers compared with other Races.

Come forward a decade or so later and we still have that problem here without any apparent abatement:

> *18.9% of Black households were made up of a single parent with dependent children, the highest percentage out of all ethnic groups for this type of household; the lowest percentage was found among Asian households, at 5.7% (2019)*

Even the concerned Black Community Leaders feel the need to speak out about the problem, for me the more notable - Dr Tony Sewell, CEO of the Charity <u>Generating Genius</u>,

> *'This problem of absent dads isn't going away: in Britain, the black ethnic group has <u>the</u> highest proportion of lone parent households at 13 per cent. There is a culture among some black men of producing children without taking responsibility. Inevitably, these children end up paying the price.*

- Other factors have worsened this problem in recent years.
- The steady decline of male adult authority outside the family has been undermined by worries over child abuse.
- The availability of welfare and housing provided to single working-class mothers has also lessened the risk of – or need for – putting up with flaky men.

The result has been that a new generation of black and white boys have been raised without the much-needed permanent presence of their fathers.

Half of black children have no father living at home.

This absence is sorely felt and has arguably been the root cause for poor school performance and the rise of knife crime...'

He had his own trying to turn the tide solution (how many listened?) but as usual sufficient resources would be a perennial stumbling block e.g. *...more needs to be done to provide other black boys with mentors who can inspire them!*

I leave it to those who can give him the support he craves for those he feels can make a difference.

MYA

[EH?] *Although I myself have come across an instance where one black woman allowed herself to be impregnated twice by the same man, although he wasn't considered marrying material and also suggested to her female friend to couple copulate with him to produce her a baby, but again neither a mention of settling down with him?*
Perhaps a beau but nothing else to commend him but his looks?!

There again perhaps there is a simpler, going back centuries, genetic history/mores/answer link which was covered in Chapters 7 + 11 of Book 2, *The No-Change-Here Sex Anthropology of Homo Sapiens?*

AND LAST OF ALL ◇ YOU ALL KNOW....

SABRINA GUINNESS GOT HACKED!

If you were to key in *'Sabrina Guinness Hacked'* it is likely that you will be led to the Daily Telegraph (Mandrake) Site like the one which has an article dated 2nd March 2011.

There is the article's beginning with talk of her being blackmailed & targeted by Romanian Criminals...

But the main player was ALEX.

And it all actually started one week in 2010, 25-29 June.

Imagine the scene where you get home to check your emails and find some already opened and you could swear you didn't open them!?

And as the days unfold you find your access denied despite the/your correct password being used!?

Then you get a threatening phone call where your access would be restored if you...!?

The voice is foreign with a Baltic State type Accent so definitely not known to you at all!?

The Police get called in and ask did you record the call?

Obviously the answer would be, no!

Then the obvious panic even though you now have control restored to you!?

The address book and other personal detail must have been copied (And stored somewhere?)!

What about all those whose detail you hold!?

Would the criminal(s) get in contact with them and threaten them too with what I had about them!?

>>The last would be problematic if some intimate or very secret detail had been included in any email exchanges!?

John had been a person of interest but the interest dissipated as he produced those *'unknown source'* he received 30th June.

He got the nod from the Police, but it was well after the event that he could contact her ex Ladbroke Hall Pupils...

>>>>>>>>

YCTV FACEBOOK PREDICTABLY

18 October at 12:50 did you hear what happened to her at the end of June? Poor woman it must have really shaken her...

....no i don't know. what happened?

19 October at 21:49
Some person(s) hacked into her computer,
if that was not dreadful enough for her and all those she had dealings with on her computer (the latter because if the hacker(s) got their personal detail then they could also be attacked) –
I had previous dealings with her and her family and it seems the day after she regained full control of her computer I got some strange emails to my 2 personal accounts I had used in the family correspondence) from someone purporting to be Guinness.camilla@gmail .com (ever heard of her?)
(the police have the details) but the real evil twist is that the hacker (Alex, some foreign sounding guy) rang her to give her a password to regain full access to her PC which he/they had gained access to through what she thinks is her poor password control? –
coupled with some comments I cannot repeat here!!!
If she were alone when he called it must have been really upsetting - poor woman!
Hope this isn't the type of attention he has to regularly endure. (don't mention the source as we broke contact a while back even though she wished me a Facebook * happy easter xx
but even when we did meet those times at Ladbroke Hall and talk there was also tension between us - inquisitive people are not those she takes to for all her obvious reasons then (and now), although there are very few family secrets/skeletons in cupboards that she and her sister have apparently not made public in newspaper interviews.
Trust if you feel like making contact with her you (after all you are one of her Facebook friends) you will treat this with the sensitivity it requires and not post it on your wall read by many.
Despite several requests over the weeks the police have not told me if they caught anybody and contrary to someone's opinion of me I too do not know the hackers identity either, other than the above?!
Thanks
(Facebook own everything on their site so keep anything private somewhere else) that's why I doubted the authenticity of that 'camilla guinness' e mail with dodgy attachments to both my personal e mail addresses only known to a select few and perhaps one of them found to their cost to make their passwords all different & hard to crack!

...

18 October at 12:30 sorry to relate I heard from the Chelsea Police, Sabrina Guinness that kind lady who was always willing to help any of you when you had problems had her computer hacked!

I was told about the incidents (yes there is more) but waiting if I can divulge more. Poor woman if this is what she has to suffer!? regards hope your media career is on the rise...

Hi "John Baker", applogies, Sabrina got hacked!
by whom/what? is being hacked such a big deal nowadays, surely they just mess with her Facebook?

no I gather it was more serious than that, her personal address book may have been interrogated/copied etc you get my drift?
then there was a more sinister turn of events by the hacker - will let you know later ..
30 September at 11:38
Chelsea Police told me something befell her recently - interested?
... Really what happened?

2010...I received some strange e mails on a personal aspect to my e mail accounts - private & otherwise - on 30th June this year - the source could only have been her - especially when I found out she was hacked during 25/6 - 29/6.
The Police made me privy to her statement of the event(s) but of course I cannot give you all the details suffice to say her personal data could have been viewed/used/stolen e.g. her address book etc (you get the drift).

Why would they let me have the detail?
Well what with all my YCTV etc investigatory work she thought it might have been me!
I don't hold it against her; her recollection of our meetings those years back had become blurred and presumably mixed up with someone else she seems to have met down on the farm near Hook!
Not so, but I did however meet another member of her family there (A bit of an aberration by her. None of us are perfect and that apparently even applies more so in her choice of password protection!)
And coincidentally there have been a series of arrests this Monday by the Met's e-crime unite around London/Essex of an east European gang * involved in a large scale hacking operation and I hope they are the same as hacked her PC and that a certain infamous person with a foreign accent called Alex/Alec? is among those arrested.
I am awaiting objections from the Chelsea Police (and her - if they forwarded the request, but (and forgive the pun) they are a law unto themselves) that I intend to let ex YCTV people on Facebook know of the incident who then can offer her words of comfort and support this weekend.

....

lol... that is an interesting story. Nothing but drama and bad karma surrounds that woman. To be honest I am surprised and genuinely relieved the news was not much worse

....

04 October at 16:45
not sure what you meant by 'drama'? are there other similar incidents?

....

17 March at 20:50
h8 ideastap loved YCTV!! Nothing like it anywhere!

why not post it on sabrina's Facebook page - she'd really appreciate it!

Whilst writing would you like to contribute more (like others are doing)? I am sure you have more to tell about YCTV success etc >
Your name/moniker; when & why joined YCTV; when left; what learnt/studied; your current job & type or name of employer.
Comment on YCTV set up; the trainers; who was in charge; was 'S' hands on or off; her good/bad qualities (I've heard of 1 in particular).
Shoot locations and experience (were you one of the lucky ones she let work near her country cottage)?
Did YCTV spread and be replicated elsewhere/nationwide (I heard of the Toxteth venture) or were the students only Londoners?
The characters you met; the friends you made; share with us experiences good and bad (gang member infiltration or attacks on staff/students.
The addition of the new studio ~ 2006 * (where was it situated?) – did you attend the fund raising?
*I understand that after this event the lack of funding contributed to the end of YCTV as you knew it
In general any fundraising activities by YCTV students
Post YCTV – is ideataps as good? Comments why?
do any of you have 'S' e mail/phone detail to keep in touch?
Any of you a member of her Facebook page? What is she doing now? Future reuinion plans?
Lastly add what you think might be missing from above; your own personal views .e.g. what it did for you, its legacy if there is one e.g. what has it spawned; and anything else you feel relevant.
Please e mail reply to me Thanks, John: bakerjohn@hotmail.co.uk

....
26 April at 17:49
notice she isn't on any YCTV Facebook page - more details please
....

Hi John, she is one of my friends - not quite sure how I link you up though! Will send you and she a message. Can chat with you any time about YC stuff. Tomorrow not so good. Weds Ok. Cheers! E.
27 April at 13:36
expect call tomorrow night but I find one can't get everything jotted down so to assist here is a sample of the topics I might cover so you are prepared: period you were there; general feeling/comments; specific YCTV success/failures; was it funding problems &/or other factors which contributed to the decline - from the accounts 2006 onwards were not good years?; how did the 'folkstone billionaires' & ideastap get involved; quality of

staff; pupil numbers and course variety; SG hands on or hands off; mistakes made over the years/lessons learned; did the aid get to the targeted youth group or did some (not so underprivileged) manipulate the system to get on? anything you wish to ad e.g. life after YCTV for you, SG, staff, pupils - some don't reckon ideastap - well hope this is not too much too handle PS if you have any photos to send over?

28 April at 16:46
we spoke so long my battery finally gave out - but we were nearing the end. One thing that I have since thought of, although not sure if applicable, but she should also try to ascertain the project in the USA which prompted Sabrina to do something similar here. I am sure there are studies on its efficacy or lack of, success or failure, lessons learnt etc there & maybe include her targeted group.
Thanks John I will pass suggestion on to her. It would be good to chat soon. I'm developing a YCTV inspired idea and would love to hear the feedback you are getting from members. Best, E.

....
24 May at 13:12
how about Thursday after 6.
Pick a venue where I can buy you dinner as we speak
John
cool. can we do a bar in Ladbroke Grove? There is a nice one called the Elgin just by the Library.
25 May at 11:26
OK 7pm This Thursday - beforehand do you want me to send you a list of things which interest me?
25 May at 11:29 Report
S. yes 7pm is great. please send me your list.
26 May at 12:24
how you got into YCTV & Ideastap/workplacement; did the study cost you anything? who did the training & where? general impression of how good the training was; the surroundings; intermixing with others - staff & students; how many you know got work as a result of YCTV training; who was in charge? did Sabrina Guinness get involved in any way - with the training or socially with the students? why do you think it failed? links with local schools/bursaries/funding if known;
you mentioned depression - were you treated any differently from the others? look at the following link and comment >
http://www.thefreelibrary.com/I'm+not+rich+like+the+other+Guinnesses.+I+do+the+Lottery+every+week;...-a0110762116 (I will bring a copy) Thanks John

Why are not those apparently previously close to you at YCTV not on your friends list - ? E.? and no ex students? well that's a quandry I won't be unable to unravel.
Why not get back into philanthropic acts - no future Charity connection on the horizon for you?
....

MYA Why 'Don't You Believe anything I Say!'...JOHN ↓

Between Sabrina Guinness and You

18 March at 12:49

it's quite incredible the lasting wonderful impression YCTV had on their lives - they miss it terribly - and

ideastap is not a patch on it.

a great tribute to all your work and effort on their behalf.

That apparent reply> 03 April at 19:55

AND SO NOW YOU ALL KNOW ALL I KNOW-APPARENTLY!?
<u>But the final irrefutable evidence is just around the page corner...</u>

354

....

Author's Postscript: And the true identity of the hacker is still a mystery!?
But, the answer might lay within the 2000-page Trilogy k/a
Plain JANE Guinness & I Once...

Eh Alex?

....

Final Info Update:-

Nomenclature comes from a Latin word meaning "the assigning of names." English's *name* and *noun* are rooted in the Latinate *nomen*...

For those unaware of a certain someone's nomenclature!

It's **Sabrina *JANE*, Lady Stoppard (née Guinness; born 9 January '55)**

YCTV - THAT'S A WRAP.......................... THE END

+ MYA's SPECIAL IN MEMORIAs

BOTH > (Author Copyright Photography)

BUT ONE THING HIDDEN FROM YOU ALL UNTIL HERE:

The password Alex phoned Sabrina to input to regain control of her PC was **WANTED22**

She was their 22nd...So who were the previous 21?
They're out there somewhere, but by now all the Gossip Columnists would have already emblazed their periodical with Banner Headlines warning of the hacking Threat!?

But you'd be totally wrong!!!

They'd have been treated as SG's with secretive kid gloves.
And depending on their status *like hers* their case(s) would be placed in those, only for certain eyes, *'Restricted Case Files'!*

John, with his RBK&C Constabulary Contacts ^PC, easily ascertained such, when asking the Local Sergeant to change a phone contact therein – he couldn't as the request had to go upstairs for approval for the amendment access!

*So only the type only their Senior Police Officers could Access! – **Perhaps Not?** * ^PN
^PC *In case you've forgotten John was once its Local Taxmen, and also being on the Prosecutional side, there were many times he'd ask the Local Bobbies to execute Arrest Warrants on his behalf! Additionally, his last Central Government was at the Ministry of Justice, so the Legal Maze System was no bar to him!*
^PN *NB His Govt. Security Access Clearance was **well above** RESTRICTED!*

AND SO, THE HISTORICAL TRUTH IS FINALLY OUT

IN THE OPEN..........

AND AGAIN *,FOR ANY DISBELIEVING MYA*

↓

PART 18: JOHN's MEMORABLE (YCTV) REGARDS TO ALL - MYA

↓

FROM THE END

↑

John wanted more for his books and the YCTV creator's opinion mattered to him and so he sent the standard request he had to so many...

Dear Sabrina

I was there the year after it started - full of donated PCs - the room on the 1st floor where budding film makers practiced story writing - the dingy basement. Well I now fancy writing about YCTV's history: its successes, – failures, the effort; the rewards etc. witty comments about the founder and examples of innovations like 'pass the mike'...how it mushroomed - how it is now sorely missed & why. The kids I spoke to said IDEASTAP was not as good? They all miss YCTV!
How do you feel about it all?

HERE THE REAL DEAL REPLY:-

Sabrina sent you a message.

Pretty Yellow top and more So a pretty smile unlike so many press intrusive photos!

Sabrina Guinness April 3, 2010 at 7:55pm

Re: ex yctv students comments about you and YCTV

thank you john..i miss it too

happy easter

xx

To reply to this message, follow the link below:

http://www.facebook.com/n/?inbox%2Freadmessage.php&!
b3e0b9fG157cd8G0&n_m=bakerjohn%40hotmail.co.uk

Find people from your Windows Live Hotmail address book on Facebook!

This message was intended for bakerjohn@hotmail.co.uk. If you do not wish to receive this type of email from Facebook in the future, please click on the link below to unsubscribe.
http://www.facebook.com/o.php?k=1f1ea7&u=1000007174747198&mid=2218c51G5af33b3e0b9fG1
57cd8G0 Facebook's offices are located at 1601 S. California Ave., Palo Alto, CA 94304.

NB The addresses have been blanked out for the obvious reasons!
And should the photo interest you, view those cloned ones about...
John never said who took it,
BUT
I think he knew more than he let on!

And to put the hacking record straight:- John said it was always the email/address book correspondence content which the blackmailer/hackers Alex & Co were after.

The Facebook account then, 15 years+ back was in its infancy and security controls not 100% secure, if you understand me – it goes to prove then and now make sure your passwords are difficult to crack and virus software always up to date!

Additionally, according to John, then, there might have been several dozen names attached to her (<u>open to the public</u>) Facebook account,
BUT no real big hitters or persons of note: the most notable would have been her Samuel nephew/nieces.

So quite mundane!
And adding to the security lapse note:- before the hacking incident which happened after the demise of YCTV, but during YCTV's existence, the office staff were known to use post-it notes above their work areas showing SG's contact detail & whereabouts!

BUT she doesn't have all that to worry about anymore!

The 3rd & Last Carousel of Remarkable Coincidental *Nonsense* - - - -

And so now to end up jovially joining up some *relatively* connected dots using one of Michael's Chapter linked words – Quirky ^(OFF-CENTRE – Hope Not)

Here Goes >

Michael

Married a Guinness

Named Julia

↑
...
↓

Julia

Had 4 Siblings

– One Named Sabrina

↑
...
↓

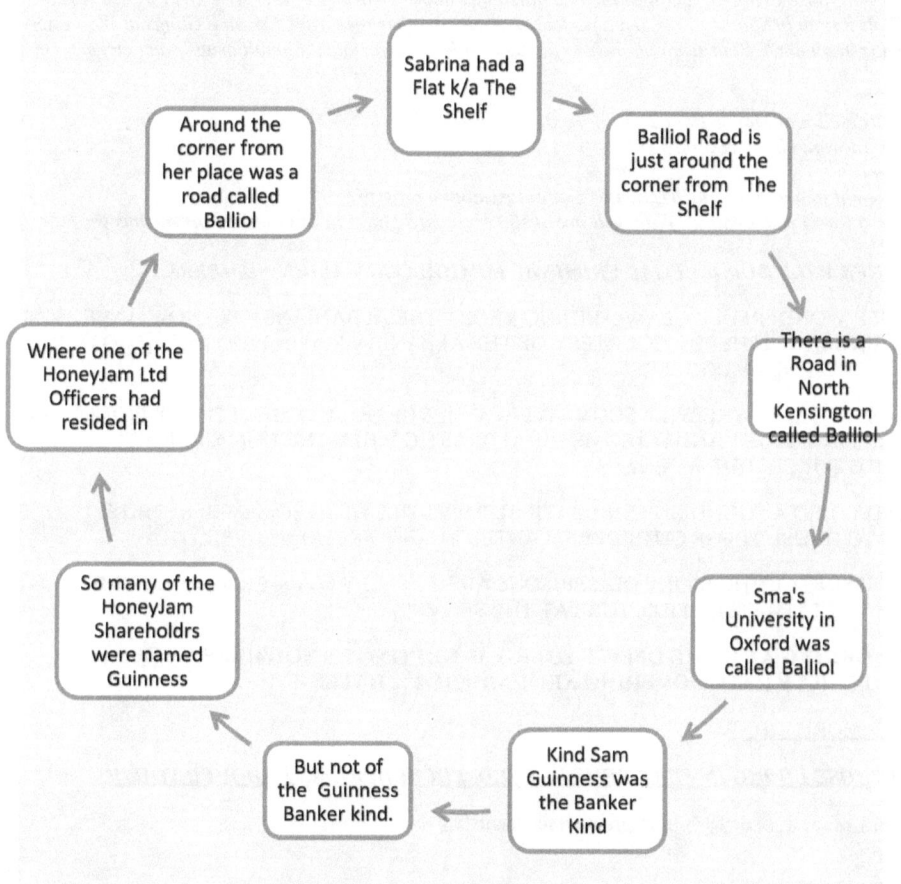

SOMEWHERE IN ILFORD... OCT0BER 2022

AND ANOTHER DRILLING POST SCRIPTED SHOOTING UPDATE:-
TWO SOMALIAN ^{S} YOUNG MEN WERE DRILLED DOWN WHILST FIREWORKS DROWNED OUT THE BULLETES AND THEIR DEATH PRELUDING SCREAMS!

^{S} NB A point of info, when in Africa the Somalians are painted as crooks & thieves etc. so it will come as no surprise here that those who get past our holed Immigrant Border Controls end up housed in Tower Blocks together to assist those Criminal amongst them to quietly go about their import lucrative Drug Trade – The Pennines Flats Estate in Southend-on-Sea a perfect example; another the Crack Cocaine Gangs in Worcester; and Boscombe in quiet (?) Bournemouth is also facing problems with violent Somali drugs gang etc. etc. etc..

The above hits a case of Manor Park 2 Drillford 0
The 2 murdered were Giddy & Shifty
2 drill rappers
They were caught in another Drug Trade turf war assassination crossfire
The killing just won't end – will it? With well over 1500 organised gangs in England I think the answer patently obvious!?
AND NEITHER WILL OUR ILLEGAL CRIMINAL IMMIGRATION ALIEN NUMBERS...

THAT OTHER WONDERFULLY LAW-ABIDING RACE – THE ALBANIANS – WE NOW HAVE 10000 OF THEIR SINGLE MEN HERE – COURTESY OF THE ALBANIAN MAFIA WHO ARE **ALSO** OUR FOREMOST COCAINE SMUGGLERS!

THAT FINGER IN THE DYKE WILL SOON GIVE WAY IF THE GOVERNMENT DON'T *IRONICALLY* PULL THEIR FINGER OUT AND DO SOMETHING DRASTIC WHEN THE HUMAN RIGHTS ACT IS KICKED INTO TOUCH! BUT WHEN?

SO, RWANDA DIED A SOUND BITTEN DEATH BUT WE STILL NEED SOMEWHERE BIG & ISOLATED TO HOUSE THOSE OUTSIDERS WANTED TO GET *FREELY* IN HERE.

OUR PROCESSING CENTRES LIKE OUR PRISONS ARE TOTALLY OVER-CROWDED & WILL CONTINUE TO ULTIMATELY FRACTURE AT THE SEAMS!

NB THIS WORKING AT HOME OFFICE POLICY IS GETTING US NOWHERE WITH OUR ANNUAL CLEAR UP RATE HOVERING AROUND THE 4% RATE!

NEED I SAY MORE JOHN?

WELL TO THOSE LIVING IN FEAR BEHIND THEIR LOCKED DOORS IN DOVER YOU DO!

But, not to any of these, once Irish Immigrant Descendants!? >>>

↓

↓

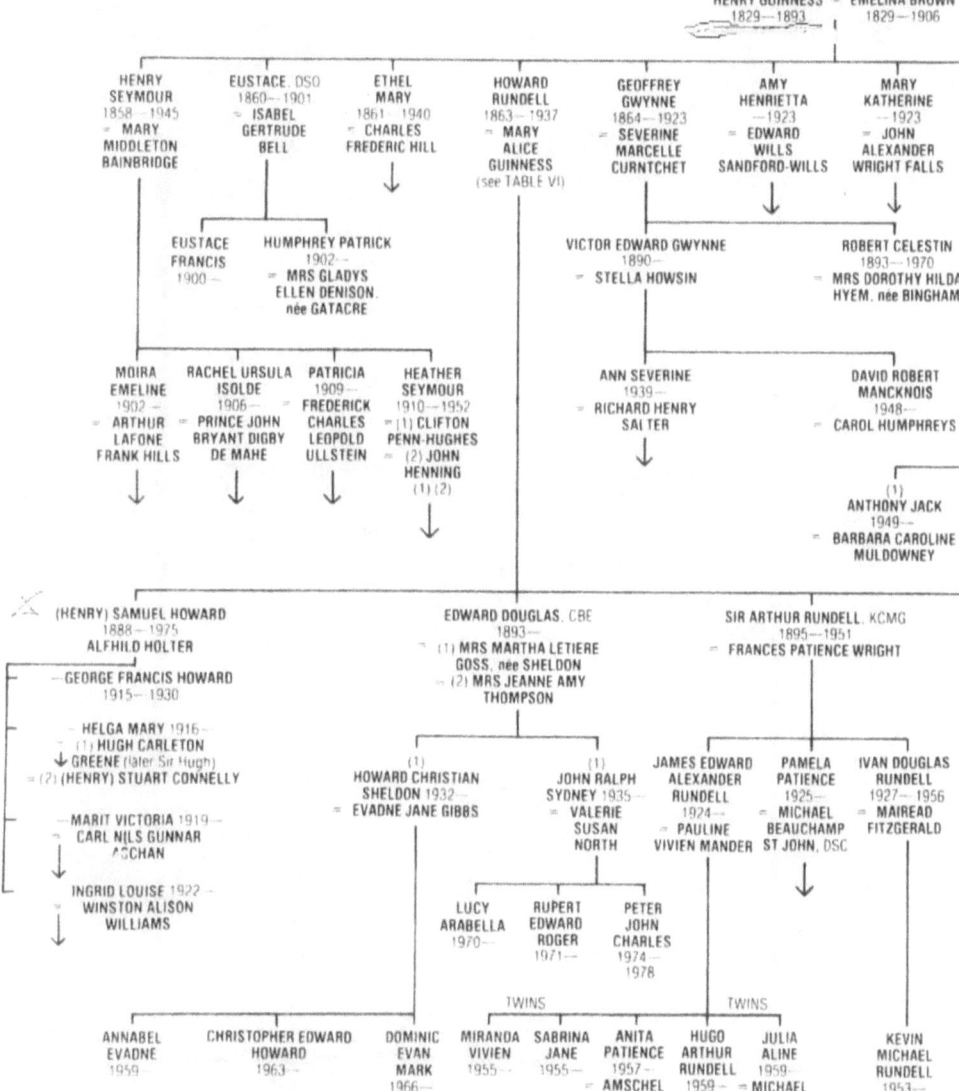

A PERSONAL THANKYOU IN MEMORIA

> It was so very kind of you to send me such a wonderfully generous message following the death of my beloved mother. Your most thoughtful words are enormously comforting, and I cannot tell you how deeply they are appreciated at this time of immense sorrow.
>
> *Charles R*

NB ENDING

One thing one doesn't hear is that oddity that both Sabrina and her twin sister both got married...

BUT
Neither apparently gave birth....
Well, perhaps both already had a ready made set of step children and thereafter the step grand children...etc!

BUT
One got married at child bearing age, whilst the other didn't!

So, the problem before us is, was this a conscience decision by either, or both, or something else? ***

And let us not forget there was no shortage of linked-family suitors as enumerated above and elsewhere in one my other Books: And here is a reminder extract from Part 10 of my *'Legal Sanctity of Book Series...*
"It is interesting to go back centuries and sort out the Rich wheat from amongst the rabble chaff and, apart from the Royal Patronage links, see the interconnections, here the Churchills/Marlboroughs/Spencers and via marriage Sunderlands below.

NB Cadogan Estates is linked with the Marlboroughs:- ↓
The 1st Earl Cadogan ↓ (1672-1726) was Marlborough's Quartermaster during the Spanish War of Succession, where the success got Marlborough to be given Blenheim by Queen Anne!
And if cash got scarce:- But when the UK Landed Gentry cannot help, then that simple outsider Marriage expedient:- ***
A Blenheim Palace example being - *At the end of the 19th century, the palace was saved from ruin by funds gained from the 9th Duke of Marlborough's marriage to American railroad heiress Consuelo Vanderbilt!*

And in recent times the Royals > Spencer wife > Guinness girlfriend *** > the interconnectivity friend links between the last two named, leading to the Somerset Samuels via Marriage and God parents of the Royal progeny!

Here (1) a Samuel/Guinness offspring once a (2) Wiliam playmate and he/his wife being Sponsors of Samuel's favourite Mental Health Charity:- Anna Freud Centre, which got multi million new build (3) makeover via another UK outsider, here a Russian Jew (4) ** ...!

Ah well can't win em all!? Oddly enough the Duke of Westminster has a Russian Past link:- Via his mother, Westminster descends from the Russian ** Imperial House of Romanov, which had a notable historical past:- after their Anastasia married Ivan the Terrible! (And yet as before, another Royal Historical Link!)

But there again we could continue with the Samuel – family seat in Somerset and the link with Northumberland Estates (Duke/Duchess owners) who might be one of the many *largest* UK land owners. *(Duke of Northumberland (House of Percy) = (The Regal Scotland/England links:- His maternal first cousin is Richard Scott, 10th Duke of Buccleuch, one of the largest private landowners in Scotland, while his paternal first cousin was Angus Douglas-Hamilton, 15th Duke of Hamilton. His first cousins once removed are Prince Richard, Duke of Gloucester & Prince William of Gloucester, both members of the Royal Family hence no shock that his brother Henry Percy, 11th Duke of Northumberland FRS (Died 1995) was a British peer, heir to the dukedom of Northumberland and a godchild of Queen Elizabeth 11.)*

To name a few:- Both Samuel and Northumberland had 2nd homes in Central Homes: one which overlooked Marble Arch, whose address was later mirrored by the Blairs, where the central garden square was for owner/residents use only. The Duke of Northumberland main London Residences ◇ Syon House/Park...

(Ignoring our King Charles ***) *The richest* UK landowner is likely to be the Duke of Westminster (Hugh #) (Grosvenor Estates) (a few bob short of £10 billion!) – although his Property Portfolio is world wide! (And ? Third? = Cadogan Estates a mere £ 5 Billions!) Hugh # was later to have King Charles 3rd as one of his children's God parents! And he reciprocated being godfather to 2 children in the current Royal family set up!– And we must not forget the other linkages/marriages to such as the Goldsmiths & Rothschilds!

*** And ignoring all the gossip column nonsense of the time, perhaps the real reason for the Sabrina/Charles Split was her unwillingness to do a Diana and would not be an Heir Producer, possibly later castoff (?) when Camilla took his eye her way?!

Author copyright

Like Diana, Sabrina was a free spirit but also enjoyed her privacy:- she'd always refuse to pose for photos, although had to tolerate the paparazzi at glittering functions!

Hence the paucity of her during her ordinary, behind the scenes, life!
And yes both as a Royal and a Dynasty Regal Guinness she could have had total seclusion...well apart from such as my interrogatory John of this world!

BUT
One would come at the price that she could not venture outside Palace conclaves, whereas her comings and goings between *chosen* friends and relatives and also YCTV, were done at her own volition and pace, not some agenda set by Royal Duties! As was her choice of out of the limelight boyfriends!
So Sorry Charles No Heir There!

BUT
There would be a Future Sabrina Heart **_Stoppa!_**
And here a brief additional comment....
She's kept her # Ladbroke Grove Flat, whilst Tom sold his Chelsea pad:- they relocated to Dorset, although SG's flat comes in handy for the occasional London Town visit/invite/glamour event/award ceremony etc..
Coincidentally, Stoppard used to also live in the Ladbroke Grove area with an old friend, Derek Marlowe, who was there when times were tough for old Tom.
NB Although where property prices go through the roof, like its Notting Hill Neighbour, the area has its unsightly underbelly, which often explains the police + sniffer dogs in the Ladbroke Grove Tube ticket office foyer!

BUT
Away from al the glitz, at home the social lady shows deference to her new man, as you'll find her asking his opinion of this and that before doing whatever.
Really one could class them as both modest now suited individuals.
And to prove the point when photographed they put on such a smiley pair show!

*(Sabrina in the past had been know to scowl at constantly being put out by the paparazzi – the worst incident John was aware of was when she had just vacated her car & was about to enter her front garden, then to climb the stairs to her flat, some notcareadot fella just jumped in front of her from behind a large bush and stuck the lens literally up her nose!) + (She was not one to freely have her photo taken by individuals at any time, as she felt unfairly ? put upon, being a (? Unwilling ?) celebrity and all, which tag she wasn't enamoured of, as John discovered when they met & spoke those times at YCTV HQ. - where also a certain JB, who **got his** meeting date all wrong, **got her** real moody silent treatment!)*

BUT
He's a different **Principal Plain Jane Guinness & I Once Story Subject**!
And everyone thought him loathsome!
Especially a Whitemoor Mental Institution Inmate!

BUT
The Gang Got rid of him **well & truly**, as all those types of gangs do – *so well!*

BUT
YET AGAIN
THAT'S ANOTHER
PLAIN JANE GUINNESS & I ONCE...STORY!

POST MORTEM >>>>

In the end, his body riddled with the Big 'C' such that his fingers could not make the words walk onto the pages; his previous lifestyle excesses, whichever was the culprit, like for example his chain-smoking as opposed to his sweet chain-eating only diabetes contributing – then he was gone!

Sir Tom Stoppard is buried at St Mary's Church in **Tarrant Gunville, Dorset, United Kingdom**.

>Should you want to visit like I did, just get in touch with
>Mrs Lizzie Patterson
>Churchwarden
>01258 830216

This file is licensed under the Creative Commons Attribution-Share Alike 2.0 Generic license. Thanks to: Chris Downer <> Chris Downer / Tarrant Gunville: parish church of St. Mary / CC BY-SA 2.0

He was laid to rest there on Monday, December 15, 2025

And Covid couldn't get him, but it did his favourite local theatre, just a few miles away, The Tivoli, in Wimborne, which itself passed in 2019!

Tarrant Gunville does not have a train station, with the nearest options being Gillingham (approx. 10-12 miles), Blandford Forum (no station, relies on buses), or Salisbury, served by South Western Railway and Great Western Railway. Gillingham station provides direct hourly trains to London Waterloo.

Closest Train Stations to Tarrant Gunville:

- **Gillingham (Dorset) (GIL):** Roughly 10-12 miles north, this is generally considered the most convenient station for the area, offering direct services to London Waterloo and Exeter.
- **Salisbury (SAL):** A major station northeast of the village, providing broader regional connections.
- **Dorchester West/South (DCH):** Located further southwest, about a 20-30 minute drive, suitable for travelling along the Dorset coast.

2026 CAME…

AND OFF HE WENT TO VISIT THE GRAVE…

THERE WAS ONLY ONE OTHER SOLITARY FIGURE THERE…

THAT PERSON LOOKED UP…

AND FOR THE FIRST TIME SMILED HIS WAY…

WELL HI AGAIN PLAIN JANE GUINNESS LADY

I DIDN'T EXPCT YOU TO BE HERE

THE SELF-SAME DAY I CHOSE…

HOW'S LIFE?

AND YET AGAIN NO PHOTO CAME ABOUT…

BUT WHAT FOLLOWED NEED NOT BE TOLD…

THIS BOOK IS LARGE ENOUGH ALREADY!!!

MYA

www.ingramcontent.com/pod-product-compliance
Lightning Source LLC
LaVergne TN
LVHW091619070526
838199LV00044B/856